To

Tom.

Hope you enjoy the classes

This book will help you

to master the cooking

Nov. [illegible]

Rice and Kari

Traditional Sri Lankan/Asian cooking adapted for modern living in the West

by

Sivakamy Mahalingham

Title : Rice and ~~Curry~~ Kari

Author : Sivakamy Mahalingham

© : Sivakamy Mahalingham

Publisher : Esredelk
Cambridge
United Kingdom

1st Edition : December 2009

Cover Design & Layout : K. K. Rajah

Photographs: S. Mahalingham
K. K. Rajah

E-mail : sivakamy@talktalk.net
sivabookrk@googlemail.com

ISBN : 978-0-9564289-0-5

The Proceeds of this Cookery Book

100% of all profits from the sales of 1500 books printed in this edition will be donated to Cambridge Addenbrooke's NHS Trust Oncology unit R+D Fund 9250,Great Ormond Street Childrens Hospital (registered charity number 235825) in memory of Meera, and the Sri Murugan Temple (registered charity number 271097).

I dedicate this book to my late parents: To my mother, Mrs Ruby Sivananthan (Hallock) who inspired my interest in cooking but passed away in 1963. Some of the recipes are from remembering her cooking. To my father, Mr P Sivananthan who passed away in 1994 in Sri Lanka after suffering a stroke in 1988; I wish I could have been there to look after and cook for him. I am sure both will shower their blessings from above.

Contents

Essential ingredients

- Bottle of roasted chilli curry powder from Sri Lankan shops
- Roasted fennel powder (see spices section)
- Grains: rice, red lentil, rice flour

- Spices: cumin seeds, coriander seeds, fenugreek seeds, mustard seeds, red dried chillies, turmeric powder.

- garlic and root ginger (paste, powders are available)

Lentil/Dhal

A variety of lentils can be purchased from Supermarkets or Asian food stores.

The common ones used in day to day cooking are listed below with the different names used.

Toor dhal:
Tuvaram paruppu in Tamil , yellow colour available in plain or oily

Chana dhal:
Split chick peas, kadalai paruppu in Tamil. Used in cooking and vadai (recipe in finger foods)

Whole chana:
Chick peas

Green gram/Mung dhal:
Moong dhal, whole green gram, Payarü in Tamil. Can be used as a whole or split and husked to make several dishes.

Split mung/moong dhal:
Split green gram, Pasi paruppu in Tamil, cream/yellow colour. In Jaffna the roasted dhal is cooked on special days, included in the menu for weddings. At home the first course of rice and dhal is served with a teaspoon of ghee or gingerly oil.

Urad dhal:
Ulunthu, ulutham paruppu is the Tamil name. The whole urad is the black gram. You need to soak and wash the husk and skin before cooking. My recipes include the split white urad dhal. (Thosai, vadai etc.)

.

Masor/Mysoor dhal:
Red lentil

Coconut

1. Scraped coconut
2. Desiccated coconut
3. Coconut milk
4. Coconut powder
5. Coconut pieces
6. Coconut cream or cream coconut
7. Coconut water
8. Ground coconut known as kootu

Coconut scraper
Coconut scraper is a tool used to scrape coconut.

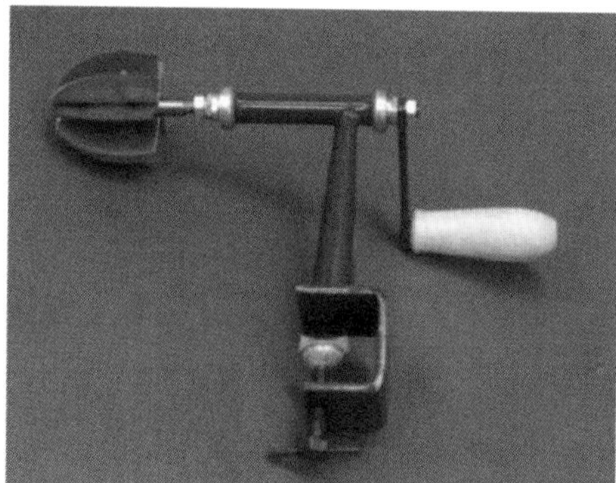

1. Scraped coconut:

To prepare scraped coconut, have the coconut cut in two halves.
Using the scraping machine scrape the coconut.
Can be stored in the freezer. Scraped coconut is available in the freezer section of Asian stores and supermarkets.

2. Desiccated coconut:

Available in supermarkets. Soak in a bit of warm milk to make it like fresh scraped coconut.
Can get sugared sweetened coconut for sweet dishes.

3. Coconut milk:
This is a very important item in Sri Lankan, and South Indian dishes.The coconut gives richness to the prepared dishes. It also takes off some of the heat from the dishes. Put the scraped coconut in a bowl with a cup of hot water and squeeze well with fingers. Using a colander strain the first extract. Repeat it four times and keep the milk from each extraction separately.

If using a blender put the scraped coconut or chopped pieces into a blender, add a little warm water and grind it fine. Take out and strain the first milk and keep it aside. Add more warm water and run the electric blender. Do the same for 2nd, 3rd and 4th milk. The milk can be frozen or left in the fridge for two or three days. Use the 4th milk for cooking vegetable where you require more liquid sauce.

Karis cooked in coconut milk have a distinctive taste.
The first milk is added towards the final stages of the cooking.
The second extract is used when you need a lot of sauce.
The third and fourth is used at the begining of the cooking process (for vegetables and in cooking fish) instead of water .

You can use desiccated coconut but you need to soak the coconut in hot water for a few minutes and then put in a blender. But instead of this you can use canned coconut milk which is readily available.

4. Coconut powder:
Available in packets can be stored in bottles. Mix powder in warm water or warmed normal milk and add to the dish before the final cooking.

5. Coconut pieces:
The scraper cannot cut the coconut into pieces. You break the coconut in half then get the flesh out and chop this to large pieces and then put in the blender for a few seconds till it is chopped. You can eat this as well. These finely chopped (½ inch) pieces are added to boiled chickpeas and boiled dark brown gram, and eaten with Palmyra tree products from Jaffna, such as pullukodiyal, which is available in some Sri Lankan shops.

6. Cream coconut:
Available in a small rectangular box, you can get it from supermarkets. At the final stages of the cooking you can add a small piece (¼" slice) to make the sauce thick.

7. Coconut water:

This is the juice that comes when you cut the coconut in half. Used for dishes like bitter gourd, green banana curry and the banana flower 'valai potthi' dish. It is tasty to drink too.

8. Ground coconut known as kootu

Famous and an important ingredient in Jaffna and South Indian cooking. Traditionally, the scraped coconut was put on a grinding stone and ground with a heavy grinding roller until very fine. This was done daily and a spoonful was put into every Kari prerpared. Now the blender/liquidiser does the job. Use a little water and grind it to a paste.

Daily cooking in the West

For health reasons, in my day to day cooking I add semi-skimmed milk. But on weekends and for special dishes, I use coconut powder, cream coconut, and full cream evaporated milk.

Essential utensils

- An electric grinder/liquidiser/food processor. Worth investing in a good brand.

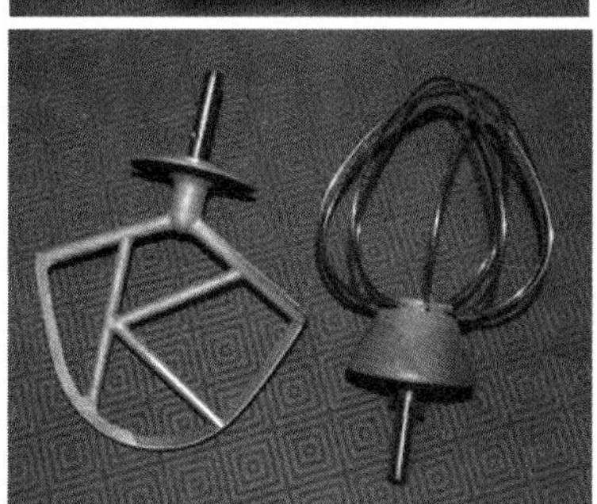

- Mortar and pestle: Useful for crushing and grinding ginger, garlic, cumin, pepper, mustard seeds etc.

- An electric cake mixer/beater.

- Pressure cooker: Now available in many sizes and would halve the time you spend in the kitchen. Can be used to boil pulses,vegtables,soups etc.

- Wok or a Karahi/thava (known in Tamil as a tharchi or a karahi in India). Made of cast iron aluminium which will retain the heat. I use a Karahi for most of my cooking, I find that there is a difference in cooking certain items in a saucepan and a karahi/thava. A useful item to have, which is available in different sizes from Asian shops.

- I have tried to keep to metric weights, but as I grew up using imperial measurements, there may be few imperial measurements included. The chart below may be of help.

- The oven temperature used is for an electric oven - circotherm fan assisted oven based on a maximum heat of 190°C . You may need to check and adjust accordingly.

List below gives a guide.

Fan assisted	celsius	fahrenheit	gas mark	description
190°C	220-230°C	425°F	8	very hot
160°C	190°C	375°F	5	moderate
140°C	160°C	320°F	3	low
120°C	150°C	300°F	2	very low

- Cup measurements used in the book is of a tea/coffee mug used in the UK homes. I have weighed the items where appropriate and included in gms.

  1 inch = 2.5 cm
  I have used 2 cm as an approximate measurement

  1 cup = 225g lentils, split peas, 200gm caster sugar
  1 cup = 225ml liquid

Glossary

<u>Some are explained in the introduction section</u>

Asafoetida: Perungayam (Tamil), Hing (Indian)

It is a pungent spice extracted from a plant of the giant fennel family
It is frequently used in Indian and Middle-eastern cookery.

Coriander:

Thaniya (Indian) Kothamalli (Tamil) Its leaves are used as an herb and the seeds are ground to make curry powder with other spices. Used to prepare Rasam .Boiled corriander water with a bit of honey is given to children for cold .

Cumin:

Jeera (Indian) Natcheeraham(Tamil) Small, crescent shaped seeds. They have a strong pungent aroma and a warm flavour – can be used whole or ground into a powder.

Curry leaves:

These are small, shiny pointed leaves along a central stem.
They are used to add flavour and fragrance in Indian/Sri Lankan cooking.

Fennel seeds:

These greenish brown seeds are from an aromatic herb. In Jaffna fresh ground roasted fennel is used towards the end of the cooking. See the spices section of the recipe to make this special fennel powder.
Fenugreek: An aromatic plant that produces long pods containing brownish seeds. The seeds and the leaves have a strong flavour.

Gingelly/Sesame seeds:

Indian sesame seeds are cream coloured, small and glossy; Chinese sesame seeds are black. Gingelly oil is used in stir frying. served.
Some have a teaspoon of oil with hot rice and dhal as a starter.

Rampe:

Rampe (Sinhalese) Pandan leaves (Thailand)
Similar to curry leaves, these are added to give a flavour to the cooked dish. Can be purchased frozen from Sri Lankan shops.
Sera (Srilankan name - Lemon grass is also added to dishes for flavour.

Saffron:

Dried stigmas of the saffron flower. They are used for the bright orange-yellow colour and strong intense aroma and flavour.

Tamarind:

Comes from the long bean-shaped fruit of the tamarind tree. It is sold as a pulp and is used as a souring agent. Dark brown or black in colour. Can be bought as pods, paste or a rectangle block. It requires soaking in hot water to loosen.
Tamarind is used to flavour fish, vegetable dishes, chutneys and a kind of soup called 'Rasam'. A similar fruit used in southern Sri Lanka is called Gorakka .

Turmeric:

A bright yellow spice from a plant in the ginger family. It is usually sold dried and ground in powder form.

Roasted Chilli /curry powder

Roasted chilli powder used in this section refers to the Sri Lankan mixed curry/chilli powder which has the spices mixed in proportion.
There is a recipe on spices section to prepare the powder.

Plain chilli powder: Ground dried red chilli, used in various recipes. For a Kari you may need to add cumin,coriander and tomatoes to reduce the extra hotness.

Spices: Cardamom, Cinnamon and Cloves. Worth having a small quantity of these ground. Used in cooking meat, stir fry and fried rice etc.
Cloves have a pungent taste, so it is better to remove these from the dishes before you serve.

Garam masala: Includes above spices and large cardamom, ani seed etc

Ingredients used in this book (Sri Lankan- Asian cooking) are available from Asian Supermarkets and Sri Lankan food stores. Some leading Supermarkets have started to stock these too.

Tempering:

This is done at the start of the cooking. Heat a frying pan add oil then chopped onions stir fry or sauté. Then add mustard seeds, cumin, or fennel seeds, curry leaves, dry red chillies. I may have used the words as frying, stir-fry sauté or tempering.Traditional method is to heat the oil or ghee, add the mustard seeds and when it stars to pop add cumin and others. It is also done as the last garnishing, add tsp of the fried items to the cooked vegetables. ("Thalitham" in tamil). Mostly done on special days, religious functions when there are several dishes.

Acknowledgements

My thanks to all those who have provided encouragement for the completion of this book, which is now twelve years overdue:

My sons for the constructive suggestions which made me look again at some of the work. Also for coming up with the title and writing the introduction.

The many friends who helped me to set out these recipes in a coherent manner, and who tried, tasted and tested the recipes over the years.

Alex, Elaine and Keith for proof reading.

Viji, for her constant support.

Mr Nithiyananthan, for his guidance and encouragement, and for persuading me to write a comprehensive cook book in the first place. The book has grown from 160 pages to 578, packed with information and references.

Mr Mahalingasivam (Mali) for his support, and for seeing this book through to print form.

Mr Krishnarajah (Rajah) for the colour plates, cover design and layout, and for his patience and time when changes were required.

Seelans Superstores of East Ham, for allowing us to take the photographs of ingredients and utensils which are included in the book.

My friend Malar, for her continued support, and for proof reading.

My extended family, my friends and their children, for sustaining my passion for preparing and perfecting these recipes.

Niru BRAND, for getting the books from Chennai to London.

Finally, my eternal gratitude to my husband, who encouraged me to donate the profits from this book to cancer research, and for his discerning palate despite ill health. Without his constructive comments, suggestions and support, my cooking could not have been honed over 41 years. This book is the result.

INTRODUCTION

"Nothing will benefit human health and increase chances for survival of life on Earth as much as the evolution to a vegetarian diet."

- Albert Einstein
on the benefits of a vegetarian lifestyle.

"The thought of two thousand people crunching celery at the same time horrified me."

- George Bernard Shaw
(who incidentally was a vegetarian)
on turning down an invitation to a vegetarian gala dinner.

Some practice pure vegetarianism for moral, religious or health reasons, and some merely wish to supplement their diet with a healthy proportion of vegetarian food. However, it is sometimes difficult to effectively prepare a nutritionally balanced but at the same time tasty meal.

South East Asia is renowned for methods of preparing food that produce both nutritious and delicious results; there can be few living in the West who have not sampled the delights of a well prepared curry. There is much disagreement as to the etymology of the word 'curry' but it is interesting that in the language of Tamil, spoken widely in South India, there exists a word '**kari**' which denotes a spicy gravy.

The recipes in this book are likely to be quite different from anything the reader has seen before, as the recipes have been handed down from generation to generation and perfected over many years within a small group of families. The advantage in preparing one's own meals is that spices and herbs can be added subject to individual taste; whilst the recipes in this book are tried and tested, I would encourage the ambitious reader to experiment with combinations of spices that suit their own palate. I would also caution readers to have due regard for allergies/intolerances when selecting ingredients and recipes.

The core aspects of each of the recipes will have survived for hundreds of years but each has been adapted by recent generations to ensure:

- Healthy eating for the health-conscious modern world
- Ingredients are readily available in supermarkets
- Preparation and cooking times are not excessive, so as to suit the lifestyles of the modern family

What inspired this book?

Some 15 years ago, my son left home for University to fend for himself and rather than sending him parcels of food each week, his father and I encouraged him to try and cook for himself. He was quite adventurous and wanted to try his hand at the delicious South Indian dishes that he had grown up on. He would often call me asking, "Mum how do you cook that curry and how do you make cutlets?" I would scribble the recipes down for him and try to ensure that they would be easy to follow. He suggested that I collate my recipes into a book and give all the profits to charity.

Who would benefit from this book?

As a working mother, I am aware that when you get home from work, the last thing you want is to spend hours in the kitchen. You may therefore opt for a take-away, which of course can be quite unhealthy and even costly. With this in mind, the average preparation and cooking time for the meals in this book is 30-45 minutes and the recipes have also been compiled to ensure that they are healthy.

Complete beginners to cookery who do not want to spend hours preparing and cooking food (but would still like to experiment with exotic recipes and tastes) would find these recipes of great interest.

The recipes will also be useful to students or busy professionals who are looking for healthy, tasty meals that are quick and easy to prepare.

What are the basic ingredients?

The basis for each of the recipes will be:

- Root vegetables, such as potatoes, carrots and yams
- Fruit vegetables, such as courgettes, aubergines and pumpkins
- Leaves such as kale and cabbage
- Lentils and beans

Many of the herbs and spices traditionally used in Sri Lankan/ South East Asian cooking are thought to have significant health-enhancing and medicinal properties (based upon anecdotal evidence).

Consider the following ingredients (used throughout this book) and their corresponding Ayurvedic medicinal property:

- *Pundu or Garlic – believed to help lower cholesterol and also to have hepataprotective and pharmacodynamic properties.*
- *Inji or Ginger – believed to be useful in treating asthma and heart palpitation. Ginger is also believed to have antiemetic and anti-inflammatory properties.*
- *Kottamalli or Coriander – believed to be useful in treating allergies and also to aid digestion. Its leaves are used as a herb and the seeds are ground to make kari powder with other spices.*
- *Jeera or Cumin – believed to have carminative properties.*
- *Tamarind – believed to have anti-inflammatory properties. It is from a long bean-shaped fruit of the tamarind tree. It is sold as a pulp and is used as a souring agent.*

- *Vendhiyum, fenugreek or Methi – believed to have carminative and aphrodisiac properties. An aromatic plant that produces long pods containing brownish seeds. The seeds and the leaves have a strong flavour.*

- *Asafoetida: believed to help with digestion. It is a pungent spice extracted from a plant of the giant fennel family. It is added to vegetables and dhal.*

- *Haldi or Turmeric – believed to have antiseptic properties and to help moderate stomach ulcers.*

- *Mulluha or Chillies – believed to increase metabolic rate, which of course can help with weight loss as part of a calorie-controlled diet and fitness programme.*

- *Curry leaves – believed to have stomachic properties. These are small, shiny pointed leaves along a central stem. They are used to add flavour and fragrance in Indian/Sri Lankan cooking.*

- *Vengaiam or Onion – believed to have aphrodisiac properties.*

The six Ayurvedic tastes

In defining the taste sensations of a particular meal, the English language provides us with an arsenal of four* basic descriptions (which originated from the believed number of receptors on the human tongue):

- **Sweet** - the taste experience of sugar often identified with a pleasurable taste sensation.

- **Sour** – the taste experience of a vinegary or citrus item that may involve a moderately unpleasant sensation.

- **Salty** – categorised by a mild sensation on the tip of the tongue.

- **Bitter** – a harsh and sharp taste experience that may be unpleasant to many palates. Bitter gourd, as the name suggests, would be an excellent example of a food providing such a taste.

Ayurvedic literature presents two additional tastes:

- **Spicy** - almost a synonym for "peppery" but a softer, more rounded flavour is intimated

- **Astringent** - a puckerish taste experience which has the effect of drying out the mouth. Lentils or beans would fall in to this taste category.

"Spicy" and "Astringent" are in fact two descriptions that are frequently used by wine connoisseurs to define respectively the aroma and tannin content of particular wines.

The aim for the reader of this cookery book is to encompass all of the above tastes in a particular meal using a combination of ingredients. It is this complexity and variety of taste that attracts many to South East Asian cuisine.

*Another taste sensation is often cited in East Asian cookery, termed "umami", from a Japanese word applied in relation to a "savoury" or "meaty" glutamate taste.

Rice

Rice is a staple food for a significant number of individuals, especially those living in (or those originating from) South East Asia. It is the centrepiece of a meal, as opposed to the accompaniment. There are also many cultural traditions in South East Asia that involve rice:

- The question 'When are you going to provide us with a rice meal?' is sometimes posed to an eligible bachelor. This question is synonymous with the question 'When are you going to get married?'
- Traditional marriage ceremonies involve a bride and groom feeding each other rice. After the ceremony is concluded, well wishers bless the newly-married couple by showering grains of rice upon them.
- Rice is the first solid food given to a 6-month-old baby, a custom which is becoming prevalent in Western cultures as well.
- When performing last rites, a few grains of rice are offered as a symbolic final meal.

Rice - Index

Page N°

Cooking Rice:

Wash rice in cold water until water is clear (2-3 washes).
Simmering: For basmati rice: To 1 cup rice add 2 cups of water.
For easy-cook brown rice: To 1 cup rice add 2.75 cups water.
(Size of the cup does not matter as long as the same cup is used for the rice and water).

Place the rice and water in a pan, bring to the boil, stir once with a fork, reduce to a very low heat, cover with a tight fitting lid and cook for 18-20 minutes until all the water is absorbed. Remove from the cooker and serve.

Draining: Boil 2 cups basmati rice in a pan, adding plenty of water. Continue boiling on fairly high heat for about 18minutes.
Cover the pan and drain the water by tilting the pan sideways or using a colander. Leave the rice covered until required. For recipes where further cooking is needed in the oven, boil the rice for about 14-15 minutes and drain the water (do not over cook).

Rice cooker: Measurements are given, inscribed in the inside of the cooker. Here, to get the correct consistency, for every cup of rice add an equal amount of water and little bit extra. For two cups basmati rice the water level should be 2.5 to 3.
Brown rice, par boiled easy-cook rice, Sri Lankan "kutharisi" brown rice: These take a longer time, and you will need to add an extra cup of water to the given measurements. The easy way is to cook in plenty of water and drain.

Measurements used in this chapter
1 cup basmati rice - 150gms
2 cups water - 310ml (appx)

Salt is not essential when you cook rice, the recipes do not include salt as I do not use salt. You may add salt to your taste, it is best to add salt towards the last steps of cooking /boiling rice.

Add salt and drain the water. For simmering add less salt and stir once.

Ghee Rice

Preparation and Cooking: 30 minutes
Serves 4-6

Ingredients:

- 2 cups basmati rice
- 4 onions, sliced
- 6cm cinnamon stick, chopped
- 4 tbsp ghee
- 4 bay leaves
- 2 cardamoms and 2 cloves

Method:

1. Wash the rice, drain the water and leave it aside.
2. Melt the ghee in a heavy-bottomed saucepan until hot.
3. Add the onions and sauté for a few seconds. Then add the spices and stir until the onions are slightly brown and cooked.
4. Add the rice and stir-fry for 30 seconds or so. Add 4 cups of water and bring to boil, then lower the heat, cover and cook for approximately 18-20 minutes or until the rice is cooked to your taste.
5. Flake the cooked rice with a fork to separate. Remove the cloves and cardamoms and serve.

★ If you are giving this to young children you can omit the cardamoms and cloves which bear strong flavours.

★ If using a rice cooker, transfer to the rice cooker with water after step 3.

All In One Rice

This is a dish I was introduced to when I visited Malaysia in 2006. A very easy preparation when you return from work and you are too tired to cook. It is apparently popular with students who live away from home.

Preparation & cooking time: 45 minutes
Serves 3-4

Ingredients

- 2 cups, basmati rice (300g)
- 1 onion, chopped
- 1 small aubergine, cut into small cubes
- 1 large potato, cut into small cubes
- ¼ cup red lentils (6tbsp)
- 1 tsp tamarind paste
- 1 tsp ground ginger paste, 1 tsp garlic paste
- 2 tbsp butter
- 2 tsp roasted chilli powder
- 1 sprig curry leaves
- ¼ cup milk (75ml)
- 2 green chillies, cut up (optional)
- 1 tomato, cut into small cubes

Method

1. Wash the rice and red lentils, place in a heavy-bottomed saucepan (or rice cooker) add five cups water (750ml), bring to boil, then reduce the heat and cook for appx. 8 minutes.

2. Add the vegetables and all other items (stirring once) and cook for a further 20 minutes. Add butter to the cooked rice and stir it once more before serving.

★ Serve with natural yoghurt or chutney

★ Increase or decrease the amount of vegetables and the amount of chilli to suit your taste.

Rice Pongal

Preparation & cooking time: 45 minutes
Serves 4-6

Ingredients

- 2 cups basmati rice
- ½ cup split green gram
- 15 pepper corns
- 2 dried red chillies
- 1 tsp cumin seeds
- salt to taste
- 1 tsp ginger paste (or chopped ginger)
- 10 roasted cashew nuts
- 300ml milk, 1 tsp ghee

Method

1. Dry roast the green gram in a heavy-based saucepan until slightly brown in colour. Add the rice and roast for few minutes, then add three cups of water and cook for about 15 minutes (until the rice is almost cooked).
2. Grind the ginger, cumin, dried chillies and 10 pepper corns into a paste in a blender (or with a mortar and pestle).
3. Add the ground paste to the rice with the milk and the rest of the whole pepper corns. Add the roasted cashew nuts, ghee and mix well.
4. Cook for a further 5 minutes and serve.

★ Serve with chutney

Vegetable Bhiriyani

Preparation & cooking time: 45 minutes (excluding marinating time)

Serves 6-8

Ingredients

- 3 cups basmati rice
- ½ cauliflower, cut into florets
- 150gm petit pois peas
- 2 carrots, cut into thin matchstick-size strips
- 5 french beans, cut into thin diagonal strips
- 10 shallots, sliced (or 2 red onions, sliced)
- 3 tbsp butter or 2 tbsp ghee
- 4 cups natural yoghurt (appx 350g)
- 2 tsp ginger paste
- 2 tsp garlic paste
- 2 tsp roasted chilli powder
- 2 tsp garam masala powder
- 4 large green cardamoms
- pinch of saffron or 1 tsp turmeric powder
- 1 tsp mixed spice powder (cinnamon, cardamom)
- 8 peppercorns, 1tsp cumin seeds
- 3 bay leaves
- salt to taste

Method

1. Place the cut vegetables on a plate and cook in the microwave for one minute. Place the vegetables in a clean dish cloth to take the moisture out.

2. Mix the yoghurt, ginger paste, salt, chilli powder, and garam masala in a bowl. Add the vegetables and marinate for 40 minutes.

3. Heat the butter in a wok and fry the onions until brown. Remove the contents and leave aside in a dish. In the same pan, fry the vegetables and all the spices for a few minutes until slightly dry.
4. Cook the rice in a saucepan of water for about 18 minutes, drain the water and spread the rice on a large plate.
5. Dry roast the saffron strands in the wok, crush and sprinkle over the rice (alternatively use turmeric mixed with little water and sprinkle over the rice).
6. Switch on the oven, place foil paper in a baking tray (cover the sides), and place half the rice into the tray. Then arrange half the vegetables over the rice. Repeat with the rest of the rice and vegetables. Top with the fried onions, ghee, mixed spice powder, and bake for a further 20 minutes in a preheated oven at 180°C.

★ Serve with salad and other side dishes.

★ You can add freshly ground or crushed cinnamon, cardamom and cloves.

Yellow Rice

Sri Lankan name 'Khabath' meaning yellow
Preparation & cooking time: 1 hour
Serves 4

Ingredients

- 2 cups basmati rice
- 5 small red onions or shallots, chopped
- 10 green chillies, chopped
- 2 tbsp moong dhal, urad dhal and sesame seeds
- 2 tbsp coriander seeds or a small sprig of coriander leaves
- 3 tsp butter or ghee
- 1 tsp turmeric powder or saffron
- 6 cm cinnamon stick, 8 cardamoms, 4 cloves
- 1 rampe stick, cut into pieces, 3 bay leaves
- 1 can thick coconut milk (300ml)
- 10 roasted cashew nuts
- Salt to taste

Method

1. Soak the rice in water, leave for 15 minutes and drain thoroughly.
2. Fry the onions and chillies in the butter and leave to one side.
3. Roast the dhal and coriander in a pan, remove and then grind into a fine powder in a blender/grinder.
4. Grind the cinnamon and cardamoms (leave a small piece of cinnamon to cook with the rice).
5. Add the ground ingredients and turmeric to the rice. Heat a saucepan and melt 2 tsp of butter. Add the rice and fry for a few minutes. Add the rampe stick, bay leaves and fry.
6. When the rice is fully coated in the ground powder, add 2 cups of water and bring to the boil. Add the cloves and then reduce the heat, cover the pan and cook.
7. After approximately 10 minutes add the coconut milk, butter, cashew nuts and cover the pan with a lid. Cook on a low heat for a further 10 minutes.
8. Remove the cloves from the rice and serve

★ Serve with salad/seeni sambol/sambar. Can use freshly blended coconut milk, use the first two extractions (2 cups). Evaporated milk can be used according to your taste.

Hot Savoury Rice

Preparation & cooking time: 45 minutes
Serves 3-4

Ingredients

- 1 cup rice
- 1 cup split moong dhal
- 50g cashew nuts
- 5 green chillies, chopped
- 125g butter
- salt to taste
- 1 tsp mustard seeds

Spices to be ground

- 1 tsp cumin seeds
- 1 tsp coriander seeds
- ½ tsp turmeric powder
- 4 cardamoms, 3cm cinnamon stick
- 2 dried red chillies

Method

1. Melt 1 tablespoon butter in a heavy-bottomed saucepan. Add the cashew nuts and roast slightly. Remove and add a bit more butter and roast the moong dhal until slightly golden colour.
2. Wash and drain the rice and then add it to the pan and fry for a few minutes. Add two cups water and bring to boil, reduce the heat, cover with a lid and then cook for approximately 18-20 minutes. Set aside and then grind the relevant spices in a mortar and pestle.
3 In another pan, heat the remaining butter, add the mustard seeds ground ingredients and the green chillies. Keep stirring and add the rice. Stir well so the rice becomes covered in the paste.

★. Serve with chutney.

Lemon Rice - (1)

Made for special auspicious days

Preparation & cooking time: 45 minutes
Serves 4-6

Ingredients

- 2 cups cooked rice
- juice of two lemons
- 3 sprigs curry leaves
- 5 red chillies, chopped
- 2 green chillies, chopped
- 1 tbsp mustard seeds
- 3 tbsp sesame oil or vegetable oil
- ½ tsp turmeric powder mixed in 1 tbsp water
- salt to taste
- 2 tbsp split chick peas (fried)

Method

1. Heat the oil in a large wok, add the mustard seeds and allow this to splutter.
2. Add the chillies, curry leaves and fry for a few minutes.
3. Add the mixed turmeric to the fried ingredients. Reduce the heat and add the lemon juice and channa dhal. Stir well.
4. Add the rice gradually, stirring until yellow in colour. Remove from heat.

★ Serve warm.
★ You may fry chopped shallots and add to the rice.

Lemon Rice (2)

Preparation & cooking time: 45 minutes
Serves 4-6

Ingredients

- **Same as for Lemon Rice (1)**
- **Additional: 10 roasted cashew nuts, chopped.**
- **1 tbsp oil**

Method

1. Spread the cooked rice on a plate to cool it.
2. Cut the lemons and squeeze out the juice. Strain and remove the seeds.
3. Heat the oil and fry the cashew nuts and mustard seeds together. Add the green chillies, turmeric powder and fry for another minute.
4. Add the lemon juice and stir gently, reduce the heat, cook for a further minute.
5. Remove from the cooker, pour the paste over the rice, spreading evenly, and cover with a lid for a further 10 minutes.

★. Add stir-fried curry leaves last to provide a special flavour.

Rice with Urad dhal

Preparation & cooking time: 45 minutes
Serves 5

Ingredients

- 2 cups rice
- ¼ cup urad dhal
- 2 tbsp butter or oil
- ¼ tsp asafoetida powder
- 1 tbsp black pepper seeds for tempering
- 1 tsp mustard seeds
- 1 tsp cumin seeds
- 1 dry red chilli chopped
- 1 sprig curry leaves, chopped
- salt to taste
- 3 tbsp dried fried onions
- few crisps or fried poppadoms to garnish
- 5 roasted cashew nuts, chopped

Method

1. Wash the rice, place in a pan of water and bring to boil. Then reduce the heat cover and cook (simmer) for about 20 minutes or until the rice is cooked. Add asafoetida powder and leave it to cool in a large, wide plate.
2. Roast the urad dhal in a frying pan, remove, grind it in a mortar and pestle and set aside. Roast the pepper in the pan in a little butter and set aside. Then add little more butter, the mustard seeds, cumin seeds, red chillies, curry leaves, roasted cashew nuts, and temper for two minutes.
3. Add the rice, ground urad, roasted black pepper to the above and mix well.
4. Finally add the fried onions, garnish with crisps or few small poppadoms.

★ Can substitute ghee or sesame oil instead of the butter. Gingelly oil (Tamil name "Nallennai" is used in Sri Lanka; it is similar to sesame oil.)

Sesame Rice

Preparation & cooking time: 45 minutes

Serves 4-6

Ingredients

- 250g sesame seeds
- 125g urad dhal
- 10 dried red chillies, chopped
- 1 tsp asafoetida powder
- 5-6 curry leaves
- 1 tsp mustard seeds
- 4 cups rice
- 2 tbsp butter or 1tbsp ghee
- salt to taste

Method

1. Slightly dry roast the urad, sesame seeds and the chillies in a pan (leave one chilli and a tsp of urad aside for step 3). Remove contents and grind in a mortar and pestle. Add the asafoetida.
2. Cook the rice in a saucepan of water and drain (appx 20 minutes).
3. Heat the butter in a separate pan. Add the mustard seeds, dried chilli and urad dhal. Remove from heat and pour this over the cooked rice, add the ground powder and a little more butter and mix thoroughly.

Quorn Bhiriyani

Preparation & cooking time: 45 minutes

Serves 4-6

Ingredients

- 3 cups rice
- 200g (packet) quorn cubes
- peas (optional)
- 200g tub natural yoghurt
- 1 tsp masala paste
- 2 tsp crushed garlic & ginger paste
- 2 onions, 2 green chillies
- 2 tsp mixed coriander and cumin powder
- 1 tsp ground mixed spice powder, 2 tbsp butter

Method

1. Grind the onions, masala paste, garlic, ginger and green chilli in a blender and add to the yoghurt. Soak the cubes of quorn in this for 2 to 3 hours.
2. Half cook the rice and drain the water. Move this into a roasting dish lined with foil.
3. In the mean time cook the quorn and the sauce on a high heat for 5 to 8 minutes. When the mixture is slightly thick, remove it from the cooker. Stir fry the peas in little butter and mix with the quorn.
4. Spoon this mixture on to the rice and cover with the rest of the rice. Sprinkle the mixed spice powder (cardamom, cinnamon, nutmeg) and a bit of butter all around the rice, cover with foil and cook in a preheated oven on 160°C for about 20 minutes.
5. Remove and mix it well, serve with salad or any cooked side dish.

★ Can also use paneer or tofu; if using these, first cut into cubes and fry then add with yoghurt and peas and cook in the oven.

Rice Porridge

Known as kanji, you may treat this as a breakfast cereal for a Sunday morning

Traditional recipe is with Sri Lankan red rice, coconut milk, and half split moong. Having two bowls of it will make you full and not think of a meal for the next 6-8 hours.

Preparation & cooking time: 1 hour

Serves 4-6

Ingredients

- 1½ cups red rice (about 200g)
- ½ cup roasted split moong dhal(50g
- 400g (can) coconut milk
- and 500 ml cows milk
- salt to taste.

Method

1. Wash the red rice and the moong dhal well in water.
2. Place the rice and moong in a large heavy based saucepan, add about 500ml water and bring to boil. (You may need to boil water in a kettle and keep it ready). Reduce and cook for 15 minutes. If water evaporates, top it up with little more boiling water (1 cup-150ml). Dhal and red rice,require more water and should get cooked in 20-25 minutes.
3. When the rice is almost cooked add the milk, bring to boil and reduce the heat and let it simmer for further 5-8 minutes.
4. Add salt as per your taste.
5. The finished product will be similar to cooked porridge, but a little bit watery. Serve hot in bowls.

★ Substitute full creamed evaporated milk (400g) and 1 pint cows milk. Can also prepare with semi skimmed milk but taste differs.

★ Some prefer to add sugar instead of the salt.
Prepare and enjoy a healthy breakfast. It is one of my favourites.

Fried Rice

Preparation & cooking time: 1 hour
Serves 4-5

Ingredients

- 2 cups basmati rice
- 1 large carrot
- 6 cloves
- 1 leek (with the green leaf)
- 100g small peas (frozen)
- 100g sweet corn (frozen)
- 5 button mushrooms, sliced
- 10 mange tout peas, thinly sliced
- few baby corns cut into ½cm pieces
- 1 tsp of mixed cinnamon and cardamom powder
- 3 tbsp sesame oil
- ¼ tsp turmeric powder
- 1 tsp ginger and 1 tsp garlic paste
- 1 cube vegetable stock
- salt to taste (to be added to the vegetables)

Method

1. Wash the rice and bring to boil in a pan of water. Add the cloves, reduce the heat slightly and cook for about 18 minutes until the rice is just ready and not overly cooked.

2. Add the turmeric powder, stir it once and drain the water. Place the rice in a colander. Remove the cloves, cover and leave it aside.

3. In the mean time, while the rice is getting cooked, clean the leek by removing the leaves and wash. Slice it finely.

4. Scrape the carrot skin and grate it or cut into fine strips of matchstick size.

5. Microwave the vegetables, spread out on a plate, for a minute or two minutes, depending on the microwave power. If using frozen vegetables cook for a bit longer.
6. Heat a wok and add oil, then add the vegetables, ginger and garlic paste and fry. Sprinkle salt and stir fry. When the vegetables are slightly cooked start adding the rice little by little and mix with a long handled fork. Add the vegetable stock and mix well.
7. Finally add the ground cinnamon and cardamom powder, stir well to mix and remove from the cooker.

★ **Serve with salad and any favourite kari**
Can use 2 tbsp butter or 1 tbsp ghee instead of the oil

Variations:

With egg
You can beat 2 eggs in with a little milk and divide this into two or three portions and fry each like a thin pancake. Then cut these into strips and add to the rice before removing from the cooker.

With Tofu
Tofu or Quorn pieces are to be fried and added to the rice.

Soya mince
Fry this in a frying pan with a little oil and add this last to the rice.

Jeera Rice 1

South Indian preparation S
Preparation & cooking time: 45 minutes
Serves 4-6

Ingredients

- 2 cups basmati rice
- 1 tbsp cumin seeds
- 2 tbsp ghee
- 4 tbsp dried onion flakes
- paste made with 2 garlic cloves,
- 1 inch root ginger,1 small onion, 1 tomato
- salt to taste
- ¼ tsp turmeric powder
- 3cm rampe leaf, chopped
- 4-5 curry leaves, chopped
- 4cm cinnamon stick, 6 cloves

Method

1. Wash the rice and cook in a large pan of water. Add cloves. After 12 minutes add turmeric powder and boil for another 3-4 minutes until the rice is just ready grains start to split). Drain the water and leave the rice in a colander.
2. In a wok, stir fry the cumin seeds in a little ghee, add the cinnamon, cloves, rampe, curry leaves and dried onion flakes.
3. Add the garlic, ginger, onion paste to above and stir it for few minutes. Add the rice little by little and mix with a fork to ensure the rice is mixed well.

★ **Ready to serve hot with chutney or sambar**

Hyderabad Bhiriyani

Preparation: 15 minutes, Cooking: 45-50 minutes
Serves 7

Ingredients

- 3 cups basmati rice
- ½ tsp turmeric powder
- vegetables – 2 carrots, 1 leek, sliced
- 15 button mushrooms, cut into quarters
- 3 medium size potatoes, sliced
- 2 medium onions, sliced
- 20 roasted cashew nuts, cut in half
- 10 almonds (soak in water for 10 minutes)
- 12 large sultanas (optional)
- 1 tsp chilli powder
- 1 tsp garlic paste, 1 tsp ginger paste
- 1 tsp saffron (if you cannot get this use turmeric)
- 2 tsp masala paste or powder (cumin, pepper, coriander powder)
- 1 cup natural yoghurt (250ml)
- 3 sprigs of coriander leaves, chopped
- few bay leaves
- 3 green chillies, sliced
- 3 tbsp rose water
- 4 tbsp coconut milk
- 2½ tbsp ghee
- 5cm cinnamon stick, 5 cardamoms, 2 cloves (grind all)
- salt to tasteλτ το ταστε

Points to note

Saffron: If using saffron, first mix this in a little warm milk. You can grind the cinnamon etc. and sprinkle, or break the cinnamon into pieces and add to the vegetable.

Method

1. Wash the rice and leave it aside in a colander for 15 minutes.
2. Boil the rice in a large pan of water, add 2 cloves bring to boil and cook on fairly high heat for about 12 minutes until the rice just starts to get fluffy (but not fully cooked).
3. Add ½ tsp of turmeric powder and mix well. Drain the water and leave the rice in a colander covered.
4. Cook the vegetables in the microwave for 2 minutes.
5. Heat a large wok, Add little ghee and fry the onions until slightly brown, then add the vegetables, ginger garlic chilli powder, chopped coriander leaves, salt, green chillies and stir fry for 2-3 minutes. Add half of the spices and salt to your taste.
6. Add the yoghurt, mixed saffron and bring to boil. Add the cashew nuts, almonds, sultanas, ground cinnamon etc. and when this starts to thicken remove from heat.
7. Line an oven tray or dish with foil to cover the sides. Spread one-third of the rice as one layer and spread some vegetables. Repeat the rice and vegetables and finally add a layer of rice. Sprinkle rose water.
8. Add one or two teaspoons of ghee over the rice. Add the rest of the spices, the cinnamon and ground cardamom.
9. Cover with foil and cook in a preheated oven, on 160°C for 20 minutes. Mix well before serving.

★ Serve with chutney, salad, dhal etc.

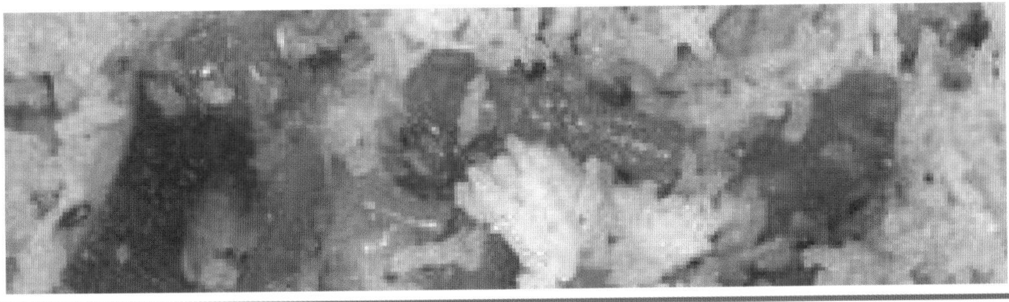

Yoghurt Rice

Called Thayir satham or Curd rice in South India

In the early 1960's when I was in Sri Lanka my dad used to mix rice, yoghurt/curd and vegetable hot sauce and the children got a treat of what he called "curd rice". I learnt that curd rice was different from this when I visited South India. There are several recipes, the one below was given to me and I regularly prepare this.

Preparation & cooking time: 35 minutes
Serves 4-5

Ingredients

- 2 cups basmati rice
- 1 large (500g) carton natural yoghurt
- 3cm root ginger finely chopped
- 1 tsp mustard seeds
- 1 tsp cumin seeds
- 1 tsp urad dhal
- 1 tsp channa dhal
- salt to taste
- 2 dried red chillies, chopped
- 3 tbsp oil or 1 tbsp ghee
- ¼ cup milk (100ml) (optional)
- 3 sprigs coriander leaves, chopped

Method

1. Boil the rice in a pan by adding 4 cups water, reduce heat and simmer for 20 minutes until the rice gets cooked. Add salt and leave in a fairly large bowl.

2. Heat a frying pan add 1 tsp oil or a little ghee and stir fry the mustard seeds and cumin seeds for a minute, till the seeds splutter.

3. Then add the red chilli, channa dhal, urad dhal and fry for few minutes.

4. When the dhal turns slightly brown add the ginger and coriander leaves. Stir once and remove from the cooker.

5. Transfer the fried contents to the bowl of rice and stir well.

6. Finally add the yoghurt and if the mixture is slightly thick add the milk and serve warm.

★ Chopped green chillies can be added with the coriander leaves.
If you want it mild, you may omit the chillies.

If you like it sweet, add white sugar and a bit of honey (and leave out the chillies).

★ Can add pomegranate seeds to either the sweet or hot preparation

Pilau Rice

Preparation & cooking time: 45 minutes T
Serves 2 io

Ingredients

- 1 cup basmati rice
- 2 garlic cloves, grated
- 2cm piece ginger, grated
- 2 tbsp ghee • salt to taste
- 1 red onion, sliced
- 3 cardamoms, 3 cloves
- cinnamon stick - 4cm size, chopped
- 10 cashew nuts, chopped, or a few almonds
- few strands of saffron or ¼ tsp of turmeric powder mixed in little water

Method

1. Wash the rice, place in a pan of water and bring to boil. Reduce the heat to medium and cook for about 18 minutes until the rice grains begin to slightly split. Half way through the cooking add the cloves and the cardamoms.
2. Add the turmeric, stir for few seconds and drain the water. Keep the rice covered.
3. Heat the ghee in a frying pan, add the onions, chopped cashew nuts, garlic, ginger, curry leaves, bay leaves and then add the cinnamon pieces.
4. Add the cooked rice little by little and stir well. Leave it covered and cook for a minute.

★ Serve with any vegetarian/non-vegetarian dish and a salad.
If using the rice cocker, add the fried items half way of the coocking.

Pongal - (Savoury Rice)

Preparation & cooking time: 45 minutes
Serves 4-6

Ingredients

- 2 tbsp butter
- 1 medium-sized onion, finely chopped
- 2 cups red rice (Sri Lankan) or basmati
- ½ cup roasted split moong dhal
- salt to taste
- 400g coconut milk (1 tin) or milk made from ½ a coconut
- 1 tsp ground cardamom
- 15 roasted cashew nuts
- ½ coconut

Method

1. Carefully remove the inside flesh of the coconut using a knife. Then cut this up into thin flakes.
2. Heat the oven to190°C Circotherm.
3. Arrange the coconut flakes on a baking tray lined with foil and place this in the oven and cook for 12-15 minutes until coconut turns slightly brown in colour.
4. Wash the rice, moong dhal and place in a heavy-based large saucepan. Add appx. five cups water and bring to boil. Reduce the heat to medium and cook until the rice is fairly cooked, about 15 minutes.
5. Add the butter, salt, coconut milk and cook for another 10 minutes, until the rice mixture is thick and absorbs the water. Add the roasted cashew nuts, cardamom powder and mix well. Remove from cooker.
6. Transfer the rice on to a serving dish and top it with the flaked coconut.

★ Suggested items to serve with rice are fried aubergine, sambar, lentil dish, red chilli-onion sambol.

★ Can substitute semi skimmed milk or full cream carnation milk according to your taste.

Rice and dhal

North Indian name is Khichri
This can be cooked with moong dhal, red lentil or any other dhal. I have used red lentil in this recipe. This is a dish children like to have instead of plain rice. Add ginger, garlic to taste and omit the chillies.

Preparation & cooking time: 40 minutes
Serves 2

Ingredients

- 1 cup basmati rice
- ½ cup red lentil (masoor dhal, preferably whole with husk)
- 1 onion, sliced
- 2 tbsp ghee
- salt to taste
- 2 sprigs fresh coriander leaves, chopped
- 2 green chillies,chopped
- 1 tsp garlic and ginger paste
- ½ tsp turmeric powder

Method

1. Wash the rice and dhal and soak in water for 10 minutes.
2. Heat 1tsp ghee in a heavy-based deep saucepan and fry the onions.
3. Add turmeric, garlic and ginger paste. Drain the water from the rice and add the rice to the pan and fry for few minutes.
4. Add three cups of water, bring to boil and reduce the heat. Half cover and cook for 15 minutes.
5. Add the coriander leaves, chopped green chillies and cook for another 5 minutes. Add 1 tsp ghee and stir.

★ Have it hot with salad or any side dish.
More water is used as it is tasty when slightly moist and sticky.

Tomato Rice

Preparation & cooking time: 30 minutes
Serves 4

Ingredients

- 2 cups boiled rice
- 2 fresh tomatoes, chopped
- 2 tbsp split moong dhal
- 3 green chillies, chopped
- 1 onion, chopped
- 1 clove garlic, crushed
- small piece of ginger, crushed
- 8-10 curry leaves
- 1 tsp mustard seeds
- 1 tsp cumin seeds
- pinch of fenugreek seeds
- pinch of turmeric powder, 3cm rampe stick
- oil/butter for frying
- 1 tsp chilli powder

Method 1

1. Fry onions in a little oil, add mustard seeds, crushed garlic, ginger, curry leaves and moong dhal.
2. When all of this is fried and golden in colour, add the chillies, tomatoes, chilli powder, and stir fry for few seconds.
3. Add the rice to the fried ingredients and stir it well. If required, sprinkle a little water and stir.
4. Add cut-up rampe stick, stir well and remove from cooker.

Method 2

Use ingredients as in the above recipe except for the rice. Use 1 cup uncooked basmati rice and 20 cashew nuts, roasted and chopped.

1. Fry all the ingredients in a pan adding 1 cup basmati rice. Add 2½ cups of water and bring to boil. Reduce heat and simmer for 15-18 minutes and cook the rice. Add roasted, chopped cashew nuts and serve hot.

★ I like to add some fried dry red chillies.

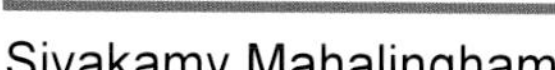

Sweet Rice

Tamil name: Sakkarai satham or pongal
Preparation & cooking time: 45 minutes
Serves 5

Rice dish prepared for auspicious occasions and festival times. This can also be served as a dessert.

Ingredients

- 1 cup red raw rice
- ½ cup roasted split moong dhal
- 2-3 cups water
- 1 cup cows milk
- ½ can evaporated milk
- 4 cardamoms crushed
- Pinch of salt
- 3 tbsp butter or 2tsp ghee
- 150 g soft brown sugar or sakkarai (jaggery)
- 20 cashew nuts, 1tbsp sultanas.

Method

1. Wash the rice until the water is clear and add 2 cups water, place the rice and water in a heavy based saucepan and bring to boil. Add the washed roasted moong dhal.

2. Reduce the heat and cook for 10-12 minutes. You may need to add another cup of hot water until the rice is nearly cooked.

3. Add cows milk, soft brown sugar and stir well. If using jaggery, mix the jaggery with milk, sieve through a fine net to remove any unwanted items etc and add it to the rice.

4. Roast the cashew nuts in ½ tsp butter and add the sultanas. Chop the cashew nuts.

5. Add butter or ghee to the rice and stir well. Add the cashew nuts, sultanas, crushed cardamom

6. Finally stir in the evaporated milk and cook over slow heat for further 5 minutes until the rice and milk form a sticky texture with almost no liquid.

★ Using a heavy based pan is essential to avoid the rice from sticking to the base

Alternatives to Rice

Alternatives to Rice - Index

Page N^o^

Alternatives to Rice - Index

Cup measurement included in this chapter refers to UK standard. Cup included refers to a coffee/tea mug

1 cup plain flour	165gm
1 cup water	330ml
little water	3-4 tablespoons

Cheese Potato Pancake

Preparation & cooking time: 1 hour

Serves 4

Ingredients

- 360g (2 cups) plain flour
- 300-400ml milk
- 1 egg beaten
- pinch of salt
- little butter or oil

Filling

- 1 courgette
- 30g plain flour
- 2 large onions, chopped
- 1 green pepper, diced
- 250g grated cheese
- butter or oil for frying
- ½ tsp chives or any spice to your taste
- 1 green chilli, chopped
- 2 tbsp rice flour
- 1 leek
- 10 button mushrooms
- 100g sweet corn
- 1 tsp garlic paste,
- 150ml milk
- 1 tsp pepper powder
- 250g potato, grated

Method

1. Heat a pan and melt butter or oil.
2. Add the onions, vegetables, potato, salt, garlic and the spices. Cook for a minute, add 30g flour and stir fry.
3. Add the milk and ¾ of the grated cheese (save a bit for later).
4. Bring to boil and let it thicken.
5. Make the pancake batter with egg, sieved flour, milk and ¼ tsp salt. Beat well with a hand beater or a fork.
6. Heat a frying pan, brush with little butter or oil. Pour one spoon of the batter and swirl the pan to make a pancake (or move the back of the spoon around to get the shape). Cook for 30 seconds.
7. Turn the pancake over, cook the side and leave it on a plate.
8. Pour the next pancake and whilst this is cooking spread the vegetable mixture on to the cooked pancake, fold in half and leave on a baking tray.
9. Do the same with the rest of the pancakes. Sprinkle the rest of the cheese and bake for 20 minutes in a preheated oven at 170°C.

★ Can place the tray under a grill and cook until it turns slightly brown.

Savoury Pan Cake -1

Preparation & Cooking time: 40 minutes

Appx - 20 pan cakes.

Ingredients:

- 200g plain flour
- ¼ cup water
- 1 egg
- ½ cup milk, full cream
- salt to taste
- little oil

Filling:

Savoury mashed potato mixture or chick peas mixture. Recipe included in the vegetable section

Method:

1. Combine all the pancake ingredients (except the oil) and mix thoroughly.
2. Heat a frying pan, brush with a little oil.
3. Pour a large spoon of the batter into the pan. Prepare the pancake, cooking both sides.
4. Leave on a plate, spread one tablespoon of the filling, roll it up and serve.

Pan Cake with Sweet Filling

Preparation & cooking time: 40 minutes

Appx - 20 pan cakes.

Ingredients

- 200g plain flour
- ¼ cup water
- little oil or butter
- ½ cup milk, full cream
- 1 egg
- salt to taste

Filling

- 125g desiccated coconut/fresh coconut scraped
- 100g soft brown sugar
- 3 cardamoms, crushed

Method

1. Melt a little butter in a pan and roast the coconut until golden brown. Remove from cooker. After a minute add the sugar, crushed cardamoms and mix well.
2. Cook the pancakes, spread a tablespoon of the filling on each and roll.

★ Good to serve with a cup of tea.

Savoury Pan Cake - 2

Preparation & cooking time: 40 minutes
Makes 25 pancakes

Ingredients

For the batter

- 360g plain flour or equal amounts of plain and self raising flour
- 1 cup cows milk
- 1 egg optional
- pinch of salt

For the filling

- 10 small mushrooms
- 1 tsp chilli powder
- 1 potato boiled and mashed
- salt and pepper to taste
- 1 small onion, chopped
- 1 green chilli, cut finely
- 200g cream cheese

Method

1. Sieve the flour and place in a bowl. Add egg and beat with a fork. Add the milk and beat well using a whisk. Add little water to get the correct thickness of batter and leave it aside.

2. Cut the mushrooms finely and fry in little butter or oil with chopped onion. In a bowl mix cream cheese, salt, pepper, chilli powder, fried mushrooms and potato to form a paste.

3. Heat a 10cm diameter frying pan and cook the pancake by pouring 1 largespoon of batter and swirling the pan or use the back of the spoon over the batter to make a circle.

4. When cooked turn it over. After a minute serve on to a plate. Brush or wipe the pan with little oil and prepare another pancake.

Savoury Pan Cake - 3 (Bengal preparation)

Preparation & cooking time: 45 minutes

Serves 4

Ingredients

- 2 cups gram flour - sieved
- ½ cup self raising flour
- 1½ tsp garlic paste
- 1 tsp ginger paste
- 3 green chillies, chopped
- 1 tsp cumin seeds
- 1 tsp ajwain seeds
- 1 medium onion, finely chopped
- salt to taste
- water
- 1 egg (optional)

Method

1. Grind garlic, ginger, chillies, ajwain seeds and cumin.
2. Mix the ground paste with the flour. Add the onions and salt. Beat an egg and add this (optional).
3. Add water to the flour, beat it well to prepare a batter as for pancakes and leave for 15-30 minutes.
4. Heat a frying pan or an iron girdle and brush with little oil or ghee.
5. Pour a spoon of the batter and make a circular pancake.
6. Cook both sides and remove and place on a plate
7. Serve with dhal, chutney, coconut sambol or dry potato kari.

★ Can chop the green chilli and add to the flour.

Toor Dhal Thosai

Preparation: 2-3 hours Cooking time: 30 minutes for 25 thosai pancakes

Ingredients

- 100g toor dhal
- 200g rice
- water
- salt to taste
- 45g (¼ cup) self-raising flour
- water to mix
- spring onion, green chilli,
- 2 shallots
- 2 cloves garlic
- piece of ginger
- ¼ tsp turmeric powder.
- ghee or butter (2 tsp)

Method

1. Soak the dhal and rice for at least 2 to 3 hours. Wash and using a blender grind to a paste, adding water.

2. Mix with salt and the self-raising flour. The batter should be a bit thick at this stage.

3. Leave for an hour or so.

4. Add finely chopped spring onions, chilli, shallots, grated garlic.turmeric powder and ginger to the batter. Mix well.

5. You may need to add a bit more water to get the batter to the correct consistency to make the thosai/pancake.

6. Place a frying pan on cooker brush with little oil or ghee.

7. Pour the batter using a small ladle or a large spoon and spread it in a circle like a pancake. Whilst cooking add ¼ tsp of ghee, turn it over, cook for a minute or so and remove from pan.

★ Serve with chutney or sambol

Thosai - 1

Preparation: 7-8 hours before or overnight
Cooking time: 30 minutes to make 25

Simple method without tempering

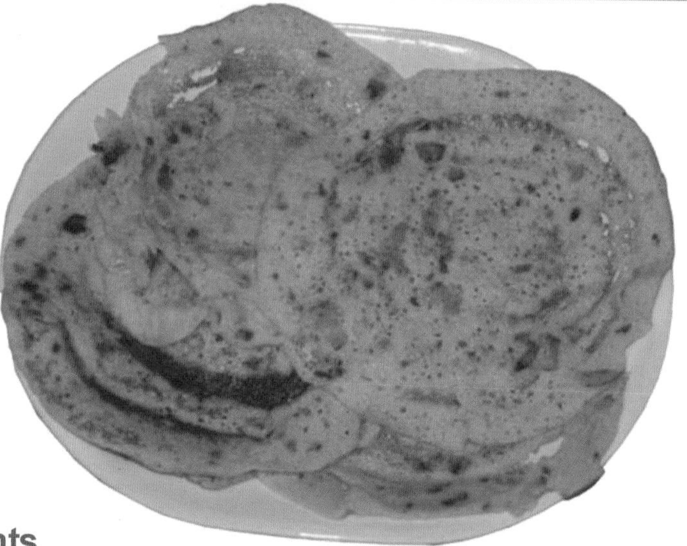

Ingredients

- 1 cup rice flour
- pinch of fenugreek powder
- 1 cup urad flour
- pinch of turmeric powder
- ½ cup semolina
- salt to taste
- 1 tsp of yeast
- 1 tsp pepper and cumin powder

Method

1. Mix the flour, semolina and yeast, adding water to form a thick paste (in between a dough and batter). Leave in a warm place for at least 7 to 8 hours.

2. When the mixture has doubled in size and fermented, add more water, pepper/cumin, fenugreek powder, pinch of turmeric powder and mix to bring into a batter-like consistency for pancake.

3. Heat a frying pan or a griddle and wipe the surface with an oil cloth.

4 Pour 1 large spoon of the mixture and make circular movements quickly with the spoon to make a large circle.

5. When one side is cooked turn over; you may add a little butter or ghee before turning over to make the thosai slightly crispy.

★ Eat with sambol (made with coconut), or sambar.

More time-consuming preparation

- 1 cup white raw rice
- ½ cup urad dhal
- 4 tbsp boiled rice cooked the previous day or ½ tsp yeast

Soak rice and urad for a few hours.
Wash and grind using a blender,
add the boiled rice and grind (or add the yeast).
Follow method 1-5 above.

Thosai - 2 (South Indian method)

Preparation: 7 hours before or overnight
Cooking: -half an hour for 15-20 large thosai.
Crispy pancake.

Ingredients

- 150g white rice
- 50g urad dhal
- 3 tbsp cooked rice
- 1 coconut scraped and milk extracted, about 2 cups or 375g canned coconut milk mixed with ½ cup warm water
- 1 tsp of mixed cumin and pepper powder
- ½ tsp of ground fenugreek or few methi leaves
- 125g natural yoghurt
- salt to taste, ½ tsp sodium bicarbonate
- oil, a large frying pan
- tempering ingredients: 1 onion, chopped; pinch of cumin seeds, 1 tsp mustard seeds, 10 curry leaves

Method

1. Soak the urad dhal and rice in plenty of water overnight.

2. Next day wash the rice and urad and place in a colander. Warm the coconut milk. Grind the urad, rice, cooked rice by placing in a blender and adding the warmed coconut milk.

3. Make the batter slightly thick. Add salt, yoghurt, sodium bicarbonate, pepper, cumin and fenugreek. If using fenugreek leaves chop fine. Mix well and leave it to ferment for 6 to 7 hours.

4. In a frying pan pour a little oil. When hot, add all the tempering ingredients and fry until golden brown. Add this to the batter.

5. If the batter is thick add a bit more milk to get the correct consistency.

6. Heat a frying pan or a griddle, brush the surface with oil.

7. Pour a large spoonful of batter in the centre, spread with the back of the spoon to a thin large circle.

8. Sprinkle ¼-½ tsp ghee or sesame oil over it. Turn over to cook the opposite side. Cook and remove when crisp (1 minute).

★ Serve hot with chutney or sambar

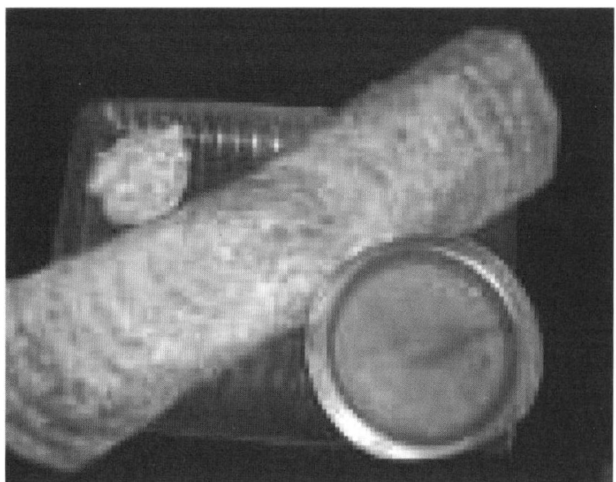

Thosai, a dish served for breakfast or an evening meal, includes several preparations and varieties.

- plain thosai • masala thosai - with potato filling
- ravai thosai - with semolina, • ghee thosai
- paper roast (thin crunchy thosai) • egg thosai

★ The above are speciality of Tamil Nadu (South India), where the ratio is 1 cup urad to 3 cups rice.
The rice gives the crispiness.

Rava Thosai

This is my mother's recipe with small amendments

Preparation & cooking time: 45 minutes Serves 4

Ingredients

- 200g fine semolina
- 100g rice flour
- 60g self-raising flour
- 2 cups butter milk
- salt, pinch of sodium bicarbonate
- 1 cup water
- gingelly/sesame oil
- 1 onion, chopped, 1 tsp grated ginger
- 1 green chilli, few curry leaves
- 2 tbsp chopped coriander leaves
- few mustard seeds, cumin seeds
- 2 tbsp chopped coriander leaves

Method

1. Mix the semolina and flour with butter milk. Add water as required to get a thick consistency, add sodium bicarbonate and put it aside for one or two hours.
2. Heat a tsp of oil in a frying pan and temper chopped onions. Add mustard seeds, cumin seeds and the finely cut curry leaves. Add it to the mixed batter, add the chopped chillies and coriander.
3. If the batter is still thick add more water or buttermilk.
4. Heat a frying pan, brush the base with little oil, pour one ladle of the mixture and spread it around as for a pancake.
   Cook one side, spread ¼ tsp of oil over the thosai. Turn it over with a spatula and cook the opposite side for a couple of seconds and remove from pan.

★ Serve with chutney.

★ You can omit the tempering and add freshly chopped onions as long as these are very finely chopped.
Can substitute natural yoghurt and water instead of the butter milk.

Chapatti/Naan/Poori

I learnt to make this after coming to the UK and now prepare it once a fortnight. I am told by my North Indian friends (Gujarat/Punjab) that a girl's cooking capability is judged by how well she can prepare a perfect round chapatti.

My mother-in-law wasn't aware of this in Sri Lanka in 1968. I have not tried this out on my two daughters-in-law who are British but of Gujarat origin. I have a round cutter which I use to get a perfect round shape.

For the dough you can use different types of flour that are available in super markets or use the traditional chapatti flour known as Atta.

Poori:

Add atta flour and self-raising flour. Can also make it in self-raising flour alone. See individual recipes. Prepare the dough, roll it out, cut discs of 7cm, and deep fry.

Chapatti:

Add salt to the flour, rub the butter into the flour, add water, knead the dough and leave it aside. Make into small balls roll it out and cook on a non-stick pan or special griddle available to cook the chapatti.

Chapatti / Naan

Preparation & cooking time: 30 minutes
Makes 10 chapattis

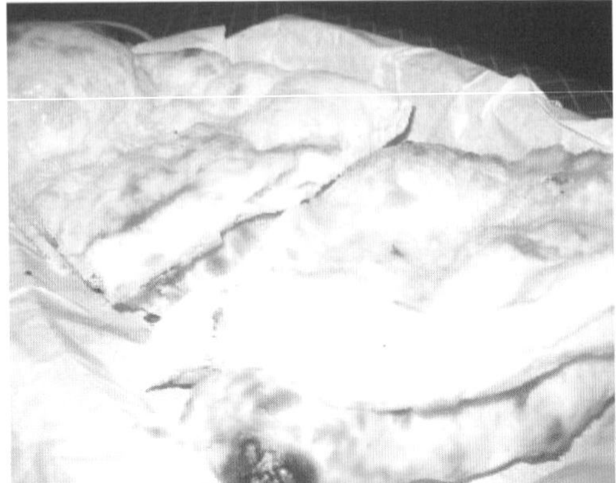

Ingredients

- 2 cups flour (360g)
  (1 cup each self raising and atta flour)
- pinch of salt
- water
- 2 tbsp butter

Method

1. Add salt to the flour, rub the butter into the flour, add water and knead well to prepare a dough. Leave covered for 5 minutes.
2. Make into small balls, roll out on a board sprinkled with flour. Make discs of appx 7cm diameter.
3. Place on a warmed non-stick pan or special griddle available to cook the chapatti.
4. Cook both sides.

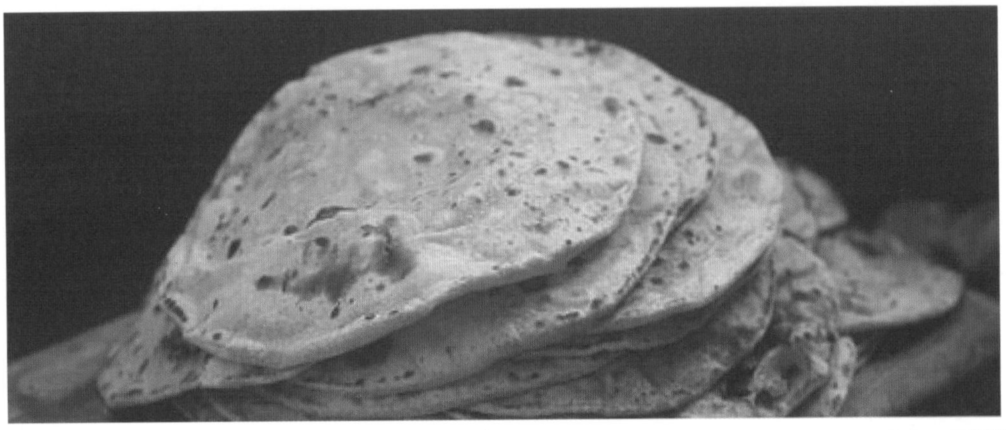

Poori

Preparation & cooking time: 25 minutes
Serves 4

Ingredients

- 180g (1 cup) atta flour or mixture of half each self-raising flour and atta flour
- 2 tbsp butter
- salt to taste
- water for mixing
- oil for frying

Method

1. Put the flour in a bowl, add butter, salt and rub the butter into the flour. Add a little water at a time and knead the flour until it is mixed well and forms a dough. Cover and leave for 5-10 minutes.

2. After 10 minutes take a small amount (size of a lime or golf ball), dust the board with flour or little oil, roll into a round shape. Do a few and leave spread out on a plate.

3. Heat fresh oil in a pan. Carefully slide the poori into the hot oil. Using a slotted spoon gently sprinkle the hot oil over the surface and the edge of the poori. Turn over quickly and remove from oil within a few seconds. Leave on a kitchen paper to drain any oil.

★ This is tasty with potato kari or sambar.

Poori with onions

To the flour in the above recipe add a bit of finely chopped onions, garlic and mushrooms. Knead and leave, roll out and deep fry as above.

Cheese & Veg Bake with Bread

Preparation & cooking time: 1 hour
Serves 4

A favourite dish

Ingredients

- 150g small mushrooms, cut fine
- 1 tbsp Worcester sauce
- 2 tsp of tomato purée, 3 tsp butter, herbs
- sauce made up of 2 eggs, 1 cup of milk
- 1 green pepper, cut fine
- 1 tsp crushed ginger, pepper powder (optional)
- ½ tsp salt
- 6-7 slices of white bread
- 1 vegetable cube (oxo)
- 250g cheese, grated
- 1 leek, cut fine

Method

1. Sauté the mushrooms, pepper, leeks in a little butter, add tomato purée, crumbled vegetable cube, ginger, Worcester sauce and pepper or any spice you like.
2. Cut the bread slices into 4-5cm strips and arrange this in a medium size baking dish.
3. Spread a layer of the mushrooms, leeks and pepper mix.
4. Arrange another layer of bread and spread the rest of the vegetables.
5. Mix milk, 2 eggs, chives (herbs of your choice), little butter, 2 tsp cheese. Heat for 2-3 minutes. Pour over evenly. Top it with grated cheese and bake for 45 minutes at 170°C.

- ★ Can use lasagne sheets instead of the bread.
- ★ Children who are not keen on having veggies will like this.
- ★ You can add grated carrots, chopped green chillies, etc.

Cous Cous

Made from durum wheat. Can be prepared very quickly.

Basic preparation

1. Prepare by soaking one cup of cous cous in two cups of boiling water or stock.
2. Set aside for 5 minutes.
3. Use a fork and rake the cous cous to avoid any lumps.
4. You should finally get swelled up separate grains of cous cous.

- ★ **Can add coconut and steam (equivalent to pittu/puttu, a Sri Lankan recipe)**
- ★ **Veg with couscous**
- ★ **Meat with couscous**
- ★ **Indian spices/lentil/chick peas with Couscous**

Cous Cous with Chick Peas

Preparation & cooking time: 40 minutes Serves 4

Ingredients

- 1 onion chopped
- 220g (1½ cup) cous cous
- 2 green chillies, chopped
- 4 tomatoes, chopped
- few fresh spinach leaves.
- oil for frying
- 450g chick peas (1 can)
- 1 tsp ginger and 1 tsp garlic paste
- 1 tsp chilli powder (optional)
- 1 large potato, cut into cubes
- 1 courgette chopped,1 green and 1 red capsicum pepper, chopped
- ¼ small cauliflower cut into small florets, few curry leaves

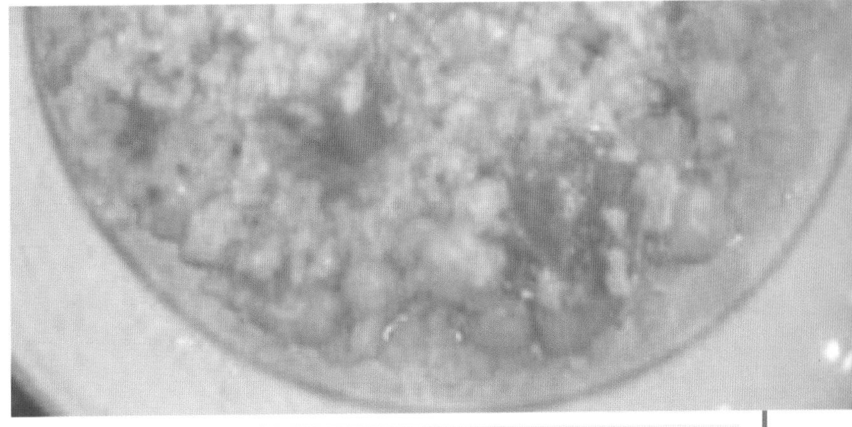

Method

1. Prepare the cous cous as per the main recipe, adding boiling water and rake with a fork to avoid lumps.
2. In a frying pan put some oil, add capsicum, cauliflower, potato and stir- fry for 2 minutes. Add the drained chickpeas and cook for another 4 minutes. Add the spinach, cook for a minute and serve the vegetables onto a dish.
3. Using the same pan add 2 tsp oil and fry the onions, tomatoes, ginger, garlic, curry leaves until slightly brown and soft. Transfer the vegetables and stir fry on low heat.
4. Add the cous cous in small quantities to the vegetables, stir well to mix and remove from cooker after a few minutes.

★ Serve with sauce or chutney.

★ Can sprinkle roasted chopped nuts, chopped coriander leaves. Can add aubergines, mange tout, carrots etc.

Cous Cous with Vegetables

Preparation time: 20 minutes. Cooking time: 15 minutes
Serves 2-3

Ingredients

- 150g cous cous
- 1 carrot, grated
- 1 onion,chopped
- ½ tsp cumin seeds
- 3 tbsp oil for frying
- 12 mange tout, finely cut
- 2 green chillies, chopped
- ½tsp mustard seeds
- 1 leek, cut fine
- 2 cloves grated garlic
- 20g butter (small slice)
- salt to taste, 8 curry leaves

Method

1. Soak cous cous in water as in main cous cous recipe.
2. Fry onions in 2 tsp oil or little butter, add the mustard and cumin seeds, then add the vegetables, garlic and stir fry. Add chillies and curry leaves.
3. Add the cous cous, keep stirring and fry. Add the butter and cook for 3-4 minutes. Remove from cooker.

★ Serve with chilli sauce, coconut, tomato chutney.

Hoppers

It is a traditional Sri Lankan item, looks like a cup-shaped, crispy wafer all round for about 4cm depth with a spongy cake (like crumpets) in the centre. It is a most popular breakfast, but is time consuming and best left for weekends.

In Jaffna hoppers are prepared with milk, whereas in the Southern part of Sri Lanka plain hoppers and egg hoppers are cooked, and eaten with seeni sambol or chilli sambol.
Egg hoppers are popular too. Other varieties are made with jaggery and with sweet pani (sweet toddy), which is now available in cans.

Another variety is the 'chatti appam', prepared in the early 1950's in Jaffna, which is baked over a slow fire for 30 minutes. It turns out like a cake. Not many prepare this now. The recipe consists of adding a little jaggery, ground rice granules and a bit of coconut milk to the last spoon of batter and then pouring this into a hopper pan (tharchi). The tharchi is then placed on very low heat on open firewood. A tray of burning coconut husk is placed over the lid and cooked. The dish turns out like a baked muffin, which you cut and serve.

Hopper pan: This is a small round-bottomed, half-sphere-shaped pan with two handles and a lid, and is called a thava or tharchi. It is better to have two sets of thavas.

I have included the traditional recipe for hoppers and the one that I follow.

For milk hoppers, coconut milk gives a distinctive taste. You can also use single cream, double cream or normal dairy milk. To ¼ cup of any of the above, add sugar to taste, mix and keep this aside to pour in the centre of the hoppers. (see recipe)

Jaggery: This is a type of special hardened brown sugar bought from the Sri Lankan shops. Grate it using a grater or scrape with a knife. You may add a little milk. Pour two table spoons of this in to the centre of the hopper, cover and cook, or use 1 table spoon of the scraped jaggery without the milk, cover and cook.

Hoppers - Traditional Method

Preparation: Mix and leave overnight or 7 hours before

Cooking time: 30 minutes to prepare 10 hoppers

Ingredients

- 2 cups red raw rice (from Sri Lankan shops)
- ¼ cup urad
- 3 slices of white bread with crusts removed
- 6 tsp sugar, coconut water
- 1 coconut - scraped
- salt
- pinch of bicarbonate soda
- 1 tsp yeast in place of toddy
- tharchi/thava

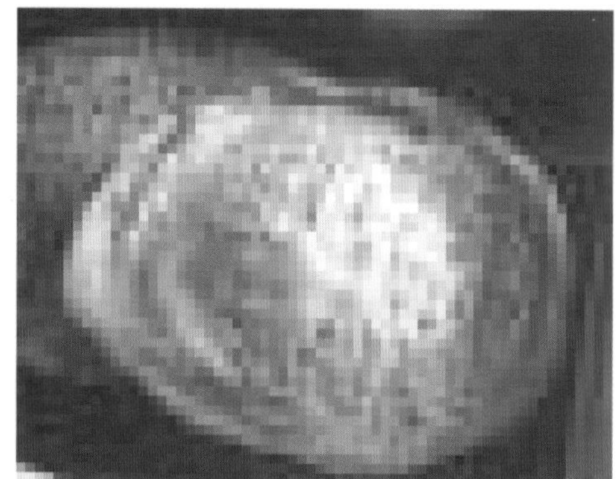

Method

1. Soak rice in water for few hours.
2. Soak the bread in coconut water and 1 tsp sugar for about 20 minutes.
3. Drain the rice and leave it in a colander. Using a blender/liquidiser grind the rice, add the bread and urad and grind it fine.
4. Knead the ground items, adding a little water and prepared yeast, and leave to ferment forabout 8 hours.
5. Put the scraped coconut in a blender, add a little warm water and grind. Put through a netted colander and collect the milk.
6. Keep the first milk separately. Use more warm water and grind the coconut again, to collect the second milk. Try once more to extract any milk and keep this separate.

7. To the first lot of milk, add the rest of the sugar and set aside.

8. Next, mix the second lot of milk to the fermented batter, add salt and beat well with a whisk. Add a pinch of bicarbonate soda and leave for 15 minutes.

9. The batter should be a bit thicker than for pancake. If not add a bit of milk.

10. Heat the hopper pan (tharchi), coat with a little oil using a small piece of cloth or a brush.

11. Use one spoon of batter and pour into the pan, remove pan away from the flame and give it a quick swirl rotation (once) for the batter to cover the sides. Place the pan back on the cooker.

12. Cover and cook for 2-3 minutes or until the sides are crispy.

13. After pouring the spoonful of mixture and doing the rotating /swirling movement, you can add 1 table spoon of the milk and sugar mixture. Cover and cook. When it is ready carefully take out with a flat metal spatula and leave on a plate.

★ Sieve the ground rice and take a spoon of rice granules and mix with water and bring to boil. This can be mixed with the batter instead of the yeast.

Hoppers: Easy Preparation - Milk Hoppers, Egg Hoppers

Preparation: 6-8 hours for fermenting
Cooking: 30 minutes to prepare 15 hoppers

Ingredients

- 1 cup fine white rice flour
- ½ cup bread mix (from any supermarket)
- 560ml cows milk or 375g can coconut milk mixed with 150ml cows milk
- water,
- ¼ tsp salt
- ¼ tsp bicarbonate of soda
- small carton, single cream (150g)
- oil brush or piece of cloth and 3 tbsp oil

Method

1. Mix rice and bread mix flour with about ½ cup of water. Knead and make into a dough as you would do for bread. Leave in a warm place for about 6 hours to ferment and rise.

2. Once the dough has risen pour some milk, add a pinch of salt and mix with a metal spoon. Keep stirring and try to spoon the mixture up and down (like basting). Alternatively use a hand whisk/blender and make sure there are no particles.

3. The mixture should be a slightly thick batter and not of watery consistency. Add the bicarbonate of soda and leave for 15-20 minutes.

4. Next heat the pan and wipe the base and sides of the pan with an oiled cloth or brush. Whilst it is fairly hot, spoon a medium ladle of batter and give the pan a full swirl/twist; a rotating movement in order that the batter comes on to the sides of the pan. Cover and cook until the sides are crispy and turn light brown in colour. The centre should be cooked but soft to touch, similar to a crumpet.

5. Carefully using a spatula remove the hopper from the pan and place on a plate.

Milk Hoppers

Mix single cream and caster sugar and leave in a bowl.
For a few hoppers, after rotating the batter in the pan add two teaspoons of the mixed cream to the centre, cover and cook.

Egg Hoppers

After pouring the batter and rotating, break an egg into the centre cover and cook on low flame for 3 minutes.

★ Eat plain hoppers with chutney or seeni sambol.

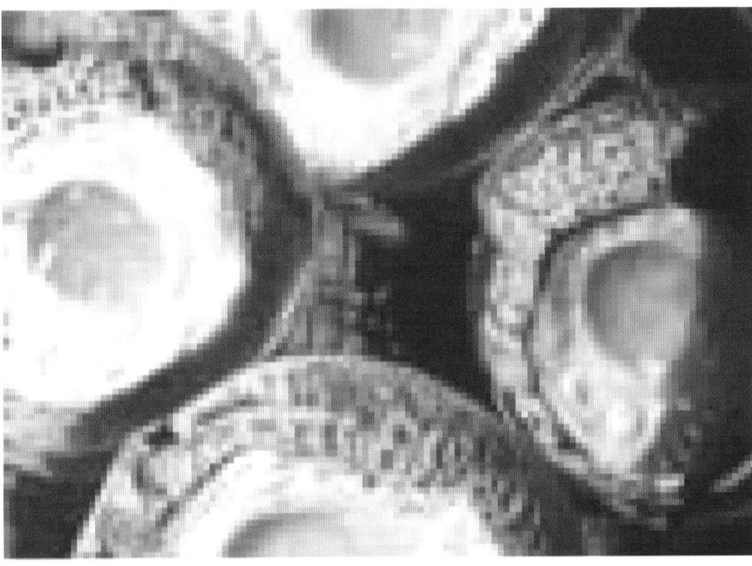

Khata Dhokra (North India)

A North Indian favourite

Ingredients

- 220g basmati rice or patna rice
- ¼ cup channa dhal (appx 60g)
- ¼ cup urad dhal (60g)
- ¼ cup semolina (60g)
- 1 large carton natural sour yoghurt (400g)
- 2 tsp salt
- ¼ tsp asafoetida powder
- 4–5 green chillies and ginger, crushed or chopped to small pieces
- 2 sprigs, coriander leaves
- 5-6 cloves garlic, crushed
- 2 tbsp cooking oil
- 1tbsp bicarbonate of soda
- 1 tsp chilli powder

Method

1. Soak rice and both dhals together overnight in lukewarm water.
2. Clean and wash the rice and dhal four or five times. Leave in a colander to drain the water.
3. Grind the rice and dhal in a blender adding the yoghurt and make a paste/batter. If it is runny add semolina and mix. Leave for 5-6 hours.
4. Add salt, asafoetida, green chillies garlic and stir well.
5. Spread a little oil on small cereal bowl dishes or a high sided baking tray or a flan dish.
6. Add ¼ teaspoon of bicarbonate soda to a quarter of the batter, mix well and fill the oiled dish to ¾ of the bowls depth. Repeat this process for the rest.
7. Sprinkle red chilli powder on top of the batter evenly.

8. Steam the dhokra batter by placing the tray in a steamer (similar to idlis). Dhokras will be ready in 15 minutes.
9. Remove from the steamer and let it cool down for 2-3 minutes and cut in to squares or diamond shapes.
10. Add the chopped coriander leaves and serve hot with garlic chutney or green chilli chutney.
11. **To garnish:** In a pan heat 2 table spoons of oil, add 2 tsp of mustard seeds and allow to splatter. Pour this over the cooked dhokra. This is tasty but can be oily.

Variations

- Substitute 180g (appx 1 cup) gram flour for the rice.
- Also add the following to the previous recipe:
  1 tbsp each of lemon juice, coconut powder, 1 tsp mustard seeds and 1 tsp cumin seeds.
- 1tsp sugar (optional), few dry red chillies to your taste.
- Mix gram flour, lemon juice, salt, ginger paste, yoghurt, turmeric, (sugar is optional) and mix well. Add the ground dhal. Add boiling water to make the paste smooth. Add sodium bicarbonate and stir well.
- Pour the dhokra into a prepared tray and steam
- As soon as you take it out cut into shapes and set aside. Heat a thava and add oil, the mustard seeds, cut dry red chillies etc. and cook for ½ minute. Pour this in with the oil over the cut up dhokra. Garnish with chopped coriander leaves and coconut powder.

Kothamba Rotti (Sri Lankan preparation)

A thin sheet like rotti prepared in a rectangular shape.

Ingredients

- 3 cups plain flour
- 1 tsp table salt
- 2 cups oil (vegetable or corn)
- 1 cup warm water

Method

1. Add salt to the flour and sieve it once.
2. In a large bowl put the sieved flour, add ½ cup of oil and mix to a dough. Mix well and add warm water little by little and knead to form soft dough. Can use an electric beater with a dough hook.
3. If the dough sticks, add a little more oil to your fingers and knead well. It should be a soft dough.
4. When it is very soft make a few small balls and then flatten each slightly.
5. In another small square dish pour the rest of the oil so that the oil is about ½ inch from the bottom.
6. Now place the flattened balls in the oil and soak for 3 hours. Turn it once so that all the sides are soaked and covered.
7. Place a large frying pan or a rectangle griddle on the cooker and heat it.
8. Meanwhile roll the pastry on an oiled board by flattening it and spreading out using your fingers and palm.
9. Raise the flattened rotti and with a swinging movement turn over to the other side. Fold over the edges by approximately 2cm .
10. Brush a large heavy bottomed frying pan with oil. Put the rotti on the pan and cook. Can add 1 tsp of oil all over the rotti while cooking. Turn over and cook for few minutes.

★ Can break an egg on to the first side of the rotti, whilst it is cooking and spread it. Cook both sides. Serve with plain red onion salad or any kari.
Can add an egg to the flour when you prepare and knead it.

Kottu Rotti (Vegetarian)

Kottu Rotti meaning chopped bread

Ingredients

- 10 kothamba rotti cut into 1-2 cm strips
  Can use the tortilla thin sheets or any thin rotti
- 1 red onion, finely chopped
- 1 tsp grated ginger
- 1 tsp grated garlic
- 2 green chillies, finely chopped
- 10 fresh curry leaves, finely cut
- 1 small leek, finely sliced
- 3 tbsp vegetable oil
- 1 tomato chopped
- 1 cup of cooked tofu, cut to strips
- 8 small mushrooms, finely sliced
- mock chicken kari or veggie mince, cooked as per recipe on vegetarian section
- 1 tsp of mixed spice (cinnamon and cardamom)

Method

1. Heat a wok or a heavy based deep saucepan.

2. Add oil and fry the onions, garlic, ginger, leeks, mushrooms, green chilli, tomato and mix well. Add salt and mixed spice.

3. Add the finely sliced rotti, and the prepared tofu or mock chicken. Stir for few minutes and remove from cooker.

★ . If you prefer,the recipe can be adapted to use pasta instead of the rotti.

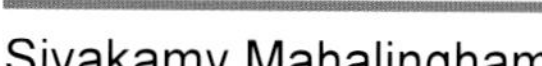

Lasagne with Spices

Ingredients

- one box of lasagne sheets
- ¾ cup red lentils boiled in a cup of water
- 250g fresh spinach leaves washed and cut
- 250g small mushrooms, finely cut
- 150g tofu (steam cook)
- 2 carrots, grated
- 1 can chopped tomatoes (400g)
- 2 fresh tomatoes, chopped
- 5-6 large florets of cauliflower, broken to smaller pieces
- 1 courgette, finely cut
- 125g parmesan cheese grated for topping
- 150g cheddar cheese, grated
- 1 medium potato, grated
- 2 tbsp butter
- 1-2 tsp corn flour
- 1 onion, chopped
- 1 tsp chives, 1 tsp chilli powder and 2 green chillies, chopped (optional)
- 3 garlic cloves and a small piece of ginger crushed
- 1 cup milk to make the sauce (appx)
- few coriander leaves (optional)
- 4 tbsp bread crumbs

Method

1 Cook the lentil in 1 cup of water. After 5 minutes, add a pinch of salt and the spinach and cook for 2 minutes. The mixture should be fairly thick after it is cooked, but should be moist with a bit of water for further cooking to be done in the oven.

2 Stir fry the onions, add the mushrooms and chopped fresh tomatoes.

3. In a separate pan warm the canned chopped tomatoes, add the spices and salt, cook for 4-5 minutes. Add the flavouring you prefer - chilli, cumin or chives.
4 Cook the cauliflower and courgette in microwave for 3 minutes. Steam the tofu and slice into thin sheets.
5 Place the lasagne sheets on to a medium size oven-proof dish and brush this with milk.
6 Place the spinach and lentil mix; smooth this and cover it by arranging a few lasagne sheets
7 Next layer add the mushrooms and tomato mix. Pour the chopped tomato sauce over this. If it is too watery add 2 tablespoons of grated potatoes.
8 Place one sheet of tofu and cover with lasagne sheets.
9 Next layer is the mixture of carrot, cauliflower, grated potato, ginger and garlic. Use the rest of the tofu to cover the top.
10 Warm two parts of the grated cheese. Add a bit of butter, milk and heat up. Add corn flour and remove from cooker.
11 Pour the cheese sauce over the cauliflower and courgette and cover with the last tofu slice and lasagne sheets
12. Spread the rest of the grated cheese; pour the remainder of the sauce, sprinkle with breadcrumbs and chopped coriander leaves. Add little knobs of butter over the cheese and bake in a preheated oven for 20- 25 minutes at 170°C

★ If you like veggies minced, thid can be cooked with tomato and some spices and added as a layer.
Aubergine: Should be chopped to small cubes and microwaved first, then mixed with tomato and cooked on the cooker for few minutes.

Noodles or Rice Stick

Ingredients

- 250g fine noodles /rice stick
- 1 carrot • 1 leek
- few cauliflower and broccoli florets
- 6 large fresh spinach leaves
- 10 button mushrooms
- 100g bean sprouts
- 4 square pieces of fried tofu, sesame - gingelly oil
- 3 cloves garlic, 4cm piece ginger, Chinese oxo cube flavouring
- 1 tsp soya sauce/chilli sauce
- salt to taste

Method

1. Clean the vegetables. Slice the carrot to small matchstick size strips or grate it on the large section of the grater.
2. Slice the leeks, florets of broccoli and cauliflower.
3. Wash and clean spinach, cut this into strips. Slice the mushrooms.
4. Cut the ready fried tofu to thin strips.
5. Cook the packet of noodles/rice stick in water as stated in packet drain and rinse in cold water (3-4 minutes).
6. Heat a wok, add 2 tsp sesame oil, add the cauliflower, broccoli, then leeks and lastly the carrot and stir-fry. Remove and serve on to a dish.
7. Add 1 tsp of oil, sauté/stir fry the bean sprouts, then add spinach, grated garlic, ginger, tofu and the flavouring mixed in 2 tbsp of water.
8. Add the cooked vegetables and the noodles. Keep stirring with two forks to ensure the vegetables and noodles are mixed well.
   Add chilli and soya sauce mix until it gets coated and is well mixed.

★ If using fresh tofu, first steam, then slice and dry on kitchen towel. Stir fry seperately adding chilli sauce. Mix with noodles and vegetables.

For frozen vegetable:

I usually cook the vegetable in the microwave first and then stir fry it.

★ Bamboo shoot, mange tout, sugar snaps are tasty too.

★ Non vegetarians can add strips of egg omlette or roasted/stir fried meat.

Ondhwa (a savoury cake for breakfast)

Dish from North India - Gujarat

This is a baked savoury cake, which is served for breakfast on weekends or as a snack for tea. Ondhwa flour is grainy milled flour made from rice, gram dhal and corn.

Preparation: 6-7 hours to soak
Cooking: 20 minutes and baking 40 minutes

Ingredients

- 2 cups ondhwa flour
- 1 cup warm water
- 1 cup shredded cabbage
- 1 tsp soft brown sugar
- ½ tsp fenugreek seeds
- 2-3 tbsp oil
- 1 cup of yoghurt (140g)
- 1 medium onion chopped
- ½ tsp turmeric powder
- ½ tsp of ajwain seeds
- ½ tsp bicarbonate of soda
- salt to taste
- pinch of asafoetida
- handful of sesame seeds to garnish
- 3 green chillies, cut fine
- 3 garlic cloves, chopped
- 1 medium marrow or 2 courgettes, grated
- 1 bunch methi (fenugreek) leaves, cut fine
- 3 sprigs coriander leaves, chopped

Method:

1. In a bowl mix flour, yoghurt, water, fenugreek seeds, ajwain and leave for 6-7 hours.
2. Next add shredded vegetables, onions, chilli, garlic, salt, sugar, bicarbonate of soda to the above mixture.
3. Heat a pan, add oil and fry the mustard seeds and asafoetida. Pour this onto the mixture. Mix well and taste for salt etc.
4 Line a medium baking tray (22cm square or rectangle) with non stick parchment paper. Pour the Ondhwa mix to 2-3½ cm thickness and sprinkle the sesame seeds.
5 Place the tray in a preheated oven at 190°C for 10 minutes. Reduce the heat to 150-160°C and bake for 40 minutes.
6. Check by inserting a knife which should come clean. The sides and top should be slightly brown as well.
7 Slice into squares or wedges and serve hot.

★ Serve with chutney.

Paratta

Another North Indian dish similar to Naan bread

Preparation & cooking time: 30 minutes

For 6 parattas

Ingredients

- 160g brown atta flour
- 100g self-raising flour
- 70g butter
- cooked potato dish (recipe in vegetables section)

Method

1. Make the dough by adding the flour, most of the butter and follow the recipe for poori. Leave a little butter for the final cooking.
2. Take some dough (smaller than a tennis ball) and roll out to say 10 cm diameter circle and ½ cm thick.
3. . Put a spoonful of mashed filling in the centre bring the edges towards the centre to cover the filling and form a bundle.
4. Roll it out to a fairly thick circle about 10 cm diameter.
5. Heat a frying pan, place the paratta and cook for few minutes.
6. Turn over the paratta, add a bit of butter and cook both sides for few minutes.

★ Filling can be varied: chopped onion and finely cut chilli or any other dry kari.

Pittu Introduction

Another dish with roasted rice flour. A popular food in Sri Lanka. Usually eaten at breakfast or for an evening meal.

Preparation & cooking time: 1 hour
Easy to make.

Can be prepared from any of the following:

- Roasted red rice flour mixed with steamed plain flour.
- Mixture of roasted white rice flour and roasted atta flour.
- Roasted, stone-ground whole meal flour from supermarkets.
- If using plain flour, I usually steam a packet of plain flour for about 45-50 minutes. Pierce with a knife to allow the steam to get to the flour. Next take it out and sieve the flour breaking the large lumps. Alternatively use an electric food processor or blender, which will help to grind the pieces and make it easy to sieve. This flour can be stored and used to prepare pittu and iddiyappam.

- For atta flour, stone ground etc., I usually roast it either by placing the flour in a tray and baking in the oven for 30 minutes on high, or I put in a frying pan and dry roast it until slightly coarse to touch.

- Freshly grated coconut is tasty; if using desiccated coconut, add milk and soak the coconut first. Mix it with the pittu and steam in a steamer for 20 minutes.

- You can steam in a traditional pittu kulal bamboo steamer, which consists of about a foot-long sturdy hollow mould, covered with coir strings and a cloth at the base so that it is easy to handle whilst cooking. Cover the top with a coconut shell or a lid.

Pittu is tasty and is a well liked dish.
Served with sugar, scraped coconut, fruits like mango or banana, any hot kari, egg omelette
My favourite is Marmite on very hot pittu with chopped shallots and green chillies

Pittu

Preparation & cooking time: 45 minutes

Ingredients

- 2 cups, roasted red rice flour (from Sri Lankan shops)
- 1 cup, steamed plain flour
- ½ tsp salt
- 1 cup hot water (appx)
- 1 cup scraped coconut or desiccated coconut

Method

1. Mix the salt and flour by placing in a bowl. Add the water little by little and mix with a handle of the wooden spoon so that the flour absorbs the water.

2. Next using your fingers try and knead so that all flour is coated with water and no dry flour is seen. But the dough should be fairly firm and coarse. Make sure you mix and hold all the flour together in a sphere, ready to crumble.

3. Place half the dough on a sheet of paper and with the open end of a can (tin) keep tapping on it to make it crumble. The food processor can also be used and is quick. Use the cutting blade, put quarter of the flour and run the mixture for 1 minute. You will see small tiny balls. Transfer to a bowl. Do the same with the rest.

4. Traditional way is to steam in a bamboo steamer sitting on a tight-fitting pan/vessel, ¼ filled with water and placed on a cooker.

5. Place the perforated disc in the bamboo steamer, follow with 2 tsp coconut, then a handful of pittu. Repeat and fill to the top. Place on the vessel; once you see the steam coming through the top, cover with a coconut shell or a lid and steam for 3 minutes.

6. Remove the bamboo steamer from the vessel, slightly tilt it and slide the pittu on to a dish by pushing the cooked pittu with the handle of the wooden spoon through the bottom of the bamboo steamer (see photos).
Repeat and steam the rest.

7. If you are to use a steamer, mix the coconut with the prepared crumbled pittu.
Place a small tumbler in the middle of the steamer, and distribute the pittu evenly around the tumbler. Cover and steam for few minutes and gently remove the tumbler allowing the steam to come through the middle. Steam for further 7-8 minutes.

★ **For Milk Pittu (Paal Pittu)**
Add 1 cup roasted urad flour to the ingredients in the main recipe
1 can (400g) thick fresh coconut milk, little bit of sugar.
Mix the flour and follow the recipe as on previous page .
Once steamed, place on a tray and pour a cup of warm coconut milk when the pittu is hot. This is called milk pittu, eat whilst warm, add sugar to taste.

Pizza Hot and Spicy

Ingredients

- 250g plain or whole meal flour
- ½ tsp dried mixed herbs
- ¼ pint milk
- 2 tsp baking powder
- pinch of salt

for the topping

- 2 tomatoes, 1green pepper
- 125g grated cheese
- 1 tsp crushed red chillies
- few mushrooms, 2 shallots
- 2 green chillies, cut fine

for the paste for base

- 1 large onion sliced
- 2 cloves garlic and piece of ginger, crushed
- 2 tomatoes

seasoning

- ½ tsp chilli powder, ¼ tsp basil.
- 3 tsp breadcrumbs
- 2 tbsp oil for frying

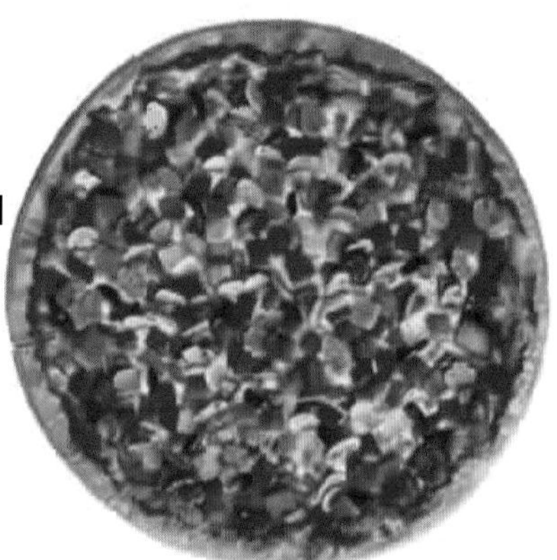

Method

1. Mix the flour, baking powder, salt and herbs. Add milk and knead to stiff dough. Leave for 10 minutes.
2. In a frying pan heat the oil and fry onions, 2 chopped tomatoes, crushed garlic and ginger. Simmer for 2 minutes and then add the chilli powder.
3. Add a spoonful of breadcrumbs to make the mixture thick. Put in a blender and grind to a thick paste.
4. Flour a work surface and roll out the dough to a large circle and transfer to a pizza-baking tray or onto a greaseproof paper.
5. Spread the paste and sprinkle basil.
6. Thinly slice the vegetables for the topping and arrange on the surface. Cover by sprinkling the grated cheese and green chillies.
7. Bake for 20 to 25 minutes in a preheated oven at 180°C.

★ Change the thickness of the base and the toppings to your liking.

Red Lentil in Pastry Case

Ingredients

For the base • 250g plain flour • 150g butter • pinch of salt • little water

Filling

- 1 cup red lentil • 1 cup toor dhal soaked in water for ½ hour
- 1 onion chopped • 2 tbsp margarine,
- 1-2 tsp butter or ghee for topping • 1 tbsp tomato purée
- flavouring: either chives/parsley or coriander leaves chopped
- 1 tsp garlic powder or paste • 1 tsp ginger powder or paste
- vegetables: 1 carrot, 1 pepper, chopped finely
- 1 tomato chopped • 1 vegetable cube (oxo)
- 125g grated cheese

Method To prepare the base

Place the flour in a bowl, add salt, rub the butter into the flour until the mixture is in fine crumbs. Then add water and knead it well, cover and leave in the fridge for half an hour.

Method

1. Wash both toor and red lentil and cook separately adding one cup of water to each. Bring to boil, reduce the heat and simmer the toor dhal for 5 minutes and the red lentil for appx 10 minutes. Do not over cook and ensure it is dry. Remove from heat, mix the dhal and spread it on a tray.
2. Chop the onions and sauté in margarine. Add the ginger, garlic and then the chopped vegetables and tomatoes. Fry for 3-4 minutes, add the dhal and the chopped leaves etc.
3. Roll the pastry on a lightly floured board and cut out circles to fit a cup cake tray or roll out to fit a flan tray /pie dish.
4. Fill the case with the lentil mixture, add the cheese, little bit of butter or ghee and bake in a preheated oven for 25 minutes at 180°C.

★ You may boil the toor dhal first for 5 minutes, then add the red lentil and cook together. Can also use ready-made short crust pastry dough

Rotti with Split Peas - Trinidad

Preparation & cooking time: 40 minutes

Ingredients

For filling

- 1 cup boiled split peas or a can of boiled chick peas (375g)
- 2 tsp cumin seeds
- ½ tsp salt
- I green chilli, chopped
- 1 clove garlic, chopped
- 4 tbsp dried onion flakes

To make the Rotti

- 3 cups fine plain flour sieved
- 4 tbsp butter or 2 tbsp ghee
- 1 tbsp baking powder
- 1 tsp salt
- ½ to 1 cup water

Method

1. Place the flour in a large bowl, add salt and baking powder. Add water in small quantities and knead the flour. Add the softened butter or ghee and knead until the dough becomes soft. Cover the top with a moist cloth and set aside.
2. To make the filling, in a pan roast the cumin adding a knob of butter. Add the chopped garlic, green chilli, salt and the boiled split peas. Remove and grind all ingredients to a paste. Add the dried onion flakes.
3. Take small amounts of dough, roll into balls and flatten to discs ½ cm thick. Place 2 tbsp of the filling paste in the centre. Cover this by bringing the edges to enclose the filling to form a ball. Roll out to ¼" thickness. Do not allow for the filling to leak out.
4. Place the rotti on a heated frying pan or a heavy thava. Can add a bit of ghee or oil and cook both sides.
5. Cook until it is puffy say about 3-4 minutes.

★ Can also prepare plain rottis. Omit the filling, add 3 tablespoon of corn flour to the rotti ingredients and knead well. Then roll out to circles and cook as above.

Rotti with Coconut

Ingredients

- 1 cup plain flour
- 2 cups self raising flour
- ¾ cup desiccated or fresh grated coconut; if using
- desiccated coconut, soak this in ¼ cup of milk or water
- salt to taste
- 2 tsp margarine
- cold water for kneading, about 1 to 1½ cups

Method

1. Mix the coconut with the flour, add salt and margarine. Add water little by little, knead well so that all the ingredients get mixed and form a dough. You may use the food mixture for this. The dough should be soft but not too watery. If the dough is too wet add a little bit of flour. Knead the dough and leave it for 5 to 10 minutes.

2. Take a portion, the size of a ball (4 or 5cm across), flatten and place on a floured board. Roll out with a rolling pin. If you want it crispy, roll it thin, otherwise leave it slightly thick.

3. Heat a frying pan or griddle, place the rotti and cook for few minutes. Turn over and cook for few minutes.

★ Serve hot, with sambol, chutney or butter and jam.

Semolina Uppuma (plain)

Uppu-ma is a Tamil name. The literal translation is 'salt flour'

Preparation & cooking time: 30 minutes
serves 4

Ingredients

- 180g semolina roasted
- 1 onion, finely chopped
- 2 green chillies (optional)
- 1 tsp mustard seeds
- 1 tsp cumin seeds
- 1 sprig curry leaves
- 2 tbsp olive oil or butter
- 1 cup hot water
- pinch of salt

Method

1. Heat a frying pan, add oil and fry mustard seeds, onion, cumin seeds and curry leaves.
2. When this is slightly brown add the water and bring to boil. Add salt and the roasted semolina little by little and keep stirring.
3. Finally add a bit more butter and stir; this will bring it to crumble consistency.
4. Serve with chutney.

Semolina Uppuma - (with tomatoes)

Ingredients

- 1 tsp chopped ginger
- 1 large tomato chopped
- 2 sprigs of coriander leaves chopped
- 2 tbsp grated coconut or desiccated coconut mixed • with little milk
- 20 cashew nuts chopped and stir fried in ghee

Method

1. To the vegetables in the previous recipe add the tomato, ginger and stir fry.
2. If you wish, leave out the peas and carrots and substitute two chopped tomatoes instead.
3. Finally serve into large bowl and garnish with fried cashew nuts, grated coconut and finely chopped coriander leaves.

Uppuma (Savoury Semolina Special)

Preparation & cooking time: 30-40 minutes

Serves 4

Ingredients

- 200g semolina
- 1 onion, chopped fine
- 3-4 tbsp olive oil or butter
- 1 tsp of mustard seeds, 1 tsp garlic granules
- 1 tbsp cleaned urad dhal (soaked for about an hour)
- vegetables: 1 small potato, 1 carrot, 1 small leek,
- 2 tbsp peas
- ½ tsp salt or to taste
- 1 green chilli, cut finely or 1 dried chilli cut (according to your taste)
- 8-10 green curry leaves cut to strips
- 1½ cups boiling water
- large flat base frying pan or Wok

Method

1. Roast the semolina until slightly brown and transfer to a plate.

2. Clean and chop vegetables, cut potatoes to very thin slices.

3. Fry onions in oil, add mustard seeds, urad dhal, few curry leaves. Sprinkle some garlic granules. Add the vegetables, chopped chillies and the rest of the curry leaves. Add bit more oil if you need it. Keep stirring for few minutes. Add the roasted semolina and let this coat the vegetables. Add salt and stir.

4. After a couple of minutes reduce the heat, add the boiling water in small amounts and stir. Keep stirring to ensure the mixture has no dry areas and the lumps are broken into small particles. Continue until you get small round crumbs.

★ Remove from heat and serve with chutney.

Savoury Vegetable Bake

Preparation & cooking time: 1 hour

Serves 4-6

Ingredients

- 1 large aubergine, skinned and sliced
- 5 medium potatoes (waxy type)
- 1-2 onion, thinly sliced
- 2 courgettes, sliced thin
- 1 leek, finely sliced
- salt to taste
- 1 tsp ground pepper
- 2 cloves garlic, grated
- 150g of grated mozzarella cheese (can be increased to your taste)
- 1-2 tsp corn flour
- ½ cup of vegetable stock made with vegetable seasoning
- 1 tsp paprika powder
- 125g butter
- 2 tbsp olive oil
- bread crumbs for topping
- 2 tsp fresh chives, sliced
- 1 tbsp finely chopped fresh coriander

Method

1. Slice the aubergine to thin strips about 1½" long and ¼" thick. Wash and leave on a kitchen paper to dry. Salt the aubergine and toss it to coat all around.

2. Do the same to the courgettes. Cut the potatoes into strips.

3. In a colander place the aubergine and immerse in a pan of boiling water for a minute. Drain and leave on a plate. Repeat the same for courgettes and potatoes. Leave these on separate plates.

4. In a frying pan add two tablespoons of olive oil and sauté the onions and grated garlic.

5. Brush the sides and bottom of a baking tray with oil or butter.

6. Arrange the potatoes in one layer then half the leeks and courgettes. Sprinkle half the spices, finally the fried onions, garlic, remaining leeks and the rest of the spices including the chives and chopped coriander leaves.

7. Mix the corn flour with a little milk and mix it with the vegetable stock. Pour this over the vegetables. Sprinkle cheese to cover the top. Slice the butter and arrange on top. Sprinkle some bread crumbs and cover the top with foil. Bake in a preheated oven at 160°C for 30 minutes.

8. Remove the foil and bake for another 5 minutes. Bake for a further 8-10 minutes by increasing the temperature to slightly brown the dish.

9. Serve hot with mash, rice and fresh salad.

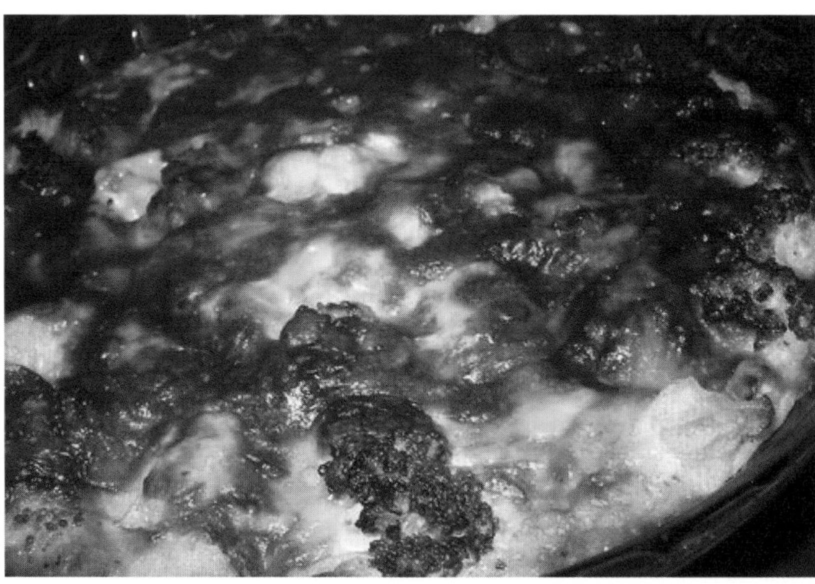

Soft Idli

Ingredients

- 2 cups white rice, basmati or idli rice
- 1 cup urad dhal
- ¼ cup self raising flour b
- ¼ cup cooked rice
- ½ tsp fenugreek seeds or ¼ tsp of the powder

Method

1. Soak the rice, urad dhal and fenugreek seeds overnight.
2 Wash the above and grind in a blender, add the cooked rice and blend to a paste.
3. Place in a large bowl and mix the self raising flour. Leave in a warm place for 8-10 hours to ferment.
4. When the mixture has risen, mix well adding water and salt. It should be a fairly thick consistency.
5. Pour into idli steamer or an egg poacher and steam.

Variation 1

Can use powdered urad dhal and ground rice flour.
1 cup urad flour, 2 cups rice flour, ½ cup self raising flour.
Mix the above with warm water and leave covered in a bowl for 8-10 hours. If it has not risen heat the oven for 5 minutes at high and switch it off. Place the bowl of the mixture in the oven for ½ hour. This will help it to rise. Next add water, salt and mix well. Pour into idli trays and steam for 5 minutes.

Variation 2

Instead of the rice flour add roasted semolina.
1 cup urad dhal soaked and ground, 2 cups roasted semolina
Mix this and keep for few hours as above, after fermenting follow instructions as in variation 1.

String Hoppers

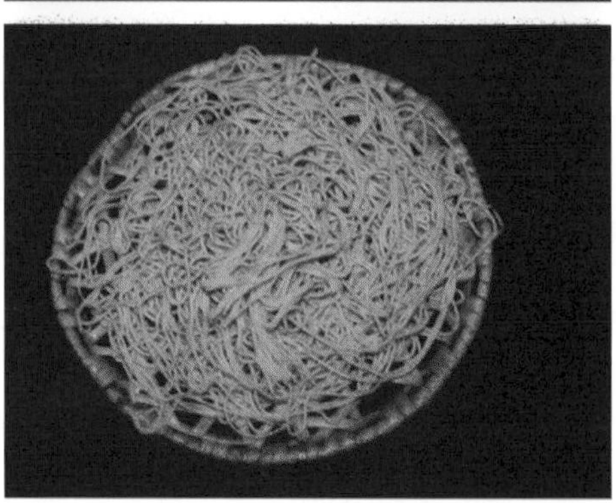

A dish prepared with a mixture of roasted red rice flour, white rice flour or steamed plain flour.

You need a mould with multiple fine holes to squeeze the dough through onto a round flat woven mat which has holes (known as Idiyappa thattu).

When squeezing you need to move your hand in a circle so that the strings of dough cover the mat.

These are placed in a steamer. Arrange so that they don't sit on each other, can place 8 in a steamer and steam for 5 minutes.

Preparation & cooking time: 30 minutes

Serves 3
20 String Hoppers

Ingredients

- 1 cup roasted red rice flour
- 1 cup steamed and sieved plain
- flour
- ¼-½ tsp salt
- 2 cups boiling water, allowed to cool for 3 minutes
- 2 tsp of oil
- 10 string hopper mats
- (Idiyappa thattu)
- steamer
- string hopper mould

Method

1. Place the flour in a bowl and add salt. Using the handle of a wooden spoon mix the flour.
2. Pour water little by little and mix it well so that the whole mixture is moist but not of a soggy consistency. Mix quickly before the water cools down. Add 2 tsp oil and mix well. The flour paste will leave the sides and will form a ball (use your palm to roll it to a ball). It should not be wet and sticky but of a smooth texture. Add more flour if it is too moist.
3. Fill the string hopper mould with one spoonful of the dough. Place the top half of the mould. Compress the two halves of the mould and the dough will come out at the bottom of the mould in fine strings. Move the mould in a circular manner and cover the thattu with the strings.
4. Heat water in a pan and place the steamer on top. Place a few string hopper thattu's and cover. Steam for 4-5 minutes.
5. Remove and carefully take out the string hoppers and place on a dish.
6. Repeat the above for the rest of the flour mixture and steam.

★ Serve with sothi, any kari, sambol, seeni sambol.
★ Ready made idiyappam can be obtained from Sri Lankan shops.

String Hopper Pilau

Preparation & cooking time: 30-40 minutes
Serves 3-4

Ingredients

- 25 cooked string hoppers
- ghee, gingelly /sesame oil
- 6 almonds
- packet of croutons (fried bread)
- fried potato sticks (crisp)
- 8 curry leaves, 2" piece rampe, cut fine
- piece of ginger, 2 clove garlic grated
- 1 tsp mixed spices powder (ground cinnamon, cardamom & cloves)
- small amount of peas and corn (50g each)
- 1 carrot, grated, 1 leek finely sliced
- 4 shallots finely cut
- 3 eggs
- 20 cashew nuts
- 3 tbsp sultanas

Method

1. Shred the string hoppers into small pieces. If it is too dry sprinkle a little water to slightly moisten it.
2. Beat the eggs, add salt and make two omelettes. Serve it on a plate and cut into strips.
3. Sauté the halved cashew nuts, almonds and sultanas. Leave on a plate.
4. In a wok put 2 tablespoons of oil or ghee, stir fry the vegetables and onions. Add garlic, ginger, curry leaves and the rampe.
5. Add the string hoppers little by little and keep stirring. After about 3-4 minutes add the ground spices, fried cashew and bread croutons. Keep stirring; dish out and before serving garnish with potato and strips of omelette.

★ You can use rice stick instead of string hoppers; it needs to be cooked as per instructions on the packet (appx 4 minutes in boiling water). Drain and wash in cold water. Then follow the above recipe.

★ To make crunchy croutons cut up bread into slices, then into cubes. Deep fry in oil until crispy.

Stuffed Parathas - 1

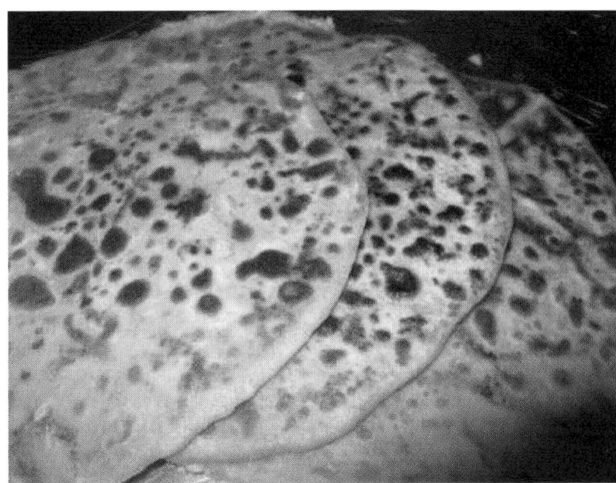

Ingredients

- 3 cups atta (wheat flour)
- 1 tbsp cooking oil or little ghee to fry
- 1 tsp salt
- 3 medium boiled potatoes
- ½ cup boiled and crushed peas
- 1onion chopped.
- 1 tsp lemon juice
- 1 tsp garam masala paste
- 2 tsp mixture of crushed garlic, ginger and green
- chillies (optional)
- 2 tsp chopped coriander leaves

Method

1. Boil and mash the potatoes. Add the boiled peas, garam masala, crushed chillies and mix well.
2. Add all the ingredients to the flour and make a medium dough by adding some water if needed. Divide the dough into balls of equal portions.
3. Apply some flour on the surface and roll it gently into a round shape 'paratha'.
4. Now cook on a frying pan or heavy thava by applying little oil or ghee to each side until light brown.
5. Serve hot with chutney, pickle or yoghurt.

Stuffed Parathas - 2

Ingredients

- 200g potato
- 1 small onion, chopped
- 2 cloves garlic, grated
- small piece of ginger, grated
- 1 tsp chilli powder
- 1 tsp butter

Method:

1. Boil potatoes, skin and put through a grater.
2. Add the ingredients mix and set aside.
3. Mix the atta flour with water following the recipe to make dough for chapatti.
4. Take some dough the size of a tennis ball and place it on a slightly floured work surface or a board. Flatten to form a circle.
5. Place 2 spoons of the filling in the centre, bring the edges of the dough to the centre to cover the filling, then roll it out to a medium sized disc which holds the filling.
6. Heat a frying pan, place the disc and and cook on both sides for few minutes. Brush the sides with very little butter after cooking and leave on a plate.
7. Repeat the same procedure with the rest of the dough.

★ If you like a crispy paratha use more ghee or butter.

Vegetables

Vegetables - Index

Page Nº

Vegetables - Index

Vegetables - Introduction

Some of the traditional native Sri Lankan and Indian vegetables are now available fresh from Supermarkets. The rest can be purchased from Asian grocery shops. Cans and frozen packets are available.
Some require a longer preparation time. Kari's are tasty, they are served as a side dish (not eaten in bulk) for plain rice, string hoppers and pilau rice.

Snake gourd: Long light green, pointed at both ends and hollow in the centre.

Bitter gourd: Also known as Karela/pavakkai. Bitter, as the name says, good for diabetic patients, of medicinal value and green in colour with rough edges on the surface. Chinese shops stock a light green variety which is not so bitter. To cook this you need lot of tamarind juice and coconut water. Serve in small quantities.

Long beans - Payathangai: Thin long bean about one or two ft in length with soft skin; you can break it with your fingers.

Yam – Karanai kilangu: Dark brown with hard skin like a turnip. Be careful when you cut the skin as sometimes fingers can get itchy. Inside it is light orange colour. Clean and cut up in to strips or cubes. Wash it in two lots of water to get rid of the sticky surface (cleaned pieces are available in tins and frozen packs).

Cassava: Brown inner skin and outer light purple skin. It is hard, about a foot in length, a rounded vegetable with a two-inch diameter. The inside is white. The frozen kind is good and equally tasty. If there are any small blue lines in the fresh one these should be avoided as they can be poisonous. Reacts with ginger, so traditional cooking does not include ginger.

Pumpkin: Slightly different from the ones in supermarkets.

Sprouts: Vegetable you like or dislike. It is tasty if you follow the recipe on page 167

Drumstick – Murunga: A long green stick-like vegetable with varied thickness.

Courgette: Ridge gourd referred as "Dodka" or "karuku" is dark green, ridged and tapers at both ends. It can be cooked like the courgette.

Small red onions: Sinna vengayam in tamil. These have a strong taste are like shallots.

Stir Fry with Aubergine, Celery & Pepper

Preparation & cooking time: 25-30 minutes Serves 4-6
A dish as an accompaniment to rice or alternatives to rice.

Ingredients

- 1 large aubergine
- 2 potatoes
- 1 green pepper
- 1 large onion, diced
- 2 cloves of garlic, grated
- 2 teaspoons of chilli powder/paste
- olive oil
- 2 tsp soya sauce
- 2 tsp lime juice
- water
- 2 celery sticks, finely sliced
- 2 tsp tomato purée

Method

1. Cut the aubergine into thin (matchstick) pieces about 5cm long.
2. Brush the aubergine slices with little olive oil and grill
3. Cut pepper and potato to same size (appx 5cm) thin strips, brush with oil and grill.
4. Heat a frying pan, add 2 teaspoons oil and fry the onions for few minutes. Add the grilled aubergine, pepper, potato, celery and stir fry

★ Can add or replace with mushrooms, baby corns, butternut squash

Aubergine Special

Preparation & cooking time: 20 minutes Serves 4

Ingredients

- 6 small aubergines or a large one
- 2 onions
- 1 tsp each of ground garlic and ginger paste
- 1 tsp chilli powder or paste
- 1 tablespoon of ground coriander & cumin powder
- 1 tomato
- ½ tsp of tamarind paste mixed in 2 tbsp water
- oil about 3 or 4 tbsp
- 2 green chillies
- 1 tsp mustard seeds

Method

1. Cut the aubergines and onions into small cubes.

2. In a frying pan add 3 tablespoons of oil, add the mustard seeds and when they start to splutter, add the onions and aubergine. Cook on medium heat until the aubergine gets slightly moist.

3. Add the cut up tomato, salt, green chillies. Then add the chilli powder, coriander powder and the mixed tamarind paste. If necessary add 1 tbsp water, but not more.

4. Keep stirring and cook for about 10 minutes.

5. When the mixture is just beginning to dry, but is still moist, it is the correct time to remove it from the heat.

★ Serve with plain rice or Naan bread.

★ Can microwave the aubergine pieces first for two minutes before frying. This takes less oil and also speeds the cooking.
Chilli paste: Grind 4 dried chillies, salt and garlic.

Aubergine - with Ginger

Preparation & cooking time: 30 minutes
Serves 4

Ingredients

- 2 purple long aubergines (16cm length)
- 8cm size ginger cleaned
- 1 tsp crushed chillies
- 2 cloves garlic
- 1 tsp salt
- 1 tsp turmeric powder
- ½ lime
- 1-2 tbsp oil to fry aubergines
- ¼ cup water

For tempering

- ½ tsp mustard seeds
- ½ tsp cumin seeds
- 1 red chilli, chopped
- 1 tbsp oil
- 5 curry leaves
- 2 shallots, chopped

Method

1. Cut the aubergines into rounds or thin long pieces of 4cm size. Leave on a plate and cook in microwave for 1½-2 minutes.
2. Heat 1 tablespoon oil and add the tempering ingredients, the mustard seeds first, followed by the cumin, onions, chilli and curry leaves.
3. Add the aubergines, salt and stir fry on a high heat. Reduce the heat, add the turmeric powder, sliced green chilli and water, mix well and cook over a medium heat for 10 minutes.
4. Grind or finely crush the garlic and ginger. Add this to the aubergine with the crushed chillies. Stir for a minute and remove from heat.
5. Add the juice of ½ lime just before serving.

Aubergine and Fenugreek leaves (Methi)

Preparation & cooking time: 30 minutes
Serves 4

Ingredients

- 1 large aubergine
- 1 bunch methi leaves, finely cut
- 3 shallots, chopped
- 3 to 4 tbsp oil
- tempering: ½ tsp each cumin and mustard seeds, 1 red chilli chopped, few curry leaves
- ½ tsp turmeric powder
- salt to taste
- 2 cloves garlic,1 tsp crushed chilli powder
- 1 tsp garam masala
- 3 tbsp of milk (optional)

Method

1. Heat a heavy-based frying pan, add the oil, onions and stir fry. Add the cumin and mustard seeds followed by the red chilli and curry leaves.
2. Cut the aubergine into small cubes and add it to the above and fry.
3. Add the garam masala, and then add the finely cut methi leaves.
4. Add the chilli powder and turmeric, cover and cook on a medium heat for about further 5 minutes.
5. If you think mixture is too dry you may add 3 tbsp milk, cook for a minute and remove from heat.

Aubergine Bake

Preparation & cooking time: 1 hour
Serves 4-5

Ingredients

- 1 large aubergine
- 1 large potato part boiled and sliced
- 1 onion • 2 eggs
- ½ tsp cumin powder, • ½ tsp roasted chilli powder
- 1 or 2 green chillies cut up finely (optional) • oil for frying
- small piece of grated ginger • 2 tbsp bread crumbs
- small carton of single cream
- ½ cup milk • 2 cloves garlic, grated
- 100g grated cheese
- 2 tsp butter
- salt to taste

Method

1. Cut aubergine in half length wise and rub with a little butter. Prick in a few places, wrap it in foil and bake in oven for 25 to 30 minutes at 180°C.
2. When cooked peel the skin, discard this and take the pulp.
3. Cut up the onions into small cubes, fry in a little oil to a golden colour.
4. Add the pulp, garlic, cumin powder, chilli powder, green chilli and stir fry for 3-4 minutes. Switch off the heat and allow to cool.
5. Using a hand blender, mash the pulp.
6. Beat two eggs, milk and single cream. Place in a saucepan and bring to boil and cook for two minutes.
7. Place the pulp in an oven proof dish. Add the egg and cream mixture. Arrange the potato slices on top, sprinkle grated cheese and bread crumbs. Preheat the oven to 170°C, bake for 20 minutes and remove from the oven.

★ To save time, you can deep fry the cut-up aubergine in oil and then remove the skin and follow the recipe. This will reduce about 20 minutes of the cooking time.

Banana flower or Plantain flower

Tamil name "Vaalai pothi"
A tasty vegetable but it is not prepared frequently. There is an art in cutting the plantain flower. Some hold in the hand and chop it fine, but you can use a board. The outer harder skins should be removed.

Banana flower stir fry

Ingredients

- 1 medium plantain flower
- 3 tbsp desiccated coconut
- 3 shallots chopped
- 1 tsp mustard seeds,
- 1 tsp cumin seeds
- 2 tbsp olive oil
- Salt to taste
- 2 red chillies, 4 curry leaves chopped
- ½ tsp chilli powder, ½ tsp turmeric powder

Method

1. Clean the banana flower by removing few outer skins which are too dry. You may have to remove two or three including the yellow flowers in between the skins.
2. Cut the flower into fine pieces starting from the pointed end and place in a bowl.
   Add 1 tsp salt to 2 cups water, add this to the bowl, mix well with your fingers and set aside for few minutes.
3. Heat a pan, add the oil, mustard seeds, cumin, onions and stir fry. Add the chopped red chillies, curry leaves
4. Drain the water. Squeeze the banana flower to remove the water. (Can pat dry on a kitchen paper) .

5. Add the flower to the fried ingredients, add salt to taste and cook for 5 minutes.
6. Keep stirring until the dish is dry and lastly add the desiccated coconut turmeric and chilli powder.

For the hot preparation

★ Follow the above recipe omitting the desiccated coconut and red chilli powder.

Add the following

- 1 tsp roasted curry powder
- 1 tsp roasted fennel powder
- 1tsp grated garlic
- ¼ cup milk.

Follow method 1-5 and add curry powder and cook for 2 minutes. Add the milk and cook for 10 minutes. Finally add the roasted fennel powder and remove from cooker.

Beetroot Kari (hot)

Ingredients

- 2 fresh beetroots with leaves
- 1 onion chopped
- 1 garlic clove grated
- ½ tsp ginger powder or
  ½" fresh ginger
- salt to taste
- 1 tsp roasted chilli powder
- 3 tbsp oil
- 4 tbsp water (use if necessary)
- 3 tbsp full cream evaporated milk or, if preferred, normal cow's milk
- 1 sprig of curry leaves
- tempering ingredients: ½ tsp each mustard, cumin seeds, 4 curry leaves and 1 dried red chilli (optional)

Method

1. Peel the beetroot, wash and cut to appx 2 cm cubes. Wash the leaves and thinly slice the tender leaves, discard the thick ones.
2. In a deep frying pan add oil, onions and tempering ingredients. Fry for few minutes until slightly golden in colour.
3. Add the beetroot and cook on a low heat for five minutes. Stir well and add salt, chilli powder, garlic and ginger. If the mixture begins to dry then add a little water, cover and cook for 5 minutes over a medium heat.
4. Finally add the milk, curry leaves, cook for a further minute and remove from heat.

★ Serve with rice or chapatti bread.

Medium hot

Same as above but instead of chilli powder add 1 tsp of turmeric powder and 2 sliced green chillies. Finally add milk or a piece of cream coconut, cook and remove from heat.

Stir Fry Beetroot

Traditional name: "Varai" or "Mallung"
Cooking time: 10 minutes
Preparation: 10 minutes
For 4-6 people

Ingredients

- 3 beetroots
- 1 large onion, chopped
- 1 clove garlic, grated
- ½ tsp grated ginger
- oil for tempering
- 1 tsp turmeric
- 2 tbsp desiccated coconut or fresh scraped coconut
- ½ tsp of plain chilli powder
- 1 carrot grated
- tempering ingredients: cumin, 1 red chilli cut, mustard seeds, few curry leaves chopped

Method

1. Clean the soil from the beetroot and peel the skin. Wash and grate the beetroot.
2. Heat a frying pan, add oil and temper the chopped onion mustard seeds, cumin and the cut up dry chilli.
3. Add the grated beetroot, garlic, ginger and cook on a high flame for 2 to 3 minutes. Keep stirring.
4. Add the grated carrot and stir once.
5 Add the salt, mix the desiccated coconut with turmeric and chilli powder, add this to the beetroot mixture and cook for 2 minutes. Stir fry and remove from heat.

★ Serve with rice.

Carrot Milky Kari

Preparation & cooking time: 20 minutes
Serves 4

Ingredients

- 2 medium carrots
- 1 small onion, diced
- 1 green chilli sliced lengthwise
- pinch of turmeric powder,
- 2 cloves garlic, sliced
- 3 tbsp full cream milk or 1cm piece of cream coconut
- ¼ cup water to cook the carrots
- 3 or 4 curry leaves (optional)
- 1 tsp lemon juice

Method

1. Peel and cut the carrots into small cubes. Place in a pan with the water, chilli, garlic, turmeric, onions and cook for 10-12 minutes.
2. Add the salt, milk, curry leaves and cook for 3 minutes until the milk is absorbed.
3. Remove from heat and let it cool. Add the lemon juice.

★ Serve with rice.

Cauliflower Tandoori

Preparation and cooking time: 30 minutes
Serves 6

Ingredients

- 1 cauliflower, cut into florets
- 3 tbsp ready-made tandoori paste
- small carton natural yoghurt
- 1 tsp garlic powder
- salt to taste
- 2 tsp ginger powder
- chilli paste/powder to taste

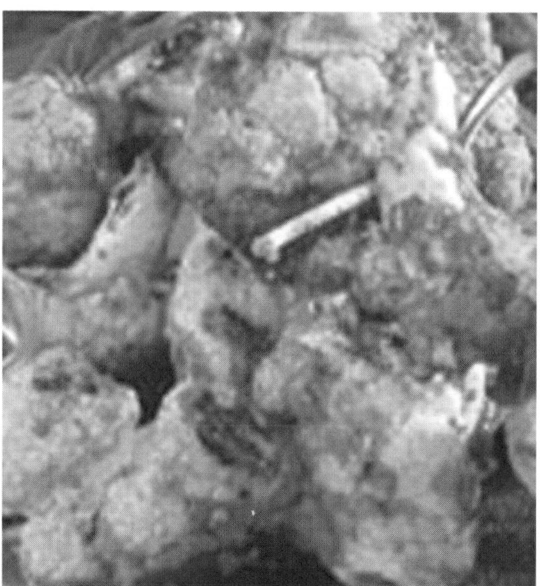

Method

1. In a bowl place the cauliflower florets and add the mixed paste prepared with tandoori paste, ginger, garlic, yoghurt, chilli and salt. Cover and leave for 5 minutes.
2. Preheat the oven at high 190°C. Place the florets with some of the sauce on a baking tray and cook for 15 minutes.
3. Take out and place the florets on another tray and brown it in the oven on circotherm setting for 5 minutes.

Deep Fried Cauliflower Florets

Ingredients

- 1 cauliflower, cut into small florets
- ½ cup plain flour, ¼ cup gram flour
- salt to taste
- 2 tsp plain chilli powder,
- oil for deep frying
- 2 tsp masala (spices) powder
- water

Method

1. Prepare the batter adding the flour, salt, chilli powder, spices and water.
2. Heat oil in a pan, dip the cauliflower florets in batter and deep fry.

Cauliflower and Cheese with Chilli

Ingredients

- 1 cauliflower, cut up
- 2 green chillies chopped
- ½ tsp ground pepper
- chives, salt to taste
- 125g grated cheese
- 4 tbsp butter
- ½ tsp ground cumin

Method

Grilling

Steam cauliflower for 2 minutes. Add butter, grated cheese, chopped green chillies, pepper, salt and grill for 5 minutes.

Baking

Prepare a sauce with milk, butter, cheese, parsley, grated garlic, pinch of cumin, pepper or chives. Pour just enough over the cauliflower and bake for 15 minutes on high 190°C

★ If you are baking then there is no need to steam the cauliflower.

Cauliflower in Tomato & Chilli Sauce

Preparation & cooking time: 15 minutes
Serves 4

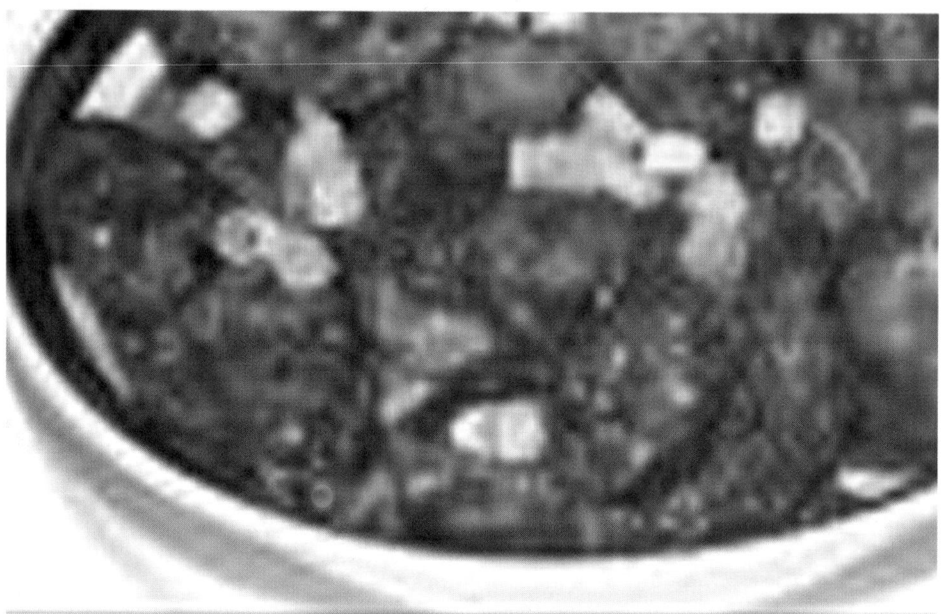

Ingredients

- 1 medium cauliflower
- 1 onion
- 2 tomatoes
- 1 tsp soya sauce
- 2 cloves garlic, 2cm ginger
- ½ tsp vinegar
- salt to taste
- 2 red chillies or 1 tsp chilli powder
- 2 tsp tomato sauce, 1 tsp tomato purée

Method

1. Cut the cauliflower into large florets and steam this for 4 to 5 minutes.
2. In a blender liquidise the onion, garlic, ginger, tomato and red chillies/ chilli powder.
3. Make a sauce with the ground paste adding vinegar, tomato purée and tomato sauce.
4. Arrange the cauliflower pieces onto flat plate. Pour the sauce over to cover the florets. Serve with roasted potatoes or noodles.

Variations

Cauliflower & parsley sauce

- 1 medium cauliflower
- ½ cup olive oil or milk to make parsley sauce
- grated garlic ginger ground to paste
- parsley
- 1-2 tsp ground pepper
- ½ tsp garam masala paste (optional)

Method

1. Cut and steam cauliflower for 4 minutes.
2. In the mean time mix the olive oil with the ground paste of garlic, ginger, salt, parsley, garam masala, pour over the cauliflower and mix.
3. Otherwise you can prepare parsley sauce by mixing little butter with milk and one teaspoon of corn flour. Add dried parsley and pour over the florets

★ To serve with naan or boiled potatoes

★ For a very hot taste add dried onions and chopped green chillies.

Cauliflower

Preparation & cooking time: 15-20 minutes
Serves 4-6

Ingredients

- 1 medium cauliflower
- 1 medium onion, chopped
- 2 cm fresh root ginger, grated
- 2 cloves garlic, grated
- 1 dry red chilli, chopped
- ½ tsp turmeric powder
- ½ tsp crushed chilli powder
- pinch of mustard seeds and cumin seeds
- 3 tbsp desiccated coconut or fresh coconut scraped (optional)
- 2 tbsp oil or 1 tbsp ghee, salt to taste

Method

1. Grate the cauliflower by using a food processor or a hand grater.
2. Heat oil or ghee in a frying pan, add the onions and cook until slightly brown.
3. Add the mustard seeds, chopped chilli and cumin seeds.
4. Add the cauliflower, the grated garlic and ginger. Cook for 4 minutes and sprinkle salt.
5. Add turmeric and crushed chilli to the coconut and rub it slightly using your fingers so that the coconut is reddish-yellow in colour.
6. Add to the cauliflower, stir-fry and remove from heat in a total of 10 minutes or less. Do not over cook.

★ This can be served with rice. Can omit the coconut from the recipe.

Cauliflower Manchuri

Kobi Manchoori - South Indian
Preparation & cooking: 30 to 40 minutes **Serves 6**

Ingredients

- 1 small cauliflower cut into small florets
- 200g self raising flour
- 3 tbsp corn flour
- 1 egg white (optional)
- water to make the batter

Finely chop the following items:

- 2 red onions or shallots
- 3 green chillies
- 3 cloves garlic
- 3cm piece of ginger
- 2 sprigs curry leaves, piece of rampe
- oil (for frying and cooking)
- 2 tbsp soya sauce
- 1-2 tbsp tomato sauce

Method

1. Mix the flour adding salt and chilli powder. Add small amounts of water and mix to prepare a thick batter, add the beaten egg white.

2. Heat fresh oil in a deep frying pan, coat the florets of cauliflower in batter and drop one by one into the hot oil and deep fry quickly.

3. Remove and drain on kitchen paper.

4. Heat a wok and add 3 tbsp oil. Fry the onions. Add chopped ginger and garlic, then add curry leaves and rampe. After few seconds add the chillies and stir.
5. Add soya sauce, tomato sauce and stir until the paste is slightly thick.

6. Add the fried cauliflower and stir well with a fork.

★ Can be served as a party food using a cocktail fork or toothpick. For more spice add plain chilli powder or extra green chillies to the tomato paste

Variations

★ **Use the same recipe for button mushrooms or broccoli.**

Dust or roll the florets in the mixed chilli powder, ginger and garlic powder. Leave it aside and dust in mixed self raising and corn flour. Deep fry these.

Without the egg white

1. Half cook the florets, adding a few grains of salt.
2. Mix in the corn flour and water (no self raising flour) and red or orange colouring. Coat the cauliflower and deep fry.
3. Fry onions with ginger and garlic paste until slightly brown.
4. Add the chopped green chilli, fry for a minute, add sauce and then the fried cauliflower.
5. Stir it once and turn off the heat.

Chinese Green Beans and Soya Stir Fry

Preparation & cooking time: 30 minutes   Serves 6

Ingredients

- 250g <u>thin</u> fresh green beans
- 2 tbsp oil
- 2 garlic cloves grated
- 1 tbsp soya sauce
- ginger - 3cm piece
- 1 tbsp sesame seeds (optional)
- pinch of salt
- pinch of sugar

Method

1. Clean the beans and cut into half. Microwave for 1 minute.
2. Heat the oil in a wok or frying pan. Add the beans and stir fry on high heat for a few minutes.
3. Add the salt, grated garlic and ginger. Cook on a low heat for 5 minutes.
4. Add soya sauce, sugar, sesame seeds and if necessary, 3-4 tablespoons of water.
5. Cook for few more minutes until the water is absorbed and the sauce begins to leave the sides of the pan.

Variation

Instead of sugar and soya sauce at 4 above include ½ tsp turmeric, ¼ cup milk
At the end, add a few curry leaves and 1 tsp lime juice. .

★ This is tasty with noodles or fried rice

Courgette Kari

Recipes include a mild and a hot preparation

Preparation & cooking time: 30 minutes
Serves 6 (side dish)

Mild milky dish

Ingredients

- 2 courgettes
- 1 large or 2 medium onions (red is tastier)
- 2 cloves garlic
- 2 tbsp oil
- pinch of asafoetida powder
- salt to taste
- 1 sprig of curry leaves
- 1 tsp turmeric powder
- 1 tsp cumin seeds, ¼ tsp black pepper corn
- 1 tsp mustard and 1 tsp cumin seeds for tempering
- 1 green chilli (optional) - slit it lengthwise
- 4 tbsp evaporated milk or full cream milk or 4 tbsp coconut milk

Method

1. Wash the courgettes, cut them in half length wise and then slice thinly.
2. In a flat based pan, heat the oil, add the chopped onions and sauté. Add the mustard seeds, cumin, and courgettes.
   Stir fry for 3-4 minutes.
3. Add salt, turmeric, sliced green chilli and continue cooking. If needed add a maximum of 2-3 tsp of water. Stir once or twice to check. It will take about 8 minutes to cook.
4. Add the curry leaves, milk and bring to the boil. Using a pestle and mortar crush the pepper, cumin and the garlic. Add it to the courgettes, stir once and remove from heat.

★ The dish should not have too much water content.

Variations

Courgettes with 2-3 chopped tomatoes

Add the chopped tomatoes to the fried onion and cook for a minute or two, then add the courgettes and follow the method for mild preparation at 2 onwards.

Hot preparation

Ingredients

Additional to ingredients for mild preparation

- 2 tsp chilli powder or paste
- 2 tomatoes, chopped

1. Add the chilli powder/paste and the tomatoes after cooking the courgettes for 2-3 minutes. Cook until any water evaporates.

Courgette with Potato and Carrot

Ingredients

To the ingredients in the mild courgette recipe add

- 2 small potatoes, cubed
- 1 small carrot

and exclude the oil and tempering items.

Method

1. Place the courgettes in a pan. Add the potatoes, carrots, chopped onions, 1 green chilli, salt, turmeric, asafoetida, chopped garlic and few drops of water. Mix well and cook over a low heat for 6-8 minutes.

2. Add the milk and cook for another 2 minutes. When the sauce thickens and the vegetables are cooked add the curry leaves and the ground cumin and pepper. Stir and remove from cooker.

Courgettes (Fried)

Preparation & cooking time: 30 minutes

Ingredients

- 2 courgettes
- 1 cup plain flour
- ½ cup fine rice flour
- oil for deep frying
- salt to taste
- 1 tsp chilli powder
- ½ tsp garlic powder
- ½ tsp ginger powder
- ½ tsp coriander powder

Method

1. Mix all the spices to the flour and leave it aside.
2. Slice the courgettes in rounds, dry on kitchen paper. First roll in the flour to take the water content. Then when ready to deep fry roll it again and fry.

★ This is tasty as a snack with any dip.To keep it crispy preheat the oven to the highest temp and place the fried courgettes in a tray and cook for 10 minutes.

Dwarf Fresh Beans Stir Fry (1)

Preparation & cooking time: 25 minutes
Serves 4-6

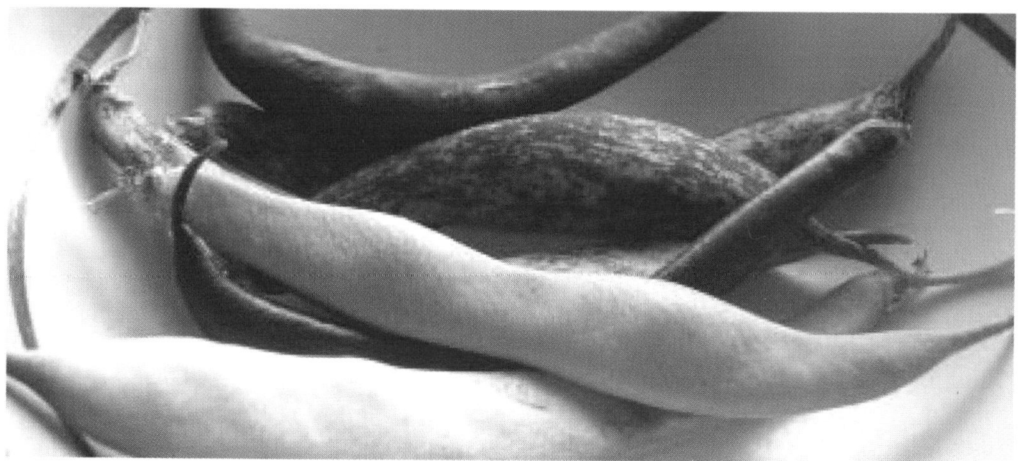

Ingredients

- fresh small dwarf thin beans (150g)
- 1 green chilli (optional)
- 1 tsp mustard seeds
- 2 tbsp of desiccated coconut
- ½ tsp ginger paste or grated ginger
- ½ tsp turmeric powder
- 1 onion, chopped
- 1 tsp fennel seeds
- 1 tsp plain chilli powder
- 1 tbsp of oil or ghee
- salt to taste

Method

1. Wash, top and tail the beans and slice thinly.
2. Heat the oil or ghee in a frying pan.
3. Add the fennel and mustard seeds. Then the ginger, green chilli and sliced beans.
4. Add the salt, sprinkle a few drops of water. Cover and cook for 5 minutes.
5. Mix the turmeric and chilli powder with the coconut and leave it aside.
6. Stir the beans so that they do not burn.
7. Finally add the mixed coconut and stir well.
8. Once cooked for about 15 minutes remove from heat and serve.

Dwarf Green Beans Stir Fry (2)

Preparation & cooking time: 15 minutes
Serves 4-6

Ingredients

- 1 packet of fresh thin green beans (200g)
- 2 onions, sliced
- 1 tbsp coriander seeds roasted and ground (fresh)
- 1 tsp of crushed chillies
- 2 tbsp olive oil
- salt to taste
- 1tsp crushed garlic, 1 tsp crushed ginger
  5 curry leaves

Method

1. Clean the beans and cut to about two-inch strips (can microwave on a plate for 1 minute).
2. Heat olive oil in a pan and fry the onions for few minutes.
3. Add the beans and stir fry, if needed sprinkle on some water.
4. After 2 minutes add the freshly ground coriander seeds, chilli, garlic and cook for about 10-12 minutes add the curry leaves and remove from heat.

★ Serve as a side dish with rice.

Green Banana skin and Toor Dhal

Preparation
& cooking time: 30 minutes
Serves 6

Ingredients

- 3 or 4 green banana skins
- ½ tsp mustard seeds
- 1 sprig curry leaves
- ½ tsp cumin seeds
- 3-4 tbsp desiccated coconut
- 1 large onion, chopped
- ½ cup toor dhal
- 2 tsp ghee
- ½ tsp ground cumin and pepper powder
- ½ tsp chilli powder, pinch of turmeric powder

Method

1. Peeling banana will be similar to peeling potatoes, but you will need to peel in a way that a little part of the banana remains on the skin. Skin and cut it deep.
2. Boil the toor dhal adding 2 cups of water. Cook till tender, drain the water and spread it on a kitchen paper to dry.
3. In a pan of water place the banana skins, bring to boil, add salt, turmeric and cook for 6-8 minutes. Drain the water allow to cool and slice finely.
4. Heat ghee in frying pan, add mustard seeds, cumin, chopped red chilli curry leaves and fry. Add the banana skin and toor dhal and cook for 2-3 minutes.
5. Add the desiccated coconut and ½ tsp of pepper/cumin and red chilli powder, stir fry for a minute and remove from heat.

★ This is a dry preparation

Ladies Fingers (South Indian style)

Other names - Okra or Bindi

Preparation & cooking time: 20 minutes

Serves 3

Ingredients

- 10 ladies fingers or 150g
- 2 tsp cumin seeds
- 1 tbsp split roasted moong dhal (payaru)
- 1 large onion, chopped
- 2 green chillies, sliced lengthwise
- 1 tsp mustard seeds
- few curry leaves.
- 1 tbsp paste made up of garlic, ginger coriander, curry powder
- 3 red chillies
- oil for frying, salt to taste
- ¼ pint full cream evaporated milk or coconut milk

Method

1. Crush the dhal with a roller for few seconds in an electric grinder.
2. Top and tail the ladies fingers, wash and cut into 2-inch pieces. Discard any spoilt ones. Cook in microwave for 1½ to 2 minutes.
3. Fry the onions in little oil. Add mustard seeds and cumin seeds. Then add the curry paste, curry leaves, ladies fingers and green chillies. Cook for 3 to 4 minutes and add the salt.
4. Keep stirring for a couple of minutes, add the milk, bring to boil and add the crushed dhal. Cook for two to three minutes and remove from heat.
5. Serve hot with rice or poori.

Ladies Fingers with Chilli

Preparation & cooking time: 20 minutes
Serves 4

Ingredients

- 250g ladies fingers
- 1 medium onion, chopped
- 3 cloves garlic and 1cm piece of ginger, grated
- salt to taste
- 4 green chillies, chopped
- 1 tsp tamarind paste
- 1 tsp urad and 1 tsp mustard seeds.
- few coriander and curry leaves roasted in little butter
- 3 tbsp oil
- ½ cup water

Method

1. Cut the ladies fingers into 3 cm (1") pieces.
2. Fry the onions in oil, add green chillies, garlic and ginger and continue frying.
3. Add the ladies fingers, salt, water and bring to boil.
4. Add the tamarind and cook for 5 minutes.
5. Add the roasted urad, mustard and coriander/curry leaves and cook for another 2 minutes and remove from heat.

★ Serve warm with boiled rice.

Ladies Fingers (steamed)

Preparation & cooking time: 10 minutes
Serves 4

Ingredients

- 200g ladies fingers (about 20)
- salt & freshly ground pepper
- 1 tsp olive oil

Method

1. Clean the ladies fingers top and tail, cut up to say about 5 cm. Can leave as a whole but by cutting you can see if any are spoilt.
2. Heat water in a pan, put the ladies fingers in a steamer and steam for 10 minutes.
3. Then heat the olive oil in a frying pan, add the ladies fingers, the salt and pepper. Keep tossing without breaking the cooked ladies fingers. Remove from heat after a minute or two.

★ Olive oil is optional, can eat without tossing in olive oil.

Fried Ladies Fingers

Preparation & cooking time: 30 minutes
Serves 4

Ingredients

- 200g ladies finger
- ½ tsp salt
- 2 tbsp mango powder
- ½ tsp turmeric powder
- oil for deep frying
- 4 tbsp gram flour
- 1 tsp chilli powder
- 1 tsp cumin powder

Method

1. Wash and top and tail the ladies fingers.
2. Cut in half. Then cut each half to strips lengthwise and place it in a bowl.
3. Mix the turmeric, chilli, salt in a bowl and add the gram flour and mango powder. Dust each piece of ladies finger in the flour. Ensure the pieces are coated well.
4. Heat the oil in a deep frying pan and deep fry by placing the ladies fingers in a metal colander or sieve and immersing it in the hot oil.
5. Remove and place onto a kitchen paper. Sprinkle a bit of cumin powder on the pieces.

★. Serve with rice or chapatti/naan bread.

Mixed Vegetable Stir Fry (South Indian preparation)

Preparation & cooking time: 20 minutes
Serves 4-6 (side dish)

Ingredients

- 1 small cauliflower, cut into florets
- 1 large onion, sliced
- 3 small potatoes, quartered
- 200g fresh thin dwarf beans
- garlic, ginger paste or freshly grated
- curry paste made of cumin, coriander, chilli
- 1 tsp of roasted chilli powder
- salt to taste

Method

1. Cut the beans in half, to about 2-inch size. Cut the potato into four quarters lengthwise. Microwave the potatoes, cauliflower and beans or steam for few minutes.
2. Heat the oil in a pan, fry the sliced onions, add mustard, cumin and curry leaves. Then, when it is slightly brown, add the tomatoes, garlic, ginger, curry paste or chilli powder, salt and a little water. Bring to boil then reduce the heat and simmer for 5 minutes.
3. Finally add the cooked vegetables and stir fry it for another 2 to 3 minutes.

★ If you want you can add 2-3 tablespoons of whisked cream or Greek yoghurt. Serve with rice, naan or bread.

Potato Kari - 1

Preparation & cooking time: 30 minutes Serves 8

Ingredients

- 150g small potatoes
- 1 large onion finely sliced
- 3-4 dried red chillies
- 2 sprigs curry leaves
- 1 tsp cumin seeds
- 1 tsp mustard seeds
- oil for shallow frying
- 1 tsp tamarind paste
- 1 small tomato
- ¼ cup coconut milk
- 1 tsp roasted fennel powder

Method

1. Peel the potatoes, prick each potato with a fork, place on a plate cover and microwave for 3-4 minutes. Remove and cut into small cubes. Alternatively boil the potatoes in water for 15 minutes and peel the skin.
2. Grind the red chillies, tamarind, tomato and salt into a paste adding few drops of warm water.
3. In a heavy-based deep frying pan, heat the oil, add the mustard seeds, cumin and allow to pop. Then add the onions and sauté on a low heat. Add a few of the curry leaves.
4. Add the ground paste, coconut milk and cook for 2-3 minutes. Add the potatoes and stir fry until the mixture turns fairly thick. Add the remainder of the curry leaves, fennel powder and remove from cooker.

For a crispier dish:

★ After adding the potatoes at 4 above add 2 tbsp of rice flour, 1 tsp crushed chilli powder and cook for a minute.

Potato Kari - 2

Preparation & cooking time: 45 minutes
Serves 4

Ingredients

- 4 medium size potatoes
- 3 large tomatoes
- oil for deep frying
- 3 tbsp butter
- 2 medium onions, chopped
- small piece of ginger, 2 cloves of garlic
- spices: 1 tsp coriander powder, 1 tsp cumin powder, 1 tsp plain chilli powder
- 5 tbsp natural yoghurt
- 2 tbsp coconut powder mixed with little warm water
- ½ cup water
- 5 to 6 curry leaves
- ½" rampe leaf cut up (optional)
- 2 green chillies sliced (optional)
- salt to taste
- pinch of special flavouring powder (roasted fennel powder)
- for tempering: ½ tsp mustard seeds, ½ tsp cumin seeds

Method

1. Peel the potatoes and cut up to small squares about ¾"cubes. Dry and deep fry in hot oil. Drain on kitchen paper.

2. Grind garlic, ginger, half of the onion, spices, one chopped tomato and salt into a paste adding some water.

3. Heat the butter, add the onions, mustard seeds and cumin seeds and fry for a minute.

4. Add the remainder of the tomatoes and cook for a few minutes. Then add the yoghurt, the fried potatoes and the ground paste. Cook for 3 to 4 minutes, add the coconut milk, curry leaves and bring to boil stirring well.

5 At this point you can decide if you want the sauce to be thick or more watery. If you want it thick cook for few more minutes otherwise just before removing from cooker add curry leaves, and rampe leaves.

6. Sprinkle the roasted fennel powder.

★ It is tasty with rice, fresh bread or noodles.
You may add ¼ cup of cows milk instead of the coconut powder or coconut milk.

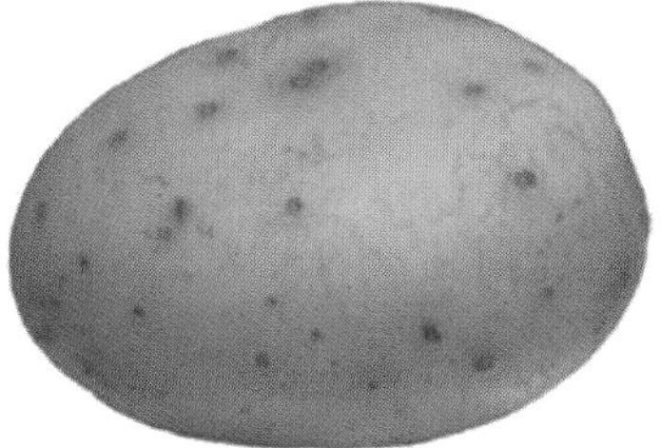

Potato Kari 'Thel'

A dish prepared in the southern part of Sri Lanka (thel meaning oil). Traditional preparation includes Maldive fish. I have omitted this and have also reduced the amount of oil.

Preparation & cooking time: 20 minutes
Serves 4-6

Ingredients

- 250g small potatoes boiled and skinned (about 16)
- 1 tsp turmeric powder
- 1 tsp plain crushed chilli powder (pieces)
- 2 medium onions, finely chopped
- 3-4 tbsp sesame oil or olive oil
- 1 sprig curry leaves, chopped
- piece of rampe, chopped
- 1 tsp mustard seeds
- salt to taste

Method

1. Cut the potatoes into small cubes, say 1" size.
2. Fry the onions until brown.
3. Reduce the flame and add the mustard seeds, turmeric, chilli powder, curry leaves, rampe, salt and stir it once.
4. Finally add the cut up potato stir, cover and cook for 8-10 minutes or until the pieces are cooked.
5. Remove and serve with rice.

★ A spicy hot dish, can increase and decrease the amount of oil. Goes well with plain rice.

Potato Kari - 3

Preparation & cooking time 20 minutes

Serves 6

Ingredients

- 500g potatoes
- 3 tbsp butter or 2 tbsp ghee
- 1 medium onion, chopped
- 1 onion chopped for the spice mixture
- 1" size ginger
- 3 cloves garlic
- ½ tsp turmeric powder

for the chilli paste

- 1 tsp coriander powder
- 1 tsp cumin seeds
- 1 tsp plain chilli powder
- 1" size ginger
- 3 cloves garlic
- normal milk or
  ½ can coconut milk (200g)
- 2 sprigs curry leaves
- 2 sprigs coriander leaves (optional)
- 2 green chillies sliced (optional)
- salt to taste

Method

1. Peel the potatoes and cut up into about ¾" cubes. Place on a plate, cover and cook in the microwave for 2-3 minutes or steam cook for few minutes.
2. Grind the garlic, ginger, onion, spice and salt using a mortar and pestle or blender. Add little water and grind to a paste.
3. Heat the butter or ghee in a frying pan or a wok, add the chopped onions, mustard seeds, cumin seeds and then the ground paste. Add the potatoes, turmeric powder and cook for 2 minutes.
4. Add the milk, bring to the boil and simmer for 5 minutes. Add the chopped curry leaves and coriander leaves and remove from heat.

★ To serve with rice, naan or any rice equivalent.

Potato Kari - 4

Preparation & cooking time: 20 minutes
Serves 4

Ingredients

- 150g potatoes, 4 medium
- 1 large onion, finely sliced.
- 3-4 dried red chillies (or to your taste)
- 2 sprigs curry leaves
- 1 tsp cumin seeds
- 1 tsp mustard seeds
- oil for frying
- 1 tsp tamarind paste
- 1 small tomato
- ¼ cup coconut milk
- 1 tsp roasted fennel powder
- salt to taste

Method:

1. Boil the potatoes, peel and cut them into small cubes.
2. Grind into a paste the red chillies, tamarind, tomato and salt, adding a little hot water (use a blender or mortar and pestle).
3. In a heavy-based deep frying pan, heat the oil, add the mustard and cumin seeds and allow to pop. Then add the onions and sauté. Add a few curry leaves, turn the heat low and add the ground chilli and tamarind paste and the coconut milk and cook until it turns to a thick paste.
4. Now add the potatoes and stir fry. Add the remainder of the curry leaves and 1 teaspoon fennel powder and remove from cooker.

Spinach

Preparation & cooking time: 20 minutes
Serves 6

Ingredients

- 500g frozen spinach
- 1 onion, chopped
- 2 cloves of garlic sliced
- 2 tbsp water
- 2 green chillies (optional)
- ½ lemon
- 4-5 tbsp single cream or evaporated milk
- salt to taste

Method

1. Put the spinach, onion, garlic, water and sliced chillies in a pan.
2. Cook on a low heat until the spinach is cooked. Add the salt and cream or milk. Cook for few minutes and remove from heat and serve into a dish.
3. When slightly warm, squeeze the lemon and stir into the spinach.

★ Serve with rice, chapatti, or naan bread.

Fresh spinach

★ There are several kinds available including leaf beet, New Zealand spinach, baby spinach leaves etc. Can buy a variety of tropical spinach from Asian shops.

Method

1. Cooking is the same as for frozen but you need to wash the leaves to remove any mud.
2. Wash individually and allow to drain. Then arrange a few eaves one on top of the other. Once you have about 5 or 6 leaves, roll it and slice it to two or three cuts. Follow the steps 1-3 of the recipe above.

★ Spinach is tasty in lasagne and noodles, see recipes. Spinach can be cooked with red lentils. For this see dhal recipe variations.

Spinach and Yoghurt

Preparation & cooking time: 25 minutes

Serves 4-6

Ingredients

- 500g frozen spinach
- 2 green chillies, slightly slit
- 2 cloves of garlic, sliced thinly
- 2 medium sized onions,chopped
- salt to taste
- ½ tsp asafoetida powder
- 2 tbsp natural yoghurt
- few drops lemon juice (from bottle) or ½ lime
- tempering: 2 tbsp oil, pinch of mustard seeds, cumin seeds, 1 dry red chilli cut up and 2-3 curry leaves.

Method

1. Thaw the spinach and squeeze some of the water out. Place the spinach with the salt, garlic, asafoetida and chopped onions (retain 1 tbsp of the onions for tempering). Cook for 10 minutes. Add the yoghurt, stir and remove from heat.

2. In a separate pan place the oil, tempering ingredients and sauté for few minutes. Add the curry leaves and then the cooked spinach. Stir well, remove from heat and dish it out.

★ The green chilli is tasty, but if you are going to serve the dish to children, you can omit it from the recipe.

★ Instead of the yoghurt you can add 3 tablespoons of milk and cook.

Spring Greens Stir Fry

Preparation & cooking: 15 minutes
Serves 6

Ingredients

- 1 packet of spring greens (500g)
- 1 medium onion
- 2 tbsp olive oil
- 1 dried red chilli cut up (optional)
- 1 tsp mixed mustard and cumin seeds
- 1 tbsp desiccated coconut or grated fresh coconut
- salt to taste
- 1" size ginger, grated
- ½ teaspoon of mixed turmeric powder and chilli powder.

Method

1. Clean the greens by removing the leaves one by one and washing them under running water to get all the soil out. Then cut the stem into half lengthwise. Place a few leaves together and roll them up. Hold with one hand and slice very finely. If you use a food processor, use the thin slicing blade to cut (put it through twice for a fine cut).
2. Chop the onions into small cubes or fine strips lengthwise.
3. Heat the oil in a flat-based frying pan. Add the onion and temper until a slightly golden colour.
4. Keep the heat at medium. Add the mustard seeds, cumin seeds and the cut up chilli. Then add the greens and sprinkle on the salt. Cover and cook for a few minutes.(If you think it is going to burn add 1-2 teaspoons of water). Add grated ginger and garlic.
5. In a small bowl place the coconut and rub the mixed turmeric and chilli powder.
6. After cooking for 5 minutes in total from the time the greens are added, add the coconut mixture. Stir well. If the greens is slightly watery increase the heat for the water to evaporate. Cook for a few seconds and then remove from heat and leave it uncovered to avoid over cooking.

★ This recipe can be used to prepare kale, broccoli and leaf cabbage. But spring greens is the best ingredient.

Stir Fry - Greens, Kale or Savoy Cabbage

Preparation & cooking time:
20 minutes
Serves 4

Ingredients

- 5 leaves of any of the above
- 1 small onion
- 2 tbsp of olive oil
- 1 dried red chilli (optional)
- 1 tbsp desiccated coconut
- ½ tsp mixed turmeric and chilli powder
- 2 tbsp split peas or channa dhal (soaked and deep fried)
- pinch of salt
- 1 tsp mixed spice (mustard and cumin seeds)
- 1 grated garlic and small piece of ginger

Method

1. Wash the leaves and chop finely. You may use the fine blade of the food processor and slice. Or, cut the washed leaves in half, then roll the leaves and hold with one hand and slice with a sharp knife.
2. Cut the onions finely and fry in the olive oil, add the mustard/cumin seeds, chopped red chilli. Then add the greens and garlic.
3. Sprinkle on the salt and cook on a medium heat for five minutes. Cover the pan and try not to over cook.
4. Finally, mix the coconut and chilli powder together and add this to the greens, stir to mix well and remove from heat. Do not cover, as the greens will get over cooked.
5. In another pan shallow fry the dhal in olive oil or prepare this first before frying the onions and set aside. Add the fried dhal just before serving the cooked greens, kale or savoy cabbage.

★ There should be enough water in the washed leaves to allow it to cook without burning. If you need to, sprinkle on a little water as salt will produce some moisture to cook.

Tender Jackfruit

Preparation & cooking time: 15 minutes

Serves 4-6

Ingredients

- 1 tin raw jack fruit (375g)
- 2 tbsp olive oil
- cumin seeds, 1 red chilli
- 1 tsp roasted chilli powder
- ½ tsp mustard
- salt to taste • 1 large onion
- piece of cream coconut or 3 tbsp milk
- piece of ginger and 2 cloves garlic • ½ tsp turmeric powder
- 1 tsp roasted fennel powder, sprig of curry leaves

Method

1. Slice the onion and cook in oil, add the mustard seeds, cumin, crushed garlic and ginger. Cut the jack fruit into cubes and add to the onion mixture and stir fry for a minute.
2. Add the chilli powder, turmeric and ¼ cup water. Cook for five to six minutes on a high heat.
3. Add the cream coconut or milk and let it cook until the sauce thickens.
4. Finally sprinkle the chopped curry leaves and the fennel powder.

★ Serve with rice. Whilst cooking do not stir a lot as the jack fruit will tend to break and get squashed/mashed.

Fresh Jackfruit

Lot of preparation is necessary. First you need to oil your fingers as the fruit produces a sticky milky liquid. Carefully remove the individual segments. Slice the fruit segments, remove seeds, wash and leave it ready to cook. It will take about 25 minutes cooking time. To remove the stickiness from your fingers, rub a piece of lemon and wash with soapy water.

★ Fresh, canned and frozen jack fruit are available from Chinese/Asian supermarkets.

Tofu and Aubergine Special

Preparation & cooking time: 20 minutes
Serves 2-3

Ingredients

- 1 packet of tofu 250g
- 1 medium aubergine
- 1 large potato
- 1 large onion
- 1 pepper
- 1 tsp of tamarind paste
- 1 green chilli
- oil for deep frying
- 2 tbsp oil for stir frying
- 5-6 curry leaves
- 1 tsp roasted curry powder.
- 1 tbsp (garam masala) Kashmir masala paste
- 1 garlic clove and small piece of ginger grated.
- 2 tsp of grated cream coconut (optional)
- salt to taste

Method

1. Wash the tofu as whole block and cut into small cubes. Pat dry and deep fry in oil. Drain on kitchen paper
2. Cube the potato,aubergine to the same size of the tofu, deep fry and drain.
3. Mix the tamarind paste with a quarter cup water, add the curry powder and garam masala.
4. Heat a frying pan or a wok, add 2 tablespoons of oil and fry the chopped onions and green pepper pieces. Add the grated ginger, garlic and curry leaves.
5. Add the tofu, fried aubergine and the tamarind juice. Cook for 4 to 5 minutes on a high heat. The sauce should be thick without much water. If too watery add 2 tsp of grated cream coconut and remove from heat.

★ You can microwave the aubergine and potato instead of deep frying but this will need to be stir fried with the chopped onions. Tofu can be steamed and then cut into slices.

White Cabbage Kari (mild)

Preparation & cooking time: 20 minutes
Serves 4

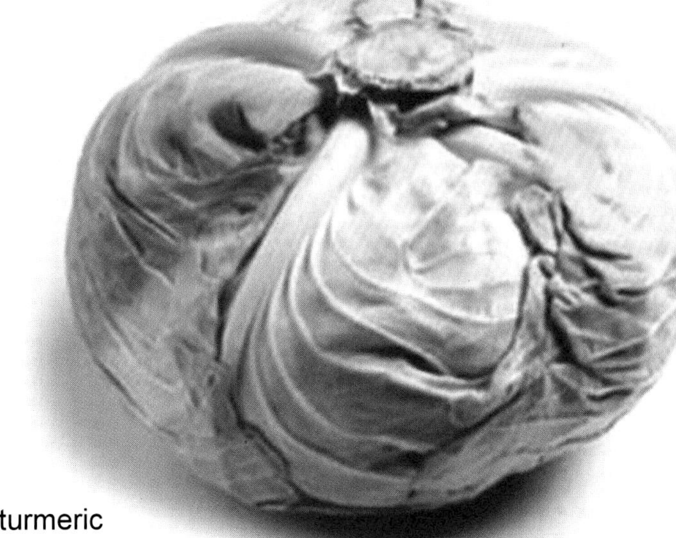

Ingredients

- 250g white cabbage
- 1 medium onion
- 1 green chilli, pinch of turmeric
- 1 clove garlic, sliced
- 5-6 curry leaves
- salt to taste, evaporated milk or piece of cream coconut
- 1 tsp pepper crushed
- 1 tsp lime juice (optional)

Method

1. Slice the cabbage finely, chop the onions and cut the chilli lengthwise.
2. Place the cabbage in a saucepan, add two tablespoons water, turmeric, garlic, green chilli and cook for 8-10 minutes.
3. Halfway through add the salt.
4. Finally add the evaporated milk or cream coconut, curry leaves and pepper.
5. Cook for a minute and remove from heat. If needed before serving add the lime juice.

★ This can be eaten with poori, rice or Naan bread.
Can omit or add extra green chilli according to your taste.

Beans Dishes

Preparation & cooking time: 20 - 30 minutes

Main types of beans dishes are:

- Stir fried beans
- Mild dish with milk
- Hot dish
- Beans with desiccated coconut

Milk preparation

Can be made for all types of beans: french beans, runner beans, dwarf beans. It is tastier if it is prepared with fresh beans, but a dish prepared with frozen beans can also turn out well.

Beans - mild preparation known as milk (paal) kari
Serves 5

Ingredients

- 250g fresh green beans
- 2 new potatoes, peeled and cut lengthwise into chips
- 2 medium onions,chopped
- 2 garlic cloves, grated
- ½ tsp turmeric powder
- 1 green chilli (optional)
- ¼ tsp salt
- pinch of asafoetida powder
- ¼ cup milk or evaporated milk
- 1 sprig of curry leaves
- ½ lime, 1 tsp ground cumin and pepper

Method

1. Clean the beans and slice at a slant/diagonally to about an inch in length.
2. In a heavy-based pan, place the beans, onions, garlic, potato, salt, green chilli, turmeric, asafoetida and add ¼ cup of water. Bring to a boil, then reduce the heat, cover and cook for about 5 minutes.
3. Add the milk and cook for another 5-8 minutes until the potato and beans are just cooked. Add the remainder of the curry leaves and finally the ground cumin and pepper.
4. Add lime juice just before serving.

★ This is tasty with rice or noodles. Suitable for children.

Variation

A: Additional ingredients.

- 3 tbsp oil
- 1 tsp chilli powder
- ½ tsp special flavouring powder (fennel)
- ¼ cup cow's milk
- small piece of cream coconut

Temper the onions, add the beans, potatoes and stir fry. Sprinkle some water, add chilli powder, cover and cook. After 5 minutes add the milk and cook for another 5-6 minutes. Add the cream coconut or evaporated milk, curry leaves and fennel powder.

★ To both the above recipes you may add chopped coriander leaves as flavouring.

Butternut Squash – Pumpkin

Preparation & cooking time: 20 minutes
Serves 6

Ingredients

- 1 small butternut squash
- 1 medium size onion
- 2 tbsp oil
- 1 tsp mixed mustard and cumin seeds
- 1 dry red chilli, chopped
- 1 sprig curry leaves
- 1 tsp roasted curry powder
- 1 tsp ground pepper and cumin
- 2 cloves garlic crushed
- salt to taste
- milk 2-3 tbsp
- water 2-3 tbsp
- 2cm ginger, crush

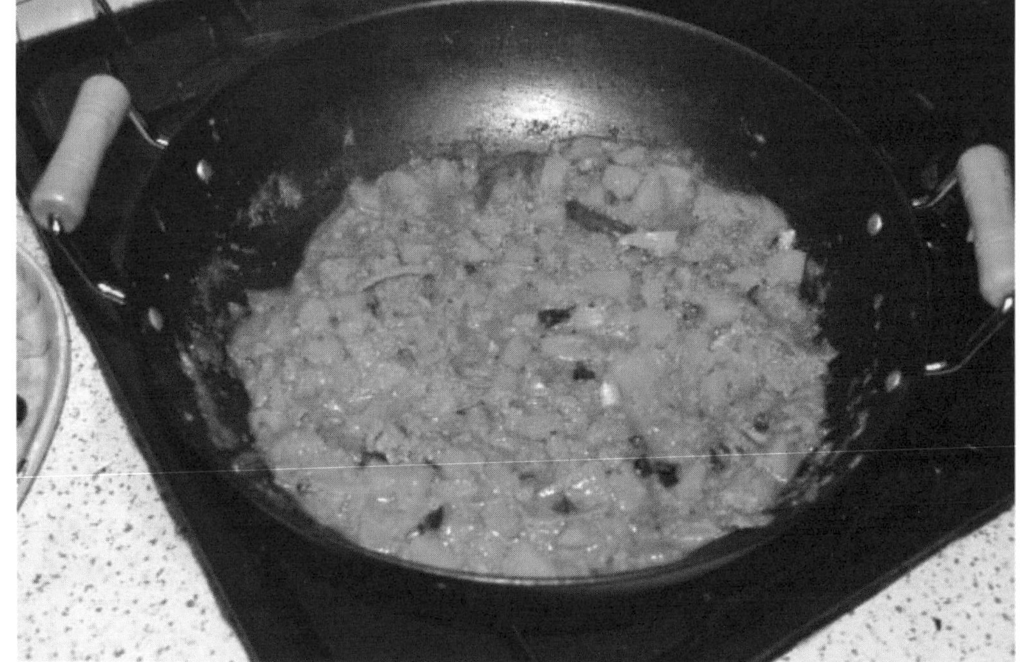

Method

1. Cut off the outer skin of the butternut squash. Cut the squash into 2" strips or small cubes

2. Heat a heavy-based frying pan. Add the oil and fry the chopped onions for 2 minutes. Add the mustard, cumin, half the chopped curry leaves and the chopped red chilli.

3. Add the pieces of butternut. Sprinkle 1 tsp of salt, add the curry powder, grated garlic, ginger and cook for a couple of minutes. Keep stirring the mixture. Sprinkle two or three tablespoons water, cover and cook on a medium heat for about 10 minutes. Keep stirring to ensure there is just enough water but not too much.

5. Add the milk and when this boils add the ground pepper and cumin powder and the remainder of the curry leaves. Cook for a minute and remove from heat.

★ Serve with rice.

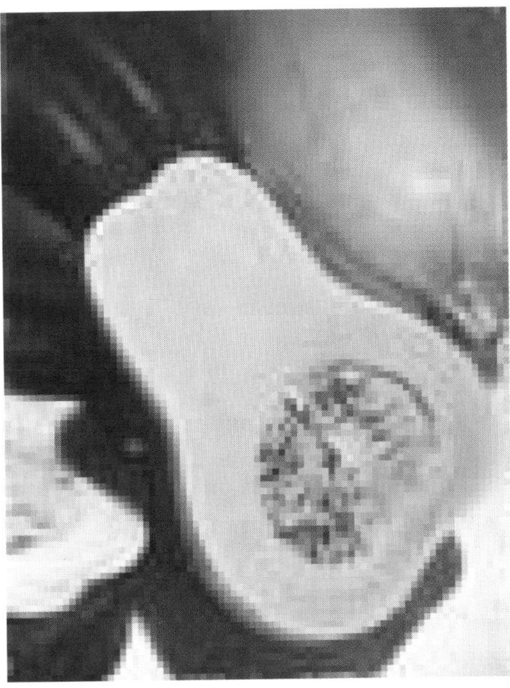

Drum stick (Sarrakku Kari)

It is a green slightly fleshy long stick

When selecting try and get the fleshy ones. Thin drumstick is deep fried and used in Kulambu - sauce. A vegetable cooked and given when someone is recovering from illness/flu etc. You may dislike it, because you don't know how to eat it. There is an art to eating drumsticks, you need to scathe the inside with a spoon or, if you are used to it, with your fingers. Some chew the drumsticks. It is tasty and I enjoy the chewing part more than the kari.

There are several preparations

★ Sarrakku kari (cumin and coriander)
★ Hot dish
★ With boiled eggs, prawns or sprats
★ Deep fried kulambu
★ With aubergine
★ Included in Sambar
★ Used in Sothi

Preparation & cooking time: 30 minutes
Serves 4-5

Ingredients

- 3 drumsticks cut to 7cm size pieces
- 1 aubergine or 2 potatoes cut length wise to 7cm
- 1 large onion chopped
- 1 tsp coriander powder
- 1 sprig curry leaves
- 1 tsp cumin powder
- salt to taste
- 1 tsp roasted Sri Lankan curry powder
- 1cm thickness cream coconut (slice)
- 3 garlic cloves
- 1 tsp tamarind paste
- 2 cups water

Method:

1 Liquidise the garlic, onion, tamarind paste and all the spice powders. Add little water and blend.

2. Peel the drumstick outer skin slightly to take the strings out. Cut into 7cm pieces and split each lengthwise.

3 In a medium size saucepan place the drumstick and potato slices or aubergine. Add the blended mixture, 2 cups water, and cover and cook for 30 minutes over a medium heat. It will take 25 minutes for this vegetable to cook.

4. Add a piece of cream coconut and cook for 5 minutes. Add curry leaves and remove from heat.

★ **Serve with rice**

Green Tomato Kari

Preparation & cooking time: 20 minutes
Serves 4

Ingredients

- 6 medium green tomatoes, cut into quarters
- 1 tsp fennel powder
- 1 large onion-chopped
- 5 tbsp coconut milk/evaporated milk
- tempering: pinch of mustard seeds, cumin seeds,
- one dried chilli cut up, 5 curry leaves, butter or oil
- salt to taste
- 2 tsp roasted curry powder (chilli & cumin mixed)
- 1 green chilli

Methou

1. Heat the oil/butter in a frying pan, add the mustard and cumin seeds, red chilli and chopped onions. Fry for 2 minutes. Add the curry leaves.
2. Then add the tomato, curry powder, salt, cover and cook for ten minutes over a medium heat. There should be enough juice to cook but if required add 2 tablespoon of water.
3. Finally add the coconut milk or evaporated milk and cook for 2- 3 minutes until the sauce thickens.
4. Add the fennel powder and remove from heat

★ This will be a slightly juicy and thick-sauce dish. Have with rice.

Variations

Can cook courgettes and green tomatoes or dhal and green tomatoes.
Can add prawns or dry Maldive fish with the green tomatoes

Green Banana - Fried dry Kari (Ash Plantain)

Preparation & cooking time: 20 minutes
Serves 3-4

Ingredients

- 2 green bananas
- 1 onion, chopped
- ½ tsp turmeric powder
- ½ tsp salt
- 1 tsp roasted curry powder
- 1 tsp ground pepper and cumin (freshly ground/crushed)
- 3-4 tbsp oil or 2 tbsp ghee
- 1 sprig curry leaves
- ½ tsp mustard seeds
- ½ tin of evaporated milk or normal cows milk
- juice of ½ lime

Method

1. Peel the banana skin using a knife. Cut the inner brown skin too. Cut lengthwise and then into cubes.
2. Add a bit of the lime juice to the banana pieces to remove any stickiness/stain. Wash these and pat dry on kitchen paper.
3. Heat a frying pan, add the oil and shallow fry the banana pieces until slightly brown in colour, remove and drain on a kitchen paper towel.
4. Now add the onion to the oil and fry this with mustard seeds and the curry leaves. Add the curry powder, turmeric, salt, milk and bring to boil and cook for 3-4 minutes
5. Add the fried banana and keep stirring for three minutes.
6. Finally add the ground cumin and pepper and remove from heat.
7. Add the lime juice before serving.

Parsnips Roast (with spices)

Preparation & cooking time: 45 minutes
Serves 4

Ingredients

- 3 parsnips
- slice of butter or 2 tbsp olive oil
- salt
- 1-2 tsp plain chilli powder
- 1 tsp garlic powder, 1 tsp ginger powder made into a paste with a little water

Method

1. Clean and cut the parsnips into long, slightly thick pieces. Place the parsnips in a pan of water, bring to boil and allow to boil for 3-4 minutes and drain the water.

2. Melt the butter in a roasting dish. If using oil, brush the base and sides with oil.

3. Mix the paste with chilli powder, garlic, ginger and salt and toss the parsnips. Arrange the parsnips to be in one layer in the roasting tray and roast for 30 minutes at 190°C.

Parsnips Stir Fry

Preparation & cooking time: 15 minutes
Serves 3

Ingredients

- 2 medium parsnips
- 1 large onion, chopped
- 1 tbsp oil
- 1 tsp roasted curry powder
- ¼ tsp garlic powder
- ¼ tsp ginger powder
- ¼ cup cow's milk
- 1 tsp of ground fennel (roasted)
- 1 tsp garam masala paste
- 1 sprig curry leaves
- ½ tsp mustard seeds, ½ tsp cumin seeds
- 2 green chillies

Method

1. Clean and scrape the skin of the parsnip and cut into small cubes or diagonal strips.

2. Heat a little oil in a wok, add the chopped onions, mustard seeds, cumin seeds and cook for three minutes.

3. Add the parsnips and cook for 2 - 3 minutes. Add the curry powder, ginger, garlic, green chillies, garam masala and mix well using a wooden spoon. You may need to sprinkle on a little water so that it does not burn. Cover and cook on medium heat for another 10 minutes.

4. Add a little milk and cook for two minutes. Add 1 tsp of fennel powder and the curry leaves and remove from the heat.

Quorn Stir Fry

Preparation & cooking time: 20 minutes

Serves 4

Ingredients

- 1 packet of quorn pieces (200g), thinly sliced
- 1 medium size onion, thinly sliced
- 1 green pepper, thinly sliced
- 1 red pepper, thinly sliced
- 1 carrot, thinly sliced
- 2 tbsp oil for frying
- salt to taste
- tomato purée
- 1 tbsp worcester sauce
- 1 fresh tomato cut into small pieces
- 1 tsp crushed chilli
- 1 tbsp soya sauce (if using concentrated use less)
- 2 cloves garlic, crushed
- 2cm piece ginger, crushed

Method

1. You may pre-cook the vegetables and quorn in a microwave for 2 minutes. In which case you can use less oil.
2. Heat the oil, and add the quorn pieces, onions, vegetables and salt. Cook the mixture for about 4 minutes.
3. Remove and serve into a dish. Into the pan add the garlic paste, tomato purée, Worcester sauce, chillies and let this boil for a minute. Then transfer the quorn mixture into the pan, stir and cook for two minutes. Remove from the heat.

Variation

Few baby corns and a finely cut leek can be added
You may add these and cook for 2 minutes.

Spinach and Onion

Ingredients

- 500g fresh spinach
- 2 cloves of garlic, grated
- 2 onions, chopped
- 1 small carton Greek yoghurt
- 1 tbsp butter
- 1 green chilli, cut up
- for tempering: pinch of mustard seeds and cumin seeds
- 1 red chilli, chopped
- 2 tsp ghee or butter
- little water for cooking (3-4 tbsp)

Method

1. Clean, wash and chop the fresh spinach leaves. Add one of the chopped onions, green chilli, garlic and boil the spinach adding little water.

2. After 5 minutes add the butter and salt and cook for a further 2 minutes. Either use a masher or put in a blender for one quick turn only.

3. Leave the spinach to cool for 5 minutes, add the yoghurt and mix well. Dish it into a serving dish.

4. Now heat the butter in a frying pan. Add the mustard seeds, cumin and the remainder of the chopped onions and fry until golden colour. Add the cut up red chilli.

5 Pour the fried ingredients over the dished out spinach and give it one stir.

★ This is tasty with rice or chapatti.

Split Peas Kari (Kadalai Parruppu)

Preparation & cooking time: 40 minutes

Serves 4-6

Ingredients

- 200g split peas
- 2 tsp urad dhal
- 2 cups of water
- 1 large onion
- 1 potato cut up into cubes and boiled
- 3 dried red chillies
- 1 tsp chilli powder
- 1 sprig of curry leaves
- 2 cloves garlic, grated
- ¼ tsp turmeric powder
- ½ tsp mustard seeds
- ½ tsp cumin seeds
- salt to taste
- 1” slice of cream coconut or ¼ tin coconut milk
- ½ tsp ground pepper and cumin

Method

1. Wash the split peas and boil in water for 15-20 minutes. Add the turmeric powder and grated garlic.
2. Place the urad dhal in a frying pan, gently heat it and let it brown. Grind it with the chillies using a grinder or mortar and pestle.
3. Heat the oil, add the mustard seeds and let it pop. Add the cumin seeds, then the chopped onions and lastly the curry leaves.
4. When slightly brown in colour, add the boiled split peas, chilli powder and potato. Cook for 5 minutes. Add the coconut milk or cream coconut, ground urad and a pinch of ground pepper and cumin seeds.
5. Remove from heat and serve with rice or bread.

Cashew nut Kari

(Sri Lankan Sinhalese) preparation

Preparation: day in advance to soak
Cooking time: 45 minutes
Serves 4-6

Ingredients

- 250g cashew nuts
- 2 cups of boiling water to soak
- 1 cup of water
- 1 onion sliced finely
- 3-4 tbsp oil
- ½ tsp turmeric
- ½ tsp of grated ginger
- ½ tsp grated garlic
- 2 tsp of plain chilli powder
- 1 can of coconut milk
- 2 sprigs of curry leaves, piece of rampe
- ¼ tsp each of mustard and cumin seeds
- ½ cup of cow's milk and 1" piece of creamed coconut
- 1 tsp of cinnamon powder or two small sticks say 1" size
- 1 tsp roasted fennel
- 1 tsp bicarbonate soda
- salt to taste

Method

1. Soak the cashew nuts in two cups of boiling water and leave for 5-6 hours or overnight. You may wish to add 1 tsp bicarbonate soda. This will soften the cashew nuts.

2. Heat a thick-based frying pan. Add the oil, mustard and cumin seeds. Then add the onions and fry until light brown in colour. Add half the curry leaves.

3. Wash the cashew nuts well and stir fry until both sides are well coated with oil.

4. Add chilli powder, one cup of water. Bring to a boil, reduce the heat and cook for 10-12 minutes on a medium heat for the cashew to become soft and cooked.

5. Add the coconut milk, and cook for a further 10 minutes until the sauce has thickened.

6. Finally add the rampe stick, remaining curry leaves, and a tsp of fennel powder and stir once. Switch off the heat and leave it covered for few minutes before serving.

★ In Sri Lanka the dish is prepared with fresh tender cashew. However the dry cashew nuts can be used, but it requires a lot of softening. Some use a pressure cooker to boil the cashew nuts, but be careful not to overcook.

Sprouting Broccoli (stir fried)

This is a vegetable available from February to April. Allotment growers will grow this vegetable. It is more of a countryside crop. The florets are either light purple or white in colour.

Preparation & cooking time: 20 minutes
Serves 4

Ingredients

- 1 large onion, chopped
- ½ tsp mustard seeds
- 1 tsp cumin seeds
- 2 dried red chillies
- small piece of ginger, grated
- 2 tbsp oil for cooking
- 1 clove garlic, grated
- 3 tbsp fresh or desiccated coconut
- bunch of sprouting broccoli with few leaves
- salt, pinch of turmeric powder.
- 1 tsp crushed chilli powder

Method

1. Fry the onions in a heavy-based frying pan in little oil. Add the mustard seeds, cumin and cut up dried chillies.
2. In the meantime wash and thinly slice the sprouting broccoli. You may cut it using a food processor (use the thin slicing blade).
3. Add the cut up broccoli to the fried onions; add garlic, ginger and cook over a medium heat for 5 minutes. If you think it is drying up, sprinkle on a few drops of water. Add salt and cook for another minute or two.
4. Mix the turmeric, crushed chilli, coconut and add it to the above. Cook for a minute and remove from heat. Leave the pan uncovered as covering will overcook it and the broccoli will lose its crispiness.

★ Sprouts can be prepared following steps 1, 3 and 4. Cut each one into a ¼ or thin slices.

Special Dishes

Special Dishes - Index

Special Dishes - Introduction

Recipes included are no different to the vegetarian dishes but some may require a bit of planning, so it is worth reading the recipe and then trying it during the weekends.
Katharikkai kulambu, Venthaya kulambu

Long beans (Payathangai) are famous dishes of the Tamils. Prepared during functions. Served with rice, alternatives such as pooris, chapatti, string hoppers pittu etc.

Sambar: A mixture of vegetables and dhal cooked in a sauce (gravy). Served with idli, thosai and rice.

Deep fried items: The recipes are not included in this section but it is also a special dish. Jackfruit seeds, Ash plantain, potatoes, sliced cassava are served with rice similar to crisps. After removing the skin, wash and cut into thin slices. Mix ½ tsp salt, chilli powder,tumeric powder in a bowl and add the cut pieces and coat well.
Deep fry in oil until crispy.

Paneer(cheese): Can be purchased in blocks from Asian shops and Super markets and the recipes include the ready-made paneer. However if you want to make your own you require a pan, muslin cloth, a colander and a square dish and tight cover. Boil 4 pints of milk and let it cool for few minutes. Add 5 tbsp lemon juice and stir. Return to heat again and stir for a minute. When the curd and whey separate it is ready to be poured through a colander lined with muslin or thin white cloth. Squeeze the water out. Then put the pieces into a small dish tight pack it and put a heavy dish or weight over the cover. Leave in fridge overnight. Next day cut into small squares. Deep fry in fresh oil and it is ready to use in dishes. Alternatively when the whey and curd are separated you can add two grated cloves of garlic and chopped coriander leaves to the mixture.

Aubergine Dish (Jaffna preparation)

Katharikkai Kulambu - Tamil name
Cooking & Preparation Time: 45 minutes
Serves 3-4 as a side dish

A traditional dish. I have included the traditional method and a modified one. Lovely thick sauce with Aubergine; serve one or two spoonfuls and have with other dishes. Good for rice, string hoppers or any bread-based dish.

Ingredients

- 2 long aubergines or 1 medium round
- 2 medium onions, sliced
- 4 cloves garlic, finely sliced
- 1 tsp fenugreek seeds
- 1½ tsp tamarind paste, soaked in hot water
- 1-2 tsp roasted chilli/curry powder
- 2 sprigs curry leaves
- 1 dried red chilli chopped (optional)
- 2 tomatoes (optional)
- oil for deep frying
- salt to taste
- 1 can coconut milk (300g) or cream coconut from block - 2cm slice

Method:

1. Cut the aubergine into 3cm-long, thin pieces. Wash, sprinkle salt and set aside. Before frying squeeze any water and dry on a kitchen towel.

2. Heat oil in a thava and deep-fry the aubergine pieces in batches until golden brown. Drain on kitchen paper. Transfer to another paper towel and get rid of the excess oil.

3. Fry the sliced onions, add garlic and fry to a golden colour. Drain and set aside.

4. Put the fenugreek seeds into a tea strainer and slowly immerse into the hot oil for 10 seconds and remove. Fry the curry leaves and drain.

5. Switch off the oil and quickly deep fry the chopped chilli and remove (see note below).

6. In a pan or thava add salt, 1½ cup of diluted weaker coconut milk, tamarind with the water, chilli powder and boil for 4 minutes.

7. Next add all the fried ingredients and cook for 5 minutes over a moderate heat.

8. Add the thick coconut milk, bring to boil and reduce the flame. Cook for another 5-6 minutes.

9. When the sauce thickens, it is ready to remove from cooker.

★ When you are frying chilli be careful, as it will make you cough. You may omit this from the recipe.

Variations

- Instead of using coconut milk in step 6 can use 2 cups of water and boil. Then follow the rest.
- If adding creamed coconut you may add another ½ cup of water at the start of the cooking. Add creamed coconut and cook on low fire. Stir to make sure that the cream is mixed.

- Can add single cream or normal milk, but watch the temperature (do not let it boil), as the cream may curdle.

Healthier option

- Roll the aubergine pieces in a little oil and bake in the oven at high temperature for 10 minutes or grill these.
- Stir fry onions in 2 tablespoons of oil, add garlic, and curry leaves, fenugreek and then the grilled aubergine pieces.
- Add hot water, tamarind, salt and chilli powder and bring to boil. Then reduce, add normal milk or half fat evaporated milk and cook on medium heat for 6-8 minutes until a thick creamy sauce is formed.
- If you do not like the aubergine mixed well in the sauce, you may keep the aubergine and add it last when you add the coconut milk or evaporated milk.

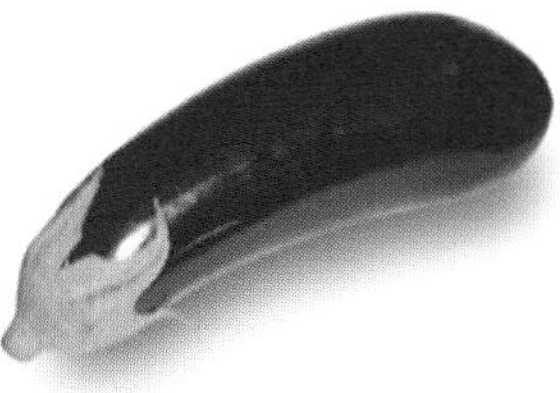

Grilled Aubergine Special

Preparation & cooking time: 30 minutes
Serves 4-6

Ingredients

- 1 large aubergine
- 200g plain natural yoghurt
- 1 tsp roasted chilli powder
- salt to taste
- 1 onion, chopped
- 1 sprig coriander leaves
- 1 tsp garam masala paste
- tempering ingredients: 1 tsp mustard seeds
- 1 tsp cumin seeds, 2 dry red chillies

Method

1. Brush the aubergine with a little oil and grill it. Keep turning until all sides are equally cooked. Peel and discard the skin. Mix the pulp with the yoghurt, garam masala paste and salt.
2. Heat the oil in a frying pan. Add mustard, cumin and the chopped red chilli. Next add the chopped onions and fry for few minutes.
3. Add the aubergine mixture quickly to the above, stir and cook for a minute. Add the roughly chopped coriander leaves and serve.

Aubergine Omelette

Preparation & cooking time 30 minutes

Serves 4 as a side dish

Ingredients

- 1 large aubergine
- 4 shallots, finely chopped and diced
- 3 green chillies, finely chopped
- 4 eggs
- salt to taste
- little oil or ghee
- 1 tsp roasted mixed chilli powder
- ½ tsp garam masala paste
- ½ tsp garlic/ginger paste

Method

1. Brush the aubergine with a little oil and grill it. Keep turning until all sides are equally cooked.
2. Peel the skin and mash the aubergine. Add the green chilli, onions, garam masala, chilli powder and salt and mix well.
3. In a bowl beat the eggs. Add the aubergine mix and beat it well.
4. In a large frying pan heat the oil and pour half of the mixture, cover and cook on low heat.
5. With a spatula (wide blade) carefully turn the egg over and cook the opposite side. Serve onto a plate. Repeat with the other half. Cut the fried egg and serve

★ If you want you can cook all the mixture in one go. It will take a long time, cover and cook. The depth will be thicker

★ If you need to cook the aubergine over a naked flame of the burner of a gas cooker, use two skewers on either end of the aubergine and keep turning until it is cooked.

Bitter Gourd (Hot Kari)

See explanations under vegetables.
This is not something everyone enjoys, but it is very healthy.
There is an art to cooking it. One can add tomatoes and tamarind while making the spicy preparation.
This is not a vegetable that is eaten in large quantities, so you serve a spoon or two.

Preparation & cooking: 30-40 minutes
Serves 3-4

Ingredients

- 1 medium bitter gourd or two small ones.
- 1 cup coconut water *
- 2 tsp tamarind paste
- 2 medium onions, chopped
- 2 cloves garlic
- 1½ tsp roasted chilli powder
- salt to taste
- 2 tomatoes, chopped
- 1 green chilli
- 1 tsp sugar (optional)
- 1 cup water .
- 1 cup coconut milk or cream coconut 2cm slice mixed in 3 tbsp normal milk

★ You need to buy a coconut and break it in half to get the water. Traditional cooking includes this and not sugar. The recipe can also be followed without using coconut water, as it cannot be obtained easily.

Method:

1. Wash and slice the bitter gourd as if cutting cucumber slices. Remove the seeds.

2. Put in salted water and leave for few minutes.

3 Chop the onions, chilli and garlic and put in a saucepan; add salt, tamarind, chopped tomatoes and 1 cup of coconut water or normal water.

4. Take the bitter gourd and drain the salted water and squeeze the pieces slightly so as to take out the bitterness.

5. Add the pieces to the pan, bring to boil, cover the pan, reduce the heat and cook for 10 minutes. Then taste and if necessary add some more tamarind as this is what gives the taste and takes the bitterness out.

6. Add coconut milk, a little at a time, not allowing it to curdle, and cook on a low flame for another ten minutes. If adding the cream coconut add it 5 minutes before removing the bitter gourd from the cooker.

7. Add the curry leaves, 1 tsp of sugar and mix well. Remove from heat when the sauce thickens.

Deep Fried Bitter Gourd Kari

Preparation & cooking time: 30 minutes

Serves 4-6

Ingredients

- 2 bitter gourds
- 2 medium onions, finely sliced
- ½ tsp fenugreek seeds
- 3 cloves garlic, diced
- 1 sprig curry leaves, roughly cut
- 2-3 tsp tamarind paste
- 1 cup coconut milk or a slice of cream coconut 2-3cm
- oil for frying
- 1 cup water
- tomato (optional)
- salt to taste
- 2 tsp roasted chilli powder

Method

1. Cut the bitter gourds into 4cm lengthwise pieces that are a bit thicker than a matchstick. Discard the seeds. Then wash and dry. Deep fry in oil. Remove and place in a colander

2. Deep fry the onions, garlic and curry leaves. Put the fenugreek into a tea strainer and slowly immerse in oil for 10 seconds. Remove and drain all fried items on kitchen paper.

3. Mix tamarind, water, salt and chilli powder. Place in a pan and bring to boil. Add the fried ingredients and cook on medium heat for 5 minutes.

4. Add milk and cook for another 2-3 minutes. If adding the cream coconut, add little bit of normal milk so that it does not burn. Allow the sauce to thicken.

5. Remove from cooker and serve with plain rice.

Butter Milk Gravy (Moor Kulambu)

Preparation & cooking time: 15 minutes
Serves 5-6

Ingredients

- 1 tbsp split peas (kadalai parruppu)
- 1 tsp coriander seeds
- 1 green chilli
- 3 tbsp chopped coconut pieces 1cm size
- salt to taste
- ½ tsp rice flour
- ½ tsp turmeric powder
- 1 tsp mustard seeds
- 1 tsp fennel seeds
- 5-6 curry leaves
- pinch of asafoetida powder
- 2 tbsp oil for frying
- 1 large pot natural yoghurt (375g)

Method

1. Heat a saucepan and add oil. To the hot oil add mustard seeds, fennel, curry leaves, coriander and fry for few seconds.

2. Mix ¼ cup water to the yoghurt. Add this to the pan and bring to boil for about two minutes. Do not over boil as it will become too watery.

3. Grind the split peas and add it to the above with salt, rice flour, turmeric, green chilli and the coconut.

4. Give it a stir and remove from the heat.

★ You may add 1 tsp gram flour instead of the split peas.

Cassava - Tapioca

Tapioca is a yam, which has a dark brown thick skin. Tapioca is also known as 'Maravalli' or cassava.
Can be purchased as a fresh Yam from West Indian, Greek, Sri Lankan and Indian shops. But nowadays you can get frozen cassava, which is clean, cut into cubes and ready for you to cook.

If using the fresh yam, you need to cut and peel the outer skin. Then cut and peel the inner skin. Quickly cut the white yam into pieces and put it in water. It is said that if you are going to eat tapioca, it is better to avoid having a lot of ginger at the same time.

Hot preparation

Preparation & cooking time: 30 minutes
Serves 4-6 as a side dish

Ingredients

- 1 packet of frozen cassava 250g
- 1 large onion, chopped
- 3 green chillies, cut lengthwise
- 2 tsp roasted chilli /curry powder
- 4 cloves garlic, crushed
- 3cm size sliced cream coconut or ½ cup evaporated milk
- 2 sprigs curry leaves, roughly chopped
- salt to taste
- ½ tsp turmeric powder
- ½ lime juice
- ½ tsp roasted fennel powder

Method

1. Defrost the cassava and cut into 4cm size pieces. Wash thoroughly to get rid of the starch and boil in water for 5 minutes. Drain the water.
2. Place the onions in a pan. Add the chilli powder, turmeric, salt, green chillies, chopped garlic, boiled cassava, ¼ cup of mixed water and milk. Bring to boil and cook for few minutes. Then reduce the flame and cook for about 8 minutes.
3. Add the rest of the milk or cream coconut and simmer for 5 minutes until the sauce thickens.
4. Remove from cooker when the dish resembles a mash. Add lime juice and serve with rice.

Variations

Boiled Cassava

- Cut into rounds of 3cm thickness and boil in a pan of water. Add salt and when the yam is soft, drain the water off. Serve with hot chilli sauce or chilli chutney.

Boiled Cassava and Pumpkin

To the ingredients in the previous page (cassava) add

- 250g pumpkin, 1 tsp freshly ground cumin and pepper; disregard the fennel powder.
- Add the cut pumpkin pieces to the cassava and cook, following step 2 onwards. Finally add the ground cumin and pepper powder.

Baking

It is safer to buy the frozen variety.

1. Thaw this, cut up lengthwise and steam it for 10 minutes.
2. Brush a baking tray or foil with olive oil. Mix a teaspoon of chilli powder and a bit of salt. Toss the cassava in this.
4. Arrange the cassava flat and bake at 180°C for 10-15 minutes until crispy. You may need to turn it once.

BBQ: Wrap the steamed pieces in foil and barbecue.

Chick Peas "Sundal"

Preparation & cooking: 10-15 minutes
Serves 2

Ingredients

- 400g can chick peas (boiled)
- 4 dry red chillies, roughly chopped
- 1 tsp cumin seeds
- 8 curry leaves
- few pieces of coconut slices (optional)
- 1 medium onion, chopped
- 1 tsp mustard seeds
- 1 tbsp oil
- pan of boiling water
- salt to taste

Method

1. Open the can and drain the water.
2. Boil a pan of water and put the chick peas for a minute and drain.
3. Heat a thava. Add the oil, sauté and fry the onions until golden brown colour. Add mustard seeds, cumin red chillies and the curry leaves.
4. Drain the water from the chick peas. Toss it in a bit of salt, add to the fried onions and stir fry.
5. Lastly, if you have small pieces of fresh coconut, cut up into small cubes, add this and remove from cooker.
6. Serve and eat this on its own.

★ You can omit step 2, but I always do this to get rid of the stickiness.

Variations

Using Dried Chick Peas

Preparation: Soak over night
Cooking: 40 minutes for boiling
Tempering: Another 15 minutes.

If you are making large quantities

1. Soak 4 cups of chick peas in water overnight.

2. Wash and put into a pressure cooker and boil for 4 or whistles and remove the pan from the heat.
   or
   You can boil in a normal large pan of water, add ½ tsp of bicarbonate of soda.

3. Drain and add salt. Then follow the tempering as in the Sundal recipe but double the ingredients.

★ There are brown and yellow grams that are cooked for religious ceremonies at temples.

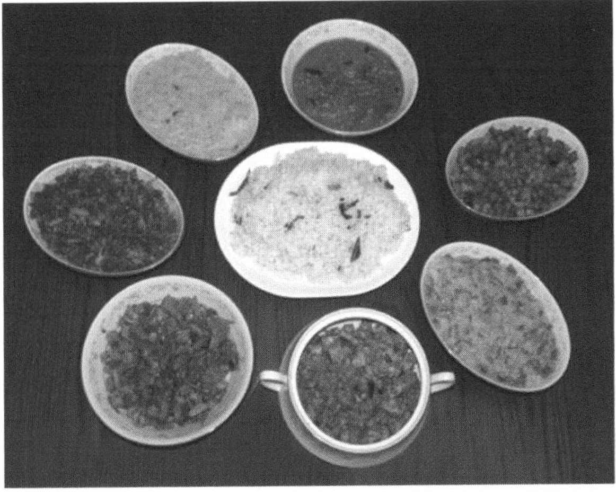

Cucumber Stir Fry

Ingredients

- 1 cucumber, sliced
- 3 tbsp flour
- 1 onion,chopped
- 2 tsp sesame seeds
- 3 tbsp oil
- salt to taste, ½ tsp garlic powder, ½ tsp ginger powder.
- 1 tsp crushed chilli powder
- 1 tsp soya sauce

Method

1. Slice the cucumber thin, leave on a kitchen paper to absorb the water. Pat dry and roll in the flour.

2. Stir fry this in hot oil in a wok or a flat based frying pan.

3. Remove and leave on a plate.

4. Into the oil add onions, sesame seeds, salt, crushed chillies, garlic and ginger powder. Stir fry for few minutes. Add the soya sauce, then the cooked cucumber. Stir fry and remove from cooker serve with hot rice.

Savoury Deep Fry (Cheese, egg, potato)

Ingredients

- 250g butter/margarine
- ¼ tsp salt, ½ tsp ground pepper
- ¼ tsp grated nutmeg, ½ tsp cinnamon powder
- 125g cheddar cheese, grated
- few chives and spring onions chopped
- 1 tsp garlic powder
- 4 eggs
- mash potato made from 4 medium potatoes (1 bowl)
- 100g rice flour
- 125g stone ground flour
- 2 tbsp corn flour
- 300ml water, 1 cube of vegetable stock
- oil for frying

Method

1. Melt butter, add all seasoning, mashed potato and half the flour mixture.
2. Keep stirring, add the stock, then the grated cheese.
3. Fold in the beaten egg and the rest of the flour.
4. Heat the oil and drop spoonfuls of mixture anddeep fry.

★ Serve with any dips.

Egg (Boiled egg Kari)

Preparation & cooking time: 30 minutes
Serves 4

Ingredients

- 4 hard boiled eggs shelled, make lengthwise slits
- 1 medium size onion
- 2 cloves garlic and small piece of ginger, grated
- 2 tbsp oil
- 1 large tomato, cut
- 2 tomatoes
- 3 tbsp milk or cream
- 1–2 tsp chilli powder
- salt to taste
- 1 cup water
- 4 small new potatoes boiled and peeled
- 1 tsp roasted fennel powder
- few curry leaves

Method

1. Chop the onion and fry in 1 tablespoon of oil. Add the tomatoes, grated garlic and ginger.
2. Add the peeled potatoes and the eggs and fry for a minute.
3. Add salt, chilli powder and water and cook for 10 minutes.
4. Add bit of milk or cream and let the sauce thicken. Add the curry leaves and remove from cooker.
5. Sprinkle fennel powder and leave it covered until you serve.

Variation

Fried whole egg

To the ingredients in the previous page, add the following

- 1 tsp each ginger, garlic powder.
- 1cm slice cream coconut, 1 tsp mustard seeds, rampe leaf 2cm

1. Prick the boiled eggs and potato with a fork all round.
2. Fry onions in oil. Add mustard seeds.
3. Mix garlic powder, ginger powder, chilli powder and salt. Add to the onions. Carefully place the eggs and potatoes in the pan and stir fry over a low flame. Keep turning the eggs until the skin gets slightly brown and the juice gets absorbed by the eggs through the little holes.
4. Now add the tomato and water, cook for few minutes, add cream coconut, curry leaves, rampe and fennel powder. Stir for 2 minutes and remove from fire.

★ My mother used to prepare this dish using coconut milk.

Omelette Dish with Sauce

Preparation & cooking time: 30 minutes
Serves 3-4

Ingredients

- 6 eggs
- 2 tomatoes, chopped
- 1 cup water
- ½ lime
- 1 medium onion, chopped
- 2-3 tbsp oil for frying and tempering
- ¼ cup milk to make sauce
- 1 tsp roasted fennel powder
- 1 tsp chilli powder, salt, 1 tsp curry powder.
- piece of ginger and 2 garlic cloves crushed
- few curry leaves or coriander leaves

Method

1. Beat two eggs at a time with 1 tablespoon milk, add salt.
2. Heat a frying pan, add oil and pour the egg mixture into the frying pan. When half cooked, roll it or fold it into a long strip.
3. Serve on to a plate and slice this across into 4cm size strips.
4. Repeat the same for the other eggs and you will have about 10-12 pieces.
5. Next heat oil, add onions and tomato and fry. Add water, salt, chilli, ginger and garlic and bring to a boil. Cook for 3-4 minutes.
6. Add the egg slices and cook. Allow for the water to be absorbed by the egg and cook for a few minutes. Add 2 tablespoons of milk and a spoon of special roasted fennel powder. Remove from the cooker and squeeze the juice of the lime over it.

YAM - Karanai Kilangu - 1

Dry preparation
Preparation & cooking time: 45 minutes
Serves 4-6

Ingredients

- 500g karanai kilangu (yam)
- salt to taste
- 2 sprigs curry leaves
- 4 green chillies
- 4cm size ginger
- 3 cloves garlic
- 1 tbsp chilli powder
- 1 lemon
- oil for frying
- ½ tsp each mustard and cumin seeds for frying

Method

1. Skin the karanai kilangu, wash and cut into small cubes about 1½ cm size.

2. Grind the green chilli, ginger and garlic into a paste.

3. In a flat-based pan heat the oil, add the spices and curry leaves and cook for few seconds. Add the yam and fry for few minutes; keep stirring and turn over the pieces so that both sides get cooked. Add the green chilli paste and cook over a medium heat.

4. Add salt, chilli powder and turmeric. Cook for further 5 minutes until the mixture is dry and is cooked well. Remove from heat.

5. Before serving add the lemon juice and stir.

Variation

Ingredients

To the ingredients in the previous add the following, and leave out the lemon juice

- 52 large onions
- 52 tsp of tamarind paste mixed in a pint of water.
- 55 garlic cloves, cut
- 51 tsp fenugreek seeds
- 5piece of cream coconut or ¼ cup normal milk

Method

1. Deep fry the diced yam and drain it on a kitchen towel.
2. Chop the onions and temper in little oil. When fried add the garlic, fenugreek seeds and the curry leaves.
3. Add the tamarind water mixture and allow to boil. Add the chilli powder and salt .
4. Add the yam pieces and cook for 5 to 10 minutes. Add the cream coconut or milk.
5. When mixture thickens remove from the heat.

★ **Traditional method:**
Deep fry the yam pieces, chopped onions, garlic, curry leaves and fenugreek seeds. Then add tamarind juice taken from soaking the tamarind in hot water and follow the rest of the recipe as above. Add coconut milk. See sections on tamarind for the different varieties available.

Karanai Kilangu - 2

Ingredients

- 500g karanai kilangu (yam)
- salt to taste
- 2 sprigs, curry leaves
- 5cm size ginger crushed
- 4 cloves of garlic sliced
- 1 tsp of mixed mustard and cumin seeds for frying
- 2 tbsp chilli powder
- juice of 1 lime
- oil for frying
- 2 tbsp roasted ground fennel powder
- ½ can coconut milk (200g) or 4 tbsp coconut powder

Method

1. Skin the karanai kilangu, wash and cut into small cubes. Deep fry in oil and drain on kitchen paper.
2. Stir fry onions, garlic, fenugreek, mustard, cumin and a few curry leaves. Add crushed ginger, chilli and curry powder. Then add 1½ cups of water, salt and bring to boil.
3. Add the fried yam pieces and cook over a medium heat for 6-8 minutes.
4. Add coconut milk or coconut powder mixed in warm water. Cook for a few minutes, add the remaining curry leaves and remove from heat. Add the fennel powder and stir it once.
5. Before serving squeeze the lime and add the juice.

Kool

A hot soup with tropical vegetables and Palmyra flour known as Odiyal ma. A good dish to have for a weekend. This is not something you would make regularly. You need company to enjoy this dish.
There is also a non-vegetarian version of it in the sea food section.
Most of the ingredients can be purchased from Sri Lankan grocery shops. Jack pieces should be the cooking type and not the fruit. Murunga leaves- leaves of drumstick tree, available in frozen packs.

Preparation: appx 1 hour
Cooking: 45 minutes

Ingredients

- 1 cup, palmyra flour (odiyal ma) from Sri Lankan shops
- 1 bunch fresh spinach leaves
- 1 packet frozen cassava (tapioca) (500g)
- 1 can of jack pieces or fresh jack pieces for cooking (400g)
- 20 jack seeds (need to soak in water and clean the skin)
- 1 bunch of long thin beans (Payathangai)
- few murunga leaves - (optional small frozen packet)
- 10-15 dry red chillies freshly ground or powdered
- 3-4 pints of water
- tamarind, ¼ block or small ball size
- ¼ cup rice
- salt to taste
- ¼ cup, split moong dhal
- 1 tsp turmeric powder
- 6 garlic cloves, ground or use the paste
- few salad potatoes
- 2 green bananas
- oil for frying
- a large pan
- corn flour (optional standby)

Method:

1. Soak the palmyra flour in plenty of water and leave it to settle for 5 minutes. The flour will settle to the bottom and you will see clear water on the top.

2. Carefully strain the water out without losing any of the flour. Pour in some more water, mix it and let it settle. You need to repeat this process three times.

3. Soak the tamarind in 1 cup of hot water, leave it for a few minutes and squeeze with your fingers to get the juice. Strain and keep the juice. Pour a bit more water over the tamarind pieces and leave it aside, in case you require it for a stronger taste.

4. Soak the jack seeds in water. Remove the outer and the inner brown skins. Wash and cut into half or quarter.

5. Cut the jack pieces to 2cm size. Break the beans in to 3cm pieces, wash and leave to one side. Cut the cassava into 3cm squares. Wash and chop the spinach.

6. Grind the red chillies and leave it in a covered dish.

7. Clean the potato and peel the green bananas. Chop into small (crouton size) cubes. Wash, add salt, 1 tsp chilli powder and deep fry in oil. Take out when it is crispy and leave it to one side.

8. In a large pan put the beans, cassava, jack seeds, jack pieces, rice and dhal.

9. Add 2-3 pints of water and cook over a medium heat. Add more water if necessary.

10. After 20 minutes when the vegetables are cooked add the spinach.

11. Mix the tamarind juice and half the ground chilli, turmeric and garlic. Add it to the vegetables and continue cooking.

12. Taste and add chillies depending on the hotness you require.

13. Add the strained palmyra flour and mix well.

14. You will see the broth thickening but the volume will be nearly the same as the amount of water used

15. To make the consistency correct, either add more hot water or more palmyra flour. A bit of corn flour mixed in water will also be okay.

16. Now add the fried potatoes, fried green banana and the murunga leaves.

17. Remove from the heat and serve while hot.

Variations

★ If you have a pressure cooker the whole process will take about 20-25 minutes.

★ Can substitute corn flour for palmyra flour; mix it with a bit of gram flour and soak it once, drain and use the flour. However the taste will be different.

★ Carrots, swede, parsnips and fresh runner beans are possible alternative vegetables to use.

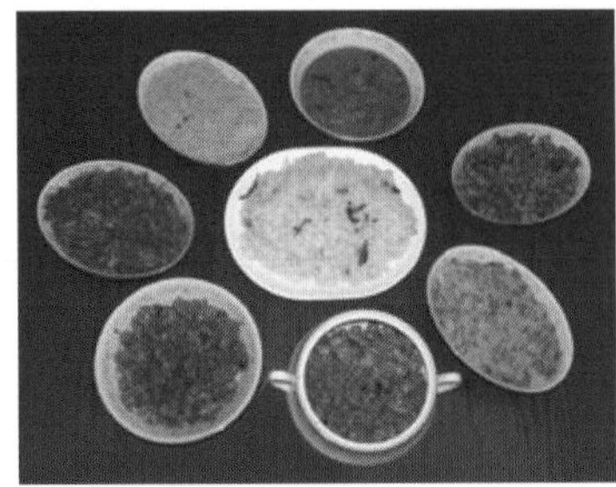

Long Beans 'Payathangai'

An Asian Tropical vegetable, now available in shops in the West

Ingredients:

- 1 bunch long beans
- 1 onion, chopped
- salt to your taste (1 tsp)
- 4cm piece ginger, cleaned and cut into strips
- 1 cup thick coconut milk
- 1-2 tsp roasted chilli powder
- 1 sprig curry leaves

Method

1. Peel the top end of the beans and pull down one side to remove the string like fibre. Chop the tail end of the bean.

2. Place a few beans on a chopping board and cut to nearly the same size, say 1½"-2". Wash and leave it aside.

3. In a frying pan place the beans, onions, ginger, salt and chilli powder with ½ cup of water and a little coconut milk. Bring to boil and cook on a medium heat for about 10 minutes.

4. Add the thick coconut milk and cook for another 5 minutes until the sauce thickens. Add the curry leaves and remove from heat.

Variations

Fried method

To ingredients on previous page add

- 4 tbsp oil
- 2 tsp of roasted fennel powder
- ¼ can of full cream evaporated milk

1. Fry the onion in oil, add mustard seeds, cumin and half the curry leaves. Then add the beans and stir fry over a medium heat. Sprinkle a bit of water, add salt and chilli powder. Cover and cook for 10-15 minutes.

2. Add the milk, mix well and cook for 10 minutes.

3. Finally, add the rest of the curry leaves and fennel powder. Remove from heat.

★ Use potato as an alternative. Cut the potato to the same size as the beans. Wash and cook in microwave for 2 minutes. Then add this to the beans just after 5 minutes and follow the above recipe.

Mango Special Side Dish

Preparation & cooking time: 30 minutes
Serves 3-4

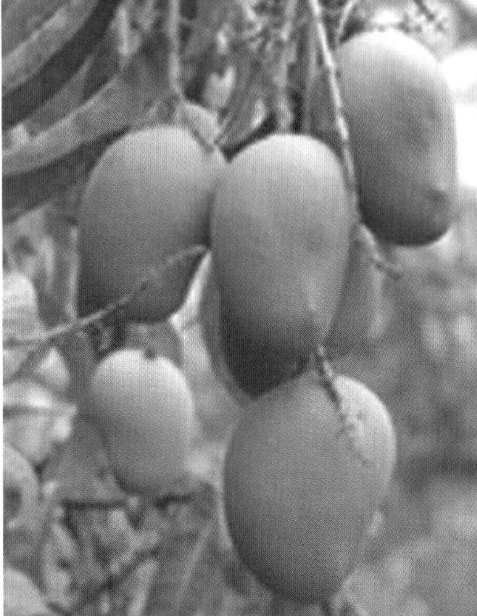

Ingredients

- 1 large raw mango (green skin)
- salt to taste
- 2 green chillies (optional)
- ½ tsp mustard seeds
- ½ tsp cumin seeds
- 1 dried red chilli, few curry leaves
- 1 tsp cumin (freshly ground)
- 1- 2 tbsp oil
- ½ tsp sugar
- 1 onion cut into small cubes
- little water

Method

1. Skin the mango and cut into small cubes.
2. Heat oil in a pan add mustard seeds and when it pops add the cumin, cut onion and temper/sauté for few minutes.
3. Add the cut red chilli, curry leaves, salt and the mango pieces. Cook over a medium flame. Add green chillies and 2 tablespoons of water if necessary and cook for 5 minutes.
5. Add cumin powder and sprinkle the sugar.
6. Toss it once and remove from cooker.

★ **If you like sour and sweet taste this is a very good dish.**

Variations

Raw mango

- For a hot dish use the above recipe, omitting the cumin powder and sugar. Add 1 tsp plain chilli powder and 2 tbsp milk towards the end of the cooking.
- Cut the mango into small cubes with the skin. Add salt, 1 tsp crushed chilli and ½ tsp lime juice. Mix well and serve.

Mock Chicken and Button Mushrooms

Kentucky style - deep fried

Preparation & cooking time: 30 minutes
Serves 4

Ingredients#

- 1 tin mock chicken (200g)
- ½ cup rice flour
- salt to taste
- oil for deep frying
- 1 tsp ground pepper, 1 tsp garlic powder
- 2 tsp mixed masala powder (cinnamon, ginger, cardamom)
- 10 small button mushrooms
- ½ cup plain flour
- 1 tsp plain chilli powder

Method

1. Clean the mock chicken pieces and dry on a kitchen paper. Cut into thin slices so that they will cook well.
2. Wash mushrooms and either boil for 5 minutes or cook in microwave for 1 or 2 minutes depending on the power of your microwave. Take out and leave on kitchen paper.
3. Mix the rice flour, plain flour and all the dry powdered ingredients.
4 Individually roll the mock chicken and mushrooms in the flour mixture and set aside. Heat the oil in a pan, when it is hot roll the pieces again in the flour and deep fry until cooked and crispy.

Variations

Dip the items in egg white or batter made of plain flour and water, then roll in bread crumbs and deep fry.

Serve with chilli sauce.

Mysore Rasam (Indian recipe)

Preparation & cooking time: 20 minutes
Serves 8-10

Ingredients

- 2 tbsp mysore rasam mix (see spice & masala section, also available in shops)
- 2 tomatoes chopped
- salt to taste
- 2 sprigs coriander leaves
- 2 tsp sambar powder (available in shops)
- ¼ cup boiled toor dhal
- 1-2 tsp tamarind paste
- 1 sprig curry leaves
- 2 cups water
- 3 garlic cloves, crushed

Method

1. Boil water in a pan. Add the cooked dhal, chopped tomatoes, tamarind, salt, garlic and heat well for 3-4 minutes.
2. Add 2 tablespoons of the Mysore rasam mix, sambar powder and leave to boil for a minute.
3. Add the curry leaves, chopped coriander leaves, sprinkle water and cover with a lid and remove from cooker.

Rasam

Ingredients

- 2 garlic cloves crushed
- 1 tsp tamarind paste
- ¼ tsp asafoetida powder
- 1 tomato cut up
- 2 cups water
- few coriander leaves finely cut
- salt to taste

Method

In a pan heat the water, add salt, tamarind, asafoetida, crushed garlic and tomato. Boil for two to three minutes. Add 2 or 3 tsp of the crushed rasam powder, sprinkle a little cold water add coriander leaves and cover with a lid. Remove from cooker. Leave to settle and pour in a glass and drink or serve with rice.

★ If you need to make it quickly, you may use a mortar and pestle and crush the pepper first, then add cumin and coriander and crush to prepare the rasam powder.

Paneer Dish with Peas - Mutter Paneer

Cooking time: 25 minutes
Serves 6

Ingredients

- 250g fresh peas or frozen petis pois
- 2 packets of paneer (appx 200g each)
- 2 medium onions
- 1 tin chopped tomatoes (400g)
- 5 garlic cloves or 1 tsp garlic paste
- 4cm ginger or 1 tsp ginger paste
- 5 sprigs methi leaves, chopped
- 1 tbsp roasted chilli powder
- 1 tsp cinnamon powder, 2 cloves cardamom
- small carton of whipping cream
- salt to taste
- 4 tbsp oil for shallow frying the paneer or oil to deep fry
- 2 tbsp ghee to fry onions
- 1 tsp turmeric powder
- 1 tsp each: mustard seeds, cumin and ajwain (omam)

Method

1. Cut paneer into small cubes and shallow fry in 2 tbsp oil in a wok or a frying pan. Keep tossing it until slightly brown. Transfer to a plate and set aside.

2. In the same frying pan add the ghee and fry the chopped onions for few minutes until it is golden brown. Add mustard seeds, cumin and ajwain

3. Grind the fresh ginger and garlic then add the chopped tomatoes and liquidise.

4. Add salt and chilli powder to the fried onions, then the ground tomatoes, garlic and ginger paste and cook for 10 minutes until the mixture gets thick.

5. Add the paneer and cook for few minutes; you may need to add a bit of water). When the sauce begins to thicken add methi leaves.

6. Cook the frozen peas in a microwave for 3 minutes, depending on the power of your microwave, until it is cooked.

7. Add whipping cream, the cooked peas and lastly the cinnamon and cardamom powder.

8. Remove from cooker and serve with rice, chapatti, poori or paratha.

Can deep fry in oil and leave on kitchen paper)

★ If you are health conscious bake the paneer pieces for 10 to 15 minutes.

Paneer Masala Grated Stir Fry

Preparation & cooking time: 25 minutes
Serves 6-8

Ingredients

As in previous recipe for paneer with peas but omit the peas, methi leaves and whipping cream

- 4-5 sprigs of coriander leaves, chopped
- 1 chopped tomato tin or 5 fresh tomatoes
- ½ tsp black pepper powder
- 1 tbsp tomato purée or sauce
- 2 tbsp coconut powder
- 2 tbsp ground peanuts

Method

1. Grate the paneer and set aside.
2. Fry onions; add the masala, chilli powder, chopped tomatoes, garlic, ginger and a bit of water. Cook to bring the gravy/sauce to slightly thick.
3. Next add the tomato purée, peanuts, powdered cinnamon and cardamom and coconut powder mixed in very little hot water.
3. Finally add the grated paneer and stir for 1-2 minutes and remove from cooker.
4. Sprinkle with chopped coriander leaves.

Paneer Manchuri

Preparation & cooking time: 30 minutes
Serves 6- 8 as a side dish

Similar preparation to Cauliflower Manchuri but with minor adjustments.

Ingredients

- 2 packets of paneer, sliced (200g each)
- oil for frying
- 1 tbsp corn flour
- 2 tbsp soya sauce
- 2 tbsp tomato sauce
- 1 tsp plain chilli powder
- ½ cup water
- salt to taste

Following items finely chopped

- 2 medium red onions are tasty or 7 shallots
- 3 green chillies, chopped
- 3 cloves garlic
- 4cm ginger
- 3-4 sprigs fresh curry leaves, sliced fine
- 2cm piece rampe

Method

1. In a heavy-based frying pan put 2 tablespoons of oil. Cut the paneer into about 2" long strips. Shallow fry both sides. Remove from pan and place on a kitchen paper to absorb the oil.
2. In a bowl place a bit of salt and the plain chilli powder. Toss the paneer in the mixed chilli whilst hot and place on a plate. The left over chilli powder can be used later.
3. To the same pan add two tablespoons of oil and fry the chopped onions, ginger, garlic and finally the chillies, curry leaves and rampe.
4. Add the soya sauce, tomato sauce and any chilli powder from the bowl.
5. Mix the corn flour with ¼ cup of water or bit more; add this to the sauce.
6. When the mixture begins to thicken add the fried paneer quickly and stir it so that the paneer is fully coated.
7. Remove and dish it out whilst hot.

Variations

If you like it hot, add 1 green chilli chopped and include 6 more green chillies cut length wise.

Tofu/Quorn

Can do the same with tofu, but it will be difficult to stir fry the tofu as it will stick.
First steam the tofu block. Cut the tofu lengthwise and pat dry.
Mix corn flour, self raising flour, salt and chilli powder.
Roll each tofu in the flour and stir fry. Then follow the above recipe.

You can also deep fry and follow the recipe.

Pasta & Soya Mince or Quorn Mince

Preparation & cooking time: 20 - 25 minutes

Serves 2-3

Ingredients

- 175g pasta
- 1 packet frozen mince either soya or quorn
- 1 onion chopped, 2 green chillies, finely cut
- 3 cloves garlic, grated
- 4cm ginger, grated
- 1 green pepper
- 1 red pepper
- 100g spinach leaves
- 2 tsp chilli oil
- 2 tsp tomato purée
- 1 cube (oxo) vegetable stock flavouring
- oil or butter
- salt to taste

Method

1. Cook the pasta in water and drain. Add a little olive oil and toss it.
2. Cut the peppers into small squares. Wash the spinach, rinse well and cut it small.
3. In a wok heat some oil or butter, add the onions, pepper, thawed mince, garlic and ginger. Cook for 2 minutes, add the vegetable stock and keep stir frying for another 3-4 minutes until it is slightly brown. Then add the spinach and stir fry. Add the green chillies.
4. Once cooked add the pasta, tomato purée, a bit of chilli oil according to the degree of spice you need and mix well; remove from fire.

★ **You may add grated carrot and quorn pieces as well.**

Potato Filling (for toasted sandwiches)

Ingredients

- 200g potato
- 1 small onion, chopped
- 2 cloves garlic, grated
- small piece ginger, grated
- 1 tsp chilli powder
- 1 tsp butter

Method

1. Boil potatoes, skin and put through a grater.

2. Add the ingredients, mix and set aside.

3. The filling can be placed in between two slices of bread and toasted in a sandwich toaster.

Potato North Indian Style

Preparation & cooking time: 30 minutes
Serves 3-4

Ingredients

- 12 baby potatoes
- 2 cloves garlic, grated
- 3cm ginger, grated
- ½ tsp mustard seeds
- ½ tsp cumin seeds
- ½ tsp fennel seeds
- 1 tsp crushed dry methi leaves
- 1½ tsp mixed spice powder (cinnamon, cardamoms and cloves
- 2 tsp plain chilli powder, 1 tbsp gram flour
- 1 small carton, natural yoghurt
- 1 cup water
- 3 green chillies, finely cut
- 2 onions, chopped to small cubes
- 2 sprigs curry leaves
- oil for deep-frying, 2 tsp oil for tempering
- 1 tsp ground kastoori masala powder
- salt to taste

Method

1. Boil potatoes and peel skin. Prick with fork and deep fry in oil until slightly brown. Drain on a paper to get the excess oil off.
2. Mix gram flour with water to form a paste, then mix with yoghurt and put aside.
3. Fry the chopped onions in little oil, add mustard seed, cumin, fennel, half the curry leaves and chopped green chillies. Then allow to cool for a while and add the yoghurt mixture, chilli powder, salt, methi leaves and kastoori masala; bring to boil and reduce to medium heat.
4. Keep stirring. Add the potatoes and salt, cook for 5 minutes.
5. Lastly add the cinnamon powder and balance curry leaves and remove from cooker

★ Serve with rice or naan bread

Potato & Veg Special (Fillers)

A filling for samosas, cutlets or toasted sandwiches
Preparation & cooking time: 25 minutes

Ingredients

- 4 potatoes (appx 250g)
- 70g peas
- 1 large carrot
- 1 medium leek
- 1 onion, cut into very fine cubes
- 1 tsp coriander powder
- ½ tsp cumin powder
- 1-2 tsp roasted chilli/curry powder(to your taste)
- 2 sprigs curry leaves
- 2 tbsp oil
- 2 cloves garlic and 2cm size ginger, crushed
- tbsp mixed mustard and cumin seeds, ½ tsp fennel seeds
- 1 red chilli cut up.
- ½ tsp of kastoori masala powder, 1 tsp spices (cinnamon & cardamom)
- 2cm rampe, cut up fine

Method

1. Clean and cut the potatoes into small squares. Similarly cut the leek fine. Slice the carrot and cut it across to small cubes.
2. In a wok heat the oil add the onions and fry for 2 minutes.
3. Add mustard seeds, cumin, fennel, red chilli and few curry leaves.
4. Next add the garlic, ginger, cut potatoes and stir well. Cook on low heat for 5 minutes. Then add the vegetables, peas, chilli powder, cumin, coriander powder and salt and cook for 10 minutes.
   If required sprinkle a tsp of water to avoid sticking to the base.
5. Add kastoori masala powder, spices, rampe and rest of the curry leaves, stir cook for 30 seconds and remove from heat.

★ To reduce cooking time and to use less oil, microwave the potatoes and vegetables first and then fry.

Snake Gourd ‘Puddalankai’

Tamil name is ‘Puddalankai’

A long tube-like tropical vegetable, light green in colour, hollow inside, with seeds. It can grow up to a metre. Available from Sri Lankan shops. Several preparations: Milky dish, hot dish, with lentils and a stir fry. A tasty side dish to have with rice; children would prefer the milky dish.

Preparation & cooking: 20-30 minutes
serves 5 as a side dish

Ingredients

- 1 snake gourd
- 2 green chillies
- salt to taste
- ½ cup water
- 2 cloves garlic
- ½ tsp fenugreek seeds
- 5 shallots sliced or 1 red onion, sliced
- 4 tbsp evaporated milk **or** ¼ cup coconut milk
- ¼ tsp asafoetida powder
- 1 tsp turmeric powder
- 2 sprigs, curry leaves

Method

1. Cut the long snake gourd across into two or three pieces.
2. Scrape the outer skin slightly. Cut each longitudinally and remove the seeds. Clean the inside, wash the pieces and cut into fine slices.
3. Put the cut snake gourd, onions, fenugreek seeds, salt, sliced green chillies, ½ cup of water and chopped garlic in a pan and bring to boil. Turn the heat down to medium and cook.
4. Half way through add the turmeric, asafoetida, milk and increase the temperature slightly.
5. Add the curry leaves cook until the sauce thickens.
6. Remove from fire and serve with rice.

Snake Gourd with Dhal

Preparation & cooking: 30 minutes
Serves 4-5 as a side dish

Ingredients

- 1 snake gourd (medium)
- 150g Mysore dhal
- 1 medium onion, sliced
- 2 green chillies, cut lengthwise
- salt to taste
- ¼ cup cow's milk or evaporated milk
- ¼ tsp asafoetida powder
- 1 tsp turmeric
- 1 sprig curry leaves, chopped
- ½-1 cup water
- 2 cloves garlic
- ½ tsp fenugreek seeds
- water to cook dhal
- ½-1 tsp chilli powder
- ¾ tsp freshly ground pepper and cumin

Method

1. Wash the dhal and place in a saucepan with ½ cup of water.
2. Prepare the snake gourd as in previous recipe, add to the dhal and cook. Half way through add the green chillies, chilli powder, onions, turmeric and asafoetida; cook until the dhal and snake gourd gets cooked. If needed add a bit more water, but not too much. Should get cooked in 12 minutes.
3. Add the milk and curry leaves. Using a pestle and mortar crush the pepper and cumin, then add the garlic cloves and crush. Add it to the cooked vegetable stir and remove from cooker.

★ After cooking, can temper onions in butter, add mustard seeds and other tempering items and pour it over the cooked vegetable.

Snake Gourd Stir Fry - Varai

Preparation & cooking: 20 minutes
Serves 4-5 as a side dish

Ingredients

- 1 snake gourd
- 1 medium onion, chopped
- 2 tbsp ghee or sesame oil
- ½ tsp mustard seeds
- ½ tsp cumin seeds
- 2 red chillies, cut into pieces
- 1 sprig curry leaves, cut up fine
- 3 tbsp desiccated coconut
- ½ tsp plain chilli powder
- ½ tsp turmeric powder

Method

1. Scrape the skin of the snake gourd, cut lengthwise and take the seeds out. Wash and cut to very fine pieces.
2. Place on a plate, cover it and cook in a microwave for 2 minutes. You can also steam the vegetable for few minutes.
3. Heat a heavy-based frying pan, add ghee or sesame oil, add the onions and fry. Add the mustard seeds, cumin, red chillies and curry leaves.
4. Add the snake gourd and cook on medium heat for 3-4 minutes.
5. Mix the turmeric and chilli powder with the desiccated coconut and slightly rub for the coconut to change colour.
6. When the snake gourd is cooked add the mixed coconut, stir well and cook on a high heat for a minute.
7. Remove from cooker and leave in the pan for 5 minutes, do not cover the pan, as it will get soggy.

★ If you want to pepare the dish without the pre cooking, sprinkle water, cover and slow cook for 15 to 20 minutes. Then add the coconut etc.

Sothi for String Hoppers

Sothi is a type of slightly watery sauce made with coconut milk.
Served as a side dish for string hoppers,rice and some have it with pittu.

Preparation & cooking 20 minutes
serves 6

Ingredients

- 4-5 small florets of broccoli
- 5 small florets, cauliflower
- 1 carrot, cut into strips
- 1 small potato, cut into cubes
- 1-2 green chillies, cut lengthwise.
- 2 tomatoes, chopped
- salt to taste (½ tsp)
- 2 cups water
- ½ tsp turmeric powder
- ½ a lime
- 3 shallots or small red onions, sliced
- 10 curry leaves and a piece of rampe about 3cm size
- 200g (½ tin) full cream evaporated milk or 300g coconut milk.

Method

1. In a pan place the onion, tomatoes, water, salt, turmeric and the vegetables and let it boil and cook for about 6 minutes. Add the green chillies and boil for another 6 minutes.
2. Once the vegetables are cooked add the milk and bring to boil, reduce the heat and simmer for two minutes.
3. Add the curry leaves, rampe and keep stirring. (Be careful not to increase the heat as the milk may curdle). The sauce should get slightly thick.
6. Remove from cooker and let it cool slightly, squeeze half a lime, stir and serve.

★ Other vegetables to add are aubergine, courgette, drumstick. Some vegetables require a bit longer to cook and may require a bit more water.

★ Can prepare plain sothi as above recipe, with tomatoes but omitting the vegetables.

★ To the plain sothi you can add 3 garlic cloves (crushed) and 5 crushed pepper corns. Add 1 tsp tamarind paste and lastly add the milk and curry leaves.

Stuffed Aubergine Deep Fried

Ingredients

- 8 small round (pear shaped) aubergines
- 1-2 onions
- 3-4 dried red chillies
- pinch of turmeric powder
- small piece of ginger, 2 cloves garlic
- 1 tsp coriander seeds
- 2 potatoes, boiled and mashed
- 1small leek, finely sliced
- for batter: corn flour, plain flour, 1 egg and water
- butter or oil
- 2 tbsp Quark or garlic cream cheese (optional)

Method

1. Wash aubergine, cut/slice a little bit from the top (enabling you to scoop).
2. Scoop the inside of the aubergine carefully without cutting the outer skin. Leave the aubergine covered in salted water so that it doesn't lose its colour.
3. Cut up the scooped pieces and the cut piece from the top to very small pieces.
4. Grind ginger, garlic, salt, coriander and dried chillies. Then add the aubergine pieces, potato and a little water; grind it to a paste.
5. Fry onions in little oil or butter then add the cut leeks and fry. Lastly add the ground paste, cream cheese and cook the mixture for few minutes.
6. Take the aubergines from the water and pat dry. Fill the aubergine with the mixture (not too soggy)
8. Make a batter with corn flour, plain flour, egg and water.
9. Dip the aubergine carefully in the batter and deep fry in hot fresh oil.
10. It takes about seven to eight minutes; take it out and put it on a sheet of kitchen paper to drain the oil.

★ Serve hot or can be warmed in hot oven

★ Traditional recipe did not include the cream cheese.

Stuffed Capsicum Kari

Preparation & cooking: 30 minutes
Serves 4

Ingredients

- 8 large capsicum chillies (available from Asian shops).
- 2 large potatoes boiled and mashed
- 5 shallots
- small carton natural yogurt
- 4 tbsp coconut milk or evaporated milk
- 2 tomatoes, chopped
- 2 sprig curry leaves, 3cm rampe stick
- 1 tsp ginger, 1 tsp garlic paste
- salt to taste
- 2 tsp roasted chilli powder
- 1 tsp garam masala powder or paste

Method

1. Wash capsicum chillies and dip in boiling water for a minute.

2. Starting from the bottom cut the capsicum like a cross to near enough the top but do not cut it in half.

3. Mix the mashed potato, masala, garlic, ginger paste, salt and chilli powder.

4. Stuff each chilli with this mixture and lay it flat in a pan.

5. Cut the shallots, mix with tomatoes, yogurt and pour over the chilli; cook for 5 minutes on high flame until the gravy begins to boil; add the coconut milk, reduce the heat and cook on slow heat for 8 minutes.

6. Add curry leaves and cut rampe pieces and remove from cooker.

Tomato and Potato Kari (Kulambu)

Preparation and cooking: 25 minutes

Serves: 4

Ingredients

- 6 medium tomatoes,
- 3 small potatoes cut into cubes
- 2 medium onions, chopped
- 1 green chilli
- 4 garlic cloves, 2cm ginger
- for tempering: 1 tsp each of mustard seeds, cumin seeds, ¼ tsp fenugreek
- salt to taste
- 2 tbsp oil
- ½ cup coconut milk or evaporated milk**
- 1 tbsp plain chilli powder
- masala made with 1 tsp coriander seeds, 1 tsp cumin seeds, ¼ tsp black pepper corns and a piece of cinnamon stick
- 1 tsp special roasted fennel powder
- 6 curry leaves (coriander leaves is optional)

Method

1. Heat a heavy based pan. Add the oil and add tempering ingredients, then the chopped onions and fry for 2 minutes.
2. Add the potatoes and green chilli and sauté for few minutes.
3. Grind the masala ingredients with ginger and garlic (use a mortar and pestle).
   Add the paste to the cut up tomatoes, add chilli powder and mix.
4. Add the tomatoes little by little to the potatoes and stir fry, add a medium cup of water and cook for 7-8 minutes.
5. Then add the evaporated milk or coconut milk and curry leaves.
6. Reduce the flame and simmer until the juice thickens slightly.
7. Add the roasted fennel powder and remove from cooker.

Serve with rice

★ Can substitute normal cow's milk but the taste will be different.
Can add ½" slice of cream coconut with little warm milk or water.

Toor Dhal (Jaffna recipe)

Time consuming, so best for week ends
Preparation: Soak for 3 hours
Cooking time: 45 minutes
Serves 4-5

Ingredients

- 1 cup toor dhal soaked in water for 3 hours
- 3 medium size onions, cut length wise
- 2 garlic cloves
- tempering ingredients: pinch of mustard seeds and cumin seeds
- 2 sprigs curry leaves and small piece of rampe leaf
- 1 dried red chilli cut to ½ cm size or broken to small pieces
- oil for deep frying
- 1 tbsp roasted chilli powder
- ½ tsp fenugreek seeds
- ½ can (200g) coconut milk or 2cm slice cream coconut

Method

1. Wash the soaked toor dhal and drain well. Using a blender grind the dhal, add a little bit of salt while grinding.

2. Heat oil in a pan (for deep frying).

3. In the meantime take little bit of toor dhal paste; make into a small ball rolling in your palm.

4. Prepare few of these and slowly drop into the oil, deep fry until golden brown.

4. In another pan heat two teaspoons of oil add the mustard, cumin and cut up dried chilli, finely cut onions and fry. Add few curry leaves, chopped garlic and fry.

5. After few minutes add two cups of water, little salt, chilli powder and bring to boil.

6. Add the fried toor dhal balls and cook for 4-5 minutes. Add milk, cut rampe, rest of the curry leaves, and cook for another 2 minutes.

7. Finally sprinkle 1 tsp of special fennel powder.

★ If sauce is too thick or insufficient, add ½ cup of normal cow's milk at step 6.

Another traditional method for reference

- First grind the toor dhal adding little salt.
- Spread the ground paste onto a string hopper mould (Idiyappa Thattu) and steam it.
- Once steamed take it out and turn it onto a plate, cut into small squares and deep fry and follow steps on previous page and above.
- This recipe is used if you need to cater for a large gathering.
- Evaporated milk can be used instead of milk.

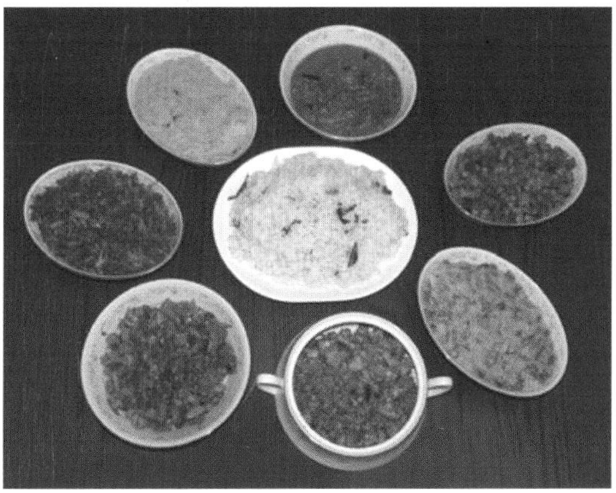

Mysore dhal

Ingredients

- 1 cup red lentils
- 2 green chillies
- 1 onion chopped
- ½ tsp peppr corns
- 1 tsp cumin seeds
- 3 cloves garlic
- ½ tsp turmeric powder
- Pincch of asafoetida powder
- 1 tbsp oil ,

Tempering ingredients:

- mustard, cumin, red chilli few curry leaves
- ½ tsp roasted curry powde (optional)
- ¼ cup milk

Method

1. Wash the lentils and soak in water for 10 minutes.
2. In a pan place the lentils, add 1 ½ cups water and bring it boil.
3. Remove the white particles that come up and reduce the heat.
4. Cut two chillies and two garlic cloves. Add it to the dhal with asafoetida, turmeric and a tsp of chopped onions.
   Cook for 5 minutes.
5. When the lentils are cooked remove and set aside.
6. In a frying pan add oil, when hot add the tempering ingredients,the rest of the onions and fry until golden colour.
7. Add the cooked dhal to the frying pan and stir. Add salt, curry powder,milk and cook on low. Crush the pepper, cumin and the two garlic cloves. Add this to the dhal and stir well.

Variations

Add spinach leaves – Chop a few fresh spinach leaves and add it half way at stage 4 above. (before adding the milk). When the lentils are cooked well, add the salt and milk and simmer.

★ **Dhal and snake gourd is a good combination.**

Toor Dhal (Simple method)

Preparation & cooking: 40 minutes
Serves 4-5

Ingredients

- ½ cup toor dhal
- 2½ cups water
- 1 onion chopped
- 1 green chilli cut lengthwise
- 3 cloves garlic
- 1 tsp cumin seeds, ¼ tsp pepper (crush this)
- pinch of turmeric, pinch of asafoetida powder
- 3 tbsp full cream milk or evaporated milk
- 2 tsp butter or ½ tsp ghee
- salt to taste

Method

1. Wash & boil dhal in two cups of water, add green chilli.
2. Add the turmeric powder, asafoetida and cook for 10 minutes. When the dhal is cooked add milk, stir and remove from cooker.
3. Crush the garlic, cumin and pepper well by using a mortar and pestle or a grinder and add to the dhal.
4. In another frying pan melt the butter or ghee, add the chopped onions, mustard seeds, cumin and sauté. Finally add curry leaves and pour the fried ingredients with the melted ghee or butter over the dhal. Stir and leave it ready to serve.

★ **Serving tips:** Dhal is served as the first course with hot rice and a tsp of melted ghee or gingelly /sesame oil.

Onion with Fenugreek (Venthaya kulambu)

Tasty dish to eat with rice, naan, bread, string hoppers

Preparation & cooking time: 45-50 minutes
Serves 5-6

Ingredients

- 4 large onions, finely cut
- 8 cloves garlic, sliced
- 2 sprigs curry leaves
- 1½ tsp fenugreek seeds
- 1½ tsp curry powder
- 1-2 tsp chilli powder
- 1½ cups water
- salt to taste
- 1½ tsp concentrated tamarind paste or juice of a 2 cm slice from compressed tamarind block soaked in hot water
- ½ bottle vegetable oil for deep frying
- 2cm piece of cream coconut or ½ can coconut milk

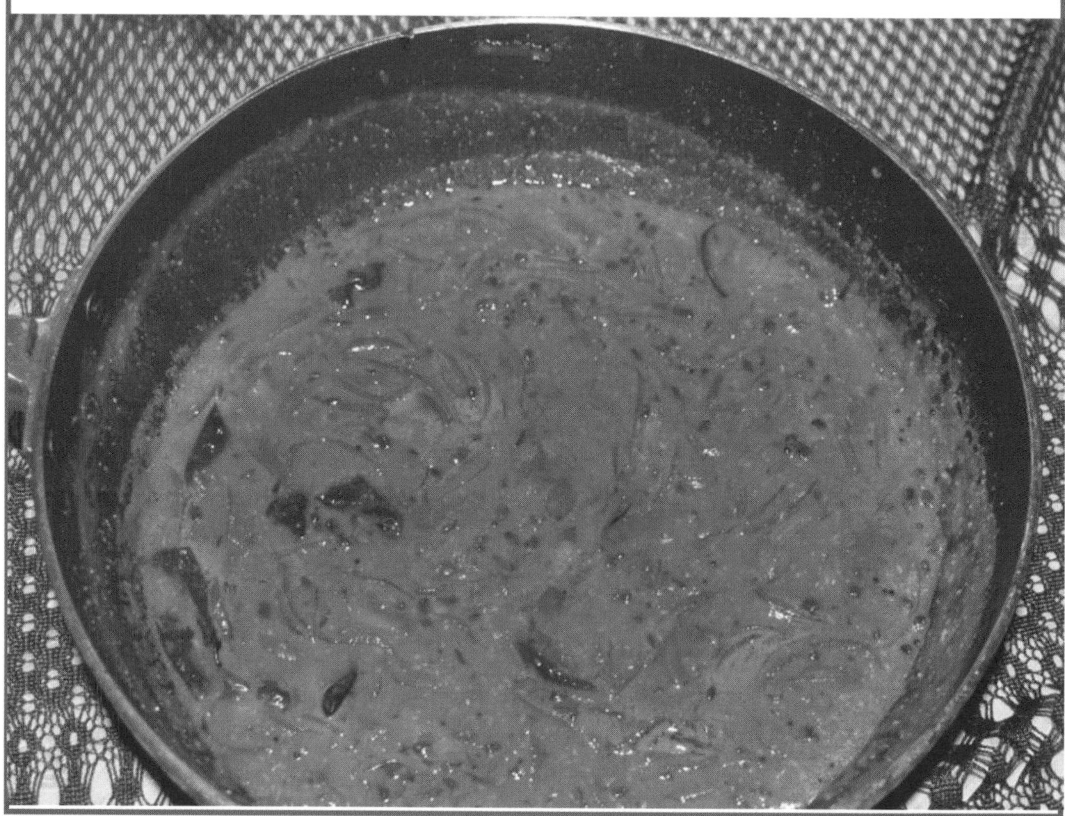

Method

1. Heat oil in a thava or pan and deep fry the onions; half way add the garlic pieces and fry until golden brown in colour and onion gets slightly crispy. Drain on kitchen paper.
2. In a small tea strainer put the fenugreek seeds and immerse in the hot oil for <u>few seconds</u> only for it to sizzle and cook. Spread it on a paper towel. Deep fry the curry leaves too.
3. Squeeze the tamarind pulp soaked in ½ cup of hot water until you get most of it. Discard the pieces and use the liquid. If you are using the paste mix with 2 tablespoons water.
4. In a pan mix water, tamarind juice, salt, chilli powder, curry powder and bring to boil. Then add the onions and other fried items.
5. Cook on a medium heat for about 10 to 12 minutes.
6. Add the cream coconut or coconut milk and allow the sauce to slightly thicken and remove from cooker.

Another method - an easy preparation for 2

Ingredients as for main recipe, but use half the quantity

Fry the onion slices in 3 tablespoons of oil, fry all the ingredients and add water, tamarind etc., cook for 10 minutes, add milk, allow the sauce to thicken and remove from heat.

Sambar

Preparation & cooking time: 45 minutes
Serves 6

Ingredients

- ½ cup toor or red lentil
- vegetables: one each of carrot, small aubergine, courgette and raw green banana, 2 potatoes, 2 tomatoes, few okras (7)
- 3 tsp of sambar powder or 3 tsp mixed masala powder made with coriander powder, curry powder, plain chilli powder, garlic powder and ground gram powder
- tempering: ¼ tsp each cumin, mustard seeds, one red chilli
- ¼ of small pumpkin cut into cubes
- 1½ medium onion, chopped
- 1 tsp turmeric
- 1 sprig curry leaves
- 1 tsp tamarind paste
- few coriander leaves
- 2 tsp of oil for tempering
- 1tsp asafoetida
- salt to taste

Method

1. Wash dhal and cook in two cups of water.
2. Wash, clean and cut the vegetables small and boil adding a cup of water.
3. Heat a deep thava-like pan. Add oil.
4. Add the mustard seeds, cumin, red chilli and onions. When onions turn slightly brown add the curry leaves.
5. Add the cooked vegetables, then the dhal, tomatoes, salt, tamarind paste, sambar powder and asafoetida; cook for five minutes, if necessary add a bit of warm water so that the mixture doesn't get too thick.
6. Cook for another 2 minutes and remove from cooker.
7. Finally add the chopped coriander leaves and remove from heat.
8. Serve with thosai, rice, semolina, uppuma, idli etc.

Finger Foods

Finger Foods - Index

Page N°

Finger Foods - Index

Asparagus Roll

Preparation time: 30 minutes
Serves 6-8

Ingredients

- 2 loaves of bread, thinly sliced
- 1 can asparagus (200g)
- 1 tsp freshly ground black pepper
- 200g cream cheese spread
- 200g soft cream cheese spread
- 2 green chillies, finely chopped
- 100g butter or soft spread
- paprika powder (optional)
- pinch of salt (optional)

Method

1. In a bowl mix the cheese spread, the butter, pepper, chopped green chillies and paprika. (Add the salt and mix). Arrange the bread slices on a board and apply the spread to one side of the slices.

2. Open the can of asparagus, drain the water and pat dry the asparagus. Take half of an asparagus flatten it lightly and place on the buttered slice.

3. Starting from one end of the slice, roll the bread with the asparagus and leave it on a plate. Prepare few more rolls and arrange these on a plate.

4. Cover with a damp cloth and leave in the fridge for about 4-5 hours.

5. Remove from the fridge, cut the crusts. Cut each rolled bread into two or three pieces. 1½" and arrange in a box or a tray.

★ Serve as a starter
Can use a medium thickness loaf, but you need to roll the slices with a roller. Cutting the crusts last makes it easy to prepare and roll.

Chat Recipe - (A North Indian Dish)

Ingredients

- 1 can of boiled chickpeas
- 2 potatoes, boiled
- 1 tsp chat masala
- 1 tsp chilli powder
- piece of ginger chopped or grated
- ½ tsp salt
- 1 sprig of coriander leaves, chopped
- 1 tsp oil
- 1-2 tbsp lime/lemon juice
- 3 shallots, chopped
- 1 tsp roasted cumin seed, freshly ground.
- ¼ tsp pepper, freshly ground
- 1 green chilli, chopped (optional)

Method

1. Boil the potatoes, peel the skin and cut into cubes of about ½" size.
2. Open the can of chickpeas and drain the water.
3. Place the potatoes and chickpeas in a bowl, add salt, chilli powder cumin and pepper and toss it to mix.
4. Heat a frying pan add the oil and fry the chopped onions for 2-3 minutes. Then add the grated ginger and chillies.
5. Add the potatoes, chickpeas mixture and toss it. Do not spoon a lot as the potatoes may break. Add the chopped coriander and lemon juice. Toss it .
6. Dish into a large dish and serve as a starter.

Variations

★ Can add 2 tomatoes, but de-seed the tomato, cube it and add to the fried potato

★ If using the fresh chick peas you will need to soak 1 cup of chickpeas first in water for at least 5-6 hours. Add ½ tsp of bicarbonate soda. Later wash the chickpeas and boil for 25 minutes. The quantity will be double. This will keep in the fridge for three to four days.

- Served as a starter with potato

Cheese Biscuits

Ingredients

- ½ cup grated cheddar cheese
- 1 cup self raising flour
- 1 tsp chilli powder
- ½ tsp each pepper chives and salt
- 2 oz butter
- milk to mix

Method

1. Sieve the flour and place in a bowl. Add the butter and rub into the flour; add cheese, salt, pepper and chives.
2. Add the milk little by little and knead so that it doesn't stick to the sides of the bowl
3. Roll it out on a board and cut into shapes with cutters or a tin (round shape).
4. Place on a baking sheet and bake in an oven on the highest temperature for 10 to12 minutes.
5. Remove from oven leave it to cool and store in an airtight tin or box until you require.

This can be served with some spreads as below

★ Cream cheese/pepper and slice of boiled asparagus on top
★ Cream cheese mixed with tomato chutney and onion ring on top.
★ Cream cheese and slice of boiled egg on top.

Variation (With Olives)

★ After mixing the dough take a small amount and wrap it around an olive to cover in full. Arrange on a baking sheet placed on a tray and leave it in the fridge for 15 minutes.
★ Bake in a hot oven 190°C circotherm for 12 –15 minutes.

Chinese Vegetable Rolls

Preparation & cooking time: appx 1 hour
Serves 7-8

Ingredients

For the pancakes

- 2 cups plain flour (200g)
- 1 egg (optional)
- pinch of turmeric powder (optional)
- pinch of salt
- 1 cup milk
- water as required

Method

1. Combine flour, eggs and salt in a large bowl.
   Using a hand whisk or an electric whisk mix the flour and milk to form a batter.

2. Add water as required
   (omit the egg for pure vegetarians).

Ingredients

For the filling

- 250g potatoes, boiled and skins removed
- 125g leeks, 125g carrots
- 1 tbsp vegetable oil
- ½ tsp chilli powder
- salt to taste
- 1 onion, chopped
- ½ tsp curry powder
- 1sprig curry leaves, chopped
- pepper

Method

Make filling (for vegetarian recipe)

1. Mash the potatoes. Finely chop the leeks and carrots.
2. Heat a large frying pan and stir fry the onions in oil for few minutes over a low heat. Add the curry powder and chilli powder. Fry for a minute.
3. Add the vegetables and stir-fry for a few more minutes. Add the potatoes, salt and pepper to taste. Remove from heat and set aside.

To make the pancakes

1. Heat a frying pan or skillet over medium heat for about a minute.
2. Coat the surface of the pan with little oil (use an oil brush or a piece of cloth dampened with vegetable oil).
3. After it gets sizzling hot, take a spoon/ladle full of batter and quickly pour and swirl it to make like a pancake.
4. Cook for a minute and take it out and leave it on a plate.
5. Brush the pan with little oil, pour the next pancake.
6. Whilst this is cooking take some filling say one or two teaspoons and place it on to the edge of the pancake. Fold the sides inwards and then roll from one end to the other. Apply a bit of water to the open edge of the pancake to stick,so that it does not open.
7. Arrange onto a plate.

Make the batter for covering

1. Mix the egg with ½ cup of flour, salt and little water. Whiskusing a hand whisk until the batter is free of any lumps of flour.
2. Dip the rolls in the batter and then in breadcrumbs.
3. Heat a thava or an electric fryer with oil. Drop a few rolls at a time, deep fry till golden brown and serve hot.

Variation

Instead of the pancakes, you can use frozen pancake sheets to prepare the roll. You only have to make the filling, fill the sheets, roll, dip in batter and bread crumbs and deep fry.

★ Serve warm.

Devilled Cashew Nuts/Almonds

Preparation & cooking time: 30 minutes

Ingredients

- 500g cashew nuts or almonds
- oil for deep frying
- salt to taste
- chilli powder

Method - Deep fried

1. Wash the cashewnuts/almonds to get rid of the floury coating. Dry by spreading onto a clean tea towel.
2. In the mean time heat oil in a pan.
3. Put a portion of the nuts in a metal mesh type colander and lower it into the hot oil (nuts should be fully immersed). Fry until slightly light brown and remove from oil. It will take about 3-5 minutes.
4. Spread the almonds on to a kitchen paper towel to absorb the oil.
5. Add salt and chilli powder to the fried nuts, shake well with the paper towel. Transfer to another tray, lined with a paper towel to absorb any oil and excess chilli.
6. Store in a bottle until use.

Method - Roasting in the oven

Place the washed almonds and cashew nuts on a tray and roast in the oven for 25 minutes at high temperature 190°C . Then melt a little butter in a roasting tray. Add salt and chilli powder, toss the roasted nuts and leave in the oven for another 5 minutes. Remove and allow to cool and store in a jar.

★ Served with drinks like crisps/nuts.
Paper towel will absorb the oil.

Fried Courgettes

Ingredients

- 2 courgettes
- 1 cup plain flour
- ½ cup fine rice flour
- oil for deep frying
- salt to taste
- 1 tsp chilli powder
- ½ tsp garlic powder
- ½ tsp ginger powder
- ½ tsp coriander powder

Method

1. Mix all the spices. Then mix with half the quantity of the flour and leave it aside.
2. Slice the courgettes in rounds, salt it, and leave for few minutes. Wash and dry on kitchen paper towel.
3. Roll the slices in plain flour, then in the spiced flour and deep fry.

★ This is tasty as a snack with chilli or tomato dip.

Variations

To fry like pakoras

With marrow

Peel and coarsely grate a marrow, add salt and place on a paper towel or a colander for 30 minutes to mdrainn the water.
Mix 1 tsp each of grated ginger, garlic, chilli powder and cumin powder; add this to a cup of gram flour. Squeeze the water from the marrow and mix it with the flour. Add a bit of water to make a paste. Take spoonfuls and deep fry until golden brown.

Fried Mushrooms

Ingredients

- 20 button mushrooms (not large)
- 1 tsp chilli powder
- ½ tsp garlic powder
- ½ tsp turmeric powder
- salt to taste
- oil for frying
- ½ cup rice flour
- ¼ cup gram flour

Method

1. Wash the mushrooms, cut in half, dry it between two sheets of kitchen paper.

2. Add salt, chilli, turmeric to the rice flour/gram flour mixture, roll the mushrooms one by one and deep fry in oil.

3. Serve hot.

Filo Pastry Sheets

Ingredients

- 200g butter
- 4 tbsp sesame seeds
- 200g grated cheese (parmesan)
- 2 tsp chilli powder
- 1 tsp garlic powder
- filo pastry sheets
- salt to taste

Method

1. Mix garlic, chilli powder, salt, butter, sesame seeds and grated cheese to a paste.

2. Apply this to the filopastry sheet and cut the sheet into small squares say 4 x 4 inch size.

3. Now keeping the spreaded side outside, scrunch each into a small ball.

4. Place on a greaseproof paper placed on a tray and bake in a hot oven for 10 minutes leaving on a greaseproof paper.

★ Serve it hot.

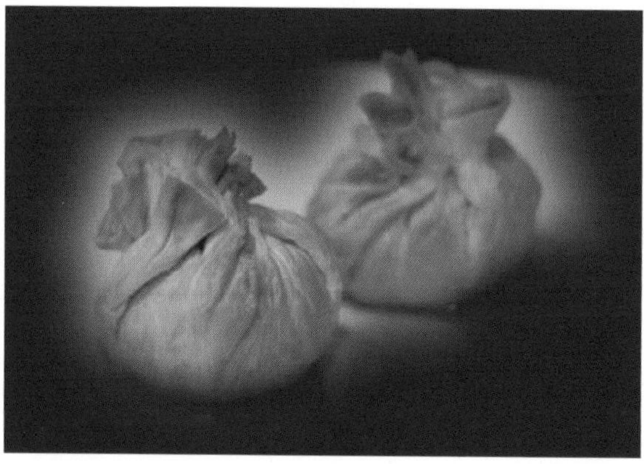

Macaroons (Sri Lankan Preparation)

Sri Lankan name “Kisses”

Preparation & cooking time: 1 hour and 30 minutes

Ingredients

- 3-4 egg whites
- 500g caster sugar
- 200g icing sugar
- 50g corn flour
- 50g cashew nuts
- few drops of vanilla and red colouring
- whipped cream to serve with kisses

Method

1. Whisk the egg whites until stiff and gradually add sugar. It should be still stiff.
2. Add the icing sugar, corn flour little by little and whisk it. Add the chopped cashew nuts. Add vanilla and colour half by adding a drop of red colouring
3. Put the mixture into a icing bag and using a slightly large nozzle, pipe circles onto a lined baking sheet.
4. Place in an oven at 140°C for 40 minutes, then reduce to 130°C and leave for another 20 minutes.
5. Remove and keep in a bottle or tin in a dry warm place.

★ Serve with tea on its own or can have with whipped cream .

You can increase the amount of icing sugar, by substituting more icing sugar and reducing the caster sugar.

Kokkis - Savoury Fried Pastry

Requires a special spoon/cutter
A short eat from the South. Sinhalese prepare this during the New Year and other special occasions

Ingredients

- 1 can (400g) coconut milk
- 1 egg
- 125g white rice flour, sieved
- 125g plain flour, sieved
- ½ tsp salt
- 1 tsp ground pepper
- ½ tsp ground cumin (optional)
- oil for deep-frying
- mould with a long (metal wire) handle, a deep pan thava

Method

1. Mix the sieved flour and place in a large bowl. Add salt, cumin and pepper.
2. Add a bit of hot water to the coconut milk and mix it well.
3. Whisk the egg and add this to the flour. Start adding the milk little by little and beat it well with a hand blender or a whisk.
4. The batter should be smooth. If you feel that any particles appear, whisk again or strain the batter through an average sieve to take out any particles of flour. The batter should be thick enough for it to cling and cover the mould .
5. Heat oil in a deep pan.
6. Take the metal mould and dip this in the hot oil to heat up.
7. Remove it and immerse the mould into the batter to make sure all sides are covered well.

8. Place the mould back into the hot oil and deep-fry until golden brown. Shake the mould and the “Kokkis” will come off the mould.

9. Fry three to four at a time, remove when it turns golden brown and it gives a clicky sound when you place a slotted spoon. Remove and place on a kitchen paper.

10. Repeat the same procedure until the batter is finished.

★ Can be kept for two to three weeks if stored in an airtight container.

Variation with sweet

To the same ingredients you may add 100g caster sugar. Add a pinch of salt and no pepper/cumin. Mix the sugar in the warmed coconut milk and follow the rest as above.

★ If you have any metal cutters with a long handle, you may try using as long as it come off easily whilst in the oil.

★ Mould is available from Sri Lankan shops. Coconut milk is what gives the taste.

Murukku

Preparation & cooking 45 minutes
Makes about 50 murukku

To make this you require a press like for string hoppers. You will get a mould with small discs of different shape cuts through which you can squeeze the flour.
Can try using the cookie press

Ingredients

- 1 cup fine white rice flour
- 1 cup roasted urad flour
- ½ cup steamed plain flour
- 1 tsp freshly ground pepper
- 1 tsp freshly ground cumin
- salt to taste
- ¼ tsp chilli powder (optional)
- 1 tbsp white sesame seeds (washed)
- 1 cup thick coconut milk
- ½ cup hot water
- Oil for deep frying

Method

1. Mix all three flours and sieve in to a large bowl. Add the ground cumin, pepper, salt, sesame seeds and chilli powder.

2. Warm the milk, pour it little by little and mix the flour with a handle of a wooden spoon. If needed add some hot water. Add 1 tbsp oil and make into a soft dough.

3. Place oil in a deep frying pan and heat it. When the oil is fairly hot, fill the mould with the flour and squeeze it over in a circle movement (as for the string hopper). Fry until golden brown and remove onto a kitchen paper towel to drain.

★ . For safety you could prepare a few by pressing it onto small squares of grease proof paper and slowly slide into the oil.

Variation

Gram flour Murukku

Omit the urad flour and coconut milk. Add 1 cup gram flour, 1tsp garlic powder, 1tsp asafoetida powder, 2tbsp butter, salt, chilli powder, cumin powder, finely ground pepper, 1 cup full cream milk, little warm water and 1/4tsp turmeric powder. Warm the milk and mix with the flour,and other ingredients to form a dough. Then using the ifferent discs can prepare a few murukku on to a plate and transfer it into the hot oil. Fry until golden colour and remove.

Mushrooms Cutlets

Ingredients

- 500g button mushrooms, finely chopped
- 1 medium onion, chopped
- 1-2 tsp chilli powder
- salt to taste
- 2cm ginger grated
- 3 tbsp gram flour
- 1 tsp turmeric powder
- bread crumbs for coating
- 1 slice bread, chopped in the blender
- 1 medium potato, boiled
- 1 green chilli, finely chopped
- 5-6 curry leaves, chopped
- 2 cloves garlic, grated
- ½ tsp pepper powder
- 1 tbsp plain flour
- ½ cup of desiccated coconut
- oil for deep frying

Method

1 Place the onion, green chilli and mushrooms in a large bowl. Add the salt, chilli powder, garlic, ginger, coconut, bread, 1 tbsp of gram flour, boiled potato chopped into small pieces and half the turmeric powder and mix well.

2. Take small amounts and roll into small balls by rolling between your palm and your fingers. Then flatten them to make small discs.

4 Mix the plain flour, remainder of turmeric and gram flour with a little water to form a paste, but not too watery.

5 Coat each shaped cutlet in the above paste and then roll in breadcrumbs

6 Heat the oil in a frying pan or thava and when the oil is hot drop in a few cutlets at a time and deep fry (oil should be hot and also cover the cutlets)

7 Serve as a starter with tomato or chilli sauce.

Variations/Useful hints

★ If you are to prepare for the next day, temper the onions and mushroom in a bit of oil and add a bit of mustard seeds.
★ Then cook all together for few minutes, before you shape the cutlets.
★ This is also good if you are to fry and deep freeze.
★ ¼ cup of chopped cashew nuts can be added, which is optional.

Party Fillers

Preparation & cooking time: 30-40 minutes

Ingredients

- 500g puff pastry
- 3 peppers
- 4 tbsp dried onion flakes (optional)
- 200g soft cream cheese
- 200g fromage frais
- 1-2 tsp chilli powder
- salt to taste
- ½ tsp powdered mixed spice

Method

1. Cut the pepper into 4cm square pieces.
2. Mix the cheese, fromage frais, salt, onion & other ingredients; the mixture should be fairly thick and not runny.
3. Roll the pastry and cut out strips slightly larger than the size of the pepper. Place the pepper on one edge of the pastry, fill the pepper with the filling and fold over with the other half of the pastry.
   Seal the sides and use a fork to dent or overlap the pastry, as for a sausage roll.
4. Brush the top with little milk. Place on a tray and bake in a very hot oven for 20 minutes.

★ If you are planning to deep fry use short crust pastry.
Can try with capsicum chilli, it willl be hot.

Pastry Dough

Pastry for deep frying.

Ingredients

- ½ cup water with salt to taste
- 1-2 tbsp butter
- 2 cups of plain flour

Method

1. In a pan, boil the water.
2. Add the butter and flour gradually, till all the flour has been used.
3. The mixture should be smooth.
4. Stir cook for 2 minutes.
5. Cool the dough.
6. Roll out on a floured board, and cut into any shapes. Use as necessary.

Prepare the above, use any filling and deep fry.
See below for the steps for frying.

Ingredients

- 1 beaten egg white
- filling of your choice
- bread crumbs
- oil for frying

Use filling of your choice. After filling the pastry pieces you will need to seal the edges, then dip in beaten egg whites, roll in bread crumbs and deep fry in oil.

Puff Pastry Savoury

Preparation & cooking time 40 minutes

Ingredients

- 500g puff pastry
- small carton of double cream (125g
- 250g grated cheese
- 1 tsp mixed spices: ½ tsp garlic powder, ½ ginger powder
- 1 tsp chilli powder
- 250g potato, boiled and mashed

Method

1. Mix the potato, beaten-up cream, cheese and all dry ingredients. Use a hand blender for few seconds to break up any pieces.

2. The mixture should be fairly thick, but not watery.

3. Roll out the pastry, cut into shapes and line a non stick pastry tin (cup cake tray) with rolled out puff pastry, spoon two spoons of mixture, sprinkle with more cheese or herbs and bake for 10 to 12 minutes at 190°C .

Method 2

With eggs and pickled courgette

Could add 2 beaten eggs, some pickled courgetts and little milk to the above ingredients. For this you may need to bake the plain case first for 4 minutes, filled with rice. Remove the rice and then add the mixture. Bake for 15 minutes.

Pakora

North indiann dish served for evening snack
Preparation & cooking time: 30 minutes

Ingredients

- 250g sieved gram flour and ½ cup rice flour
- 1 tsp salt
- 1 tsp chilli powder, 1 tsp garlic paste 1 tsp ginger paste.
- 1 tsp mixed spice powder, 1 tsp coriander and cumin powder
- 1 medium onion, finely chopped
- 1 large potato, cut into ¼" cubes
- few cauliflower florets, finely cut
- 1 small aubergine, cut into thin slices
- 3 green chillies, chopped (optional)
- ¼ tsp baking soda
- ½ tsp black pepper
- spinach leaves,sliced
- oil for deep frying
- water, enough to make paste

Method

1. Mix all dry ingredients in a bowl and add enough water to make a paste. Mix well.
2. Heat oil in a pan. Take a spoonful at a time from the bowl of paste and deep fry it in hot oil until golden brown.
3. Serve with sauce.

★ Sauce see section on dips. For a quick preparation
Mix yoghurt, grated garlic, grated ginger and salt and stir well.

★ Add any vegetable you like but try and grate it coarsley.
Adding rice flour makes it crispy.
To reheat place it under the grill.

Pakoda with Yoghurt

Preparation: Soaking the dhal for 2 hours

Cooking time: 30 minutes

Ingredients

- 2 cups split chick peas dhal (kadalai parruppu)
- 1 large onion, chopped
- 2 cloves garlic
- 8-10 curry leaves, cut finely
- 2 green chillies, chopped
- 4 dried red chillies
- 6 tbsp natural yoghurt
- 2 tbsp butter
- salt to taste
- 1 tsp fennel seeds
- 1 tsp cumin seeds

Method

1. Soak the dhal for two hours, wash and drain.
2. In a liquidiser grind this and the dried red chillies, salt, garlic, fennel and cumin seeds to a fairly coarse paste (mixture to have some small pieces of dhal).
3. Now add the chopped onions, chopped green chillies and yoghurt.
4. Take a spoonful of the mixture, slightly flatten it to look like a disc. Prepare a few and leave on a plate.
5. Heat a pan; add oil, when oil is hot deep fry the flattened pakodas.
6. When cooked remove and drain on kitchen paper. The pakoda will be crunchy.

★ Omit the yoghurt, add little water and follow the recipe to prepare a spicy pakoda.

Paneer Cutlets

Ingredients

- 250g paneer packet
- 4 shallots, chopped
- 5 florets cauliflower, grated
- grated white cabbage, a small bowl full
- 2 medium potatoes, boiled and mashed
- 3 green chillies, chopped
- oil for stir frying
- bread crumbs
- 1 tsp plain chilli powder, few curry leaves
- piece of ginger, 3 garlic cloves (grate or crush)
- flour to make batter to coat the cutlet
- 3 tbsp self raising flour
- 1 carrot, grated
- 1 leek cut fine.
- 5 tbsp peas
- salt to taste
- 3 boiled eggs
- oil for deep frying
- bread crumbs

Method

1. Grate the paneer and leave in a bowl.
2. Add self raising flour, yolk of eggs, shallots, salt, chopped coriander leaves or curry leaves, chillies and mix well. Knead it all together.
3. Use half of the boiled potato. Leave the other to mix with the vegetables.
4. Grate the vegetables and either cook in the microwave for 2 minutes or boil in water for 3 minutes and drain.
4. In a bowl mix the vegetables, chopped egg white, salt, chilli powder, garlic, potato and stir-fry in little oil.
5. Take a small ball of the paneer mixture and form into a ball then a cup shape. Place one teaspoon of the vegetable mixture and bring the sides of the cup together to close to form a ball. Make a few of these.
6. Prepare batter with 1-2 tablespoon flour and a bit of water (instead can use egg white).
7. Dip the cutlet in the batter and roll in breadcrumbs. Coat few more and deep fry.
8. Serve as a finger food for a party.

Pure vegetarians

★ Can leave out the eggs and use the rest. You may need a bit more flour and potato.

★ Can prepare with home made paneer, see recipe to make paneer.

Pattis Pastry

Ingredients

- 2 cups plain flour
- 120g butter (softened)
- cold water
- 1 egg
- salt

Method

1. Place the flour in a bowl, add the butter and mix, add salt, egg and a little water at a time and knead to form a soft pastry.
2. Knead well for the pastry to be soft and elastic.
3. Cover and leave it in the fridge for 10-15 minutes.
4. Then take it out, roll the pastry onto a board and cut small circles with a round cutter.
5. Make the filling separately add 1 tsp of the filling on to each cut out round.
6. Wet the edges slightly and bring one half of the circle over the filling and seal like for a cornish pasty. Use a fork to make markings on the edges to ensure the patties is sealed
7. Deep fry in oil.

★ Use fillings as per recipe for cutlet and rolls or make up your own. Other fillings: potato with chick peas, leeks and potato, stir fried vegetables can be used; you need to slightly mash the filling.

Potato Whirls

Preparation & cooking time: 1 hr

Ingredients

- 3 large potatoes
- 1 yolk of egg
- salt to taste
- pepper to taste
- 1 tsp chilli powder
- 2 cloves garlic (grated)
- 2 tbsp milk
- 2 sprigs coriander leaves, finely chopped (optional) or mint/parsley
- 2 tbsp oil for the tray

Method

1. Boil potatoes, peel the skins and mash them. Ensure there are no pieces, use a hand blender.
2. Add the yolk, milk and spices and mix to a thick soft paste.
3. Mix the chopped coriander leaves.
4. Use a large nozzle and prepare an icing bag. Fill the bag with the mixture.
5. Pipe a few whirls onto a baking sheet, which is already brushed with a bit of oil.
6. Brush the top of the whirls with a little milk or egg, do not allow it to flatten.
7. Bake in a preheated oven for 10 mins at 190°C and remove from cooker.

Potato Bonda

Preparation & cooking time: 45 minutes

Ingredients

- 250g gram flour
- 4 tbsp self raising flour
- 250g potatoes, boiled
- 3 medium onions, chopped
- 3 green chillies, chopped finely
- 5-6 curry leaves, chopped
- 1-2 tsp roasted chilli powder
- ½ tsp turmeric powder
- salt to taste
- for tempering: ½ tsp each mustard seeds, cumin seeds, ghee or butter
- 50g cashew nuts or any nuts chopped (optional)
- oil for deep frying
- ½ tsp bicarbonate of soda
- 1 tsp each garlic/ginger, either crushed or powder.

Method

1. Cut the potatoes into small cubes.
2. In a deep frying pan melt the butter or ghee and add the tempering ingredients, when the mustard seeds begin to pop add the cumin, onions, curry leaves and finally the chilies. Soon after, add the salt, chilli powder, turmeric and the potatoes (adding the chilies may make you cough). Cook for a few minutes and turn off the heat.
3. Place the mixture in a bowl, make sure it is mixed well but try not to mash the potatoes.
4. Take a tablespoon of mixture and form into a ball. Prepare a few and arrange them on a plate.
5. Prepare the batter, mixing the self raising flour, sieved gram flour, pinch of sodium bicarbonate, salt, little chilli powder and water. The batter should be thick.
6. Heat a pan, add oil and when this is hot, dip the potato one by one in the batter and slowly slide it into the oil and deep fry.

★ This is a tasty party snack or can be served for an evening dish.

★ You can add 2-3 tablespoons of finely cut up leeks, carrots and cabbage to the potato. Microwave the vegetables for a minute and then add it to the potatoes and fry.

Payatham Paniyaram

Sri Lankan traditional sweet served during celebration time, weddings, New Year & Diwali

Ingredients

- 250g roasted moong flour (or you roast the moong and grind it fine)
- 125g desiccated coconut
- 125g white sugar
- ½ cup water
- ½ tsp mixed freshly ground cumin and pepper
- ½ tsp ground cardamom
- pinch of salt

For the batter

- 1 cup fine white rice flour
- ½ cup plain flour
- water, pinch of salt
- oil for deep-frying

Method

1. If you are going to roast the moong dhal, do this first in a pan, then grind and sieve. If using the flour, roast the flour in a frying pan.
2. Use the same pan to roast the coconut slightly. Grind this too.
3. Place the roasted flour, desiccated coconut, cardamom and cumin in a bowl and mix well. Add a pinch of salt.
4. Bring sugar and water to boil and simmer for 7 to 8 minutes, then pour this into the flour and mix well with a wooden spoon. It should not be watery or too thick. Knead it to form a ball. Take a small amount and roll it in between your fingers and your palm to make into a small ball. Continue and prepare small balls with the mixture.
5. Prepare the batter with plain flour and rice flour. Add a pinch of salt. Add water to make a thick batter.
6. Dip the round balls one by one in the batter to coat the balls and deep fry.
7. Remove and drain in kitchen paper.

Ribbon Sandwich Squares

Preparation & cooking time: 30 minutes

Ingredients

- sliced white bread (1 loaf)
- 1 beetroot, boiled
- 1 carrot, boiled
- 125g grated cheese
- 250g butter or margarine
- soft cheese - 200g
- pinch of salt
- pepper (optional)
- green colouring

Method

1. Grate the beetroot and carrot separately, add little butter,soft cheese, salt etc. to each and mix well to a spreadable consistency. Colour the grated cheese and butter mixture green.

2. Take 4 slices of bread and spread butter or margarine to each slice on one side and place on a board.

3. Fill the first slice with beetroot filling and spread it; for the second slice spread the cheese and for the third use the carrot spread.

4. Place the second and third slice over the beetroot spread and cover with the last slice. Press well and leave on a plate in the fridge for 10 minutes.

5. Then cut the crusts and either cut in to four squares or small cubes of about 2cm squares.

★ For hotness paprika powder or finely cut green chilli can be
★ included.

Savoury Filling for Pepper

Ingredients

- 15 small baby potatoes
- 1 small onion or fried onion flakes
- 1 small leek and 2 carrots
- seasoning to include ½ tsp each of ginger powder, garlic powder and chives
- 150-200g soft cheese (mix two kinds)
- ½ small carton single cream
- 2 tbsp sesame seeds
- 2 green chillies, chopped
- 2 medium sized green and red peppers

Method

1. Boil or microwave the potatoes and skin them.

2. In the meantime cut the vegetables, add all ingredients in a pan except the cheese and cook until soft.

3. Use a blender to lightly purée the cooked vegetable mixture.

4. Cut the potato and mix with the cheese mixture, seasoning , vegetable and a little bit of the cream (not too watery). Add half the sesame seeds and chopped green chillies.

6. Cut each pepper in half. Fill the pepper with the mixture. Top it with some more sesame seeds and chives. Grill for few minutes or heat in the oven for 10 minutes.

★ The leftover filling can be used for baked Vol-au-Vent cases. Capsicum chilli is what is used in Sri lanka, these are filled and rolled in breadcrumbs and deep fried.

Savoury Bites with Semolina

"Rava bonda" south Indian preparation

Preparation & cooking time: 30 minutes

Ingredients

- 2 cups roasted semolina
- ½ cup white rice flour
- ½ cup self raising flour
- salt to taste
- 3 green chillies, chopped
- 2 tbsp dried onions (optional)
- 100g roasted chopped nuts (cashew nut)
- 125g (small pot) natural youghurt
- 2 tsp garam masala paste

Method

1. Mix all dry ingredients in a bowl.

2. Add enough yoghurt to make the flour to a dough but not too hard or watery. Leave it for few minutes.

3. Heat the oil in a pan. Prepare small balls out of the dough and deep fry.

★ Serve as a bite for an afternoon with sauce or chutney.

Savoury Gram Murrukku

Preparation & cooking: 45 minutes to an hour

Ingredients

- 1 cup split green gram
- 1½ cups white rice flour
- ½ cup white steamed plain flour (optional)
- salt
- 1½ tsp ground cumin
- 1 tsp ground pepper
- ½ cup ground coconut (desiccated)
- 1 cup coconut milk
- 1-2 tsp ghee
- oil for frying
- mould to make the murrukku

Method

1. Roast the split green gram in a pan adding little ghee. Roast until golden colour. Leave it to cool and grind in an electric grinder.
2. Grind the coconut.
3. Mix the rice flour, gram flour, ground coconut, salt, cumin and pepper.
4. Warm the milk. Add the milk little by little to the flour and mix with handle of a wooden spoon.The flour dough should be pliable and not watery.
5. Fill a murrukku mould and squeeze the murrukku on to a parchment paper to long strips. Cut the strips to 6cm size. Do a few.
6. Whilst doing the above heat oil in a frying pan .
7. Deep fry these and remove from oil. Drain it on to a kitchen paper
8. Cool and store in an airtight jar.
9. Good savoury for parties.

Stuffed Capsicum Chillies

Preparation & cooking time: 30 minutes

Serves 4-6

Ingredients

- 6 chillies of nearly same size
- 1 onion, finely cut
- 2 potatoes, boiled and mashed
- 2 tbsp soya mince or quorn mince, cooked
- 1 tsp garam masala
- 2 green chillies, chopped finely
- ½ tsp garlic paste, ½ tsp ginger paste
- bread crumbs
- plain flour/gram flour made into a thick batter
- oil for deep frying

Method

1. Blanch capsicum chilli for 2 minutes in boiling water.

2. Remove and make a small slit in the middle (about 4cm) to allow enough space for the stuffing. Do not cut it too long as this may not hold the stuffing properly.

4. Prepare the filling by mixing the potatoes, soya mince, salt, masala, green chillies, garlic, ginger paste and onion. Mix well to a paste.

5. Fill the capsicum chilli with the potato mixture, do not over fill .

6. Then dip the chilli in batter or egg white. Roll in bread crumbs and deep fry in oil.

★ This can be served for birthday parties or an evening.
★ Serve with tomato or chilli sauce.

Seeni Ariyatharam

Traditional sweet from Jaffna

Preparation & cooking time: 1 hour

Ingredients

- 2 large cups of white rice (or red rice from Sri Lankan shops)
- 500g white sugar
- water for mixing
- oil for deep frying

Method

1. Soak the rice in water for 5-6 hours. Drain and grind this in a electric mixer/wet grinder.
2. Sieve and leave aside the flour. Retain a tablespoon of the last rice particles which would not go through the sieve.
3. In a pan heat the sugar with 4 tbsp of water; add the sieved flour little by little into the sugar until the mixture becomes thick and forms like a dough leaving the sides of the pan.
4. Remove from heat and place on to a board and allow it to cool.
5. Now in the same pan add little water and cook the rice particles until it becomes slightly thick and starchy.
6. Add this to the dough and knead it well to make the dough soft, pliable without any cracks.
7. Take a small amount (1 tbsp) of the dough. Roll it in your palm and flatten this slightly to about 4cm diameter.
8. Deep fry in cooking oil, drain and serve.

Sippi - (Sweet Murukku/Acchu Palaharam)

Preparation & cooking: 45 minutes - 1 hour

An item to prepare at weekends. A sweet that can be kept for one or two weeks.

Ingredients

- 2 cups roasted rice flour (white or red)
- ½ cup roasted urad flour
- 3-4 tbsp steamed plain flour
- 1 can coconut milk
- 4 tbsp roasted sesame seed, ground
- pinch of salt
- parchment paper
- murrukku mould with discs or use a fork
- 500g white sugar
- oil for frying
- 1 tsp lime juice (optional)
- ¼ cup water

Method

1. Boil the coconut milk and leave it aside to cool for 2-3 minutes.

2. Mix the rice flour, urad, ground sesame, plain flour, salt and leave in a bowl.

3. With the handle of a wooden spoon start mixing the flour by adding the boiled milk little by little to make into a firm dough. Add 1 tsp oil to above and knead well into a ball.

4. Place a disc inside the mould (to fit the bottom).

5. Fill the mould with the dough and place the other half of the mould on top and squeeze the dough through on to a parchment paper.

6. What you will see on the parchment paper is something like a long patterned pastry ribbon. Cut this long murrukku into 6-7 cm size, bring both open ends and join it like a half bow.

7. Heat the oil in a deep pan; when the oil is hot, drop a few murruku at a time and deep fry. Remove and drain on kitchen paper.

For the coating/covering

8. In a saucepan heat the sugar adding ¼ cup of water. Boil and add the teaspoon of lime (this will make the sugar coating have a clear look).

9. Boil the syrup and it will be ready when bubbles form. The correct test is to raise the spoon and allow the syrup to drop until a thin string appears.

10. Remove the syrup from the heat, pour it over the fried murrukku and shake the bowl to ensure that all the pieces are coated with the sugar syrup. You will see the sugar beginning to solidify and leave a white coating.

11. Leave to cool and it will be ready to eat. Store in a jar or tin until required.

Variations

- If you cannot get a mould then try this

- Take very small amounts of the dough and make a ball similar to a marble.

- Flatten this to a disc; press with a fork and press. It will have a design of three lines. Slightly start to roll from one end to meet the opposite end. You will see the pattern on the surface (like a sea shell) make a few and deep fry. Then follow the sugar syrup as above.

- Can also use any small cutters or which has a design to imprint on to the flattened dough.

Tandoori Quorn Bites/Tofu

Preparation and cooking time: 45-50 minutes

Ingredients

- 1 tsp each ginger, garlic paste (or use fresh)
- salt to taste
- 1 tsp cumin powder
- 1 tsp chilli powder
- 1 onion, chopped
- ½ tsp turmeric powder
- 2 boxes tofu or quorn (500g)
- 1 tsp lemon juice
- small carton natural yoghurt
- few skewers

Method

1. Blend all above to a smooth paste (except for the yougurt, lemon juice and quorn).

2. Put in a bowl and add the yoghurt and lemon juice.

3. Cut the quorn/tofu into long or cubes of 4cm.

4. Marinate in the mixture for about 30 minutes or so.

5. Put on a tray and bake for 10 to 15 minutes at a very high temperature, 180°C

6. Then take the pieces and thread on to a skewer and grill for further 10 minutes.

★ Can add shallots and pepper to above.

Tandoori Paneer

Preparation: 2 hours to marinate
Cooking time: 40 minutes

Ingredients

- 1 block paneer (cottage cheese) (250g)
- 1 large onion, chopped
- 3 tbsp coriander and cumin powder
- 2 tbsp chilli powder
- 3-4 cloves garlic
- 4cm ginger
- 1 tbsp masala paste (Kastoori/garam masala)
- small carton of natural yoghurt
- 1 tbsp cardamom and cinnamon powder
- 2 tbsp olive oil
- salt

Method

1. Cut the paneer block into small cubes of about 2cm squares and leave it aside.
2. Mix all ingredients except the yoghurt and oil and grind this in a liquidiser. Add yoghurt and run the machine for few seconds only.
3. Put the paste into a bowl and add the paneer. Marinate for 2 to 3 hours. If it is overnight then leave it in the fridge.
4. Spread the paneer pieces onto a flat tray oiled with olive oil
5. Cook at high temperature - 190°C, for 10-15 minutes. Turn it once and cook for few minutes. Remove from the oven when the sides begin to get a bit brown.
6. Serve hot with salad; use cocktail sticks to pick up paneer pieces.

★ Can deep fry the paneer pieces in oil, drain and then marinate and cook under a grill. This gives a different taste.

★ Cut paneer to chunky cubes and marinate in chilli powder, salt and pepper. Make a batter with gram flour, dip each paneer piece in batter and deep fry in oil until it turns brown.

Tandoori Paneer - B B Q on Skewer

Ingredients

- 1 block paneer (250g)
- 1 large onion
- 3 tbsp coriander and cumin powder
- 2 tbsp chilli powder
- 3-4 cloves garlic, crushed
- 4cm ginger, crushed
- 1 tbsp masala paste (Kastoori/garam masala)
- small carton of natural yoghurt
- 1 tbsp cardamom and cinnamon powder
- 2 tbsp olive oil
- salt
- 10 small shallots
- 1 green pepper cut to 2cm square pieces
- 1 red pepper cut to 2cm square pieces
- small button mushrooms
- cherry tomatoes, halved
- oil
- salad vegetables

Method

1. Cut paneer to cubes of about 2cm and leave it aside.
2. In a bowl place the paneer, shallots, mushrooms, tomatoes and pepper. Marinate in yoghurt and the spices.
3. On the skewer thread alternate cubes of pepper, paneer, onion and mushroom. Another skewer can have tomato, paneer and pepper. Brush with oil and grill or put on BBQ .
4. Cut salad vegetables, squeeze a lemon, add salt and serve with tandoori paneer.

Vadai with Rice and Urad Dhal

Preparation: 2 hours to soak
Cooking time: 30 minutes

Ingredients

- 2 cups white rice grains
- ½ cup urad dhal
- oil for deep frying
- salt to taste
- 2 tbsp self raising flour (optional)

Method

1. Soak rice and urad for 2-3 hours.

2. Wash the urad in two or three lots of water and place in a colander to drain the water.

3. Using a food processor grind the urad and rice, adding a bit of salt and as little water as possible. The consistency should be thick and not too watery. If necessary add the self raising flour and mix well to a thick paste.

4. Heat oil in a pan, when this is hot, using a spoon, drop a spoonful of batter into the oil and cook both sides for a few minutes.

5. Take it out and leave on kitchen paper towel to absorb any oil.

★ You may also shallow fry above in melted ghee If the ground paste is watery leave it in the fridge for 20 minutes.
The reason for adding the salt first is to avoid adding too much water

★ This is a tasty quick snack.

Vadai with Vallarai (Sri Lankan Water Cress)

Preparation: 2 hrs to soak

Cooking time: 30 minutes

Ingredients

- 1 cup urad dhal
- 1 cup white rice
- 2 tbsp toor dhal
- 1 bunch vallarai leaves, finely cut
- 1 onion, chopped
- 2 cup desiccated coconut or fresh coconut
- 4 dried red chillies
- oil for frying

Method

1. Soak the dhal and rice for a few hours. Then grind all the ingredients including the salt and add the cleaned chopped Vallarai leaves too.

2. In a pan heat the oil. When the oil is hot take a small amount of the mixture in your hand make it into a ball, flatten it slightly and slowly drop it in the oil.

3. Cook on both sides, remove from oil and allow to drain on kitchen paper.

★ Vallarai is available from Sri lankan shops. It is a leafy vegetable. Water cress can be substituted.

Vadai (Point Pedro Vadai)

A popular crunchy snack,
which will keep its crunchiness if stored in an airtight tin.

Named after a village in Jaffna, where a lady had her own vadai recipe, prepared them and sold them for a living.

Cooking time: 45 minutes
Makes 35-40 flat discs of 5cm diameter

Ingredients

- 2 cups urad dhal
- 2 tsp cumin seeds
- 10 curry leaves, finely cut
- 3 tsp plain chilli powder
- oil for deep frying
- 1 tsp turmeric powder
- ½ cup steamed plain flour
- 2 cups white rice flour
- salt to taste
- 2 tsp fennel seeds
- 1 medium onion, finely chopped
- 1/4 cup hot water
- 1 cup desiccated coconut (optional)
- cellophane paper or greaseproof paper cut to 6cm squares

Method

1. Soak the urad dhal for 3-4 hours.

2. Wash and leave the dhal in a colander to drain.

3. Take a quarter or a bit less of the dhal and grind this to a paste.

4. Place the ground paste in a large bowl, add the rest of the dhal and the remainder of the dry ingredients. Mix well.

5. Now add the hot water little by little and mix to a coarse paste.

6. Using cellophane paper or greaseproof paper place about 1½ tsp of the paste in between two sheets and press to a thin disc shape.
   Prepare a few and leave with the paper.

7. Heat oil in a thava (curved pan) and slowly slide the vadai in and deep fry for few minutes.

8. Turn to the other side and fry, remove with a slotted spoon and place on a kitchen paper towel to get rid of any excess oil.

9. Store in an air tight tin.

Vadai (Ulunthu Vadai - Urad Dhal)

Preparation: 2 hours to soak dhal
Cooking time: 45 minutes

Ingredients

- 1 cup urad dhal
- 3 green chillies chopped
- 2 dried red chillies
- salt to taste
- 2 tsp grated ginger
- 2 medium onions, chopped
- 15 fresh curry leaves, cut to thin strips
- 2 tsp fennel seeds
- 1 litre oil for deep frying
- 3-4 tablespoons water
- water in a bowl

Method

1. Rinse and soak urad dhal for 2 hrs. Wash the dhal and leave in a colander to drain.

2. Using an electric blender, grind the dhal with red chilles, salt, ginger and fennel seeds. You may need to add little water whilst grinding. The mixture should be slightly coarse.

3. Put the ground urad into a large bowl, add the curry leaves, onions, green chillies and mix well .

4. Take a small amount (1 tbsp) of the paste in your fingers, form a ball and place on the other palm and flatten it into a disc shape. Make a hole in the middle with your little finger.

5. Heat a pan, add oil and bring to a fairly high heat. Take the shaped vadai and slowly drop it into the hot oil to fry. Dip your fingers in the bowl of water before preparing another vadai.

6.. You can use your palm to prepare the vadai, or prepare on cut out cellophane paper. Prepare five or six at a time and fry these. (Any plastic bag will do the trick).

7. Deep fry in oil for 4 – 5 minutes on medium heat. Fry both sides and remove from the oil with a slotted spoon and drain on a kitchen paper.

8. It will look slightly brown and crispy like a ring doughnut, but will be savoury.

★ There are lots of varieties of vadai.
★ The ones purchased in the shops are very large, but my recipe includes the small flat ones, which are crispy.

Vadai with Split Peas - (Kadalai Vadai)

Preparation: 2 hours to soak
Cooking time: 30-45 minutes

Ingredients

- 2 cups split channa dhal
- 2 medium onions, chopped
- 2 green chillies, chopped
- 3 dried red chillies
- 3 cloves garlic
- oil for frying
- 2 sprigs curry leaves, finely cut
- 2 tsp fennel seeds

Method

1. Soak the dhal for about two to three hours (not more).
2. Wash the dhal in three lots of water and drain.
3. Using a wet grinder/blender grind half the dhal adding the red chillies, salt and fennel seeds. Grind to a coarse.
4. Do the same with the rest of the dhal. Place the mixture in a bowl.
5. Add the onions, green chillies and curry leaves and mix well.
6. Take one round soup spoonful of the paste and slightly flatten it.
7. Heat fresh oil in a pan or Thava. Slowly drop into the hot oil and deep fry until golden colour and crispy. Remove by using a slotted spoon and drain on kitchen paper.
8. If you need you can cut up several squares of greaseproof paper and prepare the vadai by taking a spoonful and making into a ball or slightly flattening by placing on the palm to give a flat disc shape. You can drop 7-8 in one lot into the hot oil.

★ Served for evening tea.
You can also freeze the vadai. Warm in the oven when you need it.

Vegetable Cutlets

Preparation & cooking time: 45-50 minutes

Ingredients

- 5 medium size potatoes, boiled
- 1 medium size onion, chopped
- 1 leek
- 3-4 spring onions
- 1 tin of chick peas (400g)
- 100g soya meat, boiled
- 10 curry leaves, thinly sliced
- 1 tsp mustard seeds
- 2 cloves garlic, crushed
- 2cm ginger, crushed
- 3 green chillies (optional, finely chopped)
- 2 tbsp oil for tempering
- 50g flour (for batter) or egg whites
- salt to taste
- ½ tsp of pepper
- 1 bottle of oil for deep frying
- bread crumbs
- 1-2 tsp chilli powder
- 1 tsp roasted fennel powder

Method

1. Skin the potatoes and mash and leave in a bowl.
2. Mix the chickpeas and soya meat, run the blender for a few seconds. Add the mixture to the potatoes and mix well.
3. Heat a frying pan, add two tablespoons of oil and temper the onion, leek, spring onions, ginger, garlic and finally the potato and chickpeas mixture. Cook for a minute or two and add the chilli powder, curry leaves and the fennel powder. Cook for a minute and remove from heat.
4. Let the mixture cool slightly.
5. Take a spoonful and make it into a small ball and leave it. If preferred slightly flatten the two sides to form a flat round shape.
6. Do the same with the rest of the mixture.
7. Mix the flour, pinch of salt and little water to make the batter (if you are not too fussy use beaten egg white for coating).
8. Dip the rolled cutlet in the batter and make sure it is coated fully.
9. Then roll it in breadcrumbs and leave on a separate plate.

10. Heat the oil in a deep frying pan and deep-fry a few cutlets at a time. Make sure the oil is hot and also the oil covers the cutlet, this will prevent the cutlets from breaking while frying.
11. Remove and place on kitchen paper. Serve hot

★ Could be a starter or served with a main meal

Variations

Substitute 2 green bananas (ash plantain) instead of two potatoes.
Soya mince instead of chickpeas
Boil the banana with the skin, remove skin and mash the bananas

- 1-2 tsp of ground pepper and cumin
- 1 grated carrot
- 1 cup of boiled minced soya

Add the cumin/pepper to the mashed banana. Boil soya, drain the water; add it to the banana and potato mixture. Follow the rest as for above recipe.

Freezing

1. If you are going to freeze the cutlet then it is best to sauté/temper the onion and cook the ingredients. However if you are to going to serve it on the same day, you may add the chopped onions and green chillies without sautéing.
2. If freezing, it is best to freeze the rolled cutlet arranged on a plate and when frozen you can then put in a bag to keep. Take it out on the day you need it and leave it out for half an hour or so and deep fry.
3. You can also deep fry and then freeze. Arrange on a tray and freeze. Take it out when you need it and put in the oven to bake/reheat for 15 minutes at the highest temperature and remove from the oven and serve.

Savoury Deep Fry (Cheese egg potato)

Preparation & cooking time: 30 minutes

Ingredients

- butter or margarine 250g
- ½ tsp salt
- ½ tsp each pepper, nutmeg, cinnamon and garlic powder
- 100g cheese grated
- few chives and spring onions, chopped
- 4 eggs
- boiled mashed potato
- 125g rice flour
- 125g stone ground flour
- 2 tbsp corn flour
- ¼-½ pint of water , 1 cube of vegetable stock
- oil for frying

Method

1. Melt butter, add all seasoning including the mashed potato and half the flour mixture.
2. Keep stirring and add the stock. Add the grated cheese. Fold in the beaten egg and rest of the flour.
3. Heat the oil and drop spoonful of mixture little by little and deep fry.
4. Serve with any dips.

Bread Rolls

Known as vegetable buns

Preparation & cooking time: 2 hours

It is easier to make with the readymade flour available from supermarkets. However I have given a recipe in case you want to try making the dough.

Ingredients

- 250g packet of bread rolls flour or
- 1 sachet yeast and 250g plain flour
- ½ tsp salt
- ½ cup milk
- 3 tbs butter
- 1 egg

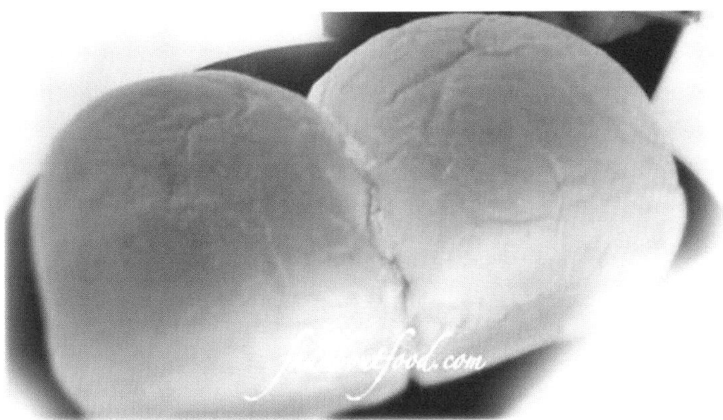

Method

If preparing from the bread flour follow the instructions given on the packet and prepare 20-25 balls, cover with a wet cloth and leave near a hot surface for the rolls to double in size. Then roll it out, use any savoury filling you like, bring back the ends to seal, place the roll facing down on a tray, brush with milk and bake in a hot oven for 20 minutes.

If you are to prepare the dough:-

1. Prepare the yeast as per the instructions on the sachet. If not add little warm water, cover and leave for 10-15 minutes in a warm place. Add ½ tsp sugar, mix and leave to ferment.
2. Beat the egg and leave it aside. Sieve the flour.
3. In a bowl place the sieved flour, yeast, salt and the egg. Knead well to get smooth dough. You may need to add little milk.
4. Make few balls out of the dough and place on a tray. Cover the tray with a wet cloth and leave it near a warm place for the dough to rise.
5. Once risen place the ball on a floured board and slightly roll out with a rolling pin. Place a spoon of any filling you have prepared and bring all the sides together to cover the open ends.

6. Place the rolls on a tray with the smooth surface on the top. Brush it with little milk and bake in a hot oven for 15-20 minutes.

Fillings

See recipes for potato dry dish, other fillings for patties, paratha, vegetable rolls, cutlets, seeni sambol which can be used here.

Non-vegetarian fillings can be of dry preparation of salmon, mince lamb or prawns.

Paneer Cutlets Variation

Ingredients

- 250g paneer cheese
- 1 tea cup corn, boiled
- 4 medium potatoes, half cooked
- 4 tbsp grated cheddar cheese
- 4 green chillies, finely chopped
- 1 onion, chopped
- 2 tbsp coriander powder
- few coriander leaves, finely sliced
- 1 tsp chilli powder
- 1 sprig curry leaves, finely sliced
- salt to taste
- 50g butter
- 200g plain flour
- 1½ cups milk
- 1 slice bread chopped (optional)
- oil for deep frying
- breadcrumbs

Method

1. Cut the paneer into small pieces. Peel the skin of the potatoes and cut these.
2. Melt the butter in a pan and add the onions and stir fry.
3. Then add ¾ of the flour and stir it.
4. Add the milk and bring to boil. Allow to thicken it as for sauce. and remove from heat.
5. In a bowl place the corn, paneer, potatoes, green chillies, cheese, coriander and mix adding the prepared sauce.
6. Add salt and mix well. If it is watery add the bread which will soak the sauce.
7. Make into small balls. Prepare a batter by mixing the rest of the flour, adding a little water. Add a bit of salt.
8. Dip the balls one by one in batter and roll in bread crumbs. Deep fry and serve.

Pakoda with Kadalai Parrupu

Pre soaking required for 2-3 hours
Preparation & cooking time: 30-45 minutes

Ingredients

- 2 cups split channa dhal
- 1 medium onion, finely chopped
- 2 tsp freshly grated garlic or powder
- 5 dried red chillies
- 3 sprigs curry leaves, finely sliced
- 2 tsp fennel seeds
- oil for deep frying

Method

1. Soak dhal for about two to three hours and rinse in two to three lots of water; allow to drain in a colander.
2. Using a blender grind half the dhal adding little bit of salt, fennel seeds and chillies. Grind it to a coarse consistency and set aside.
3. Do the same with the rest of the dhal but take it out half ground so that you can see some bits of the dhal just chopped.
4. Mix the onions and curry leaves with the minced dhal, add the rest of the fennel seeds, garlic and mix well.
5. Heat the oil in a deep frying pan or thava.
6. Take 1 teaspoon of the paste, slightly flatten it and drop it slowly into the oil. Continue to do so with the rest. Deep fry until crispy and turns to golden colour. Drain on kitchen paper.
7. To work faster, you may prepare the individual ones, arrange on a plate and slide slowly (10-12) into the hot oil.

★ Can be kept in an airtight tin or a bottle for about a month.

If it loses the crispiness, place the fried pakoda on a tray and heat in the oven at the highest temperature for 12 minutes. Leave it out for few minutes and it will get crspy.

Samosa

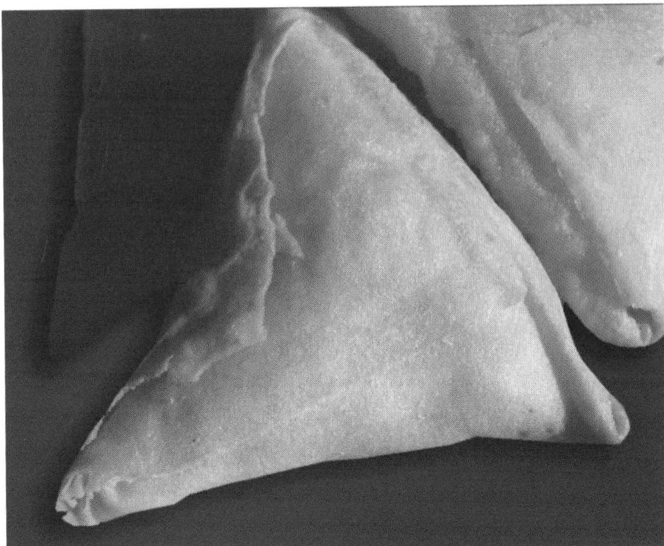

Ingredients

For filling

- 4 medium potatoes
- 5 curry leaves chopped
- 1 onion and few spring onoins, chopped
- 2 green chillies chopped
- 1-2 tsp garam masala powder
- 100g peas
- 2 carrots
- 2 tbs butter
- 1 tbs yogurt
- salt and pepper to taste

For outer covering

- samosa sheets or
  500 gms of plain flour to make the pastry
- 2-3 tbsp butter or ghee
- salt to taste
- water
- oil for deep frying

Method

For the filling

First boil the potatoes and mash it slightly. Boil the peas. Grate the carrots and cook in microwave for a minute.
Mix together the ingredients for filling and stir fry in little butter for a minute and leave it aside.

To prepare the samosa covering:

1. Sift the flour, rub in 2 tablespoons butter, salt, add water and knead to a dough.

2. Divide dough into half, cover one half and set aside. Prepare small balls from one half of the dough.

3. Take three balls and roll out to thin discs. Brush each with little ghee and place on top of each other.

4. Heat a frying pan (heavy bottomed) and place the three discs together. Heat one side for 30 seconds then turn and heat the other side.
   Seperate the discs and warm all three, leave the discs on a plate and cover with a kitchen cloth.

5. Repeat the procedure of making small discs until all the dough has been prepared.

6. Cut each round into half, take one half, place one spoon of the filling on one corner, bring the other end over to cover and seal the edges with paste made with flour and water.

7. Deep fry in hot oil until golden brown. Drain and serve hot with chutney

8. If you are going to use the readymade sheets you may need to use two sheets as they may be too thin.

   Fill them and then deep fry.

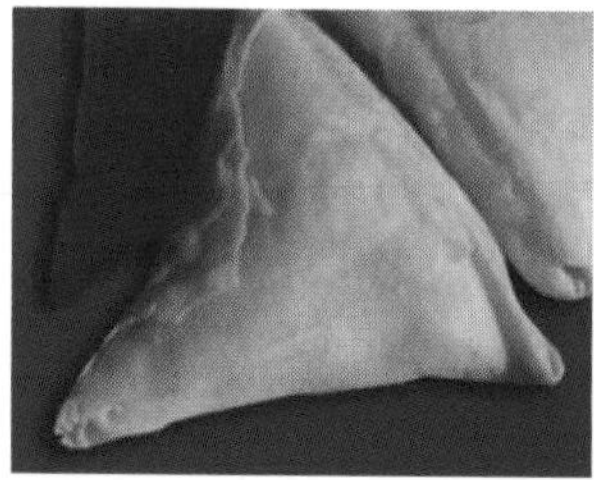

Paneer Kebab

This dish is useful when you need to cater for vegetarians on BBQ day. Easily prepared and can be grilled.

Ingredients

- 500 g paneer (cottage cheese)
- 200 g small tomatoes (cherry tomatoes)
- 15 baby corns
- 15 shallots of same size
- 2 green peppers and 1 red pepper
- 2 tsp garlic paste, 2 tsp ginger paste
- 1 tsp chilli powder
- ½ tsp turmeric powder
- 2 tsp coriander powder
- 1 tsp cumin seeds
- ½ tsp pepper corn roasted and coarsely ground
- salt to taste
- 125 gms (small carton) natural yoghurt
- ½ lemon to garnish
- wooden skewers

Method

1. Mix the yoghurt with salt, chilli powder, ground cumin pepper, coriander, garlic, ginger and turmeric.
2. Mix well and beat to a thick cream.
3. Cut the paneer blocks to 4cm pieces and add them to the yoghurt paste and allow it to marinate for 5-6 hours.
4. Cut the peppers to 4cm squares,cut the baby corn to 2 cm size dip these in the yoghurt mixture.
5. Place the wooden skeweres in hot water for few minutes.
6. On the wooden skewers alternate cubes of paneer, pepper, tomato and shallots.
7. Grill on a barbecue or in the oven until the vegetables are soft.
8. Garnish with a squeeze of lemon and serve.

Puddings

Puddings - Index

Puddings - Index

Poli

Shaped like a paratta or chapatti with sweet channa dhal stuffing

Preparation: 2-3 hours including soaking channa dhal
Cooking time: 25 minutes

Ingredients

- 250g plain flour
- 200g channa or toor dhal
- 150g sugar or jaggery
- 125g desiccated coconut
- 4-5 cardamom pods, crushed
- pinch of salt, warm water
- butter or ghee

Method

1. Roast the dhal in a frying pan, transfer to a bowl, cover with water and soak for about 2 hours.
2. Boil the dhal in enough water and drain before it gets too soggy and mushy. Spread on a plate and leave it aside.
3. Mix the flour adding warm water and a pinch of salt. Make into a soft dough and set aside.
4. Add sugar, salt, desiccated coconut and cardamoms to the dhal and mix well. You may like to very lightly mash this using a hand blender.
5. Take some dough and roll out to form a large disc about 12 cm diameter. Prepare few and leave on a plate.
6. Spread a spoon of the dhal mixture onto one, cover this with another and seal the edges carefully to avoid leaking.
7. Cook by placing it in a heated heavy-based frying pan, brushed with little ghee or butter. Cook one side for 2 minutes. Cook the opposite side for 2 more minutes.

★ Can also deep fry the prepared Poli's.

Aluwa

A Sri Lankan sweet

Cooking time: 30-45 minutes
Makes 25-30 pieces

Ingredients

- 750g red rice flour
- 250g cashew nuts, chopped
- 2 cans of coconut treacle (350g each)
- pinch of salt
- 1 tbsp butter for the tray

Method

1. Boil the treacle in a pan, add the rice flour gradually in small quantities and mix. Keep stirring and cook for 15 minutes.

2. Add the cashew nuts and keep stirring until the mixture thickens.

3. When the mixture leaves the sides of the pan and bubbles pour on to a buttered tray or board. Flatten the top using a piece of oil paper or back of the spoon.

4. Let it cool slightly and cut into squares or diamond shape.

★ **The ingredients are available from Sri Lankan grocery shops**

Bravae

This is a noughat type sweet made with semolina. Usually prepared by Christians for Christmas

I had this at a friend's house, whose family had sent it from Australia. I am sure you will find it easy and will include it as one of your favourite sweet dishes.

Ingredients

- 500 g semolina
- 200 g white sugar
- 100 g butter
- 2 eggs (white and yolk)
- 1 yolk of an egg
- 150 g cashew nuts roasted and chopped
- pinch of salt (4-5 granules)
- ¼ tsp ground cardamom (optional)
- ½ tsp rose water essence

Method

1. Roast the semolina well in a heavy-based pan until slightly brown and coarse.
2. In a bowl place the semolina, add the butter and sugar and mix well.
3 Add the egg, cashew and other ingredients and mix well to a paste.
4. Knead and leave it aside for at least one hour.
5. Take small amounts (appx 1½ tbsp) and form into balls and place these on a greaseproof paper.
6. Place in preheated oven and bake for 20 minutes at 160°C.
7. Let it cool and serve.

★ Can spread the mixture in a buttered tray, mark out squares and bake.
Remove from the oven and cut it.

Bread Pudding

Preparation & cooking time: 2 hours

Ingredients

- 6-8 slices of white bread
- ½ pint milk
- 400 g sugar
- 75 g butter
- 150 g sultanas
- 100 g cashew nuts
- ½ pint cream
- 3-4 eggs (use 4 yolks and 2 whites)
- 1 tsp freshly grated nutmeg
- 1 tsp vanilla
- ½ tsp of cinnamon powder

baking dish or dish for steaming (appx 20 cm square)

Method

1. Grease the sides of the baking dish with butter.
2. Butter each slice of bread on one side, cut off crust.
3. Slice the bread lengthwise or into triangles and place on the bottom of the dish placing the buttered side to the base. Sprinkle sugar, sultanas and cashew nuts.
4. Place the next layer of bread and sprinkle sugar and sultanas. Cover the top with buttered side up.
5. Place the eggs in a bowl and whisk the eggs lightly. Add milk.Transfer to a pan, warm mixture slightly and add half the sugar and cream and whisk lightly. Add the vanilla.
6. Pour the milk and egg over the bread and leave aside for 10-15 minutes. Once the bread has soaked in the mixture sprinkle the rest of the sugar, grated nutmeg, cinnamon and cashew nuts.
7. Place the dish in a preheated oven. Leave a tray of water on the bottom shelf and bake for 30-40 minutes at 160°C.
8. If steaming cover with a dish and steam for 1½ hours. Use a knife to pierce slightly to see if cooked.

★ This may be a recipe from the West but this is a pudding dish that was very popular with most Sri Lankans in Colombo since the fifties.

Carrot Halwa

Preparation & cooking time: 45 minutes

Ingredients

- 10 medium carrots, grated
- 4 tbsp ghee or butter
- 3 cups cows milk
- 1 cup sugar
- 25 cashew nuts or almonds
- 1 tsp saffron powder
- few drops of vanilla or rose essence
- 5 cardamoms
- 300 ml carton single cream

Method

1. Peel the carrot, wash and finely grate it. Can grate on a fine grater blade of a food processor.
2. In a deep pan fry the carrot in ghee or butter for 5–10 minutes.
3. Add milk, bring to boil and simmer until it is cooked and soft (appx 25 minutes).
4. Add sugar and let it dissolve.
5. Cook for few minutes and when the mixture thickens add the flavouring and roasted cashew nuts or almonds.
6. Serve warm adding single cream to taste.

Cheese Cakes - Individual tarts with semolina

Preparation & cooking time: 1 hour

Ingredients

- 250g short crust or puff pastry

For the Filling

- 125g cashew nuts, chopped
- 125g sugar
- 100g roasted semolina
- 2 eggs (separate whites and yolks)
- rind of one lemon
- 1 tsp vanilla
- ½ tsp rose essence
- pinch of nutmeg

Method

1. Mix the yolks and sugar and beat this well.
2. Roast the semolina, mix the butter when it is warm so that the butter melts and mixes well.
3. Add cashew nuts and flavouring to the egg yolk mixture; add the semolina and mix .
4. Finally beat the egg whites until frothy/stiff. Add the egg white peaks to the mixture and fold it in.
5. Roll the pastry on to a board dusted with flour.
6. Cut out circles with a cutter, line the cup cake baking tray with the circles.
7. Spoon the filling into each case and bake in the oven for 15-20 minutes at 160°C.

★ **Suitable to have with evening tea.**

Cheese Cake with Mango & Orange

Ingredients

For the Biscuit base

- 250g biscuit (ginger or digestive)
- 125g butter
- 4 tbsp of brown sugar

Mango - orange filling

- 200g of cream cheese
- 2 fresh mangoes finely chopped or a 400g tin of mango, finely
- chopped
- 30g crystalised ginger chopped
- 1 orange - grated rind of an orange and the juice
- 50g white sugar
- ½ packet of orange jelly or a packet of gelatine
- ½ pint of fromage frais

Method

1. Crush the biscuit; mix with sugar and melted butter.
2. Press in to the lightly oiled base of a (20cm or 22cm) round loose-bottomed cake or flan tray. Cover the base and sides.
3. Bake in a preheated oven for 10 minutes at 190°C.
4. Leave it aside to cool then remove by pushing the base up and leave it on a flat plate ready to decorate.

Filling

5. Mix the gelatine or jelly as per the instructions on the packet.
6. Mix the orange rind and the juice to above.
7. Add the fromage frais and cream cheese. Beat this well.
8. Stir in the mangoes and the chopped ginger.
9. Pour over the biscuit base and refrigerate it until firm.

★ This dish can be prepared by simply refrigerating and not cooking in the oven.

Chocolate Biscuit Gateau

Ingredients

- 1 packet of rich tea biscuit
- 2 tbsp of cocoa powder
- 125g caster sugar
- 125g butter
- 1 large carton of double cream (450g)
- ¼ tin of condensed milk (125g)
- 125g roasted cashew nuts chopped
- 3 tbsp of brandy or rum (optional)
- 100g carnation milk mixed with 2 tbsp of cows milk
- 2 tsp of gelatine

Method

1. Prepare the gelatine as normal with little less water.
2. Mix the cocoa powder in condensed milk.
3. Beat the butter and sugar till light and fluffy. Add the cocoa powder mixture.
4. Beat the double cream to thick and fluffy. Slowly add the gelatine and add it to the butter mixture. Add the nuts, rum or brandy essence and vanilla.
5. Prepare a 20cm square dish by arranging the biscuit as they are side by side and fill the base. Brush with carnation milk and normal milk to ensure the biscuit is soaked but not soggy.
6. Pour half the beaten cream mixture and spread this evenly.
7. Arrange another layer of soaked biscuits then another layer of the cream and leave it in the fridge to set.

The original recipe had two eggs. Due to fear of uncooked eggs and the risk of salmonella, I have adopted the above, but if you wish to use eggs, first beat the yolks with the butter mixture and lastly add the beaten egg white.

Chocolate Macaroons

Cooking time: 30 minutes or less

Ingredients

- 125g ground almonds
- 125g caster sugar
- 2 egg white
- 3 tbsp of drinking chocolate
- rice paper
- blanched almonds

Method

1. Whisk the egg whites until stiff; fold in ground almonds, sugar and the sieved drinking chocolate.

2. Keep ready a baking tray lined with rice paper. Using a spoon drop small heaps onto the rice paper (can use a large nozzle and a piping bag).

3. Place an almond onto each and bake in a preheated oven for 20 minutes at 180°C

Coconut Rock

Cooking time: 40 minutes

Ingredients

- 6 tbsp desiccated coconut
- 5 tbsp white sugar
- 1 tsp vanilla
- few drops of pink/green colouring
- one drop of rose essence
- 1 cup of water and ½ tin of condensed milk (200g)
- 1 tbsp butter

Method

1. Mix the sugar with water and condensed milk and bring to boil.
2. Lower the flame and cook for few minutes.
3. Add the desiccated coconut and keep stirring until the mixture gets stiff.
4. Add butter and mix well.
5. Add vanilla and rose essence.
6. Add pink colouring so that the mixture is pink in colour
7. Serve onto a plate and flatten it .
8. Once set, cut into squares and serve.

★ Repeat same procedure using green colouring.

Coconut Cake Squares

Preparation & cooking time: 1 hour and 30 minutes

Ingredients

- 250g roasted rice flour
- 2 tbsp butter
- 500g soft brown sugar
- 1 coconut scraped or
- 2 cups of desiccated coconut, 5 tbsp milk
- 5 yolks
- 2 egg whites
- 100 cashew nuts
- ½ wine glass of rose water
- ¼ tsp of ground cardamom
- ¼ tsp nutmeg

Method

1. Scrape the coconut and grind it to a paste. If using desiccated coconut add a bit of milk, soak it and then grind it.
2. Grind 2/3 of the cashew nuts adding a little bit of rose water.
3. Cut the other cashew nuts to long thin strips (for topping).
4. Put the yolks in a bowl and beat. Add the sugar and beat well.
5. Add the rice flour in small quantities and beat well. Add the cardamom and the rest of the rose water.
6. Melt the butter and add this.
7. Beat the egg whites to a very stiff froth and fold this in.
8. Pour into a buttered medium size square baking tray and top it with the cashew nut strips and the nutmeg.
9. Bake in a moderate oven at 160°C for about an hour
10. Cut into small squares and serve.

★ Butter is optional, the original recipe given by a friend did not have the butter.

Coffee Short Bread

Ingredients

- 250g brown sugar
- 125g butter
- 250g plain flour
- 1 tsp bicarbonate soda
- 1 egg
- 2 fl oz strong coffee chilled (¼ cup)
- 1 tsp salt
- 1-2 tsp of powdered mixture of cinnamon, cardamom and cloves
- 1 tsp of grated nutmeg

Method

1. Beat the butter and sugar, add the egg and beat well.
2. Sieve the flour after adding the sodium bicarbonate and spices.
3. Add the flour and coffee to the butter cream and mix well. Leave in a cool place for an hour.
4. Using a large icing nozzle fill an icing bag with the mixture. Pipe stars or discs onto a baking sheet, leave approximately an inch of space between each.
5. Bake in a preheated oven for 10-12 minutes at 180°C.

★ Can try the same with cocoa instead of coffee.

Cream Buns

Ingredients

- 125g margarine/butter
- 2 eggs
- 125g sifted plain flour
- ¼ tsp salt
- water to mix

Filling

- 75g butter
- 125g icing sugar
- vanilla essence

Beat the icing sugar and butter to creamy consistency. Add vanilla essence. If using chocolate flavouring add cocoa or melted chocolate and nuts.

Method

1. Mix in a pan the butter and salt and melt over a low flame.
2. Add the flour and stir until the mixture leaves the sides of the pan.
3. Remove from the cooker and leave it aside for a minute.
4. Add the eggs to the mixture one at a time. Beat well until glossy.
5. Using a piping bag or spoon, place one spoonful of mixture on to a greaseproof paper. Allow space between the buns, as they will rise during cooking.
6. Bake in a preheated oven at 180°C for 15 minutes. Then reduce heat to 140°C and bake for another 20 minutes. Remove from oven and let it cool.
7. Split each bun on the side and fill it with the butter cream.

★ If you like chocolate then fill with butter cream inside and pour melted chocolate over the bun.
★ Alternatively, double cream can be used; it needs
★ Good for parties or to serve after dinner.

Crunchy Cashew Nut Halwa/Brittle

Ingredients

- 250g unsalted cashew nuts, chopped
- 1 cup golden syrup
- 125g butter
- ½ cup water
- 2 tsp baking soda
- 2 tsp vanilla essence
- non stick parchment baking paper
- 200g caster sugar

Method

1. Add the sugar, golden syrup butter and water into a pan and mix well. Stir over low heat until the syrup, water and butter are mixed well.

2. Increase the heat slightly and bring the mixture to boil. Keep stirring and cook over moderate heat until the sugar syrup begins to crack slightly. It would take about 15-20 minutes.

3. Add the cashew nuts and cook for a further 5 minutes until the mixture comes to a slightly harder stage and leaves the sides of the pan.

4. Remove from cooker and sprinkle the baking soda. Need to be careful as it will become frothy and come up to the surface. Add the vanilla essence and mix well.

5. Pour the mixture onto the baking sheet and spread it with the back of a spoon or by moving and tilting the sheets to make it into a thin layer.

6. Allow to cool and break to pieces. Can be stored in a bottle or airtight container.

Eggless Dessert

Bengali preparation- similar to cheese cake

Ingredients

- 500g Greek yoghurt or a fairly thickset variety
- fruits in season, raspberries or strawberries
- sugar to taste
- 4 tbsp chopped pistachio nuts, or chopped roasted cashew nuts
- ½ can of condensed milk (200g)
- icing sugar for dusting

Method

1. Place the yoghurt, condensed milk and sugar in a bowl and beat together until creamy.

2. Butter a few small baking bowls or ramekin tins and pour the mixture into the individual dishes.

4. Place the dishes in a tray of water and bake for 30 minutes in a preheated oven at 150°C

5. Remove and chill in fridge overnight

6. Turn each pudding upside down onto a saucer.

7. Chop the berries very small and dust with icing sugar. Spoon onto the pudding, sprinkle with nuts and serve.

Eggless Pudding with Dates

Ingredients

- 2 cups chopped dates
- 100g butter
- ¾ cup boiling water
- 1 tsp sodium bicarbonate
- 200g brown sugar
- 1 tin full cream evaporated milk (375g)
- 250g self raising flour
- double cream or whipped cream (375g)
- 50g chopped cashew nuts roasted in a little butter

Method

1. Mix the chopped dates with the sodium bicarbonate and soak in hot water for 2 hours. When soft chop the dates.

2. Cream butter and sugar, then stir in the dates with the juice. Add flour and milk a little at a time to make sure the consistency is not too watery. May not need all the milk.

3. Pour into a 20cm square tray brushed with butter and bake at 150°C for 45 minutes.

4. Before serving, cut the baked pudding into cubes and cover with the whipped cream and toasted cashew nuts.

Flapjack

Ingredients

- 500g oats
- 200g sugar
- 200g butter or margarine
- 6 tbsp golden syrup

Method

1. Put the syrup and margarine in a pan and warm gently to mix well.

2. Take the pan off the heat, add the oats and sugar.

3. Put the mixture into a medium (20cm) greased tin and flatten it.

4. Bake until golden brown at 150°C.

5. Remove from oven let it cool.

6. Cut into rectangular pieces and serve.

Lavariya - Sweet String Hoppers

(see special food section)

Prepared in the south of Sri Lanka mostly for family functions and auspicious days.

It is rather time consuming and best left for weekend.

Ingredients

For the filling

- 250g jaggery or dark brown soft sugar
- 1 coconut scraped or 1½ cup desiccated coconut
- 1 tsp rice flour
- pinch of salt
- 1 tsp cinnamon powder
- 2 tbsp water

Method

1. Scrape the jaggery with a knife or a grater.
2. Put this into a pan, add the water and cook on very low heat until the jaggery thickens.
3. Then add the coconut, cinnamon powder and salt. Mix well.
4. Add a bit of rice flour to make the filling less runny.
5. If using brown sugar you may need less water and also add a bit more rice flour
6. Set mixture aside.

For the Flour covering -

similar to string hoppers in “alternatives to rice” section

- 1 cup of roasted white rice flour
- pinch of salt
- ¾ cup hot water

7. Place the rice flour in a bowl. Add salt and mix well.

8. Add the water little by little and mix using the handle of a long wooden spoon. Once the flour is mixed well, add 1 tsp of oil and mix well to form a soft dough.

9. Take a few large leaves from your garden or have a polythene sheet ready; can also use parchment paper.

10 Keep ready a couple of string hopper mats, a mould to make the string hopper and a steamer.

11 Put some dough into the string hopper mould, press and prepare like string hoppers onto the leaf or parchment paper.

12 Place 1 tablespoon of the filling mixture in the centre.

13 Now fold the leaf by bringing it over so that the string hopper folds and looks like a patty.

14 Gently slide this onto a string hopper mat.

15 Do two more and place on the mat.

16 Place the mat with the three and place in a steamer and steam for 5 minutes.

Fruit Salad - (Sri Lankan Preparation)

Serves 20

Ingredients

- 2 medium ripe papayas
- 4 ripe mangoes
- 3 ripe bananas
- 2 oranges
- 2 pears
- 2 red apples
- 1 can of peaches (400g)
- bunch of grapes
- 1 large pineapple or a 450g can of pineapple rings in juice
- ¼ tin of full cream condensed milk (100g)
- 5 tbsp honey
- 3 tsp lemon juice

Method

1. Wash fruits and peel/cut the skin for all except the grapes.
2. Discard seeds and cube papayas and mangoes to 2cm.
3. Open the cans and cut pineapple into small pieces. Cut the peaches to small pieces. Save ¼ cup of juice.
4. Halve the grapes.
5. Cut the bananas to 1cm or 2cm cubes, leave in a bowl and sprinkle lemon juice over.
6. Cut apples and pears into small pieces.
7. Put all the cut fruits into a bowl and mix together.
8. Beat the condensed milk, honey and the saved pineapple juice and lightly fold into the fruits.
9. Cover with cling film and refrigerate until ready to serve.

Ginger Cookies/Snacks

Preparation & cooking: 30minutes

Ingredients

- 250g plain flour
- 125g soft brown sugar
- pinch of salt
- 1 tsp of ground ginger powder
- 175g butter
- 6 tbsp golden syrup (about 125g)
- 1 egg
- greaseproof paper

Method

1. Soften the butter, add the syrup, egg and beat well.

2. Sieve flour into a bowl, add ginger, salt and brown sugar. Mix well. Add the syrup, butter and egg mixture in small amounts and knead to form a dough. Chill this for 5-10 minutes.

3. Roll out dough on a lightly floured board and cut into shapes using any cutters.

4. Place on greaseproof paper and bake in a preheated oven at 180°C for 10 minutes.

Gulab Jamun

Ingredients

- 100g of powdered milk (full cream or low fat to your choice)
- 3 tbsp self raising flour
- 2 tsp semolina
- 2 tbsp ghee
- 2-3 tbsp milk to mix the powder
- pinch of salt
- oil or ghee for deep frying

For the Syrup

- 500g white sugar
- 4 cardomons, crushed
- rose essence few drops
- ¼ to ½ cup of water

Method

1. Mix the milk powder, semolina, salt, self raising flour. Add milk, ghee and knead to form a dough. Leave it aside.

2. In the meantime heat the sugar in a pan adding few drops of water and rose essence, add crushed cardomons. Let this simmer on very low heat.

3. Take a small piece of the dough and roll it into a ball (bit smaller than a golf ball). Prepare a few more and deep fry in oil or ghee.

4. Remove from oil and drain on paper. The colour of the gulab jamun should be light brown.

5. Put the cooked gulab jamun in the syrup, bring to boil, remove from fire, leave to cool and serve with the syrup.

Indian Ice-cream - Kulfi - 1

Serves 6

Ingredients

- 800g evaporated milk
- 1 can condensed milk (400g)
- 2 tsp vanilla flavouring
- 300g icing sugar
- 1 tsp cardamom powder
- 150g pistachio nuts
- 50g sultanas
- 50g almonds
- 10 glazed cherries, halved
- ½ tsp ghee
- 2 egg white (optional)

Method

1. Place the two evaporated milk tins in a pan. Pour water into the pan to cover the cans and bring to boil. Reduce the heat and boil for 20 minutes.
2. Take out and leave in the freezer overnight (about 7 hours).
3. Chop the nuts, slice the almonds to thin strips and lightly roast both in a pan with ½ tsp ghee. Leave it aside.
4. Open the cans of evaporated milk and leave for 10 minutes at room temperature. Using an electric beater whisk until it doubles in quantity.
5. Add the condensed milk, sugar in small quantities and fold lightly with a spoon.
6. Add the nuts, sultanas, halved cherries, vanilla, rose essence and whisked egg white.
7. Transfer into a box and freeze for 2 hours.
8. Take out and whisk again when half set.
9. Leave in the freezer for 4 -5 hours.
10. Remove from freezer 15 minutes before serving and serve with wafers.

Indian Ice Cream - Kulfi - 2

Ice-cream for a large gathering

Serves 20

Ingredients

- 2 cans of evaporated milk (800g)
- 250g sugar (to your taste)
- 1 large carton (450ml) double cream
- 200g ground almonds
- 4 pints full cream milk
- 150g rice flour
- 2 tsp vanilla, 3 cardamoms ground
- 100g pistachio nuts chopped

Method

1. Warm the full cream milk. Warm the rice flour separately.
2. Boil evaporated milk and sugar for 5 minutes. Add the warmed full cream milk.
3. Add 3 tbsp milk to the rice flour and make into a paste. Then add it to the rest of the milk and stir. Reduce the heat slightly and stir and cook for 3-4 minutes. Keep stirring.
4. Add almonds and the double cream. Bring to boil and simmer.
5. Heat until the mixture becomes thick (appx 20 minutes).
6. Add vanilla, chopped pistachio nuts and cardamom.
7. Pour into a tray and freeze.
8. After 3 hours take out of the freezer and whisk with a fork and refreeze.
9. Leave at room temperature for about 10 minutes before serving.

Kesari

Sweet with semolina)
Cooking time: 30-45 minutes

Ingredients

- 1 cup semolina (coarse)
- 2 cups sugar or little less depending on your taste
- 2 cups water, if required use a little bit more
- 250g butter or 150g ghee
- 5 cardamoms roasted and crushed
- 70g cashew nuts chopped and roasted
- 60g sultanas
- pinch of salt (few grains)
- deep-based heavy frying pan, large chopping board or plate

Method

1. Roast semolina in a frying pan. Add 2 tsp butter to this and roast until it turns a golden colour. Leave it on a plate.
2. Pour 2 cups of water into the pan and bring to boil. Add a pinch of salt and reduce the heat.
3. Stir in the semolina little by little, keep stirring until the semolina absorbs the water and it is cooked. If water is not sufficient add a little hot water from your kettle.
4. Stir for 5 minutes and then add the rest of the butter and keep stirring/folding so that butter is mixed well (if using ghee use a little less than the butter).
5. Then add the cardamoms, cashew, and sultanas.
6. Finally, add the sugar in small quantities and stir. Once it is mixed well and leaves the sides of the pan, it is ready to be spread onto a dish which is lightly buttered.
7. Leave for few minutes and cut into diamond or square pieces.

★ Served at parties either before or after the main meal.
For crunchiness use the grit/coarse semolina. For a soft consistency try with fine semolina.

Cheese Cake - (Lemon/Mandarin)

Ingredients

- 200g cream cheese
- packet of lemon or orange jelly
- 1 can evaporated full cream milk (400g)
- 200g can of mandarin oranges
- 1 tsp of grated rind of lemon
- juice of a lemon
- 75g butter
- 125g digestive biscuits
- 2 tbsp sugar (optional for base)
- 2 tbsp sugar for the jellly
- 2 tbsp marmalade

Method

1. Place the evaporated milk tin in a pan of water, boil it for 15 minutes and then leave it in the freezer for about 2-3 hours.

2. Prepare the base by mixing butter and crushed biscuit with sugar. Press into a loose bottomed round tin and leave it in the fridge.

3. Mix jelly as per packet instructions using the sugar and a bit less water. Leave it in the fridge to cool for few minutes.

4. Mix the lemon rind and cream cheese with the jelly. Whisk well.

5. Beat the evaporated milk in an electric beater, using a whisk blade, till it is thick and creamy.

6. Then add the jelly mixture, whisk and pour over the cheesecake base and leave in the fridge to set.

7. Once set transfer to a dish. Arrange the mandarin pieces around the edge and brush the middle with marmalade.

Lemon Curd Sweet

Ingredients

- 1 cup of scraped coconut
- 150g sugar
- 3 tbsp self raising flour
- 2 egg whites
- 1 tsp vanilla
- 1 small carton of lemon curd 200g

Method

1. If using desiccated coconut, add a little milk to make it moist.
2. Beat the egg whites separately.
3. Mix all ingredients in a bowl and then add the egg whites.
4. Grease cup cake trays or muffin tins.
5. Place a dessert (or an icecream scoop) spoonful in each, do not flatten the top.
6. Bake in hot oven 160-180°C for 15 minutes.

★ Remove and serve hot.

Mango Ice Cream Kulfi - 3

Ingredients

- 1 tin condensed milk (405g)
- 1 tin full cream evaporated milk (400g)
- 450g whipping cream
- 2 cans mango pulp (950g)
- 75g pistachio nuts, chopped
- 2 tsp vanilla flavouring
- ½ tsp almond flavouring

Method

1 Place the evaporated milk in a bowl and whip to double the quantity using a hand whisk or an electric whisk.

2 Whip the whipping cream separately.

3 Add the mango pulp and whipping cream to the milk and whisk for a minute or two. Add the other ingredients.

4 Pour the mixture into a box and freeze for 3-4 hours.

5 When partially frozen, remove from the freezer and beat well again.

6 Pour into two or three small boxes and freeze.

7 Take out about 5 minutes before serving.

Mango/Orange Dessert

Preparation: Prepare the jelly on the previous day
Cooking time: 25 minutes.

Serves 4-6

Ingredients

- 1 can sliced mango (400g) or a large fresh mango
- 1 packet of orange jelly
- 500g double cream
- 100g toasted chopped cashew nuts
- 4 tbsp sugar

Method

1. Make the jelly, adding the sugar and allow to set overnight.
2. Slice the mango and cut into cubes.
3. Beat the cream and mix with the mango cubes.
4. Break up or cut the jelly into small pieces.
5. In individual stemmed glasses spoon the crushed jelly and over it the mixed cream with mango.
6. Top it up with roasted cashew nuts.
7. Leave in fridge and serve.

★ Best if prepared (on the day) a few hours before serving.

Marshmallow

Ingredients

- 30g gelatine (1 sachet)
- 500g caster sugar
- 2 cups water
- pinch of cream of tartar
- colouring/vanilla/rose essence, few drops
- icing sugar/cornflour for dusting

Method

1 In a pan add sugar and dissolve it in one cup of water and simmer on low heat.

2 Dissolve gelatine in one cup of hot water. Add this to the sugar syrup in the pan, bring to the boil.

3. Add the cream of tartar, keep stirring over low heat. You will know that it is ready when you raise the spoon to a height and the liquid drops like a thin hair.

4. Pour into a bowl and beat with a whisk or beater (preferably electric) until the mixture is frothy and thick.

5 Add the colouring, vanilla or rose essence, beat again, pour into a buttered dish and leave in the fridge to set.

★ Cut into squares and dust in icing sugar or mixture of icing sugar and corn flour.

Musket

Preparation & cooking time: 1 hour and 30 minutes

Ingredients

- 500g corn flour or semolina
- 750g sugar
- ½ cup ghee
- 250g chopped cashew nuts
- ¼ cup of water for syrup
- 3 cups water to soak the corn flour
- muslin cloth

Method

1. Mix the corn flour with three cups water and leave for 30 minutes for the corn flour to settle to the bottom. Strain the water using a muslin cloth (save the corn flour).

2. Mix sugar with ¼ cup of water and heat for 15 minutes.

3. Add the strained corn flour starch in small quantities and keep stirring over a low heat.

4. When the mixture gets thick and is begining to leave the sides of the pan add cashew nuts. Add ghee and keep stirring.

5. Pour the thick mixture into a tray and flatten the top with a oil paper.

6. Leave to cool and cut into squares.

Mysore Pahu (Indian Sweet)

Very crunchy and melts in the mouth

Ingredients

- 120g sieved gram flour
- 250g caster sugar
- 250g butter or 200g ghee
- ½ cup water
- ¼ tsp crushed/ground cardamom

Method

1. Melt the butter or ghee and leave it aside.

2. In a pan add the sugar and water, bring to boil until all the sugar is dissolved and the syrup is ready (when you spoon it from a height it should drop like a thread).

3. When the syrup is ready add half the melted butter and mix well.

4. Add one tablespoon of gram flour and stir. Then alternate by adding the butter and another tablespoon of the gram flour.

5. Keep stirring constantly so that it does not catch the sides or burn.

6. Add the cardamom. When the mixture leaves the sides and resembles a honey comb pour it on to a buttered dish .

7. **<u>Do not flatten</u>** the top, gently shake the tray (once) to get a smooth surface.

8. Cut into squares before it sets hard.

Fluff - Mousse (Pineapple or Peach)

Preparation time: One day ahead
Setting time: 5-6 hours

Serves 10

Ingredients

- 1 tin full cream evaporated milk (carnation 410g)
- 200g caster sugar
- 1½ sachets of gelatine
- green food colouring
- 2 tsp vanilla flavouring
- 1 medium tin of pineapple rings or can of peaches (375g)
- 3 tbsp roasted chopped cashew nuts
- few chocolate drops
- large glass (transparent) bowl

Method

1. Boil the unopened evaporated milk can in a pan of water for 15-20 minutes.
2. Freeze the can overnight.
3. Next morning leave the can out for about 10 minutes and open.
4. Empty this into a bowl, whisk using an electric beater for 5-10 minutes until the mixture becomes fluffy and creamy.
5. Add the sugar and continue whisking; do not let the creamy consistency go down. Add the colouring and flavouring.
6. Prepare the gelatine as on the packet instructions. Always add the gelatine to hot water and mix well, let it cool
7. Cut the pineapple or peaches to small cubes and leave it aside.
8. Add the gelatine to the beaten milk and mix gently with a spoon to ensure the gelatine is mixed. Do not run the beater as it will ose its fluffiness.

9. Pour some of the mixture to cover the base of a glass bowl which should be brushed with melted butter. Sprinkle in some of the fruits, then pour the rest of the mixture.
10. Finally sprinkle the rest of the fruits.
11. Leave in the fridge for 5 minutes. Take out and sprinkle the cashew nuts and chocolate drops. Leave to set.

★ **Coffee Mousse**

Instead of the pineapple substitute 2-3 tablespoon coffee powder and 3 tablespoon rum. Omit the vanilla and colouring.

Mix coffee in a little hot water and use this to prepare the gelatine. Add to the beaten sugar and milk. Pour into a dish and leave in the fridge to set.

Mango

Mango is a tasty fruit alternative to the pineapple.

Purple Yam - (Rasavalli Kilangu)

Preparation & cooking time: 1 hour

This is a famous sweet in Jaffna, sometimes served for breakfast too. Can be prepared easily and is a good dessert dish. The yam can be purchased from Sri Lankan or Indian shops.

Ingredients

- 1 Rasavali yam, say about 1kg
- 250g to 300g white sugar
- 420g evaporated full cream or coconut milk (1 can)
- water
- 4 cardamoms crushed
- salt - few grains

Method

1. Cut the outer hard skin of the yam. The surface of the yam is not smooth and it is difficult to use a peeler. Need to use a sharp knife.

2. Once peeled, wash and thinly slice the yam into thin pieces and not chunks.

3. Place the cut pieces in a heavy-based saucepan, add 1½ mug of water. Bring to boil, add the few grains of salt ,reduce the heat to low and cook for about 20 minutes. Stir and check so that the yam does not get burnt.

4. Add the sugar and milk and cook for a further 5 minutes until it thickens.

5. Using a potato masher, mash the yam to make sure there are no pieces.

6. Allow to thicken a bit and remove from fire, you may pour this on a plate and allow to settle; cut up into squares and serve or pour into individual small pudding dishes and allow to set.

★ Coconut milk makes the difference. If using cow's milk, add 2 tbsp coconut powder to 2 tbsp of milk or water to make a paste and then add it with the milk as the coconut gives a unique taste.I would strongly recommend that you try this recipe.

Awal for evening tea - (Rice flakes)

This is tasty and healthy to have for evening tea instead of biscuits Also prepared as a dish during religous festivals and functions.

Preparation & cooking time: 30 minutes
Serves 6

Ingredients

- 2 cups of red rice flakes (awal) available from Sri Lankan shops
- 1 cup of scraped coconut or
- 1 cup of desiccated coconut soaked in 4 tbsp milk
- 1 cup of soft brown sugar
- pinch of salt

Method

1. Wash the red rice awal in water two or three times to remove any husk, stones etc.

2. Leave for 5-10 minutes in water.

3 Drain the water, leave in a colander and add few grains of salt.

4. In a large bowl mix the sugar and coconut.

5. Stir the awal and mix well.

6. Serve in small bowls and have with tea.

Snow Balls

Ingredients

- 3 sachets gelatine (90g)
- 500g sugar
- 3/4 pint water
- 3 tsp lemon juice or any essence
- 125g desiccated coconut
- 125g melted chocolate for coating

Method

1. Soak the gelatine in ½ pint of water.
2. Boil the sugar in remainder of water for about 10 minutes.
3. Add soaked gelatine and boil for further 20 minutes.
4. Cool slightly. Flavour with lemon juice or essence.
5. Whisk until stiff; if needed use an electric beater.
6. While still warm form into balls with damp hands.
7. Drop into chocolate coating and roll in desiccated coconut.

Sweet Diamond Rotti

Ingredients

- 250g plain flour
- 125g soft brown sugar or sakkarai
- ½ coconut scraped or 100g desiccated coconut moistened with a little milk
- few drops vanilla essence
- 6 pods cardamoms, crushed
- pinch of salt, water to mix the flour

Method

1. Mix the flour with a little water and a pinch of salt. Knead like you would do for pastry/chapattis

2. Take a portion and roll it out to ½ cm thick and cut to small square or diamond shapes.

3. In a saucepan boil some water and drop these pieces in. Cover for a few minutes; when cooked the pieces will come to the surface.

4. Take them out with a draining spoon and leave aside on kitchen paper.

5. In a bowl put a few of the cooked pieces, add a bit of sugar, coconut, cardamoms and essence. Mix and serve.

★ Deep fry the pieces in oil and allow to drain on kitchen paper. Prepare syrup with 125g white sugar and 5-6 tbsp water. When the syrup is ready (drops in a thread like consistency), add the coconut and the fried rotti. Stir and serve.

Kalu Dodal - (Sweet Dish)

A famous sweet prepared in Sri Lanka with a vague similarity to Turkish delight.

Ingredients used in the traditional way include lots of coconut milk extracted from fresh coconut, rice and jaggery

Not a dish to be prepared by the faint hearted.

In the up-country in Sri Lanka you would get these wrapped in coconut palm leaf in the shape of a cucumber. Sometimes you can see ladies seated on the roadside preparing this sweet.

Ingredients

- 500g red raw rice
- 3 tins of coconut milk (375g each) or milk from 3 coconuts
- 1kg soft brown sugar or jaggery
- 250g white sugar
- pinch of salt
- 100g cashewnuts, chopped

Method

1. Soak the rice for three to four hours in water. Wash and dry for 10 minutes. Grind, sieve and keep it aside.

2. Prepare the coconut by scraping and then extracting the milk by using a liquidiser. You need to use warm/hot water for this. Strain and repeat two or three times and keep the milk separate as 1st, 2nd and 3rd.

3. Chop the cashew nuts.

4. If using jaggery you need to grate the jaggery by using a kitchen vegetable/cheese grater.

5. Add the 1st and 2nd coconut milk to the ground rice and mix well without any lumps; use a hand blender. If required use a bit of the 3rd milk.

6. Transfer the milk and rice to a heavy-based saucepan, bring to a boil, reduce heat and cook on a low flame.

7. When the mixture begins to thicken add the sugar or jaggery and stir well. Keep cooking.

8. After 5 minutes add the chopped cashew nuts and keep stirring until the mix leaves the sides of the pan.

9. Pour into a greased flat dish. The mixture shoud be 2cm thick. Leave to cool and cut into squares and serve.

Treacle Tart

Ingredients

- 200g short crust pastry
- 2 tsp grated lemon rind
- 2 eggs beaten
- 4 tbsp golden syrup
- 30g butter
- 4 tbsp single cream
- 125g small carton of double cream and piping nozzle

Method

1. Roll pastry thin. Line a round or pastry dish. Prick the base of the pastry in two or three places and bake for 5 minutes.
2. Mix the lemon rind and golden syrup. Warm this in a microwave for one minute (or heat in a pan).
3. Beat the egg and leave it aside.
4. Mix butter in the warmed syrup.
5. Add the cream and beat well.
6. Mix the beaten egg.
7. Pour into the flan case and bake for 30 minutes at 180°C.
8. Decorate with piped double cream and serve.

★ Can add 2 tbsp semolina to above and bake.

Tropical Fruit Fool

Use combination of mango and passion fruit or mango and pineapple or pawpaw.

Fresh fruit is tastier, but can use tinned fruits as an alternative.

Ingredients

- 2 mangoes
- 4 passion fruits
- 1 carton double cream 475g
- 3 tbsp caster sugar
- 4 tbsp of roasted chopped almonds or cashew nuts

Method

1. Skin the mango and cut up into small pieces. Scoop the inside of the passion fruit, take the seeds out and mix with the mango. Use a hand blender to blend the fruits.

2. Beat the cream very thick adding the sugar at the same time.

3. Gradually add the mixed pulp and fold it in (do not beat). Pour into small individual glasses and refrigerate until ready to serve .

4. Add chopped nuts before serving.

Turkish Delight

Preparation: 20 minutes
Setting time: 2 hours
Makes 30 pieces

Ingredients

- 2½ sachets of gelatine (75g)
- 500g of caster sugar
- 1 cup of water
- ½ tsp rose water
- 1 tsp butter to brush the dish
- food colouring (green)
- icing sugar for dusting
- 2 tsp of corn flour for dusting (optional)

Method

1. Mix gelatine in little water and leave it aside.
2. Melt sugar in 1 cup of water and bring to boil; remove from heat.
3. When the sugar is fairly hot add the gelatine little by little and keep stirring.
4. Add green colouring and essence.
5. Brush butter to the sides and bottom of a rectangular baking tray or dish (30cm x 20cm).
6. Pour the mixture and leave it in the fridge to set.
7. Once set, cut into square pieces and dust with icing sugar make sure that the pieces are fully covered.
8. If it is sticky add the corn flour to the icing sugar and cover/dust the pieces.

Vaiyppan

Similar to a small doughnut with no jam. Made with self raising flour and sugar for an evening tiffin, something to have whilst watching TV. I prepare the plain and everyone likes these and it gets finished soon.

For Plain Vaiyppan

Ingredients

- 500g self raising flour
- 250g caster sugar made into syrup with ½ cup of water
- pinch of salt
- water to mix
- oil for deep-frying

Method

1. Mix all the above to form a dough; if watery use some flour and knead, leave for 15 to 30 minutes.
2. Take small amounts and roll in your palm to form small balls, a bit smaller than golf balls. You may use a bit of flour to dust your fingers so that they do not get sticky. Prepare about 15 and place them on a plate.
3. Heat the oil and when it is hot, drop in at least 10 to 15 balls at a time. Cook at medium heat, remove when they turn golden brown.
4 Drain on kitchen paper and serve. Try and make the balls small, as they will swell up when you fry, and the inside will be well cooked.

★ If the colour changes quickly, reduce the heat slightly, but you require a certain amount of heat to fry. You may microwave a plate of cooked vaiyppans for 30 seconds.

★ Can add 60g of desiccated coconut, 60g semolina or a little rice flour to the mixture, knead and fry.

★ **Traditional Sri Lankan method:** It is made with mashed banana, sugar and flour mixture. Add two ripe bananas to the ngredients in the above recipe and leave for 30 minutes, then follow step 2 onwards and deep fry.

Vattilappam

This is a famous pudding prepared at Ramadan festival

Traditional preparation is with jaggery and coconut milk

Ingredients

- 500g jaggery, grated
- 10 eggs
- 2 mugs of thick coconut milk (375g each)
- 1 tsp freshly grated nutmeg
- 1 tsp vanillaessence

Beat the eggs lightly to make it frothy. Add the jaggery to the milk, warm it so the jaggery dissolves. Strain this and mix it with the egg. Add nutmeg and vanilla and steam for 1 to 1½ hrs.

I have amended the recipe to use alternatives available in the UK. It tastes equally good. A dish everyone should have a go at making and tasting.

Preparation & cooking time: 1hour and 20 minutes

Ingredients

- 8 eggs
- 300g soft brown sugar
- 400g (1 tin) full cream evaporated milk
- 4 tbsp coconut powder or a (375g) can of coconut milk
- ¼ pint cows milk
- 1 tsp of freshly grated nutmeg
- 1 tsp vanilla
- baking dish according to quantity
- 15 roasted, chopped cashew nuts

Method

1. Place the eggs and sugar. Beat the eggs and sugar in an electric beater.
2. Then add the full cream milk and run the electric beater for few seconds.

3. Warm the cow's milk, add the coconut powder and mix this to a thick paste.

4. Add this to the beaten egg/sugar milk mixture, then add the vanilla and nutmeg.

5. Pour the mixture into a buttered baking dish (rectangle or square). Top it with chopped cashew nuts and a bit of grated nutmeg.

6. Place the dish in a tray of water or leave a tray of water in the oven. Bake in a preheated oven for 20 minutes at 165°C, then reduce to155°C and bake for 40 minutes.

7. When cooled to room temperature leave in the fridge for 6-7 hours before serving.

8. Leaving for a full day in the fridge would taste even better.

★ This is a very rich dish and you only serve small portions.
★ Can add 3-4 tbsp of golden syrup and reduce a little bit of sugar. Steam in a covered container for about 1 to 1½ hours.

Eggless Vattilappam 1

Recipe with gelatine

Ingredients

- 500g jaggery scraped (can use soft brown sugar)
- 2 tsp vanilla
- ¼ tsp freshly grated nutmeg
- 60g gelatine (2 sachets)
- 400g full cream evaporated milk
- 1 cup of coconut milk or can (375g)
- 25 cashew nuts roasted and cut lengthwise in half

Method

1. Prepare the gelatine as per instructions on the packet and leave it aside.

2. In a pan add the grated jaggery or sugar, coconut milk, evaporated milk and bring to boil until the sugar is dissolved.

3. Reduce the heat and cook for 10 minutes. Remove from heat and add the gelatine and vanilla.

4. Pour into a square or oval shaped clear glass dish. Sprinkle on the grated nutmeg. Leave it in the fridge.

5. When half set arrange the sliced cashew nuts.

6. Serve when it is set.

Eggless Vattillappam 2

Ingredients

- 375g coconut milk (1 tin)
- 100g soft brown sugar
- 150g dark brown mascavada sugar
- 400g full cream evaporated milk
- small cup of fresh milk (½ pint)
- 1 to 2 teaspoon of grated nutmeg (fresh)
- 1 packet of caramel dessert powder
- 20 cashew nuts

Method

1. Mix the sugar and evaporated milk, beat this together with the coconut milk.

2. Prepare the caramel powder with milk as stated in the packet. Bring to boil and remove from heat. When luke warm add this to the above mixture. Add nutmeg and keep a bit for topping.

3. Pour the mixture in to a baking dish and sprinkle the rest of the nutmeg, cashew nuts and bake for 30 minutes in a preheated oven at 170°C.

4. Remove from the oven (it will look a bit watery) and when cooled to room temperature leave in the fridge to set.

★ You may use jaggery from Sri Lankan shops instead of the sugar.
★ Caramel dessert can be bought from supermarkets.

Green Gram/Moong (With Coconut & Sugar)

(Known as Payarru thuvaiyal in Sri Lanka)

Ingredients

- 1 cup whole seed green gram(175g)
- 1 cup soft brown sugar (125g)
- ½ cup grated coconut (50g)
- 4 cardamoms crushed
- ½ tsp bicarbonate of soda

Method

1. Over a medium flame roast the green gram in a pan for a few minutes and then soak it in water for 3 hours adding ½ tsp of baking soda.

2. Wash and boil in water for 15 minutes. Drain the water. Make sure it is cooked, but not too soft. Leave it to cool.

3. Mix the coconut, half the sugar, and the cardamom. If required, add all the sugar.

4. Mix it with the cooled boiled green gram, add four or five grains of salt. Either run it in an electric beater for a minute or mash it using a potato masher.

5. Make small balls the size of golf balls and arrange it on a plate.

★ A healthy dish for a Sunday evening tiffin and easy to make

Kollukattai

Shaped like a small Cornish pasty

A traditional sweet dish from Jaffna. Prepared with jaggery - (sakkarai)
This is also made for a family gathering when a baby has had the first two teeth showing. Arrange a day when the baby is able to sit up properly.

Sit the baby in a safe place on a clean sheet/cloth or mat. Cover the baby's head with a white cloth and any family member, usually the head of the family, will drop the kollukattai over the baby's head gently and allow it to fall on to the mat.Then take the cloth off and allow the baby to take and bite into the kollukkattai.

Avoid cardamom in the filling of the kollukkattai to be given to the baby.

Before steaming press a small coconut pieces into a few kollukkattai to resemble teeth.

Ingredients

- 2 cups roasted red rice flour
- ½ cup plain flour (steamed and sieved)
- boiling water to make the dough
- ½ tsp of salt
- 2 tbsp oil

For the filling

- 1 cup split roasted moong dhal
- 150g soft brown sugar or scraped jaggery
- 1 cup scraped coconut/desiccated coconut
- 2 tsp ground cardamom
- 2 tbsp milk to mix the desiccated coconut
- 4 string hopper mats
- steamer

Method

1. Wash the dhal in water and boil in 2 cups of water. Once the water has evaporated and the dhal is cooked, remove from the heat and spread the boiled dhal onto a plate.

2. If using desiccated coconut mix this in 2-3 tablespoon of warm milk or water.

3. Add the coconut to the cooled dhal. Add sugar or scraped jaggery and mix. Add the crushed cardamom (avoid cardamom in baby's kollukkattai).

4. Mix the two flours and add ½ tsp of salt. Add the hot water little by little and mix the flour with the handle of a wooden spoon. Mix well to form a dough, add ½ to 1 tsp of oil and make into a smooth dough.

5. Leave the rest of the oil in a saucer. Take about 2 tbsp of dough and make it into a ball. Coat your fingertips with a little oil.

6. First flatten the dough. Then using your fingers and thumb mould (move) the dough in between the fingers to form a cup.

7. Add one tablespoon of filling into the dough, bring one side over and cover, pressing the edges together. Then slightly curve the edges and do this all round the edge.

8. The finished edge will look like a scallop. Place three on each string hopper mat. Place the string hopper mat with the kollukattai in a steamer and steam for 5-10 minutes. Prepare three more and keep on another mat.

9. Remove from the steamer and slide onto a plate. Place the other mat in the steamer and steam.

★ Nowadays you can obtain a plastic mould, which is also used to make patties pastry. Continue from point 5, add the filling and close the mould. Remember to oil the mould.

Sweet Coconut Pancake

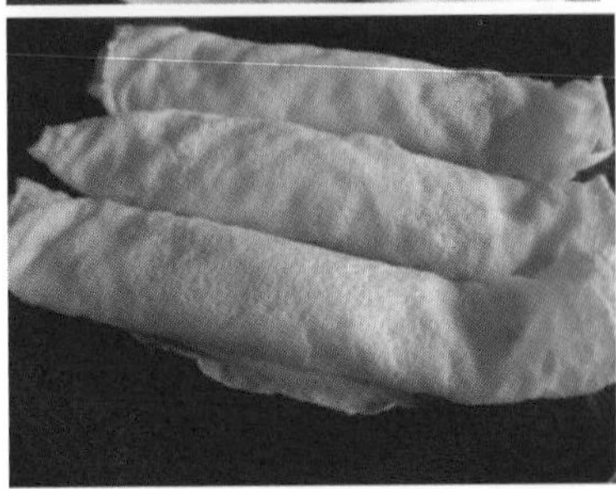

Ingredients

- 400g coconut milk (1 tin)
- 125g rice flour
- 100g plain flour
- 2 eggs (optional)
- 200g sugar
- 100g desiccated coconut
- little water if needed

Method

1. Sieve the flour and make a batter with milk egg and sugar.
2. Beat well with a hand blender or fork.
3. Add the desiccated coconut and mix well. If too thick use little water.
4. Heat a frying pan or a griddle. Brush or wipe the surface with little oil.
5. Pour one large spoonful of batter and quikly swirl it or spread with the back of the spoon to make a circle.
6. Cook both sides, remove and leave on a plate. Pour another pancake and whilst this is cooking roll the first one and serve hot.

Variations

Children like different colours so you may divide the batter and use different colouring. Make into smaller circles, roll and arrange the different colours on a serving plate.

- ★ If you have not got an oil brush you may use a piece of cotton cloth dipped in oil to clean the surface.
- ★ Can omit the eggs.
- ★ Worth having a heavy-based non stick pan or an iron griddle which will retain the heat.

Payasam

Sweet dish given at functions/weddings after a vegetarian meal

Serves 10

Ingredients

- 200g sago
- 150g sugar
- 2 cups water
- 1 can evaporated milk or coconut milk (400g)
- ½ can condensed milk (125g)
- 20 cashew nuts split in half and quartered
- handful of sultanas
- 4- 5 cardamoms roasted and crushed
- 2 tbsp butter
- pinch of salt

Method

1. In a pan roast the sago in one tablespoon of butter and set it aside.
2. In a large saucepan put the sago, add the water and slowly bring to boil.
3. Cook for about 15-20 minutes; keep stirring, as the sago will form lumps.
4. When the sago grains become glassy add the sugar and stir.
5. Add salt and the evaporated milk.
6. Bring to boil and add the condensed milk
7. Whilst the above is cooking, in another pan add a little butter and roast the cashew nuts to slightly brown, add the sultanas and remove from heat. Add it into the cooked payasam. Finally add the crushed cardamoms.
8. The mixture should not be too watery, but slightly thick. Serve warm in a bowl.

Payasam - (Variations)

Pal Payasam with rice (milk payasam)

Ingredients

- 2-3 pints of fresh milk
- 1 cup of sugar
- ½ cup white rice (pudding rice)
- 1 cup water to cook the rice
- cashew nuts chopped
- 1 tsp butter/ghee to roast the cashew nuts
- few cardamoms crushed/ground
- pinch of salt
- 200g condensed milk
- handful of sultanas (25)

Method

1. Cook the rice in water, when partially cooked add half the fresh milk, pinch of salt and cook.

2. When the rice is well cooked, mash it well and add the sugar, rest of the milk and bring to boil.

3. Add the condensed milk, cardamom seeds and the roasted cashew nuts.

4. Heat for about 2-3 minutes.

5. Serve warm in tumblers to drink or use a spoon.

Ravai Laddu (semolina)

Sweet, crunchy melts in your mouth.
Preparation & cooking time: 30 minutes

Ingredients

- 250g semolina (roasted)
- 250g white sugar (ground)
- 1 tsp freshly ground cardamom
- 100g roasted cashew nuts, chopped
- ¼ cup melted ghee or butter
- ½ cup of milk

Method

1. Heat a frying pan and roast the semolina, add the sugar and roast until slightly brown, it takes about 8 minutes. Add the cardamom and stir it well. Similarly roast the cashew nuts in little ghee, chop and leave it aside.

2. In a pan warm the melted ghee, add the semolina mix, cashew nuts and stir well.

3. Heat the milk and add this little by little to the above mixture and mix until the mixture forms into a ball. You may not need all the milk add just enough to bind.

4. Remove from cooker, whilst hot take a little mixture at a time and form small balls. Leave to cool and serve with tea.

Coffee Pudding with Dates

Ingredients

- 250g self raising flour
- 250g butter
- 225g caster sugar
- 3 eggs
- 225g chopped dates
- ½ tsp bicarbonate soda
- ½ cup boiling water
- 2 tsp coffee granules
- 1 tsp vanilla essence
- 50g cashew nuts
- 1 carton double cream (200g)
- 200g soft brown sugar

Method

1. Soak the dates in ¼ cup boiling water adding the bicarbonate soda. Leave it for four hours
2. Sieve self raising flour and leave it aside.
3. Mix the coffee in 2 tablespoons of hot water.
4. Beat caster sugar with 200g butter until creamy.
5. Beat the eggs separately and gradually add it to the butter cream, at the same time adding a spoonful of sieved self raising flour.
6. Add coffee, vanilla essence and the crushed dates to the batter to make it creamy.
7. Grease a large pudding bowl or a removable base cake tray. Pour the batter and bake in a preheated oven at 160°C for 30-35 minutes.
8. Heat brown sugar in a saucepan, add the rest of the butter, half the double cream and the chopped cashew nuts. Heat until the syrup is sticky.
9. Turn the baked cake upside down onto a serving plate and pour the syrup over. Whip the rest of the cream and serve.

★ When baking leave a tray of water on the lower shelf of the oven.

Susiyam

Very simple and easy to prepare

Ingredients

- 1 cup channa dhal (kadala parupu)
- 1 cup grated coconut or dessicated coconut
- 1 cup sakkarai - jaggery or sugar
- 4 cardamoms ground
- 1 cup plain flour
- pinch of salt
- oil for deep frying

Method

1. Roast the channa dhal in a frying pan and leave it to cool.
2. Parboil the cooled dhal in plenty of water, drain the water and spread the dhal on a tray or dish over a paper towel to remove any excess water.
3. Place the dhal in a blender and semi grind it for few seconds. Transfer to a bowl. Add the coconut and jaggery. Add the crushed cardamom seeds, pinch of salt and mix. The texture should be crumbly and not soggy (no water to be added).
4. Take small amounts (3 tsp) and roll into small balls and set aside.
5. Prepare a thick batter with the flour adding water and pinch of salt.
6. Heat oil in a pan.
7. Take the balls one by one, coat with the batter and deep fry in oil.
8. Remove and leave on kitchen paper towel and serve.

★ Prepare the balls soon after mixing as the jaggery has a tendency to make the mixture soggy. If it does, leave in the freezer for 10-15 minutes and then prepare, adding a touch of gram flour.

In South India some use thosa batter (rice flour and urad flour) to dip the balls and deep fry.

Sweet Buns/Scones

Ingredients

- 250g strong white flour
- 250g self raising flour
- 1 tsp mixed spice
- 1 tsp salt
- ½ tsp grated nutmeg
- 5 fl oz natural yoghurt
- 150g caster sugar
- warm water to mix
- 1 egg
- 50g butter
- few cherries cut up or a handful of dried mixed fruit

Method

1. Sift the flours, add salt and spices
2. Rub in the butter until the texture looks like bread crumbs.
3. Add the caster sugar and the egg.
4. Add yoghurt and warm water to bring the mixture to a soft dough but not too sticky.
5. Knead for 2-3 minutes.
6. Sprinkle the dried fruits and mix well, divide into 10-15 small balls.
7. Place the buns on a baking tray.
8. Oil a cling film sheet and cover the tray with this.
9. Leave in a warm place for the bun to double in size.
10. Heat oven to 180°C and bake for 15 to 20 minutes.

To serve:

When warm cut the scones in half and fill with double cream or jam and whipped cream

Option:

Can use butter milk instead of yoghurt.

Milk Toffee

A famous Sri Lankan toffee equivalent to noughats
Cooking time: 30 - 45 minutes

Ingredients

- 1 tin of sweetened condensed milk (400g)
- ½ tin of water (use above tin)
- 1 cup of sugar
- few drops vanilla essence
- 65g butter
- 100g roasted cashew nuts

Method

1. Into the pan empty the condensed milk. Add ½ cup of water to the tin, stir and empty into the pan.

2. Add sugar and stir well and cook on a medium flame.

3. Add half the butter (so that it does not stick to the bottom). Keep stirring. It will take about 25 to 30 minutes for the mixture to thicken.

4. In the mean time chop the cashew nuts.

5. When the mixture gets thick and leaves the sides of the pan, you will see some bubbles forming (mixture begins to leave the side and base). Add the vanilla and cashew nuts. Remove from cooker.

6. Pour the mixture on to a buttered tray and flatten it (be careful it will be hot) with the back of a spoon or a piece of oilpaper.

7. When it is half set cut into squares and leave it on the tray to set for another 15 minutes.

★ You could get about 45 pieces

Salads

Salads - Index

Beetroot Salad

I prefer to use fresh beetroot as I do not like the vinegar taste in the boiled beetroot available in supermarkets. Fresh beetroot with the leaves is tastier. If you have time you should try this in the summer when it is available.

Preparation & cooking time: 15 minutes

Serves 5

Ingredients

- 2 medium beetroots (fresh or boiled)
- 3 medium shallots, finely sliced
- 1 green chilli (optional) cut lengthwise
- 4 or 5 tbsp of thick natural yoghurt
- salt to taste
- 1 clove garlic grated
- 1 large tomato

Method

1. If using fresh beetroot, clean the outside and boil with the skin for 10 minutes in a pan of water. Alternatively you can microwave by placing in a bowl, prick with the fork in two or three places, cover and cook for 3 to 4 minutes depending on the size of the beetroot and the oven power. Leave to cool; peel the skin and cut into thin slices.

2. In a bowl mix the sliced onions, beetroot and tomato. Add the garlic, salt, yoghurt and green chilli. Mix well and serve.

★ You can add one grated carrot and salad leaves too.
It is tasty with fried rice.

Mango Salad

A dish prepared for special functions.

Preparation & cooking time: 15 minutes

Serves 4-6

Ingredients

- 1 medium green mango
- 100g grated coconut, 1 cup
- 4 green chillies,chopped
- salt to taste
- 2cm ginger
- 1 clove garlic
- 1 medium red onion, chopped,
- 3-4 curry leaves, chopped fine

Method

1. Cut the skin and chop the mango into small pieces.
2. In an electric blender put the salt, 2 green chillies, garlic, ginger, the mango pieces and grind.
3. Then add the coconut and grind. If necessary add a little water to make it easier to grind. Blend to a paste.
4. Dish out and add the finely chopped onions, the rest of the green chillies and the curry leaves.

★ Skin the mango and grate it on a carrot grater or chop it to very fine cubes. Grate the ginger and add it to the mango. Add salt, onions, chopped green chillies and mix.

Sambol

Preparation & cooking time: 15 minutes

Serves 6

Ingredients

- 1 cup scraped fresh coconut (100g)
- 6 dried red chillies or 2 tsp of crushed red chilli powder
- salt to taste
- small piece of ginger (optional)
- 6-8 curry leaves, chopped
- ½ lime, ¼ cup water
- 3 shallots, sliced

Method

1. If you are going to grind the dried chillies, first crush them in the blender (you may need to add a little water).

2. Add all the ingredients except the onions and lime juice. Run the blender for a few minutes, add water as required and grind the coconut and chilli. Then add the chopped onions and run the blender for a minute.

2 Serve into a bowl, add the lime juice and curry leaves. Stir well or mix using your fingers so that the lime juice is mixed well.

★ Can be eaten with bread/naan/thosai etc.

★ If you are going to use desiccated coconut, soak this in a little milk for 5 minutes and then follow the recipe.
Frozen scraped coconut can be purchased.

Salad with Fresh Vegetables

Ingredients

- 1 cucumber
- 3-4 radish
- 2 celery sticks
- 1 tsp salt
- 1 sprig of coriander leaves chopped
- 1 green chilli (optional)
- pinch of chilli powder, pepper powder and cinnamon powder

Method

1. Slice the salad vegetables finely.
2. In a bowl mix the yoghurt with cinnamon, chilli, pepper powder, salt and water.
3. Add the sliced vegetables. Leave in the fridge to chill and serve.

Fresh Bean Salad

Ingredients

- 250g french beans
- 2 green chillies chopped fine (optional)
- 1" size ginger grated
- 1 small tin boiled channa dhal (200g)
- 1 lime
- 1 cup grated coconut
- salt to taste
- one sprig of coriander leaves chopped

Method

1. Cut up the beans to 1" pieces. Cook in boiling water for 2 minutes, drain, rinse in cold water and then put the beans on a kitchen paper and leave in the fridge.

2. Wash the dhal and put this in boiling water for a minute. Drain and leave it in the fridge.

3. In a bowl mix the chopped chillies, grated ginger, coconut, salt, boiled channa dhal and the beans. Squeeze the lime and mix the juice into the salad.

4. Toss it, add coriander leaves and leave in fridge until serving

Pasta Salad

Ingredients

- 2-3 tomatoes
- ½ cucumber
- 1 small can boiled channa dhal (200g)
- 1 packet spiral pasta, 150g
- 2 green chillies cut lengthwise
- 3-4 broccoli florets
- 3-4 small potatoes, boiled and peeled
- few spring onions, chopped

Dressing

- vinaigrette - 4 tbsp
- fresh lemon - 2 tbsp
- salt, black pepper
- chopped parsley
- 4 tbsp soft fromage frais

Method

1. Boil the pasta, drain and leave aside.

2. Steam the broccoli florets or microwave for 2 minutes. They should remain crunchy.

3. Cut the cucumber and tomatoes into small pieces. Add the green chillies, dhal, broccoli, potatoes, spring onions and pasta.

4. In a separate dish mix all the dressing ingredients and whisk. Pour this over the salad, sprinkle with salt and pepper. Chill and serve.

Aubergine Salad (Traditional)

Ingredients

- 1 large aubergine
- 5 red onions/shallots, chopped
- salt to taste (1 tsp)
- 4 tbsp Greek yoghurt
- 1 green chilli, chopped finely
- 1 tsp oil to brush the aubergine
- oil for deep frying

Method

1. **Baking:** Prick the whole aubergine's skin in one or two places. Brush the outside with a little oil and bake this in the oven at high temperature for 20 minutes.

2. **Grilling:** Place the oiled aubergine under a hot grill. Keep turning the aubergine until the outer skin shrinks and the inside is soft and cooked (6-7 minutes).

3. **Deep fry**: Cut the aubergine into half lengthwise and then cut again to get four pieces. Heat the oil in a deep pan and deep fry the aubergine until the outside is brown and it is cooked (about 4 minutes).

4. Leave to cool and then peel off the skin, take the inside flesh and chop into small pieces.

5. In a bowl add the chopped onion, chilli, salt and yoghurt and mix well. Mash the aubergine using the back of a spoon or potato masher and add this to the onion and yoghurt mixture and mix well. Add a bit more yoghurt if needed.

★ This dish is served with rice on special occasions.

Salad Dish for a Party

Preparation & cooking time: 45 minutes

Serves 20

Very important to cut the ingredients finely, as it is then easy to serve and eat with a fork. You can use a slicer/shredder to cut.

Ingredients

- 1 green, 1 red pepper, 1 yellow pepper
- 1 cucumber, 3 tomatoes
- 4 sticks from a celery bunch
- 1 medium cos lettuce
- 1 gem lettuce
- 2 x 260g ready cut crispy salad leaves (optional)
- 1 small purple cabbage
- 6 radishes
- 3 carrots
- 1 bunch of watercress leaves

Method

1. Wash and cut the stalks of the peppers, clean the insides and slice them into thin strips, then chop to very fine small cubes. Leave them in a bowl.
2. Do the same for the tomatoes, cucumber and leave them in separate bowls.
3. Scrape the skin off the radishes and carrots. Grate these using a grater/shredder.
4. Similarly the red cabbage can be grated too. Cut the salad leaves into fine pieces to match the rest of the ingredients. Mix all the chopped salad items in a large bowl and leave it in the fridge.
5. Prepare the dressing shown overleaf and add to the salad just before serving.

Dressing Ingredients

- 2 cloves garlic grated or 1 tsp garlic paste
- 2 tbsp white vinegar
- 2 tbsp virgin olive oil
- 2 tbsp freshly squeezed lime/lemon juice
- ½ tsp of salt, pinch of turmeric
- ½ bunch of watercress leaves, chopped and liquidised
- 1 tsp each of black pepper seeds and mustard seeds. Grind into a fine powder.
- 1 or 2 tsp water to mix all the above

Using a blender liquidise the garlic and watercress to form a paste then add the remainder of the ingredients and then the lemon juice. Run the machine for a few minutes and pour this over the salad, toss it and leave it ready to serve

★ If you cannot get all of the above then use what is available and two spoons of any mild salad dressing from the supermarkets. You can include 3 tablespoons of Greek yoghurt as an alternative.

★ Try the lemon, watercress dressing and light French dressing together with a little garlic paste, ground pepper, mustard and salt

★ It is best to add the dressing just before serving. Otherwise the salad will become watery.

★ In the summer, salad should be prepared on the day. If you cut the peppers early leave this in the fridge

Variations

★ Before serving you can add some croutons/vegetarian fried bacon chips (soya) to the salad.

★ Can add 10 chopped shallots to the mixture.

★ Can add green chillies, usually I leave them halved so that they are visible.

★ Can add roasted chopped cashew nuts (check if anyone is allergic)

★ Can add ½ cup of boiled split peas or red beans together with few chopped coriander leaves.

Couscous Salad

Ingredients

- 1 cup couscous
- 2 cups warm water or little bit more
- ½ cucumber
- 3 celery sticks
- 7 spring onions
- 3 shallots chopped
- 2 tomatoes cut into fine slices and diced
- ½ green pepper, chopped into cubes
- ½ red pepper, cut into cubes
- few sprigs of coriander leaves chopped
- lemon juice
- 1 small mango grated (raw green)
- 1 tsp of dill seeds
- 2 tbsp olive oil, 2 tbsp vinegar
- salt and pepper
- 1 green chilli, cut lengthwise

Method

1. Soak the couscous in water and leave it for 20 minutes.
2. Then add the dressing, lemon juice and grated mango. Make sure that there are no lumps. Mix well and leave aside.
3. Cut the salad vegetables and mix it with the cous cous a few minutes before serving.

★ Serve as a side dish with rice.
Can add chopped nuts, red beans.

Cucumber and Dill Salad

Ingredients

- ½ cucumber
- small carton Greek yoghurt
- salt/lemon/grated garlic
- black pepper
- 1 tsp dill seeds
- 1 red onion
- 1 green chilli

Method

1. Scoop the inside of the cucumber and cut/slice into small cubes.
2. Chop the onions, mix with garlic, yoghurt, salt, dill seeds, green chilli and pepper. Leave it in the fridge until serving.

★ Can add crisp lettuce, spring onions, 2 cloves of grated garlic and coriander leaves.

Papaw Salad

Ingredients

- 1 green (raw) papaw (available in Indian shops)
- 100g thin beans
- 2 tbsp crushed peanuts
- 1tsp garlic granules
- 1 large red onion
- 15 mange tout
- small cucumber
- 4 tomatoes
- salt to taste
- salad dressing vinaigrette, 2 tbsp vegetarian bacon chips
- lime or lemon juice

Method

1. Skin a small papaw; grate this after taking the seeds out. Leave in water for 5 minutes.

2. Chop the beans to one-inch size and boil for 5 minutes in boiling water. Pour the water away and rinse in cold water.

3. Cut up mange tout finely to matchstick size pieces.

4. Put tomatoes in boiling water for a few seconds, take out and remove the skin. Chop it into quarters

5. Grate the cucumber after scooping the inner portion out.

6. Drain the papaw; squeeze the water out, mix with tomatoes, beans, mange tout, salt, garlic granules and lime or lemon juice. Can add salad cream or vinaigrette dressing.

7. Sprinkle on the peanuts and the bacon chips.

★ Serve with rice or naan bread.

Potato Salad

Ingredients

- 6 small potatoes boiled and peeled (or 2 large potatoes)
- 3 shallots or one red onion, finely chopped
- 1 green chilli, chopped (optional)
- 1 small tub fromage frais
- 2 tbsp natural yoghurt (optional)
- ½ tsp grated fresh ginger
- 1 small carton single cream or milk
- ½ tsp freshly ground pepper, chopped chives
- any salad dressing you like
- vegetarian bacon chips (can be bought in super markets)

Method

1. If using small potatoes, you may leave them whole or halve them. Large potatoes should be cut into small cubes. Leave in a bowl.

2. Add the finely cut onions, ginger, green chilies and fromage frais to the potatoes and mix well.

3. You may need to add more milk or cream to get the mixture correct.

4. Finally sprinkle the chives and bacon chips over the mixture, cover and leave in fridge before serving.

Salad with Fruits - (From Karnataka)

Ingredients

- 1 apple
- 10 green grapes
- 10 cherry tomatoes
- 2 shallots
- 1 tub natural yoghurt
- 3 tsp oil for frying
- 1 tsp mustard seeds
- ½ tsp cumin seeds
- pinch of asafoetida powder
- 2 red dried chillies, chopped
- 3-4 curry leaves cut up
- salt

Method

1. Cut the tomatoes in half, cut the apple into small triangular pieces with the skin on. Wash the grapes.

2. Transfer the cut up fruits into a bowl with the grapes. Add the chopped shallots, yoghurt and salt. Mix well

3. In a frying pan heat the oil, add the mustard seeds and when these start to pop, add the chopped red chillies, cumin, asafoetida and the curry leaves. Remove from heat and quickly pour it over the yoghurt mixture and mix.

Raita

Prepared with yoghurt, water, spices and either with a cooked vegetable or fresh salad vegetables. This is a popular dish of India. If served with hot curries then Raita balances out the heat and makes the dish milder.

Ingredients

- 1 aubergine (medium size)
- 350-400 ml pot of Greek style yoghurt (full set)
- 5-6 tablespoon of water (optional)
- 1 tsp oil

Tempering ingredients

- ½ tsp cumin seeds
- ½ tsp mustard seeds
- 3-4 curry leaves
- 1 tbsp ghee or butter
- 1 tsp salt
- 1" size ginger (grated)
- 2 sprigs of coriander leaves chopped (optional)
- 3 shallots or a red onion, chopped
- 1 green chilli, chopped

Method

1. Prick the skin of the aubergine brush with oil and bake in a preheated oven for 15-20 minutes at highest temperature (make sure it is cooked). Allow to cool and peel the skin.
2. Cut the pulp into small cubes. Mash this; add the chilli and chopped shallots.
3. Beat the yoghurt, salt, grated ginger and coriander leaves. Add water if you feel the yoghurt is too thick. Place this in a glass bowl.
4. In a frying pan, put some ghee and fry the cumin, mustard seeds and curry leaves. Quickly add this to the yoghurt mixture.
5. Add the aubergine and give it a stir and mix it well. The consistency should be fairly thick but watery enough to spoon more yoghurt than the aubergine.

★ Here you serve more yoghurt and less of the aubergine which is different from the Sri Lankan aubergine sambol.

Red Onion Salad

Ingredients

- 2 large red onions
- juice of half a lemon or ½ tsp of vinegar
- 2 green chillies sliced lengthwise or finely chopped
- ½ tsp freshly ground black pepper
- salt to taste
- 4 large eggs boiled shelled and cut into quarters

Method

1. Peel the onions, cut into rings or slices. Add salt, lemon juice or vinegar, chopped chillies and ground pepper.

2. Mix the above well.

3. Place the onions on a flat dish and arrange the cut up eggs around the edge.

★ Can leave the eggs out. Add 1 tsp lime pickle instead of the vinegar and lemon

★ Used as a side dish for bhiriyani rice, fried rice or rotti (naan).

Fried Bitter Gourd for Salads

Ingredients

- 1 medium bitter gourd or two small ones
- few shallots
- salt
- lime juice

Method

1. Wash and slice the bitter gourd across like cutting cucumber slices. Remove the seeds.
2. Put in salted water and leave for few minutes. Rinse and pat dry.
3. Deep fry in oil until slightly crispy. Remove and place in a colander.
4. Mix with chopped shallots, salt and lime juice.

Optional

Deep fry the bittergourd and sprinkle salt and chilli powder and serve as a fried side dish.

Dips
Chutney
Sambal

Dips - Chutney - Sambal - Index

Pickle - Acharru - 1

Ingredients

- 20 small red onions or pickling onions
- 10 small green chillies, each slit half way up lengthwise.
- 2 large carrots, cut into thin strips
- 1 small papaya (optional) (peel the skin and cut into thin strips like carrots)
- 15 string beans cut into 1" length
- 10 small cauliflower florets
- 1 small cup vinegar
- 3cm piece ginger, 6 cloves garlic, ground to a paste
- 2 tbsp black mustard seeds, ground
- 1 tbsp black pepper, ground
- pinch of turmeric
- salt to taste
- 2 tsp ground cinnamon and cardamom
- 10 cashew nuts, ground
- 3 red chillies, ground

Method

1. Place the peeled onions and other vegetables in a colander and immerse this for 2 minutes in a pan of boiling water.
2. Take out and put it into a glass bowl.
3. Add two tablespoon of the vinegar to the ground mustard seeds, and mix into a thick paste.
4. Add the other ground ingredients and mix, spread the paste over the vegetables.
5. Whilst hot, add just enough vinegar to hold the paste together with the vegetables. Do not create a watery consistency. Cover with a plate.
6. Bottle it and keep turning the bottle so that the vinegar and vegetables are well covered.

★ Can be served the next day.

Apple Chutney

Ingredients

- 5 cooking apples
- 4 dried chillies, chopped
- 1 tsp coriander seeds
- 2 tbsp oil
- 2 tbsp urad dhal
- 1 tsp fenugreek seeds.
- a pinch of mustard seeds, turmeric powder
- salt to taste
- 1 clove garlic
- ½ tsp asafoetida powder

Method

1. Peel the cooking apples and chop into small pieces.
2. Heat a frying pan, add 1 tablespoon of oil, add the dried chilli, garlic, coriander, fenugreek and asafoetida and roast for few minutes.
3. Remove from heat and let it cool. Grind using a mortar and pestle, adding salt and turmeric powder.
4. Purée the apple using a blender, add the ground powder and liquidise.
5. Heat the pan, add oil, add the mustard and urad dhal and fry for a minute until golden in colour.
6. Add the liquidised mixture, heat it for a few seconds and remove from heat.

★ This can be kept in the fridge and used for a few days.

Chilli Relish

Ingredients

- 1 red pepper
- 1 onion, diced
- 3 garlic cloves chopped or 1 tsp of paste
- 6 tomatoes
- 1 tsp plain chilli powder
- 1 tsp ginger paste
- salt to taste
- 2 tsp vinegar
- ½ tsp cinnamon powder
- 3 bay leaves
- 2 tbsp oil

Method

1 Place the tomatoes under a grill and cook for 1-2 minutes. Skin the tomatoes and cut into small cubes.

2 Fry the onions in the oil, add the cut up pepper and tomatoes. Add all ingredients and cook until very soft. If you have big pieces then you may use a hand blender for 30 seconds to blend.

3. If you want you can remove the bay leaves.

★ Serve in a dish and eat with bread or savoury finger food.

★ Do not put the tomatoes in hot water to remove the skin, as it will become soggy.

★ Ground crushed chillies can be added.

★ Chilli with garlic and ginger paste can also be added.

Chilli & Onion Sambol (Sinhalese preparation - Lunu miris)

Ingredients

- 2 dried red chillies or 2 tsp of crushed chilli powder
- 1 tsp salt
- 2 shallots, diced
- juice of half a lime
- 3 curry leaves, finely cut

Method

1. Grind chilli, salt and onion in a blender.
2. Add lime juice and curry leaves.
3. Mix and serve.

★ Can mix with your fingers, for this you add crushed chillies and dice the onions fine. Takes few minutes to prepare.

Katta sambol (Another preparation)

For this you do not grind the above ingredients but mix it well, you may need to use your fingers to rub well. Mix all chilli, finely chopped onions, lime juice, salt, curry leaves and serve.

In Sri Lanka this is one of the famous side dishes served with breakfast or an evening meal when you have plain hoppers, string hoppers, bread milk rice etc. Traditional dish includes maldive fish (see non-veg section for additions to this). I have omitted this here.

Clarified Butter (Ghee)

Ingredients

- 1 kg butter
- 3 bay leaves
- muslin cloth/cheese cloth
- strainer with fine net

Method

1. Place the butter in a heavy-based saucepan and melt it on a low heat.
2. Increase the heat and allow the melted butter to boil
3. Add the bay leaves and continue to heat on medium heat for 20 minutes.
4. Froth will appear on the surface. Scoop the froth with a spoon.
5. Reduce the heat slightly. You will see some particles settling on the bottom of the pan.
6. After 30 minutes, remove the pan from the cooker.
7. Slightly cool and drain the ghee through a cheese cloth or double muslin cloth placed in a colander. Allow to cool.
8. Pour the clear liquid ghee into a jar and keep.

★ Can be kept for a month or two.
Serve ½ tsp ghee with hot rice and dhal.

Date Chutney

Ingredients

- 125g dates, chopped
- 1 onion,chopped
- 2 cloves garlic
- 2 cm ginger
- 3 green chillies
- 2 tbsp sugar
- 1 tsp of mustard seeds
- 2-3 tbsp vinegar
- 1 large piece of lime from lime pickle
- 1tsp salt
- 1 tsp mixed cardamom and cinnamon powder

Method

1. Grind the mustard seeds in an electric grinder and set aside. Then grind the ginger, garlic, onion and green chilli using a mortar and pestle or a blender. Add the powdered mustard and a little vinegar and mix.
2. Add chopped dates, salt, sugar and the chopped pickle
3. Mix well with a dry spoon and leave it in a dish

Variations

Can add the following vegetables to the above

- 2 carrots, cut up to thin strips of 1"
- 2 capsicum chillies, cut to 1" strips
- 125g beans, sliced to 1"
- 3 onions, diced small

1 Cut the vegetables and add to the above ground paste.
2 Add a little bit more spices and extra spoon of vinegar according to your taste.
3 Mix and leave it for a day before serving.

Dip (Garlic and Quark)

Ingredients

- 250g quark (soft white cheese)
- 250g crème fraiche
- 1 tsp freshly ground pepper
- salt to taste
- 1 shallot, finely cut
- 1 tsp lemon juice
- 3 cloves grated garlic or garlic powder
- chopped herbs (coriander, watercress/cress)
- 1 tsp of worcester sauce or any salad dressing
- ½ tsp chilli paste

Method

1. Beat the quark and crème fraiche. Add the salt, garlic, chilli paste and herbs. Add the lemon and salad dressing, dish out and serve.

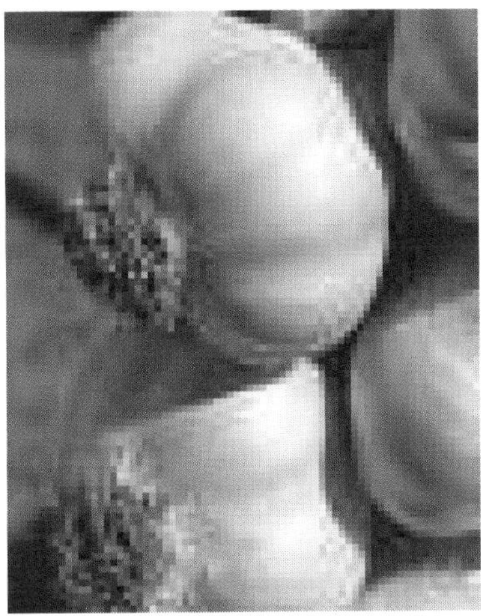

Dip - Yoghurt with Cheese

Ingredients

- 250g thick set yoghurt, small tub
- 2 small onions, chopped
- 125g cream cheese
- salt, fresh ground pepper and coriander leaves, or chopped chives and parsley

Method

1. Beat the yoghurt and cheese and add all other ingredients and beat well.

2. Add seasoning and refrigerate until serving.

★ Serve with crisps, hot potato or boiled tapioca pieces.

★ Can add chopped green chilli and chives or any seasoning you prefer.

Ginger Sambol (Traditional)

A dish prepared on special occasions and functions
Preparation: 20 minutes
Serves 6-8 as a side dish

Ingredients

- 3 cm root ginger
- 2 tsp mustard seeds
- little milk
- 2 green chillies, finely cut
- salt to taste
- 5-6 curry leaves, chopped fine
- ½ lemon
- ½ coconut scraped or desiccated coconut
- 3 shallots or a red onion chopped ino small cubes

Method

1. Scrape the skin off the ginger and grate this.
2. Grind the mustard seeds. Add ginger and salt*.
3. Add the coconut and grind for a couple of minutes.
4. Remove from the blender, add the chopped onion, chilli, lemon juice and curry leaves.
5. If using desiccated coconut, add a little milk and leave it for 10 minutes before grinding.

★ If you haven't got a blender you may like to crush the mustard seeds using a mortar and pestle. Then mix the ingredients using your fingers to rub into the coconut. Add lime and leave in the fridge until ready to serve.

★ Adding salt at the start makes it easier to grind ginger.
It gives us an idea of the water content before adding the coconut.
But some like to add the salt and lemon last.

Green Chilli Sambol

Same as for red chilli roasted Sambol with slight variations.
Preparation & cooking time: 20 minutes
Serves 4-5

Ingredients

- ½ coconut scraped
- 4 or 5 green chillies
- 1 tsp salt
- 1 clove garlic
- 1 tsp fresh grated ginger
- 1 to 2 tsp lemon juice (1/4 lime or lemon)
- 2 shallots, chopped finely
- few curry leaves, finely cut
- 2 to 3 tbsp water

Method

1. Put all the ingredients except the curry leaves, onions and lemon juice into an electric blender and grind it to a paste. You may need to use little water.

2. Add the curry leaves, onion, lemon juice and mix with a spoon.

3. Serve in a dish

★ If you want to make into a chutney, heat 1 tsp oil add the tempering ingredients - mustard, cumin, urad and curry leaves (see roasted red chillli sambal), fry and add ¼ cup of liquid (milk and water). Bring to boil, add the ground sambol and stir it.

Hot Chilli oil

Ingredients

- 2 medium onions, chopped
- 1 tsp ginger paste
- 1 tsp garlic paste
- 1 tsp mustard seeds, ground
- 8 red dried chillies
- salt to taste
- 1 tsp sugar
- 3-4 tbsp vinegar
- 2 tbsp oil

Method

1 Mix the garlic, ginger, mustard, chilli powder, salt and 2 tbsp of vinegar.

3. Heat a pan and add 1 tbsp oil and fry the onions. Add the above paste and stir fry.

4. In a blender, grind all the onions and the paste. If needed, add a bit more of the vinegar and grind. Add the crushed chillies.

5. Add 1 tbsp oil and mix well, store in a jar until required.

★ Have it with noodles, rice etc.
Can add ¼ tsp of the paste to noodles when you prepare the noodles.

Pol Sambol (Sri Lankan)

With coconut. A quick preparation

Ingredients

- 1 cup of grated coconut (half coconut)
- 2 tsp crushed red chillies*
- 2cm ginger, grated
- 1 clove garlic, chopped
- 2 tsp lemon/lime juice from ½ lemon (fresh)
- salt to taste
- 2 red onions, chopped
- 1 sprig curry leaves, chopped

Method

1. In a bowl mix the salt, ginger, garlic, coconut and crushed chilles. Mix well and add the lemon juice.

2. Add the onions, curry leaves and mix well with your fingers until the coconut turns red and the chilli is mixed well with the coconut.

3. Set aside to have with red rice, rotti etc.

★ If using desiccated coconut add 2 tbsp of warm milk to ½ cup of coconut and leave it aside for 15 minutes.
Some supermarkets now stock frozen scraped coconut

Roasted Coconut Sambol/Chutney

Serves 6-8

Recipe is for freshly scraped coconut. If you are going to include desiccated or frozen, see notes for Pol sambol.

Ingredients

- ½ coconut, scraped
- 5 dried red chillies
- 1 tsp salt
- 1 clove garlic
- 2 tbsp split channa or split green gram dhal
- ½ tsp asafoetida powder
- 1 tsp tamarind paste, mixed in little water
- 2 shallots, chopped
- few curry leaves
- few coriander leaves (optional)
- 2 to 3 tbsp water

Tempering/Seasoning

- 1 tsp mustard seeds
- 1 tsp cumin seeds
- few curry leaves
- 1 tbsp oil

Method

1. In a frying pan, slightly roast the red chillies (can also microwave), then add the dhal and the coconut and roast this until slightly brown.
2. Put all the ingredients except the curry leaves and onions into an electric food grinder or liquidiser and grind it to a paste. You may need to add some water (2-3 spoons).
3. Finally add the curry leaves and onion. Run the machine for a few seconds. Remove and set aside.
4. For seasoning heat the oil, add the mustard seeds and when it starts popping add the cumin and curry leaves. Remove from cooker and pour this over the sambol and mix it.

★ **Used as a side dish with thosa, idli, naan or even bread.**

Savoury Soup (Puli-Kanji Vegetarian)

Preparation & cooking time: 45 minutes
Serves 2

This is a good dish to have when you are recovering from flu or having a cold and have no appetite for food. It is nourishing and tasty.

Ingredients

- 75g rice (basmati)
- 3-4 cups water
- salt to taste, 1 tsp
- ½ cup milk
- 2 small shallots, chopped
- 3 green chillies, chopped (optional)
- 3 cloves garlic and 2cm ginger, crushed
- 1 fresh lime or 1 tsp tamarind paste
- ½ tsp corn flour
- ground pepper to taste

Vegetable to use

- 250g fresh spinach, small leek and 1 carrot - finely cut
- 4 strands of coriander leaves, a small pak-choi
- 1 bunch of vallarai leaves from Sri Llankan shops or a few herbs
- lemon basil - "sweet genovese", watercress
- 2 tbsp coriander seeds, 1 tsp pepper corns, 1 tbsp cumin seeds, pinch of turmeric powder. Crush these using a mortar and pestle or grind in a blender adding little milk

Method

1. In a large pan boil rice adding 2 cups of water. After 5 minutes add the vegetables, onion, green chillies and continue to cook for another 8-10 minutes.

2. Add the ground ingredients mixed in a little milk and tamarind.

3. Let it boil and add the corn flour mixed in the rest of the milk. Cook for a few minutes and remove from heat and have it whilst hot.

★ You may spoon the cooked vegetables and either squash it with a masher or blend for 10-15 seconds in a blender so the cooked vegetables would be half solidified. Then mix it with the cooked soup add ground pepper and have it.

★ If you are planning to use lime, instead of the tamarind, it is added last after removing from the heat. Squeeze the juice of the lime and add it just before serving.

★ Can add seafood, see recipe in the non-veg section.

Seeni Sambol - (A traditional dish of Sri Lanka)

Ingredients

- 6 medium red onions (can use normal onions too)
- 2 dried red chillies, chopped
- 4 tbsp oil
- 2 sprigs of curry leaves, cut finely
- salt, 1 tsp
- ½ cup thick coconut milk
- 2 tsp ground plain chilli powder
- ½ tsp garlic paste
- ½-1 tsp tamarind paste
- 1 tsp freshly ground cinnamon
- ½ tsp cardamom powder
- small piece rampe, cut up
- ½ tsp of sugar

Method

1. Peel and slice the onions finely, then cut diagonally to appx 2cm length pieces.
2. Heat oil in a heavy-based frying pan, add the onions and fry on medium heat for 5 minutes. Add the red chilli pieces and salt.
3. When the colour changes to golden brown, add the coconut milk, garlic paste, tamarind, crushed chilli powder and ½ tsp of sugar. Cook until the onions begin to dry up and have less water content. Add chopped curry leaves and rampe.
4. Stir once, add the cinnamon, cardamom and remove from heat. Remove from the cooker.

★ **Use as a spread on bread/toast, hoppers/naan**
It can be kept in the fridge for a week or two.
Can keep in a jar for a longer period but ensure it is cooked well and has no water content.
Looks like a chutney but the taste is spicy, hot and slightly sweet.

For non-vegetarians add two tablespoons of ground Maldive fish or dry prawns to this and cook (can purchase the Maldive fish from any Sri Lankan shop).

Acharru (Pickle) -2

This is one of my favourite dishes, a good side dish for parties.

For a party - serves 20

Ingredients

- 250g shallots or similar red onions from Sri Lankan shops
- 2 carrots
- 100g thin french beans
- 1 small cauliflower (crunchy)
- 10 cashew nuts, 3 tbsp peanuts
- 175g fresh green chillies or bullet chillies
- 50g dates; add ½ tsp bicarbonate of soda and a little water to soften the dates.
- 1 tbsp freshly ground spice (4cm cinnamon, 6 cardamom, 3 cloves)
- 3 tbsp mustard seeds (grind it fresh)
- small bottle of pickling vinegar
- salt to taste 1 tsp
- 4-5 red chillies, 1 tsp coriander seeds, 2 green chillies, 1 tsp each ginger and garlic paste
- 1 tbsp urad dhal

Method

1. Soak the dates in a little water and bicarbonate of soda for about two hours, then chop and liquidise the dates.

2. Peel and clean the onions, halve these and quarter the large ones.

3. Clean the carrots and cut into small sticks slightly thicker than a matchstick.

4. Cut the beans to a similar size.

5. Clean cauliflower and separate into small florets.

6. Slit the chilli lengthwise from the tip towards the stem, or if using bullet chillies, quarter these.

7. Next, in a grinder, grind the mustard seeds and leave it aside. Then grind the cashew nuts and peanuts, add the other dry spices and grind.

8. Mix in the ground mustard and the other ground spices. Add the dates too.

9. Pour about ¼ -½ cup of vinegar into a bowl, add the dates, mustard and all other ground powder to form a slightly thick paste.

10. Place the cut up vegetables into a large glass bowl, add the paste and stir it well. Cover and leave it aside. The thick paste should cling and hold on to the vegetables.

11. For the first few hours keep turning the vegetables and paste every half hour or so.

12. On the next day you can transfer into a glass bottle and keep rolling the bottle so that the paste is distributed evenly. This should be ready to eat in 2 days.

★ If you want it for the same day you may steam or par boil all the vegetables for 2 minutes and add to the paste.
It is tastier when it is crispy and crunchy.

★ 1 small green papaw (optional), but it may not be available throughout year.

Aubergine Chutney

Ingredients

- 2 large aubergines (12cm long)
- 1 tsp each of the following spices: cumin seeds, fenugreek seeds, coriander seeds, mustard seeds, urad dhal
- 8 dried red chillies
- salt to taste
- ½ tsp turmeric powder
- 2 or 3 tbsp oil
- 1 tsp tamarind paste

Method

1. Apply a little oil to the skin of the aubergine and grill this.
2. Skin the aubergine and mash this slightly.
3. Roast all the dry spices in a frying pan and grind it finely in an electric grinder.
4. Mix this with the aubergine, turmeric, tamarind and salt. Using a blender blend this into a paste.
5. Finally add the chopped coriander leaves and serve with rice.

Hints

Instead of grilling you can cook the aubergine over the gas flame of the cooker, using skewers or a fork to turn the aubergine.

It will have a better taste if it is barbecued. If none of these can be done you may cut in half and deep-fry in oil, remove the skin and take the pulp.

Chutney (Onion and Chilli)

Ingredients

- 2 onions
- 3 tbsp oil
- 2 dried red chillies, chopped
- 1 tsp tamarind
- 5-6 curry leaves

Method

1. Chop onions and fry until golden brown, add the chillies and the curry leaves. Grind it in a blender adding tamarind and salt.

★ Serve as a side dish.

Chutney (Channa dhal) from South india

Ingredients

- 120g channa dal
- 1-2 tsp ghee
- 7 green chillies
- ½ coconut scraped
- salt to taste, 3 shallots chopped, 1 sprig curry leaves,
- 1 sprig coriander leaves
- 2 tsp mustard seeds

Method

1. Grate the coconut and grind it with the green chillies, salt and the fried dhal.
2. Heat a pan, add ghee and fry the mustard seeds, then pour the hot ghee and the mustard seeds over the ground chutney. Add the cut curry leaves, chopped coriander leaves and stir once .
3. Serve with tamarind rice, savoury rice, thosa or idli.

Dhal Chutney

Ingredients

- 3 tbsp urad dhal
- 3 tbsp split channa dhal
- 3 tbsp split moong dhal
- 3 dried red chillies
- 1 onion chopped
- 5-6 curry leaves
- 1 tsp salt
- 1 tsp tamarind paste

Method

1. Roast the dhal in a frying pan.
2. Grind this with the chillies in a blender, add salt, chopped onion, tamarind and run the blender for a minute, serve with rice or chapattis. If necessary add 1 tbsp water to make it easy to grind.

Another Coconut Chutney (dry)

Ingredients

- ¼ cup urad dhal
- ¼ cup toor dhal
- 1 tsp asafoetida powder
- ½ tsp mustard seeds
- 1 coconut scraped or use 1½ cups of desiccated coconut
- 4 dried red chillies
- salt to taste
- 1 tsp ghee
- 1 tbsp oil

Method

1. In a frying pan, heat the oil add the mustard seeds, chillies, dhal and asafoetida until it becomes dry and reddish in colour and dish it out.

2 In the same pan, add the ghee and the scraped coconut (or desiccated coconut) and try and dry roast without any water.

3 Using a dry blade of a blender, grind all these together including the salt.

4 Store in a bottle and it will keep for a week or two.

★ Serve with thosa, idli, bread etc.

Can serve dry or add 1 tsp of the powder to few drops of melted ghee, mix and serve.

Garlic Butter/Garlic Bread

Ingredients

- butter 125g
- garlic paste or garlic granules 3-4 tsp
- 1 french stick
- foil

Method

1. Mix butter in a bowl until soft, add the garlic granules and mix.
2. Cut up a french stick diagonally, apply this butter liberally onto each slice. Wrap it in foil and bake in a preheated oven at the highest temp 190°C for 10 minutes.

★ Can use any variation of chopped herbs, parsley with garlic.

Carrot Chutney

Ingredients

- 3 large carrots, grated
- 3 tbsp desiccated coconut or fresh scraped coconut
- 3 tbsp milk (to soak desiccated coconut)
- 2 cloves garlic
- 3 green chillies (to taste)
- 1 sprig curry leaves cut up finely
- 1 tsp oil and 2 tsp mustard seeds for garnishing
- salt to taste, 2 tsp lemon juice.

Method

1. Soak the desiccated coconut in milk and set aside for 5 minutes.
2. Wash and clean the outside skin of the carrots and grate it.
3. Grind the carrots, garlic, green chillies and coconut into a paste. Milk should be sufficient to grind and no need to add any water.
4. Transfer into a dish and add the chopped onions.
5. Heat oil in a pan and add the mustard seeds and curry leaves. Pour the fried ingredients over the ground chutney. Add lemon juice and stir it.

Ginger Chutney

Ingredients

- 5cm root ginger
- 5 dried red chillies
- 2 tsp tamarind paste
- 1 tsp each fenugreek, coriander, mustard seeds
- ½ tsp asafoetida powder
- 2 tsp urad dhal
- 1 tsp vinegar
- salt to taste
- 1 tsp sugar
- little oil

Method

1. Roast all ingredients in a little oil.
2. Add the salt and tamarind. Place in a blender and grind into a paste.
3. Add 1 tsp sugar and the vinegar.

Green Banana Chutney

Ingredients

- 1 large green banana
- salt
- 1 medium onion, chopped
- 1 clove garlic, chopped
- 1 cup desiccated coconut soaked in milk or scraped fresh coconut
- 2 tsp crushed chilli powder
- 5-6 curry leaves,
- ½ tsp lemon juice

Method:

1. Steam the banana or boil with the skin. When the banana is just cooked and not mushy, remove and peel the skin and discard this.

2. Chop the banana pulp into small pieces. Add the salt, crushed chilli powder, onion, garlic and all other ingredients. Grind for a few seconds using a grinder.

3. Dish it out and before serving, add ½ tsp lemon juice and mix well.

Hummus (Chickpeas)

Ingredients

- 1 can boiled chickpeas (400g)
- 4 tbsp sesame seeds, ground
- juice of 1 lemon
- 1½ tsp ground cumin and pepper
- 1 tsp garlic paste
- salt to taste
- chives/parsley, chopped
- 2 tsp olive oil

Method

1. Open the can of chickpeas and empty into a pan of hot water.
2. Drain the water and leave in a colander.
3. In a blender, put the chickpeas, ground sesame, garlic, salt and blend it into a thick paste.
4. Add lemon juice, cumin and pepper mix, chopped parsley and chives and olive oil. Stir well and serve as a dip.

★ Add 4 tablespoons of Greek yoghurt to the above; this is also tasty.

★ If you like it hot, add two fresh chillies/hot pepper and blend.

Sambol Chutney - a side dish

South Indian preparation

Ingredients

- 2 cups grated fresh coconut (½ coconut)
- 1/3 cup gram dhal (pottu kadalai)
- 4-5 green chillies
- 1 tsp salt
- 1 tsp tamarind paste or ½ lime
- 1 tbsp peanut peeled, crushed
- 4 sprigs of coriander leaves
- 2 tbsp water
- **For garnishing:** 1 tsp oil, 1 red chilli, chopped up, ¼ tsp mustard seeds, ¼ tsp cumin seeds, 4-5 curry leaves finely chopped, pinch of asafoetida powder

Method

1. In an electric blender, grind all the ingredients except for the items of garnishing.
2. Add a little water so that the machine does not clog up and grinds smoothly.
3. It should be well ground into a paste without any big particles. If needed add a little bit more water but do not make it too watery.
4. Serve it onto a serving dish. If using lime, squeeze the lime into the mixture and mix well.
5. Heat oil in a frying pan or thava, add the mustard seeds, cumin, chilli, curry leaves and pinch of asafoetida. Pour this over the sambol mixture and give one stir with a fork.

★ Serve with naan bread, thosai, idli, uppuma, vadai and rice Pongal (see the recipes).

Sweet Chilli Sauce

Ingredients

- 2 cloves garlic
- small piece ginger
- 4 red chillies
- alt to taste
- 1 tsp soya sauce
- 1 tomato

Method

1. Liquidise all the ingredients in a blender to form a paste.
2. Leave in a dish and serve.

★ Tasty with noodles, rice, any savoury rice, or when you are grilling any vegetables spread this on and grill.

Thaniya Chutney - Coriander Chutney

Ingredients

- bunch of coriander leaves
- 2-3 mint leaves
- 1 apple skinned
- salt to taste
- 1 tsp brown sugar
- 2 green chillies
- 2 cloves garlic
- small piece of ginger
- 1 tsp tamarind paste or juice of one lime
- 2 tbsp water

Method

1. Cut the apples into small pieces, wash and towel dry then do the same with the coriander leaves.
2. Grind all the items into a paste. Add little water if you want.
3. Serve in a bowl to have with samosas, dhokla and any other snacks.

★ Can freeze the ground chutney.

Tomato Chutney

Ingredients

- 1kg tomatoes
- 3 tbsp chilli powder
- 2 tsp salt
- 250g sugar
- 4 fl oz vinegar
- garlic cloves 4
- ginger 4cm size
- 3 cloves, 3 cardamoms
- 2cm cinnamon ground to a powder

Method

1. Put the tomatoes in boiling water for 10 minutes.
2. Take out and peel the skin.
3. Put the pulp into a blender and liquidise with garlic, ginger and salt.
4. Add the chilli powder.
5. Boil the sugar and vinegar in a large pan, add the puréed tomatoes, and ground cinnamon, cardamom and cloves.
6. Bring to a boil and cook until the texture is thick.

Vallarai Sambol (1)

Vallarai leaves (available from Sri Lankan shops)
The substitute in the West could be watercress.
This is supposed to be good if you have a cold.

Ingredients

- 1 bunch of vallarai leaves, washed individually
- 2 small shallots peeled and chopped
- 3 dried red chillies
- ½ cup scraped coconut or desiccated coconut
- ½ tsp tamarind paste
- 2 cloves garlic
- little butter or ghee

Method 1

1. Drain the washed leaves, cut about two inches of the stalk off.
2. In a pan, heat the butter, add the leaves and cook for a few minutes.
3. Add the dried chillies, coconut, salt, tamarind and other items, stir until it is cooked, but the leaves retain the green colour.
4. Remove from the cooker and allow to cool.
5. Put the above into a blender and blend it to a paste. You may need to add a little water but not too much.
6. It will be a green soft paste.

★ Can serve with rice. This is very good if you have a cold.

Vallarai Sambol (2)

Ingredients

- 1 bunch vallarai leaves
- 3 shallots, chopped fine
- 2 green chillies, chopped
- 2 tbsp scraped fresh coconut
- salt to taste
- lemon juice

Method 2

1. Wash, cut the stalk off and finely cut the leaves. Add the chopped onions, chillies, and coconut and lastly squeeze in a small piece of the lemon.

2. Mix well and use as a salad with a rice dish.

Spices - Masala

Spices - Masala - Index

Page N^O^

Masala Paste (Balti)

Ingredients

- 3 dried red chillies
- 1 onion, cut into fine cubes
- 2 tsps ground ginger
- 2 cloves garlic
- 1 medium can of tomatoes (375 gms)
- 3 tsps coriander seeds
- 1 tsp cumin seeds
- salt to taste
- 2 tsps ground spices (garam masala - cloves, cinnamon, cardamom)

Method

1. Dry grind the chilli, cumin and coriander in an electric grinder.
2. Add the other ingredients and grind to a paste.

★ This can be kept in the fridge for a few days.

Chat Masala - (North Indian Speciality)

The name "Chat" refers to various snacks.
See the finger foods section for a recipe

Ingredients

- 8 red chillies or 3 tbsp chilli powder
- 3 tbsp mango powder
- 2 tbsp ginger powder
- pinch of asafoetida
- 1 tsp ajwain seeds
- black* salt to taste
- 75g cumin seeds
- 80g coriander seeds
- 2 tbsp crushed mint
- ½ lime or 2 tbsp vinegar

Method

1. Dry roast the cumin, coriander and ajwain seeds for few minutes. Add the red chillies, stir it once and remove from the cooker.

2. Grind the above to a fine powder and mix it with the other ground spices (mango, ginger, asafoetida) and store in a jar.

To serve

Mix the powder and sprinkle onto snacks, salads and fruits.
Add a bit of lime juice or vinegar before serving.

★ This is a tasty starter, the hotness and tangy taste with the lime juice makes it tempting to lick your fingers.
*Black salt is reddish in colour and can be purchaed from Asian supermarkets. You can also use normal salt.

★ Ready made masala is also available in packets now.

Roasted Fennel Powder - 1

Peruncheeraham Thool (Special flavouring powder)

The difference in Sri Lankan cooking is the addition of the roasted chilli powder and the above special flavouring powder

The powder is added to the dish at the final stage of the cooking just before removing from the cooker. It gives a lovely taste and flavour. Used in vegetarian and non vegetarian dishes.

Ingredients

- 125g fennel seeds
- 3 tbsp uncooked white rice
- 2 tbsp urad dhal
- 2 sprigs curry leaves
- piece of cinnamon stick - 7cm size
- 3-4 cloves
- 6 cardamoms
- 1 long rampe stick leaf cut up
- oil for deep frying (optional)

Method

1. Roast the fennel seed in a frying pan until light brown colour.
2. Wash and dry the rice. Then roast this separately with urad dhal or deep fry in oil and put it aside.
3. Roast the curry leaves and the other ingredients.
4. Add the fennel, rice and all other ingredients, stir well and roast until slightly golden colour.
5. Alow to cool and grind it in an electric grinder to a fine powder.
6. Sieve this and grind again if there are any particles left.

★ Store in an airtight bottle, can keep for 3-4 months .
Tasty when added to dry potato curry, meat, dhal and pumpkin dishes.

Roasted Fennel Powder - 2 (Traditional)

Peruncheeraham Thool - a speciality from Jaffna

Traditional preparation

The tradition was to prepare this powder at the time of cooking and add to the Kari.
Later, everyone started to prepare and store it.
The traditional recipe does not include the urad or rice.

Ingredients

- 125g fennel seeds
- 2 sprigs curry leaves
- 1 rampe leaf cut up

Method

1. Roast the fennel seeds in a frying pan.
2. When slightly brown add the curry leaves and roast until it is golden brown in colour.
3. Grind to fine powder and store in a jar.

★ Used in potato, pumpkin, tomato and non veg dishes.
★ See the previous page which I have adapted and is quite popular.

Channa Podi

Ingredients

- 50g channa dhal
- 5 tbsp desiccated coconut
- 2 tbsp cumin seeds
- 2 tbsp pepper corns
- salt to taste
- 1 tsp chilli powder
- pinch of asafoetida
- 2 tsp garlic powder
- 1 tbsp oil

Method

1. Heat the oil in a pan, add pepper, cumin, channa dhal and stir over a low heat.
2. Add the coconut and roast it, add salt and the chilli powder and remove from the heat.
3. Grind it and keep it aside to have with your meal

For serving

To make chutney: roast mustard seeds in little oil, allow it to pop, add little water or milk to the above ground powder, and add to the pan, mix well. Have it with any dish.

Dhal Podi - Chutney

Other common names used are kadalai parruppu/channa/chickpea
Preparation & cooking time: 30 minutes

Ingredients

- 200g split chick peas
- 4 dried red chillies
- 4 tbsp desiccated or freshly scraped coconut
- salt, pinch of garlic powder
- little milk or water
- ½ tsp mustard seeds
- ½ tsp cumin seeds
- 4-5 curry leaves
- 1 tsp urad dhal
- 2 tbsp oil
- 1 tbsp ghee or butter

Method

1. In a frying pan roast the split peas for few minutes. Add two tablespoon of oil and three of the dry chillies, garlic, coconut, salt and roast it until slightly brown.
2. If using fresh coconut then you need to roast until it becomes a bit dry. Set aside to cool. Grind to a paste using a blender, you may have to add a bit of water or milk to grind to a paste. Leave it aside.
3. Heat the frying pan and melt the butter or ghee .
4. Add the urad dhal and mustard seeds. When the mustard seeds start to pop add the cumin, cut red chilli and curry leaves.
5. When it turns slightly brown remove from cooker and pour it over the ground dhal paste.

★ Serve with thosai, rice and bread. Can keep for a week in the fridge.

Ground Dry Savoury Powder

Ingredients

- 100g coriander seeds
- 5 dried red chillies
- 5g cumin seeds
- 25g urad dhal
- 2 tsp oil
- salt to taste
- 1 sprig curry leaves

Method

1. Heat oil in a pan and roast the dry ingredients until brown.
2. Lastly add the red chillies, stir for a minute and remove from heat. Add salt.
3. Using an electric grinder/blender grind the above .
4. Keep in an airtight bottle, use one teaspoon of the podi with meals.

★ Can add Greek yoghurt and make it a dip.
Can use this in any stir fry cooking or vegetable dishes.

Milahai Podi (Chilli Powder)

Milahai Podi (meaning chilli powder) is made to have with thosai, idli or buttered toast.

Ingredients

- 6-8 dried red chilies (depending on your requirement)
- 100g urad dhal
- 100g split channa dhal
- 1 tbsp sesame seeds
- salt to taste
- ¼ tsp asafoetida powder

Method

1. Dry roast the urad, channa and sesame. Add the red chillies and roast it well. Add asafoetida whilst hot.
2. Remove from heat, leave it to cool and grind. Store in a jar.
3. The ground powder will be slightly coarse.

★ Mix 1 tsp of the powder with warm ghee and have it with idli, thosai, rice, savoury semolina dish etc.

During a visit to India, I learnt that the first course or starter for a main meal is to eat hot rice, ghee and the above podi.

Sambar Podi

Ingredients

- 6 tbsp coriander seeds
- 2 tbsp toor dhal
- 1 tsp mustard seeds
- 1 red chilli
- 6 tbsp split green gram seeds
- ghee
- turmeric powder
- 1 tbsp fenugreek seeds

Method

1. Roast all the above in a little ghee until slightly brown.
2. Leave to cool and grind it to a fine powder.
3. This can be used as an additional side dish with chutney for samosas or idli.

Dhal Powder

Ingredients

- 1 cup split gram dhal
- 1 cup toor dal or pottu kadalai
- 5 whole dry red chillies
- ½ tsp asafoetida powder
- salt

Method

Dry roast the above without oil, add salt and asafoetida and grind into a very fine powder and store in a bottle.

★ Add yoghurt and use as a dip. Can add to vegetable milky dishes to make the sauce thick.

Ground Spicy Powder (Podi)

Ingredients

- 15 dried red chillies
- 50g urad dhal
- 50g channa dhal
- 2 tbsp mustard seeds
- 1 tsp garlic powder
- 4 tbsp coriander seeds
- 2 tsp oil
- 1 sprig curry leaves

Method

1. Heat the oil and roast all the ingredients and grind it and keep it aside to eat with lemon rice, tamarind rice (puli satham).

★ Try it on buttered toast.

Lemon Podi

Ingredients

- 3 lemons
- piece of ginger grated
- 1 sprig curry leaves finely sliced
- 3 red dried chillies
- salt
- 3 cloves garlic grated

Method

1. Slice the lemon into small pieces. Add ginger, garlic, salt and leave it to dry for a day or two.

2. Heat oil in a pan and roast the chillies, curry leaves, and add the dried lemon.

3. Using a blender, liqudise the above to a paste.

★ If you are feeling sick this will taste good to have with your meal. In the winter, to dry the lemons, try leaving them near the boiler or place in a hot oven for 10-15 minutes.

Garam Masala

Ingredients

- 3 tbsp coriander seeds
- 3 tbsp cumin seeds
- 1 tbsp black pepper seeds
- 4cm cinnamon stick
- 4 cardamoms
- 1 tsp garlic powder
- 1 tsp ginger power
- 2 dried red chillies
- 2 cloves
- 2 star shaped ani seeds (optional)

Method

1. Grind all the ingredients and keep in an air tight jar.
2. Use in recipes where garam masala powder is included.

Variations

★ Roast the cumin, coriander and pepper seeds in a dry pan for 5 minutes and then grind, this gives a different taste.

★ If you are going to prepare the powder to use in a recipe the same day, then add 3 garlic cloves and a 1" piece of ginger instead of the powder, 1 green chilli and 1 tsp tamarind paste.

Put all into a blender including the ingredients given in the above recipe and grind to a paste. This can be kept in the fridge for two weeks or so.

★ This paste is used in vegetarian, fish and prawn dishes and also for barbecue or tandoori paste.

Masala for Cooking - 1

Ingredients

- 1 large onion
- 1 tbsp coriander seeds
- 1 tbsp cumin seeds
- 2 tbsp plain chilli powder
- ½ tsp peppercorns
- ½ tsp turmeric powder
- salt to taste
- juice of ½ lemon or 1 tsp tamarind paste
- 3 cloves of garlic and a piece of ginger

Method

1. Dice the onion to small pieces. Grate ginger and garlic.

2. Grind all the dry ingredients first then add the onion, garlic, ginger and lemon juice or tamarind. Add a little water.

3. It is ready to use in cooking.

Variations

To above add cinnamon, cardamom, coriander leaves,
and blend to a paste.

Options

★ This masala is used in cooking instead of the different powders For some vegetables, you can omit the tempering side and include this paste in cooking.

Masala for Cooking - 2 (Hot)

Ingredients

- 3 onions sliced
- 1 tsp each garlic and ginger paste
- 2 tsp roasted chilli powder
- 2 tsp garam masala powder
- 2 tsp coriander seeds
- salt to taste
- 1 tsp cumin seeds
- 2 tbsp desiccated coconut
- 2 tbsp lemon juice or 1 tsp tamarind paste
- 2 tbsp peanuts (optional)
- 3 green chillies

Method

1. Blend everything together in a liquidiser or food processer.

2 Use the paste in cooking where you require a thick sauce

3. You may omit the cumin, coriander and chilli powder included in the recipe and add above.

★ If using lemon juice, add this last after grinding the above.

Sri Lankan Roasted Chilli Powder

Special Kari Powder

This is a traditional Sri Lankan chilli/curry powder used in Jaffna. The ready made powder is available in Sri Lankan shops. There are three grades - mild, hot and very hot.

Roasted chilli powder included in the recipes refer to this unless specified otherwise.
In case you are going to prepare it, try this recipe.

Ingredients

- 100g dried red chillies
- 150g coriander seeds
- 100g cumin seeds
- 50g turmeric powder
- 75g black pepper corns
- 4 sprigs curry leaves
- 1 rampe stick

Method

1. Roast all ingredients in a frying pan except the chilli until slightly brown.
2. After 5-10 minutes add the chilli, curry leaves, rampe and stir for few seconds and remove from heat. Leave it to cool.
3. Grind using a dry grinder (coffee grinder) and store in a bottle.

★ Take care when you do this as the whole house will smell and youmay start to cough.

★ <u>An easy preparation:</u> Roast in a pan or oven the following ground powders: 100g of plain chilli, cumin, 150g coriander, 50g pepper, and 25g turmeric and fennel, few sprigs curry leaves.

Introduction to Rasam

Rasam : A spicy watery soup

- ★ Good to drink, as an appetiser. It is good to have when you are tired and have a head ache, not feeling too good or recovering from a cold and flu.
- ★ Coriander is the main ingredient; cumin, black pepper, garlic and tamarind are also added in the preparation.
- ★ A South Indian meal and a traditional Sri Lankan "Rice and Kari" meal will have a bowl of rasam.
- ★ Rasam is served as the last part of the meal probably to cleanse and digest.
- ★ However, I find the next generation Sri Lankan children brought up in the West (including my sons) serve rasam at the start.
  The response I get is, "it doesn't matter when you have it". There may be a point there.
- ★ There are several preparations but the basic recipe is without red chillies. I feel that this is tasty and good as a drink for those who are not keen on very spicy food.

You should try making rasam.

Rasam Powder - Traditional recipe from Jaffna

Ingredients

- 6 tbsp coriander seeds
- 2 tbsp cumin seeds
- 1 tbsp pepper corns
- ½ tsp asafoetida powder

Method

1. First grind the pepper for few seconds, then add the cumin and coriander seeds and grind for few seconds only. The powder should be crushed and not finely ground.
2. Store in a bottle, this should last for 5 servings for two or three people.

South Indian Rasam Powder

Ingredients

- ½ cup toor dhal
- 2 tbsp pepper seeds
- 6 dried red chillies (increase or decrease to your taste)
- 4 tbsp cumin seeds
- ½ tsp asafoetida powder
- ½ tsp turmeric powder

Method

Roast all ingredients, grind and keep in a jar. Use one or two teaspoons for four people.

To prepare the Rasam

- 2 cloves garlic crushed
- 2 tomatoes cut into cubes
- 1 tsp tamarind paste
- 1-2 cups water
- few coriander leaves
- salt to taste

1. Boil water adding salt. Add tamarind, crushed garlic and tomatoes.
2. Boil for one or two minutes and add 2 teaspoons of the ground powder.
3. Sprinkle a little cold water, cover the pan with a lid and remove from heat.
4. Allow to settle and you can serve with rice or have it as a drink.

Variations

Rasam with dhal

1. If you prepare dhal, leave the dhal pan with 1 tbsp of the cooked dhal to prepare the rasam. Follow the steps below.
2. In the dhal pan put 1 tsp of oil, fry 2 spoons of chopped onion and mustard seeds. Reduce the heat, add water and other ingredients - garlic, tamarind, salt etc., bring to boil, add 2 tsp of the ground spice and coriander leaves. Once it has boiled, sprinkle water and cover it.

Mysore Rasam Powder (Indian recipe)

Ingredients

- 1 tbsp coriander seeds
- 1 tsp black pepper seeds
- 1 tsp split channa or gram dhal
- 1 tsp cumin seds
- 1 dry red chilli
- ½ tsp asafoetida powder
- 1 tbsp desiccated coconut
- 1 tsp ghee

Method

1. Roast the above in ghee and grind and keep aside.
2. Follow the recipe for rasam below and add 3 tbsp of the ground Mysore rasam powder.

Cakes

Cakes - Index

Page N°

Introduction

The story of how I began baking and decorating cakes

When I first came over to UK I was only able to make plain sponge cakes. Decorating is something I wanted to learn in Sri Lanka but couldn't for many reasons.

In 1974 my husband and I had been to a first birthday party. The cake was beautifully decorated, but bought from a shop. It was a bit dry and some people started to cough as the crumbs got into their throat. At that time I decided that I should bake and ice cakes for my children. I started with my eldest son's first birthday in 1975. I did not stop with baking both my sons' birthday cakes; I made their wedding cakes in 2001 and 2004, which included sugar flower sprays and structures. I have also made cakes for occasions for my family members, close friends and their children. I am still continuing to bake and decorate cakes for my family and friends.

The wedding cake recipe in this book is a speciality of Sri Lanka. Usually it is boxed in a **1" x 2" piece** that is wrapped up and given as a token in Sri Lankan weddings. It is a big task as it needs lots of preparation and effort. The recipe included in this book has been devised over the years.

Home-made cakes taste better. The secret is to use butter, to beat it well and take care with the baking. I have a Kenwood beater, which I use.

The recipes that follow are my favourite ones. Most of them are from Sri lanka. Now why don't you have a go at these?

I have not given the exact measurements/sizes of the cake trays. The trays I use are a medium square 8" x 8", a loaf tin, an 8" round tray or a rectangular baking/roasting tray. Baking times vary according to the mixture. For a butter cake, at least 40 minutes is required at 160°c. The oven temperatures given are for an electric circotherm oven.

Butter Cake

Preparation & cooking time: 1½ hours

Ingredients

- 250g butter
- 250g caster sugar
- 250g self raising flour
- 5 medium or 4 large eggs
- 1 tsp of vanilla essence

Method

1. Beat the butter and sugar until it is very fluffy and creamy. If using a mixer,beat for 15-20 minutes.
2. Sieve the self-raising flour twice and leave it aside.
3. Now break one egg into a small bowl. Beat this with a fork and slowly add it to the mixture and beat well.
4. Add a table spoon of flour and then run the beater on a slow speed. If not using a beater, fold with a wooden spoon.
5. Repeat this procedure with the remaining eggs and flour, finally add any remaining flour and the vanilla essence. Run the beater on a slow speed or fold with a wooden spoon.
6. Prepare a medium square and a loaf tin by lining each with parchment paper or oil paper. If you are using a single round tin then brush it with melted margarine and then dust with flour.
7. Pour the cake mixture into the two trays and bake at a moderate heat of 160°C (circotherm) for 45 minutes. Do not open the oven door for atleast 30 minutes or the cake will sink.
8. Check if the cake is cooked by inserting a skewer or knife. If it comes out clean the cake is ready. Otherwise leave for appx 5 more minutes.

Enjoy the butter cake.

Butter cake Variations

Dates & Semolina

Can add 100g of chopped dates, 100g of roasted semolina and 150 g of self raising flour to substitute for the 250g self raising flour.

Cherries and Cashew nuts

Additional ingredients are

- 125g glazed cherries
- 125g cashew nuts, chopped
- 15-20g semolina
- 2 tablespoon milk

Quarter each cherry and dust in some flour to prevent the cherries from sinking. Mix the flour, semolina and lastly, add the cherries and fold in.
If the consistency is too thick, add milk. Mix and pour into the trays. Sprinkle on the chopped cashew nuts and use a fork to turn slightly so that they don't sink.

Cooking may take about an hour.
First cook at 160°C then reduce heat to 150°C after 30 minutes.

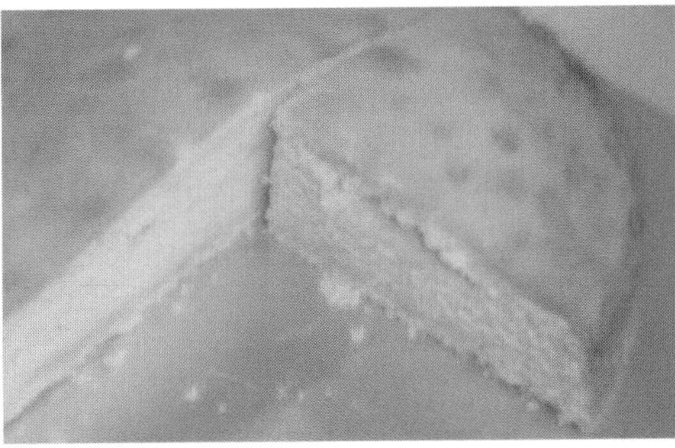

Chocolate Cake

Preparation & cooking time: 1½ hours

Ingredients

- 2 tbsp milk
- 1 tbsp cocoa
- 125g butter
- 150g caster sugar
- 2 eggs
- 125g self raising flour
- small round cake baking tray

For icing

- 100g icing sugar
- 50g butter
- 1 tbsp cocoa powder

Method

1. Blend the cocoa and milk in a pan and slightly warm on gentle heat until smooth and thick.
2. Cream the butter and sugar well. Beat in the eggs one by one and the chocolate mixture. Fold in the flour.
3. Pour into a baking tray (lined with parchment paper or brush the tray with butter/margarine and dust with flour).
4. Bake for 25 minutes on 160°C Circotherm or gas mark 4. Then reduce to 150°C and bake for another 15 minutes.
5. When cool, cut in the middle (lengthwise) to get two cakes. Spread with chocolate or cream icing, dust the top with icing sugar or decorate using chocolate icing.

★ Icing: Mix the butter, cocoa and icing sugar.

Moist Chocolate Cake

Preparation & cooking time: 1 hour

Ingredients

- 250g butter
- 250g caster sugar
- 125g self raising flour
- 85g cocoa powder or drinking chocolate
- 5 eggs, well beaten
- 2 tbsp hot milk
- pinch of salt

Method

1. Sieve the flour and chocolate powder adding a pinch of salt.
2. Cream the butter and sugar together until light and fluffy.
3. Beat in the eggs separately, add a little at a time to the butter and sugar mixture. Add one or two spoons of flour mixture to prevent curdling. Fold in the remaining sieved flour and stir in the hot milk.
4. Grease and line two round sandwich tins. Pour the mixture into two trays and smooth the tops.
5. Preheat the oven to 160°C (350°F) and bake for 30-40 minutes.
6. The surface of the cake will spring back when pressed lightly. Remove the cakes from the tins and allow to cool on a wire rack.
   Use butter /chocolate icing as in the previous recipe, spread and sandwich.

Date Cake

Preparation: 15 minutes (plus 5-6 hrs to soak the dates)
Mixing: 30 minutes
Baking: 50 minutes

Ingredients

- 500g seedless dates
- 1-2 tsp bicarbonate soda
- 250g caster sugar
- 4 eggs
- 100g roasted cashew nuts, chopped
- 250g butter
- 200g self raising flour
- 100g roasted semolina
- ½ tsp rose essence
- 1 tsp vanilla flavouring
- 1 cup hot water

Method

1. Put the dates into a bowl, add the water and bicarbonate of soda and soak for about 5-6 hrs. Take out and chop the dates finely
2. Sieve the flour twice, add the semolina and leave it aside.
3. Beat the butter and sugar until creamy.
4. Gradually add the eggs one by one, alternating with one tablespoon of the flour andsemolina. Fold the mixture with a spoon or run the beater at a very slow speed.
5. Then add the chopped dates.
6. Run the beater at a slow speed for a few seconds for the dates to get mixed well. Add the flavouring/essence.
7. Line a medium square tray and a loaf tin with greaseproof or parchment paper. Pour in the mixture, sprinkle on the cashew nuts and stir once using a fork. Preheat the oven and bake for appx 40 to 50 minutes at 160°C.

Eggless Date Cake

Preparation & cooking time: 1 hour

Soaking the dates: 4 hours

Ingredients

- 200g chopped dates
- 1 cup hot water
- ¾ tsp bicarbonate of soda
- 250g self raising flour
- 200g soft brown sugar
- 75g butter or margarine
- 1 tsp vanilla
- 75g chopped cashew nuts
- 200g (½ tin) full cream evaporated milk

Method

1. Soak the chopped dates in boiling water, add ¾ tsp of bicarbonate soda and leave it overnight or for 4 hours. Chop the dates and leave it aside.

2. Cream the butter and sugar well, add the date mixture with the water and beat well.

3. Add the flour and milk little by little and fold in. Mix well, add the vanilla and chopped nuts.

4. Pour into a greased baking tray and bake for 20 minutes at 180ºC, reduce the heat to 150°C and bake for another 35 minutes or until done.

★ Some soak the dates in hot tea instead of the water (soak a tea bag in the hot water). This gives a darker colour. However I have not tried this.

Eggless Date Cake (Another Recipe)

Preparation & cooking time: 1½ hours
Soaking the dates: 4 hours

Ingredients

- 250g dates
- 50g roasted semolina
- 200g self raising flour, sifted
- 250g butter or margarine
- handful of almonds soaked in water
- 3 tbsp sugar
- 60g candied peel
- 125g glazed cherries
- 25g ginger preserve or crystalised
- 50g sultanas
- 4 tbsp golden syrup
- 400g condensed milk, ½ cup aerated water (soda or lemonade)
- ½ tsp cinnamon, pinch of nutmeg, 1 tsp vanilla essence

Method

1. Follow the recipe as for eggless cake, chop the soaked dates and almonds. Chop the fruits and cashew nuts.

2 Beat the sugar and butter then add the milk, sifted self raising flour and semolina. Add the chopped fruits, golden syrup and lastly, open a can of lemonade and add this and blend slowly. Add the essence, cinnamon and the nutmeg.

3. Pour into a large rectangle tin lined with parchment paper, bake at oven temperature of 150°C for 45 minutes.

4. Then reduce to 130°C-135°C and bake for another 20 minutes. Remove from the oven and let it cool. Cut and serve.

Eggless Chocolate Cake

Preparation & cooking time: 1 hour and 20 minutes

Ingredients

- 250g butter
- ¾ tin condensed milk or tin of evaporated milk (410g)
- ½ cup normal milk or water
- 3 tbsp cocoa
- 250g plain flour
- 2 tsp baking powder
- 1 tsp sodium bicarbonate
- 100ml of soda water/lemonade
- 100-125g sugar (optional)

Method

1. Add the bicarbonate soda and baking powder to the flour and sieve it three times.
2. Sieve the cocoa and mix this to a smooth paste, adding a little milk, and set it aside.
3. Mix the water and condensed milk (evaporated) in a bowl and whisk it. Add the sugar and mix well.
4. Slightly moisten the butter, beat it with the milk and add cocoa mix . Keep whisking for 2 minutes.
5. Spoon the flour into the milk and mix. Add the lemonade or soda water and mix well.
6. Pour the mixture into a lined medium cake tray and bake for 45 minutes. First at 160°C for 20 minutes and then at 150°C for the rest.

For eggless cake

- ★ It is better to divide the eggless cake mixture between two medium square trays as the cake does not rise much.
- ★ Do not try to spread the top level as this will also stop the cake from rising.
- ★ To avoid breaking, cool the cakes before taking them out of the tins. Then take them out slowly.
- ★ Sandwich with chocolate icing and serve.
- ★ Can substitute self raising flour and ½ tsp each of baking powder and bicarbonate soda. Cake will be a bit softer.
- ★ To make a butter sponge leave out the cocoa and follow the recipe.
- ★ Instead of condensed milk you can use, Carnation full cream evaporated milk and substitute ½ cup of normal milk for water. Also add 125 gms of sugar.

Ginger Cake

Preparation time: 30 minutes
Baking: 45 minutes to 1 hour

Ingredients

- 250g self raising flour
- 1 tsp bicarbonate of soda
- 1 tsp ground ginger powder
- ½ tsp cinnamon powder
- pinch of salt
- 2 large eggs
- 175g butter
- 175g butter
- 1 tbsp ground almonds
- 50g cashew nuts chopped
- 150g golden syrup
- 2-3 tbsp milk
- 175g caster sugar (see notes if using brown sugar)
- 75g crystallised ginger or ginger in syrup chopped

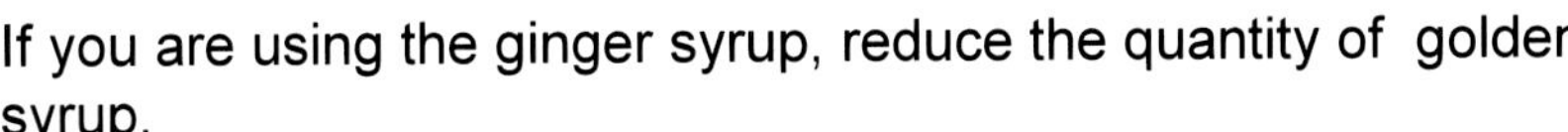

If you are using the ginger syrup, reduce the quantity of golden syrup.
Brown sugar: Use 150 gms mascavada sugar instead of the caster sugar.

Method

1. Prepare a medium square cake tin by lining it with parchment paper.
2. Preheat the oven to 160°C or gas mark 4.
3. Sieve the flour, adding all the dry fine ingredients except for the almonds.
4. Beat the butter and sugar until creamy.

5. Whisk the two eggs; add this to the butter mixture.

6. Add the flour little by little to the above mixture. Save one third of it for later on.

7. Then add the golden syrup and ginger syrup.

8. Fold in the remainder of the flour, ginger and ground almonds.

9. Add the milk to make sure the mixture is creamy and not too watery.

10. Pour this into the prepared tray, sprinkle on the chopped cashew nuts and slightly smooth with the back of a spoon.

11. Bake in the oven for 30 minutes at 160°C, then reduce the temperature to 135°C for another 20-25 minutes.

12. Do not open the oven for at least 45 minutes. When the cake is firm in the centre remove from the oven. Leave for a few minutes then take it out and leave on a wire rack.

Jaggery Cake

Preparation & cooking time: 2 hours

Jaggery can be purchased from Sri Lankan shops. Mascavada sugar is a good substitute.

Ingredients

- 250g semolina
- 125g caster sugar
- 1 tsp vanilla essence
- 1 tsp rose essence
- ¾ cup coconut milk (375g)
- 2 tbsp self raising flour
- 75g pumpkin preserve, chopped
- 100g cashew nuts, chopped
- 1 tsp ground mixed spices (cinnamon, cardamom)
- ½ tsp freshly grated nutmeg
- 125g jaggery (grated)
- 125g butter
- 4 eggs
- 2 tbsp brandy

Method

1. Place the chopped pumpkin preserve and cashew nuts in a bowl, add brandy, mix well and set it aside.
2. Roast the semolina well in a frying pan and allow it to cool.
3. Cream the butter and semolina for 10-15 minutes.
4. Place the yolks in a bowl and beat lightly until they break and then add sugar and beat well for the sugar to dissolve. Then add the butter and semolina and beat well.
5. Warm the coconut milk and mix with the grated jaggery and allow to dissolve.
6. Mix the jaggery and coconut milk to the butter cream mixture.
7. Add on the finely chopped pumpkin preserve and chopped cashew nuts and add the self-raising flour.
8. Beat egg whites separately until stiff and fold this in with the above.
9. Add the flavouring, spices and the nutmeg. Mix well.
10. Pour into a square lined baking tray and bake at 155°C for 35 minutes. Reduce to 140-145°C and cook for about an hour.
11. Take it out of the oven, remove the cake by sliding and let it cool.

Love Cake

Preparation: 30 minutes
Cooking: slow oven for 1 hour and 30 minutes

Ingredients

- 200g butter
- 450g caster sugar
- 10 yolks and 4 egg whites
- 250g roasted semolina
- 3 tbsp self raising flour
- ½ tsp almond essence
- 2 tsp hone
- 1½ tsp rose essence or 2 tbsp rosewater
- 275g cashew nuts, minced or finely chopped
- 250g pumpkin preserve, finely choppedy
- 2 tsp freshly grated lemon/lime rind
- ½ tsp grated nutmeg
- 1 tsp cinnamon and cardamom powder (freshly ground)

Method

1. First prepare a large rectangle tray or two medium square cake trays, lined with two layers of newspaper and greaseproof paper.
2. Slightly roast the semolina in a dry pan. Leave it to cool.
3. Mix the butter and semolina. Beat well using a beater. Sprinkle on the lemon rind.
4. In a bowl mix the cashew nuts, pumpkin preserve, honey, spices, essence and leave it aside.
5. Beat the yolks and the sugar. Beat in the butter and semolina mixture and the self raising flour. Beat the egg whites until stiff and fold this into the mixture. Add the pumpkin, cashew, spices mixture and mix well.
6. Pour into a tray, cover the top loosely with a foil paper. Bake at 150°C for 20 minutes and bake for a further hour and 15 minutes at 145°C. You can remove the foil for the last 10 minutes or so.
   The centre of the cake will be slightly moist but a skewer should come out fairly clean.
7. Cool the cake well before cutting. Cut into pieces, say 1" or 1½" squares, and serve.

Rich Cake (Wedding Cake)

Preparation: 2 days prior, to cut the fruits
On the day: 30 minutes
Baking: 2 hours

Ingredients

- 375g raisins
- 375g sultanas
- 375g cashew nuts
- 375g cherries
- 500g semolina
- 500g butter

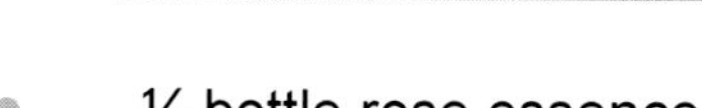

- ½ bottle rose essence
- juice of ½ lemon
- 1 bottle vanilla essence (30ml)
- 1 bottle almond essence (30ml)
- ¼ tsp salt
- 60g flour
- rind of 1 lime grated
- 2 tsp ground mixed spice (cinnamon, cardamom nutmeg)
- 125g golden syrup
- 2 oz sherry
- 1kg caster sugar (can use soft brown sugar)
- 250g strawberry jam (medium bottle)
- 250g pineapple jam
- 250g candied peel
- 500g ginger in syrup or 400g crystallised ginger
- 400g pumpkin preserve
- 375g chow chow
- 4 oz honey
- 4 oz brandy
- 24 eggs (24 yolks and 10-12 whites)
- (for large quantities you can use 1lb of chopped dates)

Method

1. Cut up all the fruits, place in a large bowl, add the jam, honey, syrup, half the essence vanilla, almond, rose, brandy and sherry and mix well. Transfer into two large bowls and allow to soak for two days.
2. Roast the semolina and beat with the butter. Leave it aside for at least 5-6 hours or over night.
3. Mix the yolks and sugar, beat it well until creamy.
4. Beat the butter and semolina for a few minutes. Add the sugar and yolk mixture and beat well.
5. Spoon in the mixed fruit little by little and mix well.
6. Whisk the egg whites until very stiff, add this little by little and fold it in with a wooden spoon. Mix but do not beat it.
7. Finally add the rest of the flavouring. Add the self raising flour.
8. Pour into two large rectangular (roasting trays) cake trays, which should be lined with two layers of paper and then a non stick parchment or greaseproof paper.
9. Warm the oven on 160°C for 5 minutes. Place a tray of water on the bottom shelf and place the cake trays in two shelves and bake at 160°C circotherm for half an hour and reduce to 140°C for another hour and 15 minutes. Check and if necessary reduce it to 135°C for another half hour and not more. Oven temperatures vary so check so that it does not get burnt.

Helpful Hints

★ Baking time: Usually 2½ hours depending on the height of the cake and the oven temperature. To check use a knife or a skewer and if it comes out clean then it is done.

★ Soft brown sugar is tasty for the eggless cake, but it may make the cake settle a bit. Lately I have started using caster sugar.

★ Can substitute 100 gms of dried mixed pineapple and melon and reduce the sultana and raisins by this amount.

For Eggless cake

a. Substitute for eggs - 1 tin (400g) of carnation milk, ½ -1 tin condensed milk and ½ tin of normal fresh milk
b. Follow all the steps of the above recipe, except for the eggs, add the milk and mix.

Eggless Cake with Butter Milk

Preparation & cooking time: 1 hour

Ingredients

- 100g butter
- 175g caster sugar
- 250g self raising flour
- ½ tsp baking powder
- ½ tsp bicarbonate soda
- pinch of salt
- 1 cup butter milk
- 1 tsp vanilla essence
- 1 tsp almond essence
- 8 half cashew nuts or almonds

Method

1. In a bowl mix the sugar and butter. Add the butter milk and beat it well.
2. Sieve the flour, adding the baking powder, salt and bicarbonate soda.
3. Mix the flour with the butter mixture.
4. Add vanilla and almond essence.
5 Make sure the flour and butter milk are mixed well. If using an electric beater beat on a medium speed.
6. Pour the mixture into a prepared, medium-size cake tray (lined with parchment paper).
7. Place the cashew nuts or almonds on the surface of the cake.
8. Bake in a moderate oven 160°C circotherm for 30-35 minutes.
9. To see if the cake is cooked in the middle prick it with a wooden skewer, which should come out clean, otherwise cook for another 5 minutes.

Butter Icing

Preparation: 10 minutes

Ingredients

- 250g butter
- 500g icing sugar
- 1 tsp vanilla essence
- 1 or 2 tbsp warm milk

Method

1. Sieve the sugar. Soften the butter and add the icing sugar little by little and mix well.
2. If the consistency is too thick to spread or pass through a nozzle, add little bit of warm milk. Add vanilla essence.
3. Now spread it on the cake or pipe using an icing nozzle.

Chocolate Icing

Preparation: 10 minutes

Ingredients

- 250g butter
- 500g icing sugar
- 3-4 tsp cocoa powder
- warm milk, 1 or 2 tbsp

Method

1 Mix as for butter icing, add cocoa and finally the milk.
2 Can spread or sandwich the chocolate cake with this icing.

Butter Cream Filling

Ingredients

- 110g icing sugar
- 50g butter
- 50g drinking chocolate
- water or milk

Method

1. Mix all the ingredients together until smooth and light.
2. Spread on one of the cakes and sandwich together.

Glace Icing

- 170g (6oz) icing sugar
- 50g (2oz) drinking chocolate
- 2 tbsp hot water to mix (appx)

Method

1. Add the hot water to the sugar and the drinking chocolate to form a thick paste.
2. Coat the top of the cake before serving.
3. Use a knife dipped in boiling water to spread the icing.

Beverages

NO PULP
ORIGINAL
Tropicana
100% Juice
Apple Juice
Tropical Fruit
Tropicana
Fruit Smoothie
BYRNE DAIRY
Milk
Pint

Appetisers - Index

Tropical Fruit Punch

Ingredients

- 3 cups orange juice
- 3 cups pineapple juice
- 3 cups grapefruit juice
- ¼ cup lime or lemon juice
- ½ cup honey
- 4 cans ginger ale or soda water
- 1 cup rum or white wine
- 1 cup finely chopped pineapple
- 1 cup small melon pieces or balls
- 1 lime or orange seeded and thinly sliced

Method

1. Open the packets and mix orange, pineapple, grapefruit and lime juices in a bowl. Add honey to taste and chill for few hours.
2. Scoop melon balls using a small fruit scoop or an ice-cream scoop.
3. Just before serving stir in ginger ale, rum, pineapple pieces and melon balls.
4. Pour into glasses, add crushed ice, lime or orange slices and serve.

For alcohol-free punch

- Leave the alcohol, ginger ale and lime out.
- Substitute a can of fruit salad or cut up fresh apple and pears into small cubes.
- Add 3 cans of Jamaican ginger beer* and mango juice.
- Finally just before serving add the apples, pears and ice cubes.

★ *Jamaican Ginger beer is quite strong, there are also mild varieties.

Jal Jeera (Cumin - drink)

Recipe from Bangalore India

A note about the drink

★ For those who do not consume alcohol this is a good drink.
I tasted this when I was in Bangalore two years ago and would say that it is different from the usual squash, which is sweet.
This is slightly salty and tangy but very refreshing to have on hot sunny days. It is an appetiser too.
I liked it so much that I asked for the recipe to include it in my book.
I have made it at home in UK during the summer time.

Ingredients

- 4 tbsp cumin seeds
- 1 tbsp tamarind paste
- ½ tsp freshly ground black pepper
- ½ tsp mango powder (optional)
- pinch of salt
- ½ tsp sugar
- 3 cups water
- 1 sprig mint or coriander leaves

Method

1. Roast the cumin seeds and leave ½ tsp of seeds out and grind the rest.
2. Boil the water add tamarind paste and ½ tsp cumin seeds.
3. Chop the mint or coriander to very small pieces and add to the above with salt, sugar, pepper, ground cumin and let it cool.
4. Strain the drink and either serve with ice cubes or as it is.

Variation

★ Instead of the tamarind you can use 2 tbsp of lime juice.
★ For this you can just add cold water and mix all the ground ingredients. Chill and serve with ice.

Lassi Sweet

Preparation: 10 minutes
Serves 4-6

Ingredients

- 1 large carton of yoghurt
- 20 fl oz water
- few drops of rose water essence, pink or green colouring
- 125g caster sugar
- ½ tsp of ground cardamom seeds
- chopped pistachio nuts
- few glasses

Method

1. Mix yoghurt and water using a whisk or hand beater and beat well.
2. Add all ingredients and liquidise it. Pour into individual glasses.
3. Sprinkle pistachio nuts and chill in the fridge.

For a function/party

If making for a large gathering can leave the mixed lassi in the fridge and spoon it out into glasses before serving.

Cup of tea

- ★ My friends have often said that I prepare good cups of tea. I am not sure if they really meant this or just wanted me to make them a cup of tea.
- ★ The secret is that you need to have good strong tea. Also add one extra spoon of tea for the pot.
- ★ In our house we buy different types of loose tea and mix it with either Sri Lankan or Indian tea and keep it in a container.

Sri Lankan preparation

For 4 people

Ingredients

- 4 tsp of tea leaves or 5 tea bags
- boiling water
- 1¼ cup of boiled milk
- sugar to taste

Method

1. In a teapot place the tea leaves or the tea bags. Pour boiling water equivalent to two cups.
2. Heat the milk in the microwave or on the cooker.
3. Pour the milk into the cups so that they are a third full.
4. Stir the tea well and pour it into the cups using a strainer. Add sugar and serve hot.

With condensed milk

Having tea with condensed milk gives a different taste.
For this you may need a bit more of boiling water in the pot.
Pour the tea into the cups, add 1-2 tsp of condensed milk and stir well and serve.

For a quick preparation use the microwave. Place milk in a cup add a tea bag, cook for 40-45 seconds and add boiling water.

Barley Water

Ingredients

- 4 tbsp barley seeds
- 1½ pint of water
- 1 cup of milk warmed
- salt

Method

1. Wash barley seeds and soak in water for 10 minutes. Wash thoroughly and throw the water away. Add 1½ pints of water in a pan, add the barley seeds and bring to boil. Reduce the flame and boil for further 20- 30 minutes.
2. Strain the water into a jug.
3. Mix a cup of warmed milk, and a bit of salt to 1½ cup of barley water.
4. Drink it warm.

★ **This is good when you are just recovering from illness.**

Variation

To the strained barley water you can add sugar and a bit of lemon juice and serve.

Buttermilk (Known as 'Moor')

Ingredients

- 1 large carton of natural yoghurt
- water, of an equal quantity to the yoghurt
- pinch of salt
- 3 shallots, chopped
- 2 green chillies, chopped fine

Method

1. Mix yoghurt, water, salt and beat well. You can use a hand blender or whisk. Add the chopped onions and chilli

2. Pour in glass and serve. This can be kept in the fridge for a day.

★ This is tasty during the summer time to drink at mid-day.

Ice Coffee

This is a famous drink served at parties in Sri Lanka
Sri Lankans living in the west still want to keep this tradition and serve it in the summer times for an afternoon party. An enjoyable drink.
I believe that it is served in the UK during the cricket matches when the Sri Lankan cricket team plays.
Traditionally, it is made with condensed milk. I have adapted it slightly

Ingredients

- 8-10 tablespoon of strong coffee (Nescafe granules).
  You can mix two types of coffee, according to your taste.
- 4 pints milk
- 1 can (410g) carnation milk
- 1 can (450g) condensed milk
- sugar to taste
- 2 pints boiling water
- few drops of vanilla essence
- 3 oz brandy
- empty milk bottles (3 x 4 pint milk bottles)

Method

1. Mix coffee in about ½ pint of hot water, add the sugar and mix it well.
2. In a large pan pour the milk and bring to boil. Let it cool and remove the skin (the top layer).
3. Mix the carnation milk and the condensed milk to the boiled milk. Stir in the coffee and mix well. Add more boiling water by tasting the coffee.
4. Add vanilla and brandy.
5. Let it cool before pouring into the milk bottles. Leave in the fridge and serve cold.

★ It is better served in small glasses or clear plastic glasses.

Lassi Drink with Mango

Serves 4

Ingredients

- 400 ml milk
- 7 fl oz single cream
- 4 tbsp caster sugar (fine powdered)
- 1 large can of mango pulp or three fresh mangoes

Method

1. If using mango pulp, put all the ingredients into a blender and run the machine for two minutes. Serve in tall glasses and refrigerate for 24 hours.
2. If using fresh mangoes, peel the skin, take out the seed and cut up the mango into small pieces. Liquidise the mango and other ingredients.
3. Depending on the sweetness of the mango increase/decrease the sugar.
4. As a variation you can add a bit of salt instead of the sugar and a pinch of freshly ground cumin and cardamom seeds.

★ This is tasty on a hot day; add ice cubes and there will be no need to refrigerate it for 24 hours.

Masala Tea (Indian preparation)

Makes 4-5 cups

Ingredients

- 2 cups water
- 4 tsp tea leaves
- 2 cloves
- 10 cardamoms
- 1cm size ginger, crushed
- ½ tsp aniseed
- 4 pepper corns
- piece of cinnamon stick
- 1 cup milk
- sugar to taste
- ¼ tsp of green fennel seeds

Method

1. Heat water in a pan
2. Add all the masala and bring to boil, allow to boil for few minutes.
3. Then add the sugar and tea leaves and boil on a low heat.
4. Add milk, cook for few minutes and remove from cooker.
5. Pour the tea into cups using a tea strainer and serve hot.
6. Add more sugar if you require.

Hot spicy tea is made with boiled milk, spices and sugar. Cardamom could be ground or crushed. There are small and large cardamoms and you can use both. Crush the cardamom and cinnamon but not the pepper

★ If you are to make with teabags, add three bags to the boiled milk. Allow few minutes for brewing and serve hot.

Coffee with Coriander and Dry Ginger

Known as 'Malli koppi'

- Dry ginger is used for medicinal purposes.
- This coffee is good to have, like masala tea.
- Traditionally, back home in Jaffna, some people have this as their early morning drink.

Ingredients

For the coffee

- 50g coffee beans
- 50g coriander seeds
- ½" piece of dry ginger

Method

Roast the coffee beans and coriander and add dry ginger.
Grind and store in a jar.

To prepare

1. Add 1 tsp coffee to a cup of boiling water.
2. Cover and leave for few minutes.
3. Strain and add sugar and milk, or have it without the milk

★ 1 tsp coffee per person boling water, sugar to taste, milk .

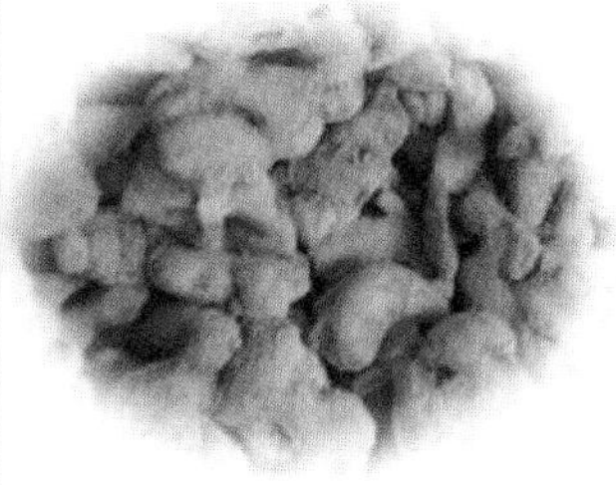

Rice and ~~Curry~~ Kari

Traditional Sri Lankan and other Asian cooking adapted for modern living in the West

Sivakamy Mahalingham

Non vegetarian

Seafood

Fish - Index

Page N°

Introduction

Fish

In the East tropical fish is bought fresh on a daily basis. There is King fish, (Travali) Seer fish, Large Mackerel, Bonito, Shark, Swordfish etc. A daily meal of rice and curry will include a fish dish.

In the West some of the tropical fish can be purchased frozen from Asian/ Sri Lankan shops. You can get vacuum-packed seer/king fish slices cut into steaks/slices. I have seen very large whole fish frozen in the large freezer section at Chinese and Bangladeshi shops. Supermarkets also have started to sell tropical fish. Mackerel, sprats, herrings, shark, salmon, halibut and mullet will be tasty for the recipes in this book. Cod Coley and other white fish are good but taste different from the tropical ones.

Deep fried fish is a favourite of most people.

During a visit to Dubai I had the experience of going to an open fish market with my late brother in law, Chandran, and his family. A large selection of different varieties, small and large fish, crabs, squid etc. were displayed in abundance.

When we came home and I prepared the fish the comment was "Acca doesn't waste time, she tucked her saree and got down to business and what a lovely meal she has prepared". He was keen that I publish a book on cookery.

Fish Preparation

You need to scale the fish by sliding a sharp knife or a scale remover. For salmon slide the knife between the skin and the flesh and remove the skin. Try to cut the fish when it is partially frozen or as soon as you bring it from the supermarkets so that the flesh does not break up. Leave in the fridge or marinate straightaway and cook.

Always use cold water to wash/clean the fish. This will take all the smell away. Even the plates should be washed in cold water and washing up liquid.

Prawns

Several varieties are available and can be purchased from supermarkets. The large tiger prawns, king prawns, small boiled prawns, and dried sprats are available in large supermarkets or from Asian/Chinese shops. Some of the prawns are frozen uncooked. Prawns can be cooked with or without the shell. When cleaning take out the head and the black thin thread of intestine which runs down on the dorsal body of the prawn. To peel cooked prawn hold the head between your finger and thumb, twist it so that the shell lifts and pull it away from the body and remove the legs.

Squid

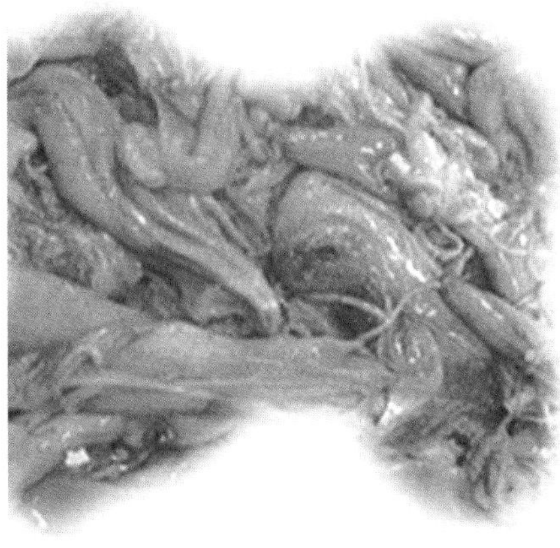

Fresh or frozen squid and squid rings are available in supermarkets. Squid rings are often ready cleaned. When cleaning a whole squid remove the white transparent cellulite “back bone”. Peel the black/grey outer skin and wash. Then cut into rounds or rectangular pieces. Take out the small hook-like piece from the mouth. Do not allow the ink bag to break, discard this.

Crab:

Tropical crabs can be bought in frozen packets. To crack the crab claw tap it gently with a hammer or a rolling pin by covering with a tea towel so that it does not shatter.

I have included a variety of recipes to prepare the seafood dishes.They are very simple and the few points/tips included will help you prepare a tasty dish.

In Sri Lanka fish is cooked using coconut milk and ground masala. First cook it in the 2nd and 3rd extracts of the coconut milk and finally in the 1st extract milk, which will thicken the sauce. An alternative is single cream or evaporated milk or even a slice of cream coconut, which is added 3-4 minutes before the end of the cooking.

Dried fish:

Prepared in the hot sunny islands. Usually prepared as soon as the fish is caught. Fresh fish of all sizes are salted and dried in the hot sun. These are used in vegetable dishes or cooked as dried fish Kari. It tastes different to the fresh fish. It is similar to the smoked fish in the West. Dried sprats are whitebait or anchovies. You will have to clean these to remove the intestine and head and then use as per recipe Can get good solid steaks of the dried fish. Some hard dried fish (Maldive fish) steaks are (pounded) ground to get flakes.

Masala Powder

Can be ground and stored in an airtight container.
See the recipes and use as required.

Ingredients

- 10-15 dried red chillies
- 1 tsp black pepper corns
- 4 cloves
- 5 cardomoms
- 4cm cinnamon stick
- 1½ tsp each ginger and garlic powder
- 2 tsp corriander seeds
- 2 tsp cumin seeds
- 1 tsp turmeric powder

Method

1. Grind all the above to a fine powder and keep.

To prepare

Add 1 tablespoon of the powder to 1tsp tamarind paste mix with water (about 1cup water), for 3-4 slices of fish.

★ If you are going to wet grind it to a paste:
Use fresh ginger and garlic, 1 tsp of vinegar (preservative)
Use a blender and grind it with other ingredients. Can be stored in the fridge for about a month.

Increase or reduce the chilli according to your taste

Fresh Sprats Kari (dry mild)

Preparation & Cooking Time: 45 minutes

Ingredients

- 10-15 sprats or sardines
- 4 shallots, finely sliced
- 2 tsp each garlic and ginger paste
- 1 tsp roasted coriander powder
- ½ cup water
- 1 or 2 green chillies cut
- 1 sprig of curry leaves
- small piece of rampe and lemon grass(sera in sri lanka)
- 1 tsp salt

Optional

- 1 tsp turmeric
- ½ can coconut milk (200g)
- ½ lime
- ½ to 1 tsp of black pepper corns - crushed

Cleaning: Leave the head on but slit the side and pull out the inner contents, intestines etc. Wash the fish in cold water.
Coat the fish with salt and turmeric powder.

Method

1. Place the fish in a flat-based pan add the chopped onion and all other ingredients including the water and bring to boil. Reduce the flame and cook. Half way through the cooking, turn the fish over so that it is cooked evenly.
2. After 10-12 minutes add the milk and rest of the curry leaves, rampe and crushed peppercorns.
3. It should be fairly dry with a little gravy.
4. Remove from cooker and squeeze the lime when kari is slightly warm.

★ Good for people who are just recovering from flu or have no appetite. Can use dairy milk or evaporated milk instead of the coconut milk.

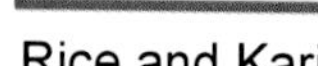

Fish Kari (Salmon cooked in spicy sauce)

"Meen Kulambu" - Tamil name
Preparation & Cooking Time: 30 minutes

Ingredients

- 2 salmon steaks
- 1 medium onion, chopped
- 1 tsp coriander powder
- 1 tsp cumin powder
- 1½ tsp roasted chilli powder
- 1 tsp garlic and 1 tsp ginger paste
- 2 cups water
- 1½ tbsp coconut powder
- ¼ cup cows milk
- 10 curry leaves, 2cm rampe
- 1 tsp turmeric powder to coat the fish
- 1 tsp ground pepper and cumin (optional)
- 1 tsp tamarind paste (can be increased depending on taste)
- 1 tsp salt

Method

1 Clean the fish, remove the skin by sliding a knife between the fish and the skin. Cut each steak to 3 or 4 pieces. Wash in cold water and roll it in the turmeric powder.

2. Place the cumin, coriander, onion, garlic, tamarind and chilli powder in a liquidiser, add ¼ cup of water and liquidise to a paste.

3. n a pan place the ground paste with rest of the water, mix well, add salt and bring to boil. Simmer for few minutes.

4. Add the fish gently with a spoon and cook on medium flame for 12-15 minutes. Stir once and make sure the fish is covered by the sauce whilst cooking. Gently stir or shake the pan to mix as stirring may break the fish slices.

5. Add the coconut powder to ¼ cup of warmed milk and mix it well. Add this to the fish and increase the heat and cook for 2-3 minutes. Add the curry leaves, rampe and sprinkle the ground cumin and pepper and remove from heat.

6. Final dish should have fish pieces in thick sauce. Total cooking time of 20 minutes is sufficient.

Variation

★ **Sarraku Kari:** Mild Masala Kari. Good for those with colds or recovering from flu etc. Use the above recipe omitting the chilli powder but add ground cumin and pepper powder. Add 1 tsp fenugreek seeds.

★ Can use evaporated milk, normal milk or cream coconut.

★ Instead of curry leaves can add 2 sprigs of coriander or methi leaves at the start of the cooking.

★ Can use herrings, mackerel or any tropical fish. Better if cut into steaks and not fillets.

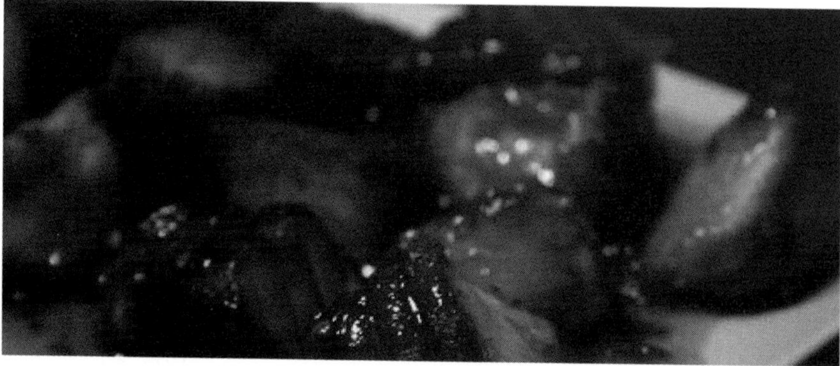

King Fish Kulambu

Kulambu is the Tamil name for sauce/gravy.
You can use any fish but salmon, mackerel, herrins, halibat and seer fish are kinds I have cooked and they taste good.

Preparation Time: 10 minutes
Cooking Time: 20-25 minutes
Serves 2

Ingredients

- 3 large king fish steaks
- 1 medium onion, chopped
- 3 cloves garlic
- 4cm ginger
- salt to taste
- 2 sprigs curry leaves
- For tempering - 1 tsp mixed mustard seed and cumin
- 2 tsp of roasted (Sri Lankan) chilli powder
- 1½" tamarind from a block; soak in warm water to get ¼ cup juice (or use 1-1½ tsp paste)
- ½ tin coconut milk or milk you have extracted from fresh coconut
- 1" piece of rampe stick
- 2 tbsp oil
- 1 cup of water or 3rd extract of coconut milk

Method

1. Wash the fish in cold water; cut each slice into four pieces.
2. In a thava or wok-type pan temper (fry) the onion in little oil, add the mustard and cumin seeds. Then add the crushed ginger, garlic and a few curry leaves.
3. Add the water or 3rd extract of coconut milk, tamarind juice, salt and chilli powder. Bring to boil for a few minutes.
4. Slowly slide the fish pieces into the boiling gravy and cook on a fairly high temperature, but not on full flame, for 12 minutes. Add the rest of the coconut milk and reduce the heat a bit.

5. Let it cook and when you see bubbles coming up it indicates that the gravy is beginning to thicken.
6. Add the cut-up rampe pieces, rest of the curry leaves and switch off the cooker.

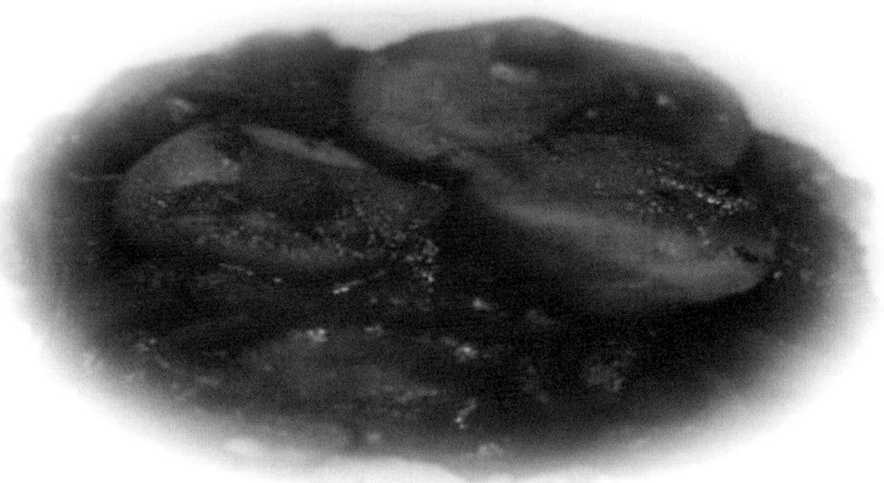

Worth knowing

- Traditional method is to cook in 3rd extract coconut milk and add the 1st thick extract milk last.
- However you can cook in water and tamarind mix, then add normal semi-skimmed milk.
- If the gravy/sauce is watery add a small piece of cream coconut and simmer or use 1 tsp of powdered dhal (see spices).

For this dish block tamarind is better than the paste. Cut a piece of tamarind about 2”x1” and soak in ½ cup of very hot water. Squeeze out the juice and discard the pieces. This process is also explained in the useful notes section.
You can also use tamarind paste.

Fish Kari (recipe from Goa)

Preparation & cooking time: 25-30 minutes
Serves 3

Ingredients

- 6 slices of fish steaks (salmon or any kind)
- 1 medium size onion, chopped
- 1 sprig curry leaves, chopped
- 1 tsp roasted chilli powder - can add to your taste
- 2 tsp fresh ground masala or masala powder
- small ball of tamarind soaked in water or 1½ tsp paste
- 1 tsp grated ginger and 1 tsp grated garlic
- 1 cup grated coconut ground to paste or ½ can coconut milk
- oil for frying
- salt to taste

Method

1. Wash the fish slices and cut in half, add a little salt and turmeric and set aside.

2. In a pan or thava heat oil and saute the onions. When it is done dish out the onions onto a plate.

3. In the same pan add 1 tsp of oil and fry the fish on low heat on both sides.

4. To the fish add the fried onions, half the curry leaves, all masala powder, rest of the salt, 1 cup water, tamarind and coconut paste and cook over a medium flame until the liquid reduces and the gets thick. Add the rest of the curry leaves and remove from heat.

★ In all it will take about 20 minutes to fry and cook the fish.

★ Preferably use seabream, king fish, salmon or mullet steaks, not filletted or smoked fish.

Fried Fish with Masala (Shallow fried)

Preparation & cooking time: 25 minutes
Serves 4

Any white fish cod or coley, salmon, halibut or mackerel

Ingredients

- 8 (slices) fish steaks
- 1 tsp garlic paste or 2 cloves, crushed
- ½ tsp ginger paste or 2cm root ginger, crushed
- 1 tsp masala powder (coriander, cumin & pepper)
- ¼ tsp ground fenugreek or pinch of seeds
- 3 tbsp oil for shallow frying
- 1tbsp desiccated coconut
- 1 tsp plain chilli powder
- 1 tbsp rice flour
- 1 tbsp plain flour
- salt to taste
- juice of ½ lemon

Method

1. In a bowl mix all ingredients except for the flour and desiccated coconut and make it to a paste by adding a few drops of water.
2. Wash and pat dry the fish steaks by placing on a kitchen tissue.
3. Place the fish steaks one by one and coat with the paste and leave to rest for a few minutes.
4. Mix the flour and desiccated coconut. Cover the fish with this mixture.
5. Heat a frying pan, add the oil and shallow fry the fish on both sides and cook for few minutes.
6. Remove from pan, add a bit of lemon juice.

★ Serve with rice and side dishes, salad or bread.

Deep Fried Fish with masala

Preparation & cooking time: 25 minutes

Serves 2

Ingredients

- 3 fish steaks (salmon)
- salt to taste
- ½ tsp chilli powder
- ½ tsp turmeric powder
- 1 tsp gram flour
- 1 tsp rice flour
- oil for frying

Method

1. Mix flour, chilli powder, turmeric and salt together. Add few drops of water and mix to a paste.
2. Depending on the size, cut the fish steaks into two or four pieces. Wash and leave to dry on a kitchen paper towel.
3. Coat the fish on both sides by placing in the mixed masala.
4. Heat oil in a small deep frying pan or thava. Fry the fish slices for 2 minutes on each side or until slightly brown.
5. One way of testing to see if the fish is cooked is if you slightly press a spoon or fork on the frying fish and remove the spoon it will spring back.
6. Remove and leave on kitchen paper.

Variation (Can use other masala)

1. Traditional method: add turmeric, salt and chilli powder only. Roll in this and deep fry.
2. For a change, you can add 1 tsp of garam masala powder and salt.
3. Coat in beaten egg white and then roll in breadcrumbs.

Tropical fish for frying

Mackerel: cut this into slices, do not fillet it.

Herrings: cut into large, say 4cm chunks.

Seer fish: halibut, kingfish slices can be fried without the chilli powder and given to children.

Shark: cut this in to 2cm square chunks, coat with chilli powder, salt and turmeric and deep fry.

Sprats / Sardines: First clean the fish by slitting the side near the neck and pull out the intestine and the residue near the head, etc. Wash in cold water. Add masala and fry as a whole fish with the head.
Fry until crispy.

Fish Varai - Stir fry - Mallung

Traditionally this is prepared with Shark/Ross.
I use a tin of salmon as shark is not always available and this tastes just as good.

Preparation & cooking time : 30-40 minutes
Serves 4-6 as a side dish

Ingredients

- 1 tin red or pink salmon (400g)
- 2 medium onions, diced
- 1 tsp mustard seeds
- 1 tsp cumin seeds
- 2 sprigs curry leaves, finely cut
- 2-3 tbsp oil
- ½ tsp garlic paste or powder
- ½ tsp ginger paste or powder
- 1 cup (6 tbsp) desiccated coconut
- 1 tsp plain chilli powder
- ½ to 1 tsp turmeric powder
- green chilli cut finely (optional)
- salt to taste ½ tsp
- a heavy-based frying pan
- 1 tsp each cumin powder and pepper powder (freshly ground)

Method

1. Open the can of salmon, drain the water and put it into a bowl, remove the bones etc. Mix and break the fish into small pieces. Mix the salt pepper, cumin, garlic, ginger and mix it well with your fingers, there should not be any large particle of fish, it should be in small fragments (crumble).

2. Heat the pan, add oil and fry the chopped onions until it turns to golden colour. Add the mustard seeds, cumin, dry red chilli and half the curry leaves.

3. Add the prepared fish, keep stirring and cook for five minutes; you need to keep stirring to ensure that all the parts get cooked. To the coconut add the chilli powder and turmeric and mix it so that the coconut absorbs the powder. Then add this to the fish and stir-fry.

4. Once the fish leaves the base of the pan and does not stick to it and is dry add the remainder of the curry leaves and remove from heat. The mixture should be dry.

Variation

- ★ **Fresh fish:** If you use fresh fish, clean the fish and boil this in water or microwave it first. Remove the skin and bones and use only the flesh.
- ★ **For children** and if you prefer mild and less fishy smell use frozen coley fish steaks.
- ★ **Shark**: Boil this in water with the skin on. Then remove the skin and bones. It tastes better if made hot; use more pepper than suggested in the above recipe and also use two green chillies finely cut.

Shark Kari

Preparation & cooking time: 30 minutes
Serves 3-4

Ingredients

- 3 steaks of shark (500g)
- 1 large onion, chopped
- 2 tsp grated ginger
- 2 tsp grated garlic
- salt to taste
- juice of 1 lime
- 2-3 tbsp oil
- 1½ tsp cumin seeds
- 1 tsp coriander seeds
- 1 tsp black pepper corns
- ½ cup water
- 2cm rampe cut
- 3 dry red chillies, chopped
- 1½ tsp roasted fennel powder
- 2 tbsp coconut powder mixed with little hot water
- 2 sprigs curry leaves, chopped

Method

1. Clean the shark remove the hard skin and cut into small cubes.
2. Grind garlic, ginger, cumin, corriander, pepper corns and chilli to a paste.
3. Heat oil in a deep frying pan, fry the onions, half the curry leaves,
   add the paste and water and bring to boil.
4. Add the shark pieces and salt and cook for 15 minutes over a medium heat.
5. Add the coconut powder mixture and cook for two minutes.
6. Add the remainder curry leaves, rampe and the roasted fennel powder. Stir and remove from heat.
7. Squeeze the juice of 1 lime and add it to the dish whilst warm and ready to serve.

★ Serve with rice, naan bread, noodles.

Aubergine and Dried Fish Pahi

A dish served in the southern part of Sri Lanka.
Dried salted fish is (pounded) ground to get the flakes. Known as Maldive fish and can be purchased from Sri Lankan shops

Preparation & cooking time: 40 minutes
Serves 3-4

Ingredients

- 2 large aubergines
- 2 tbsp dried fish flakes (available from Sri Lankan shops)
- 2 large onions, chopped
- 3 cloves garlic and 2cm ginger, grated
- 1 tbsp vinegar
- salt to taste
- 1 tbsp mustard powder
- 2 tbsp tomato puree
- 2 tsp crushed chillies (to taste)
- oil for deep frying
- 2 green chillies, chopped (optional)
- 1 sprig curry leaves, chopped
- 3cm piece rampe,cut
- ¼ tsp sugar (optional)

Method

1. Slice finely, the aubergines to about 4cm and deep fry in oil. If you are health conscious you may brush the aubergine slices with oil, place on a baking tray and cook in the oven at 190°C for 15 minutes.
2. In a frying pan or wok put two tablespoon of oil and stir-fry the finely chopped onions, garlic, ginger, curry leaves and rampe.
3. Next add the aubergine and stir-fry for 3-4 minutes.
4. Mix the vinegar, mustard powder, salt and crushed chillies to a paste.
5. Mix it with the aubergine, add the tomato puree. Cook on a low heat for 10 minutes.
6. Add Maldive fish, sugar and mix well and cook for a few minutes and remove from heat.

★ This keeps for few days if stored in the fridge.
★ Sugar gives a good taste like chutney but you can omit it.

Salted Dried fish - 'Karuvadu'

Dried fish is available from Chinese and Asian shops.

Explained in the introduction to fish. Dried fish is used in vegetable dishes or cooked as dried fish Kari. Tastes different from the fresh fish. There are several ways to prepare and cook the fish. You can add small cubed pieces of the fish to any vegetable. Tasty when added to aubergine, pepper, courgettes, tomato or potato.

Karuvadu with Aubergine Pahi

Ingredients

- 1 large aubergine
- 5-6 pieces salted dried fish
- 1 large tomato, chopped
- 2 cloves garlic, chopped
- 1 tbsp vinegar
- salt - very little
- 1 tbsp mustard powder
- 5 shallots or 1 medium onion, chopped
- 2 tsp crushed chillies
- 2 green chillies, chopped
- oil for deep frying

Method

1. Clean the dried salted fish, cut into small pieces. Wash and pat dry by placing on a kitchen cloth.

2. Cut the aubergine to thin strips. Cut to 4cm in length and deep fry in oil. Leave on kitchen paper to absorb the oil. Then place the aubergines in a bowl.

3. Fry the fish pieces and leave on a kitchen paper to drain the excess oil.

4. In another pan, fry the onions and garlic in a little oil and add to the fried aubergine.

5. Mix mustard, vinegar, salt, crushed chillies into a paste.
6. Add this to the aubergine, add the fried fish and mix well.
7. Cook the tomatoes and green chillies for a few minutes, add to the aubergine and dried fish and mix well.

Can be kept in the fridge for a week.

Variation

Ingredients

- 6 small pieces of dried fish (king fish, seer fish)
- pinch of fenugreek seeds, 6 tbsp desiccated coconut
- 1 tsp red chilli powder, 2 shallots, few curry leaves
- 1 tsp cumin, ¼ tsp pepper and 2 cloves garlic crushed
- 1 tbsp oil for frying

Method

You may try by frying the finely cut onions in oil. Add a pinch of fenugreek seeds. Then grind desiccated coconut, red chilli powder and tamarind to a paste. Add 2 cups water. Add the paste and water to the onions, add the fish. Cook for 12 minutes, add the freshly ground pepper, cumin, garlic, curry leaves and remove from heat.

Chilli & Onion sambol - Lunu miris

Speciality of the South

Ingredients

- 2 dried red chillies or 2 tsp crushed chilli powder
- 1 tsp salt
- 2 shallots, chopped
- juice of half a lime
- 6 curry leaves, finely cut

Method

1 Grind the chilli, salt and onion in a blender.

2 Add lime juice and curry leaves.

3 Mix and serve.

Katta sambol - Another preparation

For this you do not grind the above ingredients but mix them well.
Use your fingers as you need to rub well between your fingers.
Mix all chilli, finely chopped onions, lime juice, salt and curry leaves and serve.
Served with plain hoppers, string hoppers, bread etc.

Variation

To the above you can add dried flakes of Maldive fish or small dried shrimps, available from Sri Lankan or Chinese shops. It should be ground and added to the dish.

Ambul Thiyal (Dry preparation)

Speciality of the South

Preparation & cooking time: about an hour

Preferably fish steaks - such as salmon, halibut or seer fish should be used.

You need to use gorraka which is a kind of tamarind. Gorraka can be purchased from Sri Lankan shops.

This is a dish most returning from holiday in Sri Lanka try to bring with them. It can be kept in the fridge for few weeks.

Ingredients

- 3-4 fish steaks (500g)
- 7-8 pieces of gorraka
- 2 sprigs curry leaves and a 4cm piece rampe
- 1 tsp cinnamon powder, freshly ground
- 1 tsp ginger paste
- 1 tsp freshly ground black pepper
- 3 cloves garlic, crushed
- ¼ tsp turmeric powder
- 2 tsp roasted chilli/curry powder
- 1 cup water
- salt to taste

Method

1. Clean and cut the fish to 4cm cubes.

2. Place the gorraka in a pan, add ¼ cup hot water and simmer until it becomes soft. Take out the gorraka and grind or crush to a paste.

3. Put this back into the water and mix.

4. Coat the fish cubes with salt, turmeric, chilli powder, pepper, garlic, ginger and cinnamon. Arrange the fish in one layer of a heavy-based pan.

5. Pour the gorraka paste and water over the fish so that the fish pieces are slightly covered. Add the curry leaves and rampe.

6. Bring to boil and then reduce to a slow heat and simmer cook for 15-20 minutes for the fish to get cooked.

7. By this time the water should have evaporated, but if you find that there is still a lot of sauce, carefully dish out the fish onto a plate and cook the sauce alone on a high flame for it to dry. Transfer the fish back when the sauce begins to dry and leave the sides of the pan.

★ If you prefer the fish pieces coated in dry spices, you can put the fish and sauce into an oven-proof dish and bake in the oven at 180°C for 10 minutes until it completly dries up.

★ Serve with rice, bread, naan, pittu, etc.

★ If you cannot get gorraka can use tamarind paste.

★ Prepared bottled ambul thiyal is available from Sri Lankan shops

Fish Vadai

Similar to cutlets

My mother in law prepared this for my husband and me. I have used provisions available in the West to prepare this.

Preparation & cooking time: 45 minutes

Ingredients:

- 3 cod steaks or coley chunks (boiled)
- 2 shallots, finely diced
- 2 green chillies, finely cut
- 2 egg-yolks
- 2 tbsp rice flour
- 2 tbsp plain flour
- 1 slice bread, cut into small cubes
- salt to taste
- ginger and garlic (to taste)
- oil for deep frying
- chilli powder (optional)
- 1 tsp fennel seeds

Method

1. Boil and break the fish into flakes and place in a bowl. Add the egg yolks and stir.
2. Add the chopped onions, salt, garlic, ginger, green chillies, bread, fennel seeds and mix well without mashing it a lot.
3. Add rice flour and the plain flour and mix to form a dropping consistency not too watery or thick.
4. Heat oil in a pan. Drop spoonfuls and fry until brown.
5. Remove and serve as fish vadai.

★ Any white fish or shark pieces can be used to prepare this.

Fried Anchovy

Malaysian preparation - served as a snack

Popular dish in China and Malaysia.
When I visited Malaysia in November 2006, I saw children as young as 2-3 yrs old having this. It can be purchased pre-fried and packed in tins. The recipe below will help if you need to cater for a party. It can be prepared in advance and stored in airtight bottle or tins.

Ingredients

- 500g dried anchovy (about 2½" long)
- oil for deep frying
- chilli powder

Method

1. Clean the anchovy, pat dry and place in a colander or run with your palm to remove the small particles from the fish, as these will fry quickly, burn and spoil the oil. Deep fry the anchovy in hot oil and drain on paper towels.

2. After a few minutes if they loose the crispiness, heat the oven at the highest temperature and place a tray of the fried anchovy for 10 minutes. This will make it crispy.

3. Place the fried fish in a bowl and sprinkle chilli powder.

4. Serve with salad, dips, fried shallots, peanuts, etc. and with drinks.

★ An alternative method to remove the moisture is to place the washed anchovy on a tray and place in a pre-heated oven for 10 minutes at the highest temperature. Then deep fry and add chilli.

Sardines on toast

Preparation & cooking time: 20-30 minutes

Ingredients

- 5 fresh sardines, large
- white of egg, whisked
- ½-1 tsp chilli powder
- ½ tsp ground masala powder
- bread crumbs, finely powdered
- coriander leaves or parsley, chopped
- 2 bread slices, toasted and cut into strips
- butter
- oil for deep frying
- salt to taste

Method

1. Clean the sardines, remove the intestines and the head.
2. Mix salt, chilli and masala to form a paste, coat the fish in this paste.
3. Dip each fish in beaten egg white and roll in breadcrumbs and deep fry until golden brown colour.
4. Toast the bread, butter it and cut into strips.
5. Place each sardine on a slice of bread and top with chopped coriander or parsley. Serve hot.

★ Can use tinned sardine, which is readily available. Drain the oil or sauce, pat dry first, then mix the masala etc. and coat with bread crumbs. Deep fry and place on toast, garnish with lettuce/ parsley and serve.

★ Can add lime wedges.

Kool - Soup with mixed Seafood

Jaffna recipe

Something similar to a soup.
A hot soup with tropical vegetables and palmyrah flour known as 'odiyal ma'. Have it on Saturday or Sunday at lunch time.
See the special dishes section for the traditional vegetarian kool

Preparation time: appx an hour
Cooking time: 45 minutes

Serves 8

Ingredients

- 500g fish steaks
- 500g prawns
- 1 squid or squid rings
- 4 crab claws or 1 crab
- 1 cup palmyrah flour (odiyal ma)
- 1 bunch fresh spinach leaves
- 500g frozen cassava
- 250g or 1 bunch long thin beans (payathangai)
- 10-15 dry red chillies freshly ground – powdered
- 3-4 pints water
- tamarind ¼ block or small ball size
- ¼ cup rice
- salt to taste
- 1 tsp turmeric powder
- 5 garlic cloves
- a large pan
- small bunch of **murunga leaves** (optional - available from Sri Lankan shops)
- 3 tbsp corn flour (optional standby)

Few items in the vegetarian recipe are not included, but if you prefer they can also be included

Method

1. Clean the fish, cut to pieces of 4cm size. Shell the prawns, wash and leave as whole. Clean and cut the squid to 3cm size pieces. Using a hammer knock the crab claws lightly, cut the crab into 4 pieces. Place all the above in a large pan, add 2 cups of water, a bit of salt and pepper and bring to boil. Reduce heat and cook for 12-15 minutes.
   Serve in a bowl and set aside (use the pan to boil the vegetables).
2. Soak the Palmyrah flour in a large quantity of water and leave it to settle for 5 minutes. The flour will settle to the bottom and there will be clear water on top.
3. Carefully strain the water out without losing any of the flour. Pour some water again mix it and let it settle. You need to do this process three times.
4. Soak the tamarind in hot water, leave it for a few minutes, mix well, strain and keep the juice. Pour a bit more hot water over the tamarind and leave in case you need it later.
5. Cut the cassava to small squares. Wash and chop the spinach. Prepare the beans and cut to 3cm pieces. Grind the red chillies adding a little salt, garlic and enough water to make into a paste.
6. Add the beans, cassava, rice and add 2-3 pints of water to the pan and cook.
7. After 15 minutes when the vegetables are cooked add the spinach and the boiled fish etc. including any water.
8. Mix the tamarind juice with half the chilli paste and turmeric and add it to the boiled vegetables and fish and continue cooking.
9. Taste and add the remainder of the chilli paste depending on the hotness you require.
10. Add the strained palmyrah flour and mix well. You will see the broth thickening (the volume will be nearly the same as the amount of water used).
11. To make the consistency correct either add more hot water or more palmyrah flour. A bit of corn flour mixed in water will also be okay.
12. Now add the murunga leaves (optional)
13. Remove from heat and serve while hot.

★ If you have a pressure cooker, the kool will be cooked in 25 minutes.

★ Can substitute corn flour for palmaryah flour, but the taste will be different. Here the special ingredient is the palmyrah flour.

★ A packet of frozen paella mix of seafood can be used instead of the fish prawns, crabs etc. This also tastes good.

Anchovy with Potato

Halmmaso thel curry is a famous dish in the southern part of Sri Lanka. Tamil name for dry sprats/anchovy is 'Nethali'.

Preparation & cooking time: 30 minutes

Ingredients

- 20 sprats (anchovies) dried
- 2 medium onions, sliced finely
- 2cm piece of ginger, cut into fine strips
- 2 tsp plain chilli powder or crushed
- 2 medium size potato, cut into thin strips
- 1 sprig curry leaves, chopped
- 1 tsp mustard seeds
- 3 cloves garlic, finely cut
- oil for cooking (3-4 tbsp)
- 2 tomatoes, chopped
- 1 tsp tomato purée
- salt to taste

Method

1. Clean the anchovy; discard the head and the intestine (black bit) near the neck. Wash and pat dry.
2. In a flat-based heavy frying pan add oil and fry the potato for 2 minutes. Add the onions and mustard seeds and continue to cook. Remove from cooker and transfer onto a plate.
3. Add little more oil to the pan and cook the sprats until the moisture has evaporated and the anchovy starts to become crispy. Remove from the heat and transfer to a plate.
4. To the pan add the fried potato, onion, cut tomato, chilli powder, salt, garlic and ginger and cook for few minutes. If needed add tsp of oil.
5. Add the fried anchovy and curry leaves. Add the purée, mix once and turn the heat to low, cover and cook for another 5 minutes.
6. The dish will look like a thick sauce with potato strips and anchovy.

- ★ Serve with rice, string hoppers, bread
- ★ Can try making with any small fish available from the supermarkets.

Roe

Preparation & cooking time: 30 minutes

Ingredients

- 2 medium fish roe
- 2 shallots, finely sliced
- 2 tsp plain chilli powder
- salt, turmeric, few curry leaves,
- 4 tbsp of desiccated coconut
- 3 tbsp oil

Method

1. Clean roe and boil in water for a few minutes. Drain and cut to thick slices. Shallow fry in a little oil on both sides, remove and leave on a plate.
2. Fry onion adding a little bit of oil.
3. Grind the chilli, turmeric, salt, coconut and add to the fried onions.
4. Add 1 cup water, bring to boil, add the fried roe and cook until the sauce thickens.
5. Add curry leaves and remove from cooker.

★ Can deep fry roe. Dip in batter and deep fry in oil.

★ If you cannot get fresh roe try the canned roe which does not require boiling.

Mackerel with Green Mango

Ingredients

- 2 mackerels (medium)
- 1 tsp salt
- 1 medium onion, diced
- 2 small green mangoes
- ½ tsp turmeric powder
- ½ tsp fenugreek seeds
- ½ tsp mustard seeds
- ½ tsp fennel seeds
- 2 tbsp oil
- 2 sprigs curry leaves
- ½ coconut grated or (400g)1 can coconut milk
- 4 cloves garlic
- 2cm size ginger
- 2 tsp plain chilli powder
- 1 tsp pepper ground/crushed
- ½ tsp cumin seeds
- 4cm piece of rampe and 1 lemon grass, chopped

Method

1. Peel the mango and grate it.
2. Cut the fish into slices. Discard the intestines etc., wash and leave on a plate.
3. Grind the grated coconut, chilli powder, turmeric, ginger and garlic to a paste, you may need to add some water.
4. Add oil to a pan and fry the onions for 2 minutes. Add the fenugreek seeds, mustard, fennel, cumin and half the curry leaves.
5. Add the ground coconut, grated mango, pepper and 2 cups of water and bring to boil. If using coconut milk add ½ the can and 1½ cups of water.
6. When the mixture boils add the mackerel pieces and cook for 2 minutes. Reduce the heat and cook for 10 minutes.
7. Add the rest of the coconut milk, curry leaves, lemon grass and rampe. Increase the heat, bring to boil and cook for a further 2 minutes and remove from heat.

★ Can use semi-skimmed milk instead of the coconut milk, and add a small piece of creamed coconut at the end (step 7).

Fish Sothi

See the recipe for sothi in the vegetarian section page 212 and add 2 pieces of fish, fish head, ¼ tsp fenugreek seeds and prepare the sothi. Finally add lemon or lime juice.

Quick method is to boil onions, green chilli and fish with 2 cups of water. Add salt, turmeric, fenugreek,curry leaves, rampe and finally, a little milk. When warm add the lime or lemon juice and serve.

Puli kanji Soup

To the recipe included in the vegetarian section add a small packet of frozen mixed seafood or add prawns, fish slices and cook. Add lime juice.

Prawns - Squid - Crab Index

Prawns can be added to vegetables like drumsticks, aubergine, okra, mushrooms and cooked as a hot dish with chillies.

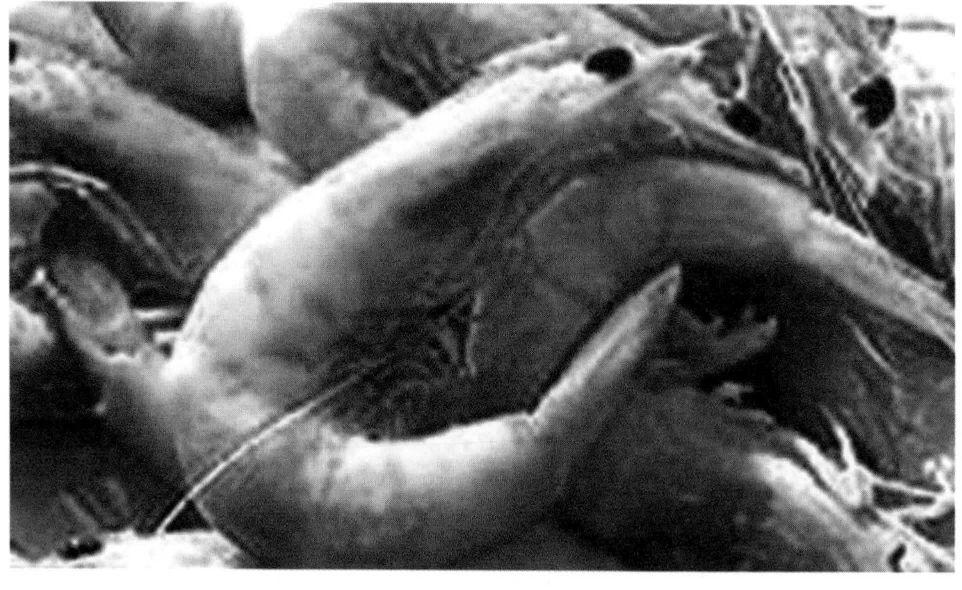

King Prawns Stir Fry

Preparation time: 3 hrs to marinate
Cooking time: 20 minutes
Serves 5

Ingredients

- 500g cooked king prawns
- 3 medium onions, sliced
- ½ green pepper, sliced
- ½ yellow or red pepper, sliced
- 2 tsp roasted chilli/curry powder
- 4 cloves garlic, grated
- 2cm ginger, grated
- 2 tbsp tomato puree, 1-2 tsp tomato sauce
- 2 green chillies, chopped
- ¼ cup water
- 3 tbsp oil
- 2 spring onions chopped
- salt to taste

Method

1. Place the prawns in a bowl, add chilli powder, salt, ginger, garlic, 2 tbsp tomato purée and little water. Mix well and marinate for 3 hours.
2. Heat 2 tablespoons oil in a thava or wok and stir fry the onions. Add the pepper and stir fry for 2-3 minutes and transfer it to a plate.
3. Add the prawns with the sauce in to the wok, add the green chillies and stir fry for 4-5 minutes. See that it is not too dry and sticking to the pan; if necessary add a little oil and fry.
4. Add the fried onions and pepper, stir and cook for a couple of minutes. Add tomato sauce and stir.
5. Add the chopped spring onions and stir. Remove from heat and serve with hot rice or noodles.

★ Instead of the pepper you can add green capsicum chillies (hot).

Prawn Rice with pillau masala

See the rice recipe for fried rice or pillau rice

To this add the following

Ingredients

- **300g king prawns, fried**
- **2 tsp masala paste or powder**
- **2 tbsp chopped roasted cashew nuts**
- **1 tsp ground cinnamon**

Mix the above with the fried rice and stir it well.

To make the Pillau Masala

Ingredients

- 3 cloves garlic
- 2cm root ginger
- 1 tsp cuminseeds, 8 peppercorns
- 2 green chillies
- 15 cashew nuts
- salt to taste

For frying

- 10 shallots,
- cinnamon, cloves, ghee,
- bay leaves, coriander leaves

Method

1. Grind the masala ingredients adding a little water.
   To this paste add 10 finely sliced shallots fried with cinnamon and cloves in a little ghee.
2. Mix all the above together, add a few coriander leaves, bay leaves and add to the cooked rice.

Prawn Kari

Jaffna preparation

The traditional method is to cook the prawns in the weaker consistency of coconut milk and then add the first thick milk extracted from fresh coconut.
For ease you can use either coconut milk from a can or creamed coconut or even coconut powder mixed in hot water. You must use coconut as this gives a special, unique flavour.

Ingredients

- 3 large red onions, chopped very small
- 400g prawns/king prawns - cleaned
- 1 tbsp concentrated tamarind
- 1 tbsp cumin seeds
- 1 tsp black pepper seeds
- 1½ tsp roasted chilli powder
- 1 tsp fenugreek seeds
- 1 whole garlic - about 12 cloves
- 10 curry leaves
- 1 green chilli and 2 dried red chillies, chopped
- 4cm size of rampe, chopped (optional)
- 1 can coconut milk (375g) or 2cm slice creamed coconut
- 1 cup of water
- salt to taste

Method

1. Wash and clean the prawns, remove the shell.
2. Clean the garlic and cut each garlic into four or five slices.
3. In a heavy-based deep pan or a thava place the prawns.
4. Add the onions, salt, fenugreek seeds, chilli powder, garlic, tamarind paste mixed in one cup of water and chillies and bring to a boil. Reduce the heat and cook for 10 minutes.

5. Add the coconut milk and slightly increase the flame and cook for a further 3 minutes.

6. Add the curry leaves and rampe.

7. Finally grind the pepper and cumin and add to the prawn dish. Stir once and when the sauce is thickened remove from the cooker.

★ Can use 1-2cm slice cream coconut instead of the milk. You may need a bit more water to cook at the start. Then add the creamed coconut, keep stirring and finally add the ground cumin and pepper.

★ If using tamarind from a block then you need to soak this in hot water and get the pulp out and use the juice.

Butter Prawn dish - Malaysian preparation

Preparation & cooking time: 20 minutes
Serves 4

Ingredients

- 20 tiger prawns, cleaned
- 60g butter or margarine
- 5 shallots, finely sliced
- 1 tsp rice wine
- ¼ tsp chilli paste, ¼ tsp garlic paste
- ¼ cup thick coconut milk or add 4 tbsp coconut powder mixed
- with hot water
- 2 egg whites
- 3 sprigs curry leaves
- 1 tsp sugar (optional)
- oil for deep frying
- 4cm rampe, chopped
- salt to taste

Method

1. Clean the prawns by removing the shell but leave the tails on. Rinse well and dry in paper towel.
2. Heat the oil in a pan. Beat the egg whites well, dip the prawn in this and deep fry.
3. Remove and drain on paper towels. Deep fry the curry leaves and leave it on a paper to drain the oil.
4. Heat a heavy-based frying pan. Melt the butter and add the sliced onions and cook for two to three minutes.
5. Add the fried prawns, stir fry and add the curry leaves. Add the ground chilli paste, rice wine and sugar. Cook for a minute.
6. Then add the coconut milk, salt and cook until the paste thickens.
7. Garnish with coriander leaves and rampe.

★ If you like the prawns crispy, cook the chilli paste etc. in coconut milk and add the prawns last before removing from cooker.

Prawns in tomato and chilli sauce

Preparation & cooking time: **20 minutes**
Serves 5

Ingredients

- 500g large prawns (boiled and peeled)
- 2 onions, chopped
- 3 garlic cloves, grated
- 3cm ginger, grated
- 2 green chillies, chopped
- 4 spring onions, chopped
- 1 tbsp roasted chilli/curry powder
- 1 tsp garam masala paste
- 1 sprig curry leaves, lemon grass, chopped
- 2 sprigs coriander leaves, chopped
- 4 tomatoes, chopped
- ¼ cup water
- oil for frying
- 1 tsp cumin, 1 tsp mustard seeds
- 2 dried red chillies, chopped
- ½ can coconut milk(200g) or 4 tbsp coconut powder mixed in ¼ cup hot water
- 1 tsp chilli sauce, 1 tsp tomato sauce
- salt to taste

Method

1. Heat 2 tablespoons oil in a pan add mustard seeds, cumin, chopped red chillies and 2-3 curry leaves. Reduce the heat and add chopped onions, garlic, ginger, chopped green chillies and cook for 2-3 minutes.
2. Add chilli powder, masala, salt, and cook for a minute.
3. Add tomatoes, ¼ cup water and 1/3 of the coconut milk and bring to a boil. Reduce the heat and cook for 8-10 minutes.
4. Add the rest of the coconut milk and increase the heat. Add the prawns, mix well and cook on low heat for 5 minutes. Add the chilli and tomato sauce and stir.
5. Add the rest of the curry leaves, coriander leaves and lemon grass. Remove from cooker and serve.

★ Can use single cream instead of the coconut milk.
★ Can increase or decrease the chilli powder to your taste.

King Prawns

Preparation & cooking time: ½ hour
Serves 3

Ingredients

For masala

- 1 tsp cumin seeds, 1 tsp coriander seeds, ½ tsp peppercorns
- 2cm size ginger, 8 cloves garlic, small piece of cinnamon, 3 cloves and 4 cardamoms, 2 tbsp desiccated coconut
- 16 king prawns cleaned
- 3 medium onions or 10-12 shallots, finely sliced
- 4 tomatoes, chopped
- 1-1½ tsp plain chilli powder
- 1 tsp turmeric
- ½ tsp fenugreek
- 2 sprigs curry leaves, 2cm size rampe
- ½ bottle oil
- 1 cup water
- 1cm slice cream coconut
- salt to taste

Method

1. Wash the king prawns and leave on kitchen paper towel to absorb the water. Add salt and turmeric powder and leave it aside.

2. Grind all the masala ingredients, cumin, coriander, pepper, coconut, cinnamon, cardamom, cloves and desiccated coconut to a paste and leave in a bowl.

3. Deep fry the onions and take it out when the onions turn colour. Fry the curry leaves and leave on paper towel. In a small tea strainer or colander place the fenugreek seeds and just lower it slowly to fry for 30 seconds and remove it.

4. Next deep fry the prawns and dish it out.

5. Heat a deep frying pan and add water, salt, masala paste, chilli powder, chopped tomatoes and bring to boil.

6. Add the fried onions, prawns, fried fenugreek, curry leaves and bring to boil. Reduce the heat and simmer for 5 minutes. Then add the sliced cream coconut and cook for 2-3 minutes. Cut the rampe into two or three pieces and add it.

7. Stir it well and remove from the cooker when the mixture is slightly thick.

★ If you want to cook this in a hurry, you can use roasted chilli powder instead of the ground masala. Add 1 tsp of mixed spice powder of cinnamon, cardamom and cloves.
Stir fry the prawns first. Then do the same for the onions and garlic (no need to deep fry). Follow the method adding 2 tomatoes and finally add 3-4 tablespoons of tomato ketchup and cook for a few minutes before removing from the cooker. Omit the cream coconut.

★ To the main recipe you can add 1 tsp of tamarind paste instead of the 4 tomatoes and follow the rest. Add either cream coconut or coconut milk.

Large Fried Prawns

Preparation & cooking time: 20 minutes
Serves 4

Ingredients

- 16 large king prawns
- 1 egg beaten or egg white
- 1 tsp ginger paste
- 1 tsp garlic paste
- 1 tsp plain chilli powder
- ¼ cup gram flour, sieved
- ¼ cup rice flour, 2 tbsp plain flour
- oil for frying
- salt to taste
- 2 tsp soya sauce
- ½ tsp each of coriander powder and turmeric

Method

1. Shell and clean the prawn, apply salt, chilli powder, ginger and garlic. Leave aside for half an hour.
2. Sieve the flour together. Add the coriander, turmeric, salt, soya sauce, egg and a bit of water to form a slightly thick batter.
3. Heat a frying pan, add the oil and bring to a high temperature.
4. Dip each prawn in the batter and deep fry.
5. Remove from oil and place on a kitchen paper to absorb the oil.
6. Serve whilst warm and crispy.

★ Can cook the prawns (covered in a dish) in the microwave for 1 minute on high power, before dipping in batter & frying.

★ Instead of making the batter you can dip the prawn in the beaten egg white and then roll in the dry flour and deep fry.

★ For crispy prawns add 2-3 tablespoons of bread crumbs to half the flour and roll the prawns in this and deep fry.

Prawn with Mango

Ingredients

- 250g shelled prawns
- 2 onions, chopped
- 1 green (raw) mango
- 1 tbsp roasted chilli powder
- 1 sprig curry leaves
- ½ cup scraped coconut or desiccated coconut
- 1 tsp turmeric powder
- ½ tsp tamarind paste
- 3 cloves garlic, piece of ginger 2cm size
- salt to taste
- 3 tbsp milk (optional)
- 2 cups water
- 1 tbsp oil

Method

1. Prepare the masala by grinding the coconut, 1 onion, salt, tamarind paste, chilli powder, garlic and ginger.

2. In a thava or a frying pan add the remainder of the onions, prawns mixed in one tablespoon of the masala and pan fry in 1 tablespoon of oil. Remove and leave it aside.

3. Mix the rest of the masala in 1½ cups of water and add to the pan and boil for two minutes.

4. Peel the skin of the mango and cut into thin slices. Add this to the boiling sauce together with the lightly cooked prawns. Cook for 5 minutes, add milk and curry leaves. Cook for 2 minutes and remove from cooker.

Prawn Kari (Venthaya Kari)

Prawn with fenugreek and onions
Recipe originated from Jaffna. It is a semi dry dish.Traditional method is to cook in coconut milk. Can use full cream evaporated milk ,cows' milk or cream coconut.

Preparation & cooking time: 1 hour 30 minutes
Serves 4

Ingredients

- 400g small or medium size prawns either fresh or frozen
- 3 large onions, sliced thin and cut to diagonal
- 6 cloves garlic, peeled and sliced into two or three
- 2 sprigs curry leaves
- 1 tsp fenugreek seeds
- 2 tsp tamarind paste or juice of tamarind soaked in hot water
- salt to taste
- 1 medium bottle oil, for deep frying
- 2 tsp roasted Sri Lankan chilli powder
- 1 cup thick coconut milk or 1 can of coconut milk
- small piece of cream coconut
- 2 cups water
- piece of rampe cut up
- few methi leaves

Method

1. Heat a thava or a wok-like pan. Add oil
2. Fry the onion slices until brown and slightly crispy, half way add the garlic and fry with the onions. Dish out the onion and garlic onto a kitchen paper placed in a colander so that any excess oil will drain .
3. Wash and pat dry the prawns. Deep fry the prawns until crispy.

4. Fry the curry leaves. Place fenugreek seeds in a tea strainer and slowly immerse into the hot oil for about 5-6 seconds. Remove and leave it aside.

5. Mix the tamarind in hot water, squeeze the juice and strain to get about ½ cup of fairly thick juice.

6. In a heavy-based pan or thava add the tamarind juice, water, chilli powder, salt and boil for a few minutes, or if you are using coconut milk instead of the water use half the coconut milk diluted in ½ cup of water. Mix with tamarind and other ingredients and bring to boil.

7. Add the fried onions, garlic, prawns, fenugreek, curry leaves and cook on medium heat for about 10 minutes.

8. Add the rest of the milk, cream coconut and cook for 2 minutes on slightly high heat for the sauce to thicken and leave the sides of the pan. Remove from heat.

★ Can be served with rice, noodles, string hoppers, bread, naan etc.

★ Instead of deep frying, can stir fry/sauté the onions in a little oil, then add the prawns and other ingredients. Then follow the rest of the method adding tamarind, milk etc. This will save lot washing and is healthy too.

Squid Kari - Jaffna preparation

Preparation & cooking time: 40 minutes

Ingredients

- 500g squid (1 large or a box)
- 1 large onion, chopped
- 1 green chilli, cut lengthwise
- 2-3 tsp roasted chilli/curry powder
- salt to taste
- 1 tsp fenugreek seeds
- 6 cloves garlic, crushed
- 4cm root ginger, crushed
- 2 sprigs curry leaves, chopped
- 3cm piece rampe, cut into strips
- small piece of lemon grass, also known as 'sara', chopped
- 1 can coconut milk (400g)
- 1½ tsp roasted fennel powder, ½ lime

Method

1. Clean the squid, take all the sand, cellulite 'back bone', ink bag, and the white fatty bits out. Wash and cut to small squares or rings.
2. In a heavy-based wok or a pan, place the squid pieces. Add onions, green chillies, garlic, ginger, chilli powder, salt and fenugreek seeds.
3. Add ¼ of the coconut milk to ¾ cup warm water, mix well and add this to the squid.
4. Bring to boil and cook for 2-3 minutes. Reduce to medium heat and cook for another 12 minutes.
5. Add the rest of the coconut milk and simmer for another 10 minutes.
6. Add the curry leaves, rampe, lemon grass and give it a stir.
7. Finally add the roasted fennel powder and stir it. Cover and remove from cooker. The sauce will be fairly thick.
8. Just before serving add the juice from the lime and stir.

★ If you want it dry then cook in a thava and increase the heat at the end for 3-4 minutes. Be careful not to let it burn.

Squid Rings Fried

Preparation & cooking time: 30 minutes

Ingredients

- 2 medium size squids or a bag of squid rings (400g)
- 6 garlic cloves, grated
- 1 tsp grated ginger
- 5-6 tbsp oil for frying
- salt to taste, pepper
- 1 tsp roasted chilli powder
- 6 fresh curry leaves

Method

1. Wash the squid, clean (as in previous recipe) and cut into rounds of ½" size. Alternatively use the ready cut rings.

2. In a frying pan put half the oil, fry the squid pieces, keep turning.

   Add the remainder oil and fry. After 4-5 minutes add the garlic, ginger, salt, pepper and fry. In all 8-10 minutes should be sufficient.
   Add the chilli powder, curry leaves and stir for a few seconds and remove from heat.

3. Serve as a bite with drinks or you can eat it with rice or bread.

★ If you like it very hot you can fry 4-5 dry red chillies with the garlic etc.

★ You can deep fry the rings; for this add powdered spice to plain flour, add salt and chilli powder. Then roll the squid rings in flour and deep fry.

Squid with Tamarind Sauce

Ingredients

- 1kg squid, clean and cut into rings or strips
- 2 medium onion chopped
- 3 cloves garlic and 1" size ginger
- 1 tsp tamarind paste
- 1 sprig curry leaves and 2” rampe
- ½ to 1 cup of water
- 2 tsp roasted fennel seed powder
- 2 green chillies cut up
- 2 tsp roasted chilli powder
- 2 tbsp ground almond
- 2” slice cream coconut
- salt to taste

Method

1. In an electric blender liquidise the onion, garlic, ginger, chilli powder, almond powder and tamarind paste mixed well in 2 tablespoon of water. Grind to a paste and set this aside.
2. In a large heavy frying pan add the oil, add the washed squid and sauté this slightly.
3. Next add the spice paste and sauté it. Add ½ or 1 cup of water and cook on a high flame. After 5 minutes reduce the heat slightly and cook for 15 minutes.
4. Add the cream coconut, curry leaves and rampe. Stir well and cook for few more minutes until the cream coconut is dissolved and is absorbed in the sauce.
5. Remove from heat and add the fennel powder and stir it. Serve with rice.

Squid with Tomatoes

Preparation & cooking time: 30 minutes

Ingredients

- 500g squid (1 box of small squids)
- 1 large onion, chopped
- 3 medium tomatoes, chopped
- 2 medium potatoes, peeled and cut into small cubes
- 1 green chilli, slit lengthwise
- 3 tsp roasted mixed chilli curry powder (Sri Lankan)
- salt to taste
- 1 tsp fenugreek seeds
- 6 cloves garlic, crushed
- 3cm root ginger, crushed
- 2 sprigs curry leaves, chopped
- 4cm rampe stick, cut into strips
- 1½ cm slice cream coconut
- 1½ tsp roasted fennel powder
- tempering ingredients: ½ tsp each of mustard seeds, cumin, 1 red chilli, chopped and 1 tbsp oil
- 1 medium cup water
- ¼ cup milk

Method

1. Clean, remove the cellulite back bones, claws near the mouth, wash and cut into small rounds.
2. Heat the oil in a heavy-based wok (thava) or a pan. Add the mustard seeds and when they start to splutter add the cumin and onions. Fry until slightly golden colour. Add half of the curry leaves, chilli and fenugreek seeds.
3. Add the squid and stir fry for 2 minutes.
4. Add salt, green chilli, ginger, garlic, chilli/curry powder and water and cook for 5 minutes.
5. Add the potatoes and tomatoes. Give it a stir and cook over a medium heat for 12 minutes adding the ¼ cup milk half way and cook. Ensure the mixture does not get burnt.
6. Add the creamed coconut and cook for further 2-3 minutes. Add the fennel powder curry leaves and rampe. Remove from heat.

Crab

Use fresh crabs or frozen Indian tropical water crabs, which are available from Asian shops/Sri Lankan shops. These are already cleaned and packed

Crab Kari

Preparation & cooking time: 45 minutes

Use fresh crabs or frozen Indian tropical water crabs, which are cleaned and packed in boxes.
Available from Asian/Sri Lankan shops.

Ingredients

- 1kg crabs, cleaned
- ½ tsp turmeric powder
- 3cm root ginger, crushed
- 2 large onions, chopped
- 8-10 curry leaves, chopped
- 1 can (400g) coconut milk
- 2 tbsp roasted chilli powder
- 6 cloves garlic, crushed
- 2 tomatoes, chopped
- salt to taste
- 1 tsp fenugreek seeds
- 2 tbsp oil
- 4cm piece rampe, cut into strips
- 1 medium aubergine, cut into small cubes
- 1 small potato, cut into small cubes
- murunga leaves (Sri Lankan shops) or methi leaves (optional)
- 1cm slice (rectangle piece) cream coconut or
- 2 tsp roasted fennel powder
- For tempering: 1 onion, chopped, 1 tsp of mustard seeds, 1 tsp cumin seeds, 2 tbsp oil
- 1 tsp freshly ground cinnamon, cardamom powder

Method

Cleaning: Wash the frozen crabs, if necessary cut into 4 pieces, keep the legs and the claws. Slightly crack the pieces and the claws with a hammer or a rolling pin.

1. Heat the oil in a large heavy-based pan or a wok and fry the mustard seeds, cumin seeds and fenugreek seeds for few seconds. Add the chopped onions and fry until golden colour. Next add the aubergine and potato cubes and stir fry for a minute.
2. Add the crab and cook for 2-3 minutes until the crab changes colour slightly. Add the crushed garlic, ginger, chilli powder, water and tomotoes (Also add the murunga leaves or methi leaves which are optional) and cook for about 12 minutes.

3. Add a little hot water to the cream coconut and make it into a paste. Add this to the crab and cook for few minutes. Add rampe, curry leaves, cinnamon powder and lastly the fennel powder. Remove from cooker and add the juice of ½ lime at the end before serving. In all 20 minutes of cooking time should be enough.
4. Serve with plain rice.

★ Can add tamarind paste or pulp. Omit the tomatoes and the lime.

Crab - With Fresh Coconut Masala

Ingredients

- 1kg crabs, cleaned
- ½ cup grated coconut
- 8 red chillies
- 1 tsp each coriander seeds
- 1 tsp cumin seeds
- ½ fenugreek seeds
- few pepper corns
- 1 tsp turmeric powder
- 6 cloves garlic and a small piece of ginger
- 1 tsp roasted fennel powder
- 2 onions chopped
- 3-4 tbsp oil
- ¼ cup milk
- ½ cinnamon powder

Method

1. In a deep pan, sauté the onion in 2 tbsp oil, add the rest of the ingredients and roast it. Let it cool and using a blender grind it to a paste. Add little water to grind.

2. Add the remainder oil to the pan, add the crabs and stir fry for 2-3 minutes until the colour changes slightly.

3. Next add the roasted masala paste, potato and aubergine and cook for twenty minutes. You may need to add ½ cup of water and cook.

4. After 20 minutes add a little milk, curry leaves, cinnamon powder and rampe and cook for 2 –3 minutes.

5. Remove from cooker and sprinkle roasted fennel powder and serve.

Chicken

Chicken Dishes - Index

Chicken Mild Sauce (for children)

Ingredients

- 3-4 cloves garlic
- 25g butter
- 1cm size ginger
- 1 onion, chopped
- ½ tsp turmeric
- 1 tsp coriander, cumin powder (roasted)
- ¼ cup water
- ½ cup normal milk
- vegetable stock cube or chicken cube
- salt to taste

Method

1 Heat butter; add the chopped onions, garlic, ginger and fry. Add cumin coriander.

2. When cool either use a hand blender or use a liquidiser and blend to a paste.

3. Set aside the ground paste until you require. Can be kept in the fridge for a few days.

4. Use 1-2 tsp of the paste depending on the quantity and the taste.

★ If you are cooking straight away, heat a little butter or margarine, add a pinch of mustard seeds, few curry leaves and add 1 tsp of the paste to the cubed chicken pieces and cook for 10 minutes. Add vegetables and milk. Finally add ¼ tsp of crushed pepper and cumin (2 pepper corns, 6-8 cumin seeds)

Bengali Chicken Kari

Ingredients

- 1 chicken breast, cut into medium size pieces (5cm)
- 2 onons, sliced
- 2 bay leaves
- 4cm cinnamon stick
- 4 cloves
- 2 tomatoes, chopped
- ¼ tsp turmeric powder
- salt to taste
- 2 tsp plain chilli powder
- 2 green chillies
- 1 tsp grated ginger
- 1 tsp grated garlic
- 4 tbsp oil
- 1 tsp cumin freshly ground
- 6 coriander leaves, chopped

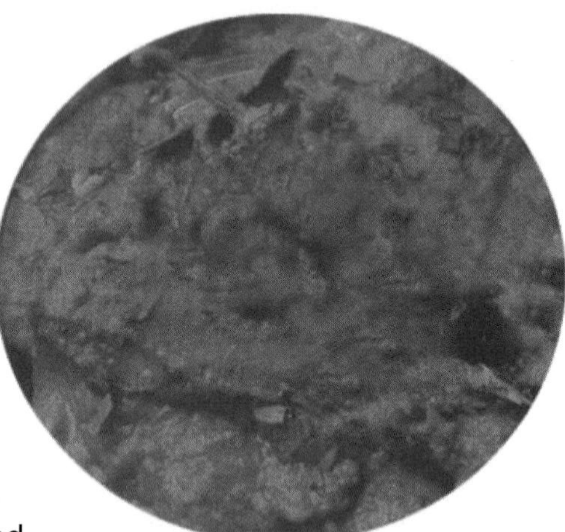

Method

1. Marinate the chicken in salt, turmeric, chilli powder, garlic, ginger and 2 tbsp of oil for about an hour.

2. Heat 1 tbsp oil in a thava and add the bay leaves, cloves and cinnamon. Then add the sliced onions and fry till golden adding oil if required.

3. Add the marinated chicken and fry on high heat for 2 minutes. Reduce the heat, cover and cook for 10 minutes without adding any more oil or water. Stir occasionally and make sure chicken is not sticking to the pan.

4. Add the chopped tomatoes, green chillies and cook for another 10 minutes. Add 1 tsp of freshly ground cumin, remove from cooker and garnish with coriander leaves.

Chicken Kari

Preparation & cooking time: 35 minutes
Serves 4

Ingredients

- 1 large chicken breast
- 1 large onion, chopped
- 4 cloves garlic, crushed
- 2 cm root ginger, crushed
- 1 tsp mixed mustard and cumin seeds
- 1 tsp coriander seeds
- 1 tsp cumin seeds
- 6 dried red chillies
- 2 tbsp olive oil
- 4 fresh tomatoes cut into small cubes
- ¼ cup milk and a slice of cream coconut
- 1 tsp roasted fennel powder
- 2 cloves, 4cm cinnamon stick, 3 cardomoms, roasted and ground
- 1 sprig curry leaves
- salt to taste

Method

1. Dry roast the coriander and cumin seeds in a pan and grind adding the red chillies.

2. Skin the chicken breast, cut to about 4cm pieces. Heat a heavy based wok type pan (thava) and add 2 tablespoons of oil. Add the onions and fry until slightly brown. Add the mixed mustard and cumin seeds, crushed garlic and ginger and fry for few seconds. Add few curry leaves.

2. Next add the chicken pieces and cook on a fairly high heat. Keep turning the chicken until the meat gets coated with the oil and is slightly sealed. This will take about 2-3 minutes.

3. Add salt and the ground powder to the chicken, add 2-3 tablespoons milk or water and cook for 10 minutes over a medium heat. Then add the tomatoes and ground masala of cinnnamon, cloves and cardomom and cook for further 10 minutes.

4. Warm the rest of the milk, add cream coconut and make into a paste. Add this to the chicken and cook for 5 minutes.

5. In total the cooking time should not exceed 25 minutes on a fairly moderate heat. Add roasted fennel powder and the rest of the curry leaves. Remove from heat and serve with rice.

Variations

★ You may use a carrot grater and grate the garlic and ginger.
★ If you prefer more sauce, add a can of chopped tomatoes. Then add ¼ cup milk towards the end.
★ 4 tbsp natural yoghurt, 4 fresh tomatoes and 125ml single cream will give a slightly different flavour. Omit the milk and the cream coconut.

Chicken and Pepper

Preparation: 10 minutes
Cooking time: 20-30 minutes.

Serves 5-6 as a side dish.

Ingredients

- 2 chicken breasts
- 2 medium red onions
- 1 green pepper
- 1 red pepper
- 3 cloves garlic, finely sliced
- 4 cm root ginger, cut into thin strips
- 2 fresh tomatoes, cut into cubes
- 3 tbsp tomato sauce
- 1 tbsp crushed chilli or plain chilli powder
- 4 tbsp olive oil or gingelly/sesame oil
- 1 tbsp chilli and jalapeno relish (hot)
- salt to taste

Method

1. Slice the chicken breast horizontally so that it is thin and flat. Then cut this into strips of about 7cm size. The onions and pepper are to be sliced to the same size as the chicken

2. Heat a wok, add 2 tablespoons of oil and when this is hot add the chicken pieces and cook over a high heat. Add a bit of salt. When the chicken pieces are sealed and the chicken is cooked, remove the pieces and place on kitchen paper. It will take 3-4 minutes.

3. In the same pan add the rest of the oil and fry the onions, pepper, garlic and ginger. Add salt and stir fry. Remove and transfer to a plate lined with kitchen paper.

4. Add tomatoes to the wok and cook until soft, add tomato sauce, chilli powder or crushed chillies and the chilli sauce. Keep cooking until the sauce gets to a thick consistency.

5. Add all the fried ingredients into the sauce mix, stir it well for the sauce to be coated.

6. Remove from cooker and serve with cooked noodles or fried rice.

Variations

★ If you want a hot dish try using capsicum chillies instead of the peppers. These are available from Sri Lankan or Asian shops. Slice these diagonally in to thin strips.

★ Grinding 6 red chillies will give 2 teaspoons of crushed chilli. Crushed chilli is available in supermarkets and Asian grocers.

★ I prefer using crushed chillies and hot jalapeno sauce for the above recipe .

Chicken Kari in Sauce

Preparation: 10 minutes   Cooking time: 30 minutes
Serves: 4

Ingredients

- 1 chicken (1.5kg)
- large onion, chopped
- 4 cloves garlic, grated
- 4cm root ginger, grated
- ¼ tsp mustard seeds
- ½ tsp cumin seeds, ¼ tsp fenugreek seeds
- 1 tbsp roasted chilli-curry powder (for a medium hot dish)
- 3 tbsp oil
- salt to taste
- 6 tbsp natural yoghurt
- 5 sprigs methi leaves
- 1 sprig curry leaves
- piece of cream coconut ½" thick piece
- 2 medium tomatoes, chopped
- ½ cup water. ½ lemon or lime
- small piece rampe and lemon grass, chopped
- 1 tsp ground cinnamon and cardomom powder

Method

1. Skin the chicken, cut into small pieces of about 5-6cm pieces.

2. Heat a heavy-based deep frying pan and add the oil. Add mustard and cumin seeds. Allow to splutter, then add the onions and fry. Add two or three curry leaves.

4. Add the chicken and stir fry until the pieces are covered and sealed on all sides. This will take about 3-4 minutes.

5. Next add the salt, ginger, garlic, chilli powder, ½ cup water and yoghurt. Bring to boil, half cover the pan, reduce the heat to moderate and cook for 10 minutes. Stir the chicken to make sure it gets cooked evenly.

6. Add the tomatoes, methi leaves and cook for another 10 minutes. Make sure there is enough sauce for the chicken to cook.

7. After 20 minutes of cooking add the grated cream coconut mixed with little hot water, the rest of the curry leaves, lemon grass, rampe, cinnamon powder and cook for three to four minutes.

8. This dish should have a fair amount of sauce. Just before serving squeeze ½ lemon and stir.

Variations

★ Cook the chicken over a medium or slightly higher heat and not on low heat. In all, the time taken to cook chicken should be 25- 30 minutes.

★ Instead of milk you can try single cream.

★ If you want more gravy/sauce, add a bit more water at the start of the cooking and slightly reduce the flame for the last 10 minutes.

Chicken Kari (Boneless)

Preparation & cooking time: 35-40 minutes
Serves 4-5

Ingredients

- 500g boneless chicken (3 breasts or thighs)
- juice of ½ lemon
- 2 large onions, finely chopped
- 1-1½ tbsp plain chilli powder
- 2 tsp garam masala powder (cinnamon, cardomom, cloves)
- 1 tsp cumin seeds, 1 tsp coriander seeds, ¼ tsp black pepper corns
- 4 fresh tomatoes or 1 can (400g) chopped tomatoes
- 80g desiccated coconut (½ cup)
- 2 tbsp vegetable oil
- salt to taste
- 4 cloves garlic, 2cm size ginger
- ½ cup water (add as required)
- slice of cream coconut (1cm thick, rectangle slice)
- 1 sprig curry leaves, 2 tbsp of fresh coriander leaves, chopped

Method

1. Grind the chilli powder, garam masala, garlic, ginger, salt, desiccated coconut, cumin, coriander, pepper and quarter of the chopped onions to a paste. Add 2 spoons of water and grind.
2. Cut the chicken into 4cm pieces, mix with the lemon juice, and he ground paste and leave it to marinate.
3. Heat the oil in a deep frying pan, add the onion and fry until it turns a golden colour.
4. Add the chicken and fry for 3-4 minutes until the chicken pieces are sealed. Cook for 10 minutes.
5. Add the chopped tomatoes and cook for another 12 minutes. If necessary add little water to avoid sticking to the pan.
6. Add the piece of cream coconut, let it melt and mix in the sauce (about 2 minutes). Stir in the chopped coriander, curry leaves and cook for a minute.
7. Serve straight away with naan bread.

Chicken Cutlet with Fromage Frais

Ingredients

- 500g chicken breast fillets
- 1 onion, chopped
- 2 green chillies, chopped finely (optional)
- 2 cloves garlic, grated
- 2cm root ginger, grated
- 200g fromage frais
- 2 tsp freshly ground pepper
- 2 tsp cumin powder
- 2 tsp chilli powder
- salt to taste
- 2 eggs
- 3-4 curry leaves or coriander leaves, chopped
- oil for shallow frying
- cling film paper

Method

1. Cut the breast meat into cubes and place in a food processor.

2. Add the chopped onions, green chillies, pepper, garlic, ginger, salt, and half the cumin and pepper.

3. Run the processor for few minutes and transfer into a large bowl.

4. Whisk the eggs and add to the chicken and mix it well. Add the curry leaves or coriander leaves

5. Take small quantities, the size of a golf ball and slightly flatten into discs.

6. Cut a cling film sheet into small squares, place the flattened discs on each and flatten it to a slightly larger circle.

7. Mix the rest of the pepper and cumin with the fromage frais. Spoon ½ tsp in the centre of the flattened chicken mixture and bring the edges to close with the filling in the centre. Cling film helps to get the cutlet into shape with the filling.

8. Heat oil in a frying pan, remove the cutlet from the cling film paper and place in the pan. Shallow fry in medium heat until both sides are fried. It will take about 10 minutes for both sides to be cooked. Serve warm.

Variations

- ★ If you are going to deep fry, dip the chicken cutlet in egg whites and roll in breadcrumbs and then deep fry. For this you need to discard the eggs added to the mixture, as raw eggs will make the oil frothy.

  Instead you may add one boiled potato mashed up.

- ★ Can try this with prawns, use the same ingredients and add one boiled potato.

Chicken Thighs/Drumstick cooked with Tomato

Preparation & cooking: 45 minutes
Serves 3

Ingredients

- 8 chicken drumsticks or thighs
- 2 medium onions, chopped
- 4 tbsp natural yoghurt
- 3 cloves garlic or 1 tsp garlic paste
- 3 tbsp oil
- 2cm piece of ginger or 1 tsp ginger paste
- salt to taste
- 1 sprig curry leaves
- 1 tbsp roasted chilli/curry powder (Sri Lankan)
- 10 sprigs of fresh methi leaves (optional), washed and chopped

For tempering

- 1 tsp mustard seeds, ½ tsp fennel seeds, ½ tsp cumin seeds
- 1 tsp roasted fennel powder
- 4-5 tablespoons normal milk or single cream
- 5 tomatoes, chopped

Method

1. Clean the chicken by removing the skin. If you prefer small pieces then cut the thighs and drumsticks into two. Add the chilli powder salt, yoghurt and the crushed garlic and ginger or the paste to the chicken and marinate for 10-15 minutes.

2 In a heavy-based thava or a heavy wok add the oil and heat. When the oil is hot add the chopped onions and cook until they turn slightly brown. Add the mustard, cumin and fennel seeds.

3. Add the chicken pieces, keep stirring. Cook for 10-12 minutes on just above medium heat. The sauce should be seen to bubble.

4. Add the chopped tomatoes, methi leaves and ¼ cup water and cook for another 10 minutes.

5. After cooking for 22 minutes in all, add the milk or single cream and cook for 2-3 minutes.

6. Finally after 20-25 minutes of cooking add the roasted fennel powder and the curry leaves, stir once and remove from cooker.

Variations

- ★ Check and adjust the heat so that it does not get burnt.
- ★ If you are not using Sri Lankan roasted chilli/curry powder then add 1 tsp each of roasted cumin and coriander powder.
  1 tsp plain chilli powder, 1 tsp Kashmir masala paste.
- ★ If you use the whole thighs or drumsticks then just give a couple of cuts into the meat so that the spices get into the meat whilst cooking.
- ★ Instead of fresh tomatoes can add a 400g tomato tin.

Served with rice, bhiriyani, noodles, naan etc.

Chicken Kari (Jaffna Preparation)

A dry dish - Recipe from Jaffna
Preparation & cooking time: appx 45 minutes
Serves 4-5

Usually a whole chicken is cut up into small pieces and the dish is prepared as a dry curry. Alternatively you can take the meat and cook a dry dish and use the bones to prepare a dish called 'Kulambu' thick sauce/gravy.

The chilli paste is formed by grinding red chilli, cumin, coriander and turmeric. But nowadays, roasted chilli/curry powder is available and this is used instead.

Ingredients

- 1 kg whole chicken
- 1 large onion, chopped
- 3 tsp roasted chilli powder (Sri Lankan)
- ½ tsp cumin seeds
- ½ tsp mustard seeds
- 2 dry red chillies
- 5 garlic cloves, crushed
- 4cm root ginger, crushed
- 2 sprigs curry leaves
- 5cm cinnamon stick and 5 cardamoms, ground
- lemon grass (4cm) and 4cm rampe cut up (optional)
- 1 can coconut milk (400g)
- 3 tbsp oil
- 1½ tsp roasted fennel powder
- salt to taste
- ½ cup of normal milk or water

Method

1. Skin the chicken and cut into small pieces about 3-4 cm size (with the bones). Wash, add salt, chilli powder, crushed garlic, ginger and marinate.

2. Heat a thava or a heavy-based pan and add oil. Add onions and stir fry until slightly gold in colour. Add mustard seeds, cumin, chillies and few curry leaves.
3. Add the chicken pieces, dilute ¼ can of the cocunut milk with little water or normal milk and add it to the chicken and cook for 15 minutes. Partially cover with lid and cook (covering full may make the milk boil over).
5. Keep stirring and add the rest of the coconut milk and cook for another 10 minutes over a medium heat. Add the cinnamon and cardamom powder,
6. Turn the heat up a bit and allow the sauce to be absorbed by the pieces. The chicken pieces covered in the sauce will begin to look dry.
   Add the rest of the curry leaves, rampe, lemon grass pieces and fennel powder. Stir once and remove from cooker (2 minutes)
7. Before serving squeeze the juice from 1 lime and stir.

★ For the above recipe, can cook by adding ½ cup semi-skimmed milk and adding cream coconut towards the end (step 6) .

Traditional way is to cook with fresh coconut milk

Ingredients

- Same as on previous page, except no oil, mustard seeds, cumin or cows' milk.

Method

See section on coconut milk for extracting milk from scraped coconut. Save the first and second milk. Add the third and fourth to the chicken pieces. Add salt, chilli powder, chopped onions, cut up red chilli, garlic, ginger and cook for 20 minutes. Then add the first and second milk, about ½ cup and cook on high flame for 5 to 10 minutes. Finally add the curry leaves and roasted fennel powder. Chicken curry should look dry with hardly any moisture.

Chicken Tikka

Preparation: marinate overnight
Cooking time: 20-25 minutes

Ingredients

- 1 Chicken breast, 400g, cut into 3cm pieces
- 200g natural yoghurt (small carton)
- 2 tbsp tomato purée, 2 tbsp oil
- 5 cloves garlic, crushed or 2 tsp paste
- 4cm piece ginger, crushed
- 1½ tsp coriander powder
- 1 tsp cumin powder,
- ¼ tsp turmeric powder
- 1 tsp garam masala powder (cardamom & cinnamon)
- 2 tsp plain chilli powder, ¼ tsp paprika powder
- 1 onion, chopped
- salt to taste

For the salad – garnishing

- coriander leaves, chopped
- tomato, sliced
- onions, thinly sliced
- green chillies, chopped

Method

1. In a food processor blend all ingredients (except the chicken) to form a paste and place in a large bowl.

2. Add the chicken pieces, stir well to coat the pieces, cover and leave in the fridge overnight or marinate for 6 hours at room temperature.

3. Pre heat the oven, place the pieces with the masala paste in a tray and bake for 15 minutes at 190°C. Remove and place the pieces in another warmed tray without any sauce and bake on circotherm setting for 3-4 minutes. Watch so that it does not get too dry or burn.

4. Serve with salad (onions, green chillies, tomato and coriander leaves).

5 An alternative method is to place the paste and chicken in a pan and cook for 10-12 minutes.

6. Next arrange 5 chicken pieces (one by one) onto a skewer. Arrange 4-5 skewers on a tray and grill it. Keep turning the skewer. It should take 3-4 minutes to cook.

7. Remove the pieces from the skewer and serve with salad.

★ If you prefer sauce add 2 tablespoon of single cream to the chicken and masala paste as soon as you take out from the oven and serve.

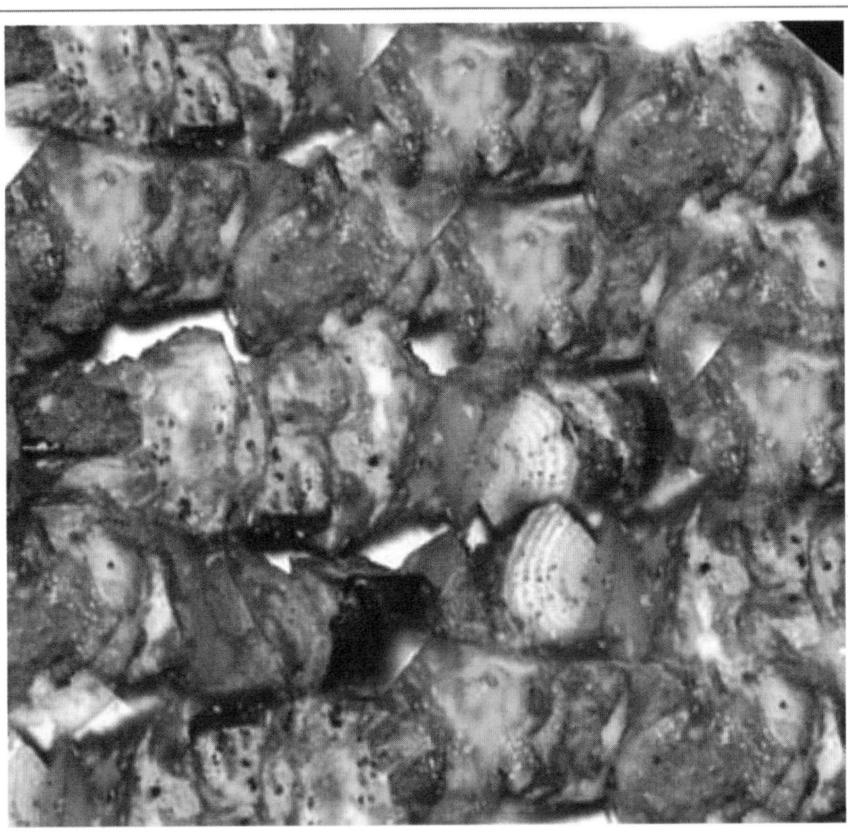

Chicken wings with sauce

Preparation & cooking time: 30 minutes
Serves 5

Ingredients

- 10 chicken wings
- 5cm ginger, sliced finely
- 2-3 tsp corn flour, salt to taste
- oil for frying, 1 tsp chilli powder
- 2 tbsp brandy and 2 tbsp sherry (optional)
- soya sauce, mushroom soya sauce (for colour)
- 3 garlic cloves, sliced
- 5 spring onions, shredded
- oyster sauce
- ½ cup water

Method

1. Skin the chicken wings clean and cut into two (delights and wings).
2. Heat oil in a pan and fry garlic and ginger until slightly browned.
3. Add the chicken pieces to the frying ingredients and cook.
4. Add salt, sherry, brandy, soya sauce and mushroom soya sauce and fry until well browned.
5. Add water and bring to boil add the chilli powder simmer for about 10-15 minutes.
6. Add corn flour and stir quickly
7. Add oyster sauce and spring onions and remove from cooker.

★ For parties can cook the chicken delights with chilli oil and soya sauce and serve as a starter.

Kottu Rotti

With lamb or chicken

Traditional method is to prepare with Kottamba rotti. Can use ordinary rotti or Tortilla sheets. See rotti preparation in the main section of the book.

Ingredients

- 4 rottis cut up to 6cm size pieces
- 2 green chillies, chopped fine
- 4-5 tbsp oil or butter for frying
- 3 shallots, chopped
- ¼ tsp salt
- ½ lemon
- 1 bowl of cooked dry kari of boneless chicken or lamb
- 15 curry leaves, piece of rampe, chopped
- 3 eggs beaten with ½ tsp of plain chilli powder

Method

1 Place a flat-based heavy frying pan on the cooker.
2. Add oil and when it is hot add the shallots, green chillies, curry leaves rampe etc. and cook until onions are soft.
3 Add the beaten eggs and cook. When the egg is cooked carefully remove and place on a plate. Cut the egg to thin slices about 4cm long and leave it aside.
5. Add the cooked meat to the frying pan and heat for few minutes, if necessary add 2 tsps oil. Add the rotti and keep stirring, add the egg strips.
6 Remove from cooker and when ready to serve squeeze the ½ lemon.

★ You can add or decrease the amount of chillies according to yourtaste.
★ Can include peas.
★ You can buy frozen rottis from Asian grocery shops.
★ An easy dish to prepare with any left over kari or roast

Paste for Chicken Kari

Grind all the following with little water and keep in the fridge

Ingredients

- 4 red chillies
- 2 green chillies
- 1 tbsp fennel seeds
- 1 tbsp coriander seeds
- 1 tsp cumin seeds
- 1 tsp black pepper
- 4cm cinnamon stick
- 4 cardomoms, 3 cloves
- 4cm lemon grass (sara)
- 4cm peeled ginger
- 5 cloves garlic
- 1 medium size onion

Method

Grind all ingredients to a paste and keep in the fridge.
You can also separate this into small portions and freeze until required.

Turkey Kari dry Preparation

Preparation & cooking time: 45 minutes

Ingredients

- 1 turkey leg (drumstick)
- 1½ large onions, chopped to cubes
- 2 tablespoon roasted chilli/curry powder
- 6 cloves garlic or 1-2 tsp paste
- 5cm ginger or 2 tsp paste
- 2-3 tbsp oil
- for tempering ½ tsp mustard seeds, ½ tsp cumin seeds
- ¼ tsp fenugreek seeds.
- 2 sprigs curry leaves (10-15)
- 5cm piece of rampe, cut
- 2 tsp roasted fennel powder
- salt to taste (1 tsp)
- 2cm cinnamon stick and 4 cardamoms, ground
- 3 tomatoes fresh or canned, chopped (optional)
- 3 small new potatoes cut into 1½cm cubes
- 2 tbsp coconut powder and 4 tbsp normal milk or
- slice of cream coconut about 1cm thick

Method

1. Clean the skin of the large drumstick and cut the meat into small pieces (2cm) size. This will be the difficult bit. If you are going to cut the meat on the previous day, then marinate with salt and 1 spoon of chilli powder and leave covered in the fridge.

2. Always try and use a thava or heavy-based frying pan. Heat the pan, add oil, then the onions and fry until slightly brown. Add mustard, cumin, fenugreek seeds and half the curry leaves.

3. Next add the cut turkey, salt, chilli powder, crushed garlic and ginger or the paste. Stir well so that all the meat pieces are evenly cooked and sealed (you will see the colour changing when the meat gets coated). Stir well and cook on a high heat for 2-3 minutes.

4. Add less than ½ cup water and continue to cook for 15 minutes on medium (not a low heat).

5. Now is the time to add the chopped tomatoes if you wish the kari to be moist.

6. If you want a dry dish skip step 5 and add the potato and cook, for a further 10 minutes.

7. Mix the coconut powder in four tablespoons of warm milk. Add this or the cream coconut to the turkey. Keep stirring and cook for few minutes. Total cooking time is 30-35 minutes.

8. Add the rampe, rest of the curry leaves, fennel powder, ground cinnamon and cardamom and remove from cooker

9. Can be served with rice, bread, naan etc.

Tandoori Chicken

It is an easy preparation which can be baked in the oven for 30 minutes. Takes 3 hrs or overnight to marinate.

Ingredients

- 4 Chicken legs (thighs and drum sticks)
- 150g natural yoghurt
- 1 tbsp ginger paste
- 1 tbsp garlic paste
- 1 tbsp coriander powder
- 1 tbsp mixed masala powder
- 1 tbsp garam masala powder
- 1 tsp turmeric powder
- salt to taste
- 1 tbsp chilli paste
- oil, few coriander leaves
- 2 tsp tomato puree

Method

1. Skin the chicken legs, cut and separate the thighs and drumsticks and leave as large pieces or cut into the size you prefer. Slit the large pieces slightly.
2. Prepare marinade with the rest of the ingredients and leave in a bowl. Add the chicken pieces, mix well and marinate overnight by leaving in the fridge or leave outside for 3-4 hours.
3. Pre heat the oven at 180°C
4. Arrange the chicken pieces on a flat dish, cover and cook in the microwave for 10 minutes. Place the cooked chicken on to a baking tray lined with foil and bake in the oven at 190°C for 15 minutes. Turn the pieces and cook for another 10 minutes.
5. Have another tray ready and arrange the pieces of chicken without any juice /sauce. Bake for another 5 minutes. Remove the tray from the oven and allow to cool and serve with salad.

★ Can use Kabab or tandoori masala from the shops. This will give the red colour.

Lamb / Mutton

Mutton/Lamb Index

Devilled Mutton

A dish for a starter
Cooking time: 1 hour

Ingredients

- 1 kg mutton
- 3 large onions
- 1 cup vinegar
- salt to taste
- 2 green chillies, 5cm ginger, 4 cloves garlic
- 6cm cinnamon stick, few cardamom pods
- 1½ tbsp roasted chilli/curry powder
- 1½ tsp paprika powder
- 2 tsp garam masala powder
- 3 capsicum chillies, blanched for ½ minute and sliced thinly
- 1 sprig curry leaves
- 2 tsp roasted fennel powder
- 1 can coconut milk (400g), 4-5 tbsp oil

Method

1. Cut the mutton into 4cm size pieces. Add vinegar and leave to marinate for 30 minutes.
2. Chop one onion and put into a blender, add the garlic and ginger and grind to a paste.
3. Spoon the mutton pieces from the marinade, drain the vinegar out and place it in a dish.
4. Heat a frying pan, add oil and fry the mutton pieces on both sides for 3 minutes. Next add the the garlic, onion, ginger paste, stir well and cook on medium heat for 2-3 minutes. Add chilli powder, paprika powder, garam masala powder and cook for 5 minutes.
5. Add the coconut milk and bring to the boil. Cover the pan, reduce the heat to medium and cook until the mutton is tender. It will take about 40 minutes.
6. Add curry leaves, ground cinnamon and cardomom, finally the fennel powder.
7. Slice the other onions and fry in little oil, add the blanched capsicum chillies, and green chillies and fry until golden brown. Have it ready to add to the cooked meat.
8. When the mutton sauce starts to dry up add the fried onions and capsicum chillies, cook for a minute or two and remove from cooker.
9. Stir well and serve with salad as an accompaniment to drinks.

Fried lamb chops - Mauritius preperation

Preparation: 15 minutes
Cooking time: 20 minutes
Marinating: 3 hours or overnight

Serves 2-3

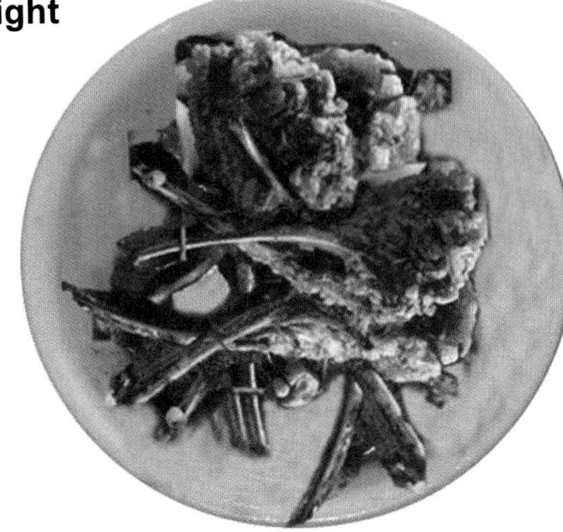

Ingredients

- 6 lamb chops - cut to medium thickness
- 1 tsp ginger paste
- 1 tsp garlic paste
- 1 tsp ground garam masala paste or freshly ground cinnamon,
- cardamom and cloves
- salt to taste
- 1 tsp chilli powder
- 2 onions, chopped (shallots)
- 2 sprigs spring onions, finely chopped
- 2 sprigs coriander leaves, chopped
- 4 tbsp yoghurt
- 2 slices of bread, to be crushed in a blender
- 2 eggs beaten up
- oil for shallow frying (6 tbsp)
- 1 lemon, sliced
- a heavy-based frying pan

Method

1. Wash and clean the chops. Place the chops between two sheets of foil paper and pat it with a rolling pin on the surface to flatten.

2. In a large bowl mix ginger, garlic, masala paste, chilli powder, chopped onions, coriander leaves and yoghurt.

3. Add the chops to the mixed yoghurt and make sure they are covered, leave to marinate overnight or for few hours.

4. Take the crushed bread and leave it on a plate.

5. Place the beaten egg in a small dish.

6. Take one chop at a time and roll in the crushed bread (to soak the sauce) and dip it in the egg.

7. Heat the oil in a large frying pan and place three chops and cook each side for 5-6 minutes on a fairly moderate heat.

8. Remove from pan, leave on a dish, garnish with lemon and have with rice or bread and salad.

9. If not serving immediately wrap the chops in foil for few minutes to retain the heat.

Variations

★ Can cook the marinated chops in the microwave for 1½ minutes. Then dip in egg and roll in either flour or bread crumbs and shallow fry for 3 minutes on each side. By doing this you use less oil and the cooking time is reduced too.

★ Can prepare with mutton instead of the lamb, this will be a bit harder and require a bit of time to cook.

Grilled Lamb Wrap

A popular item in the Western countries now.
Easy to prepare,not messy to eat.
Good to take as packed lunch or picnics

Ingredients

To prepare the lamb

- 1 medium onion,chopped
- 750g boneless lamb cut into 2cm pieces.
- small piece of ginger crushed
- 3 cloves garlic crushed
- 2 tsp roasted Sri Lankan chilli powder
- 4 tbsp natural yoghurt
- salt to taste
- 4 sprigs coriander leaves, chopped
- 2 tsp garam masala
- 2-tbsp oil or butter for basting
- wooden skewers soaked in water

For the wrap

- 1 packet of tortilla sheets (about 5)
- salad leaves finely cut
- 2 shallots sliced
- 2 spring onions sliced
- 2 tomatoes sliced
- small piece of cucumber sliced
- green chilli chutney or any flavour mixed chutney

Method

1. Liquidise all the ingredients except the curry leaves, lamb and yoghurt. Place the paste in a bowl, add the yoghurt and mix well.

2. Place the lamb pieces in the marinade mixture, cover and leave in the fridge overnight or 5-6 hours.

3. Take out from the fridge for an hour before cooking and leave at room temperature.

4. Thread the lamb pieces on to skewers and place them on an oven tray. Pre heat the oven on high 190°C for10 minutes. Place the tray in the oven and cook for 8-10 minutes. Baste with a bit of oil or butter and cook for further 4-5 minutes. Do not over cook the meat. 15 minutes should be more than enough for the 2cm size lamb pieces. Remove and leave on a plate.

5. Warm the tortilla sheets, take one and spread the chutney, place pieces of lamb on the sheets. Add chopped salad onions to your taste. Roll it up and serve, or wrap in foil and leave to take it with you as packed lunch.

Variations

★ You can also cook these under the grill.

Another method to serve

Wrap all 5 tortilla sheets in foil and place in the oven for the last five minutes of cooking.
Divide the lamb pieces into five equal portions.
Spread a little butter or margarine on the warmed tortilla sheets.
Place a portion of the cooked lamb in the centre of a warmed tortilla.
Top with sliced pepper/onion /cucumber (any of your choice) and a spoonful of tomato sauce or chutney. Roll up and serve.

Kebabs - For Parties (starters)

Preparation: 25-30 minutes
Cooking time: 10-15 minutes

Ingredients

- 1 kg minced lamb
- 1 tbsp garlic paste
- 1 tbsp ginger paste
- 3 large onions, chopped
- 2 eggs
- 2 tsp salt
- 1 tsp plain chilli powder.
- 2 green chilies, chopped finely (optional)
- 6 sprigs fresh coriander leaves, chopped finely
- 4 slices bread softened with a little water (slightly moist)
- 2 tsp ground mango powder
- oil for deep frying

Method

1 Place the minced lamb in a bowl.
2 Add the garlic paste, ginger paste, salt, chopped onions, chopped coriander leaves, mango powder, chilli powder and the softened bread to the lamb and mix well.
3 Beat the eggs and then mix it with the lamb mixture.
4 Take a tablespoon amount and shape the mince meat into a ball or flattened cutlet.
5 Heat oil in a deep frying pan
6 Place a few shaped balls at a time in the hot oil and deep fry for a few minutes.
7 Remove using a slotted spoon and drain on to kitchen paper
8 Serve hot with chutney.

Lamb Chops Kari

Loin back chops are ideal, cut to a medium size.

Serves 6-8

Preparation: 15 minutes
Cooking time: 45 minutes

Ingredients

- 1kg back chops/mutton cut to medium thickness
- 8 cloves garlic, crushed
- 7 cm size ginger, crushed
- 3 tsp of ground paste of cumin, cinnamon and cardamom
- salt to taste
- 2 tbsp roasted chilli powder (or to taste)
- 2 large onions finely sliced
- 3 sprigs curry leaves
- 2 sprigs fresh methi leaves (optional)
- oil to fry the onion and seal the chops (6 tbsp)
- 5 large fresh or canned tomatoes, chopped (400g)
- a very large pan; a heavy based wok would be ideal
- ½ carton of yoghurt
- 6cm rampe cut into small pieces (optional)
- 4cm slice cream coconut and ½ cup normal milk **or**
  3 tbsp coconut powder mixed in ½ cup of hot water.
- 1 tsp each mustard and cumin seeds
- 2 tsp roasted fennel spice powder, ½ lime

Method

1. Wash and clean the chops.
2. Heat the pan, add 2 tbsp oil and cook the chops to seal the sides.

3. You may have to cook a few chops at a time and see that they are sealed.

4. When they turn colour cook for a minute and take out and leave on a plate.

5. In the same pan add the rest of the oil and fry the onions until slightly golden colour.

6. Add the mustard seeds, cumin, half the curry leaves, ginger, garlic paste, salt, chilli and then the chops and yoghurt and cook over a high heat for a few minutes. Then reduce and cook for 25 minutes.

7. Add the chopped tomatoes, methi leaves and cook for another 15 minutes.

8. Add the cream coconut and bit of milk or the coconut powder mixed in water and cook for two to three minutes.

9. Add the rest of the curry leaves, rampe and finally the roasted fennel powder and remove from cooker. Squeeze the lime, stir and serve. The chops will be in a thick sauce.

Lamb/Mutton Kari “Pirattal”

Cooking Time: 40-45 minutes
Serves 4

Ingredients

- 1.5 kg lamb or mutton
- 1 large onion, chopped
- 5 cloves garlic
- 4cm size ginger
- 2 tbsp roasted chilli powder (adjust to your taste)
- 2 tbsp oil
- 1 tsp mustard seeds, 1 tsp cumin seeds,
- 2 dry red chillies, chopped
- 2 sprigs curry leaves
- slice of cream coconut 1cm thickness of the block
- 1½ tsp salt (or to taste)
- 2 tsp roasted fennel powder
- 2cm rampe stick sliced
- ½ cup coconut milk or normal milk
- 4cm piece of cinnamon, crushed
- a deep heavy-based pan preferably a thava

Preparation

1. Cut the meat into small cubes, 2-3cm size.
2. Crush the garlic and ginger.
3. Marinate the meat with salt, garlic, ginger, chilli powder, ¼ cup coconut milk mixed with ¼ cup water. Leave for 15-20 minutes.

Method

1. Place the pan on the cooker, add oil.
2. When oil gets slightly hot add chopped onions and stir fry until a golden colour.
3. Add the mustard seeds, cumin, red chillies and half the curry leaves.
4. Add the mutton and mix well with a spoon and cook for about two minutes.
5. Once you find that the sauce is bubbling and the meat is getting cooked reduce the heat to medium and cook for half an hour. If needed add a little milk.
6. Keep checking to make sure the base does not get burnt.
7. Lamb should be cooked in 25 minutes. Mutton takes a bit longer, 35 minutes.
8. Add cream coconut, rest of the milk, curry leaves and cook for a few minutes.
9. Finally add rampe, roasted fennel powder and cinnamon.
10. Increase the heat and when the sauce dries and the pieces start to leave the sides of the pan remove from the cooker.

Cooking tips

Mutton takes a bit longer to cook than lamb. If you want to speed up the cooking you can first cook the mutton in a pressure cooker for 3 whistles at high and then add it to the tempered onion etc. and cook for another 30 minutes.

★ Traditional cooking: no tempering as included in this recipe. Meat gets cooked in 2 cups of weaker (diluted) coconut milk and thick coconut milk is added last. Fennel powder is also freshly ground.

Mutton / Lamb Liver

Buy fresh liver and it should be cooked straightaway. It is tastier if liver is cooked as a dry dish.

Recipe below is for a dry preparation.

Ingredients

- 500g fresh liver
- 2 large onions, finely sliced
- 2 green chillies, sliced
- 7cm ginger, thinly sliced
- 4 garlic cloves, thinly sliced
- 1½ tbsp roasted chilli powder
- oil for frying 4-5 tbsp
- salt to taste
- piece of cinnamon, broken into pieces
- 2 sprigs curry leaves, piece of rampe cut up
- 1½ tsp roasted fennel or 1½ tsp ground pepper and cumin heavy-based frying pan

Method

1 Cut the liver into 5cm strips, not too thick or thin and wash in cold water. Give two or three cold rinses and leave it aside.

2. Heat the heavy-based frying pan. Add 2 tabalespoons of oil and when it is fairly hot add the liver and cook over a high heat for three minutes.
3. Next add salt, ginger, garlic, green chillies and the chilli powder and stir well. Reduce the heat very slightly and cook. Remove from cooker after about 7-8 minutes of cooking and transfer to a dish.
4. In the same pan add a bit of oil and fry the onions; add curry leaves and crushed cinnamon. When onions turn slightly golden colour add the liver and cook for a further 3-4 minutes.
5. Switch heat off. Add the fennel powder or pepper and cumin and leave in the pan covered with a lid.

★ In all it should take less than 15 minutes. Do not over cook.

Variations:

With sauce

If you require more kari sauce, to the above recipe add 1 cup of coconut milk after adding the onions, liver etc. and cook over a high heat for few minutes. Before it starts to dry add the fennel powder and remove from the cooker.

With tomatoes and capsicum chillies

Chop tomatoes, cut up capsicum in diagonal slices. Fry this with the liver, onion, garlic, ginger etc for three minutes. Add coconut milk, turn the heat low and let it simmer. After 10 minutes add the curry leaves, rampe, cinnamon and cook for a few minutes. Remove from cooker.

Mutton Chops

Preparation & cooking time: 40 minutes

Ingredients

- 1 kg mutton chops
- 1 cup natural yoghurt
- 2 medium size onions, chopped
- 6 sprigs methi leaves (fenugreek)
- 2 sprigs curry leaves
- 2 potatoes, cubed
- 4 tomatoes, chopped
- 1½ tsp mixed spice powder (cardamom, cinnamon, cloves)
- 2 tbsp roasted chilli powder (to your taste)
- ½ tsp turmeric powder
- salt to taste
- 1½ tsp each ground garlic & ginger paste
- 1tsp ground coriander powder
- oil or ghee for frying
- 1 tsp each of mustard seeds, cumin seeds
- 2 tsp roasted fennel powder
- ¼ cup milk or single cream.

Method

1 Heat ghee or oil in a heavy based pan or a thava. Add the chops and fry for a minute. Cook each side for two minutes and transfer to a plate.
2. Add little oil to the pan and add mustard seeds, when it splatters add cumin, chopped onions and fry until golden colour.
3. Add methi leaves, sealed mutton chops, salt, roasted chilli powder, garlic and ginger paste and cook for two minutes.
4. Add the yoghurt, ¼ cup water, chopped tomatoes and cook over a moderate heat for 15-20 minutes.
5. Add the cubed potatoes, keep stirring, cover the pan and cook for another 15 minutes until the mutton is cooked.
6. Add milk or cream, curry leaves, ground cinnamon powder, rampe and simmer for 5 minutes.
7. Add the fennel powder. Turn off the cooker.
8. Just before serving add 2 tsp of fresh lime juice.

Mutton Bhiryani

Preparation & cooking time: 1hour 30 minutes
Serves 8

Ingredients

Mutton for Bhiriyani

- 1kg mutton
- 1 large carton of natural yoghurt (375g)
- salt to taste
- Kari paste *see below

For Kari paste

Either use a ready made mutton bhiryani mix
Mix 3 tablespoons of this paste in yoghurt and soak the mutton pieces for two to three hours.

Prepare your own: Grind 1 tsp each of coriander, cumin, pepper, chilli powder, piece of ginger, 2 cloves garlic and 1 tsp of cinnamon and cardamom mix.

Cut the mutton to 5cm cubes soak in the above paste and yoghurt for 3-4 hours or overnight. Cook in a pan until the yoghurt is slightly thick, say about 20-25 minutes. Leave a bit of sauce.

Ingredients

- 3 cups basmathi rice
- 3 shallots, 2 cloves garlic
- 1 tsp of crushed cardomom, cloves and cinnamon
- few curry leaves, rampe, say 5cm
- 5cm sara/ lemon grass
- ghee for frying (2-3 tsp)
- pinch of turmeric or saffron, cinnamon stick
- garnishing: 10 cashew nuts, 2 shallots, 1 bay leaf

Method

1. Peel onions and slice.
2. Wash the rice and soak in water for few minutes.
3. Wash and allow the water to drain by placing in a colander.
4. Fry the onions in a teaspoon of ghee. Add the crushed cardamoms, whole cloves, and chopped cinnamon stick, curry leaves, sara and rampe.
5. Transfer to a plate and leave it for few minutes.
6. Next fry the rice for a few seconds.
7. Place the rice in a rice cooker add enough water and cook until it is half done. Add the fried stuff and cook until done.
8. Remove the cloves before mixing the cooked mutton (the cloves have a strong stingy taste and you should avoid biting one)
9. Mix the rice and the cooked mutton and sauce. Mix well and serve on to a dish. Fry finely cut shallots, add the cashew nuts and bay leaf and garnish the rice and serve.

★ If you are going to boil the rice in a pan, first add the fried ingredients, rice and water, bring to boil and reduce until rice is cooked. Once the rice is cooked take out the cloves after draining the water.

Lamb/Mutton Fried

If you buy meat from Asian shops it will be mutton unless you ask for spring lamb. Lamb is slightly more expensive and will cook quicker. It is better to cook lamb for children as it is more tender.
This is a tasty dish if fried in sesame/gingelly oil or ghee. Can be eaten with rice and one vegetable. My mum used to make this as a special treat.

Preparation & cooking time: 20 minutes
Serves 5 as a side dish

Ingredients

- 500g mutton or spring lamb
- 3-4 tbsp oil
- 3 red onions, cut into thin slices
- salt to taste
- 1-2 tsp plain chilli powder
- a heavy based frying pan
- 2 tsp mixed coriander and cumin powder

Method

1. Cut the meat into small cubes or thin slices of 2½ cm.
2. Add salt, chilli, coriander and cumin to the meat and marinate for 20 minutes.
3. Heat a pan; add oil and start frying the mutton. After 5 minutes add the onions and let it cook in the meat juice.
4. When the juice evaporates and the meat starts to turn brown and the onions turn crispy remove from the heat and serve.

★ Can fry the meat and onion separately and then mix together. Add salt, chilli powder etc. and stir fry.

Mutton/Lamb Kulambu (sauce)

Preparation & cooking time: 35 minutes for lamb, about an hour for mutton

Serves 6-8

Ingredients

- 2 kg mutton/lamb with bones
- 3 medium onions, chopped
- 5 cloves garlic, crushed
- 4cm size ginger, crushed
- 2 tbsp roasted chilli powder
- 2 sprigs curry leaves, chopped
- salt to taste
- 4cm rampe, chopped
- 2 tsp roasted fennel powder
- 2-3 tbs oil
- water for cooking
- 1 can chopped tomato (375g) or 4 fresh tomatoes
- ½ can coconut milk (200g)** see other options
- tempering ingredients: 1 tsp each mustard and cumin seeds, 1 dry red chilli, cut
- 6-8 small new potatoes, halved
- piece of cinnamon stick (6cm) – crushed or ground
- 3 cardamoms - crushed

Method

1. Cut the lamb/mutton into 2cm cubes.
2. Heat a thava or heavy-based wok type pan. Add 2 tablespoons oil and fry the mustard seeds, this will start to splatter. Add cumin, red chilli, few curry leaves and fry for few seconds.
3. Add the onions and fry until golden brown. Add the meat and fry over a moderate heat to seal all sides. It will take about 4 minutes.
4. Once sealed add the crushed garlic, ginger, salt and chilli powder, stir well and cook.

5. If it is lamb, after 10 minutes add the tomatoes, ¼ cup water and potatoes. If you are cooking mutton add the potatoes after 20 minutes. Cook on a medium heat for another 15 minutes stir frequently and check the consistency. Add the cinnamon and cardamom.
6. Add the coconut milk and cook for 10 minutes, finally add the curry leaves, rampe and fennel powder. The consistency should be a fairly thick sauce.
7. Serve with rice and other vegetables.

Traditional preparation

1. Mix the cut mutton, bones, chopped shallots, chilli powder, garlic,
ginger and a weaker consistency of coconut milk.
2. Place these in a pan and bring to boil. Reduce the heat and cook for about an hour.
3. Add 1 cup of the thick coconut milk, curry leaves, rampe, cinnamon and cardamom and cook for 5-10 minutes until the sauce thickens.
4. Then add the freshly-ground roasted fennel (no oil or tempering). Serve with rice.

Variations

1. Instead of using coconut milk can use single cream or cream coconut.
2. Can also use normal semi-skimmed milk.
3. To above recipe add 4 tablespoons of yoghurt at the start after step 4 and continue with the rest. Here instead of coconut milk add normal milk or ½" slice of creamed coconut.

Mutton/Lamb - (Hot)

With ground masala - Hot

Preparation & cooking time: 35-40 minutes for lamb, about an hour for mutton

Ingredients

- 2 kg shoulder lamb/mutton
- 3 medium onions, chopped
- 3 tsp cumin seeds
- 1 tsp mustard seeds
- 2 tsp fennel seeds
- 2 tsp fenugreek seeds
- 1 tbsp coriander seds
- 5 dry red chillies
- 3 tomatoes, chopped
- 2 tbsp roasted chilli powder (to your taste)
- piece of cinnamon stick (8cm)
- 3 cardamoms
- 5 garlic cloves
- 5cm piece ginger
- 1½ tsp salt or to your taste
- small carton of natural yoghurt (300 ml)
- 2 tbsp ghee or oil
- 2cm thick slice of creamed coconut

Method

1. Cut the lamb to 4cm pieces, mix with yoghurt and leave in a bowl.
2. In a pan roast the coriander, cumin, red chilli, fennel, fenugreek, cardamom, cinnamon. Allow to cool and grind to a powder.
3. Heat 1 spoon of ghee/oil and fry the onions for 3-4 minutes.
4 In a blender place the fried onions, garlic, ginger and tomatoes with a little water and process it. Then add the powdered spice/masala and blend it to a paste.
5 Heat the rest of the ghee or oil and add mustard seeds, then add the lamb pieces and cook for 5 minutes.
6 Add the blended paste with ½ cup water salt, roasted chilli powder and bring to boil. Reduce the heat and cook over a moderate heat for about 45 minutes.
7 Add the creamed coconut, stir and cook for few minutes.
8 Add curry leaves, lemon grass and rampe, stir and remove from cooker.

Variations

1. If you like the taste of vinegar can add 4fl oz white vinegar instead of the yoghurt.
2. Can add potatoes.

Mutton Kulambu

Preparation & cooking time: 1 hour 30 minutes
Serves 8-10

Ingredients

- 2 kg mutton
- 6 tbsp natural yoghurt
- 2 medium onions
- 5 cloves garlic, 7cm size ginger
- 7cm cinnamon stick, 4 cardomoms, and 3 cloves ground
- ½ tsp salt (add to taste)
- 2-3 tbsp oil
- ¼ tsp turmeric powder
- pinch of mustard seeds, fennel seeds, fenugreek seeds
- 12 curry leaves, small piece rampe and sara/lemon grass
- 2-3 tbsp roasted chilli powder mix (Sri Lankan)
- small carton of single cream (200ml)
- 3 tomatoes chopped

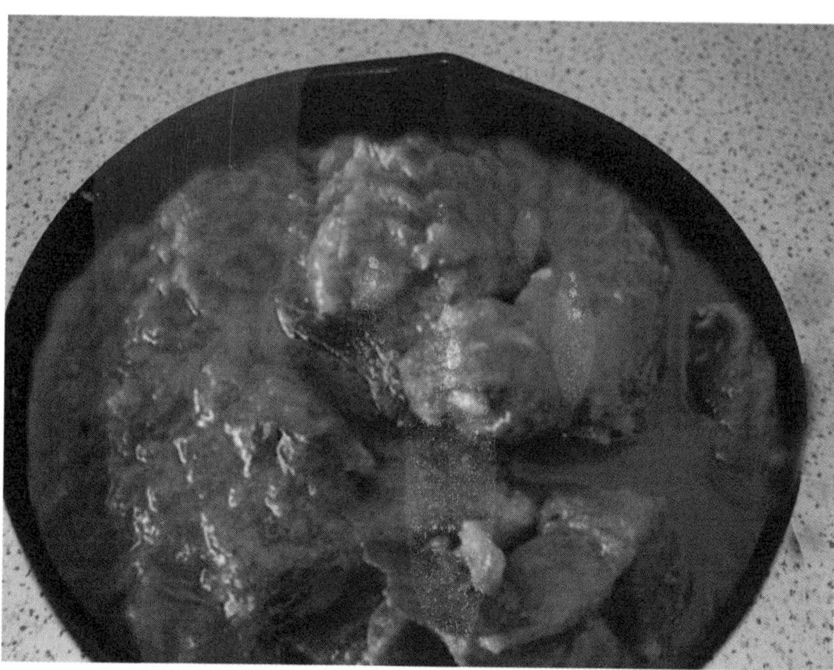

Method

1. Clean and cut the mutton into to 3½" cm size.
2. Grind garlic, ginger, 1 chopped onion, chilli powder, turmeric powder and tomatoes to a paste.
3. Grind the cinnamon and cardamom and leave it aside.
4. Mix the ground paste with the mutton pieces. Add salt, yoghurt and half the cinnamon powder, mix and marinate for two hours. Stir and mix the meat once or twice.
5. Heat a large thava, add oil and fry the onions for 2 minutes. Add mustard seeds, fenugreek and fennel seeds. Then add the mutton with the sauce and cook for 5 minutes on high heat. Reduce the heat, cover and cook for another 20-30 minutes.
6. Add the cream, curry leaves rampe and cook for 2-3 minutes. Finally add the fennel powder and cinnamon powder. Remove from heat and serve.

★ **Traditional preparation includes about ¼ cup oil added to the paste for marinade. But the above recipe is equally good and is healthier.**

Lamprais

A famous festive dish introduced by the Dutch.

Includes cooked with flavored basmati rice, cooked chicken, cooked lamb or mutton with cinnamon and Rampe, fish cutlet, boiled egg, Seeni sambol and aubergine dry dish(pahi). All of this placed in a banana leaf, wrapped and slowly baked to give this dish a unique flavour and taste.

Banana leaf is available from Sri Lankan shops. These can be stored in the freezer.

Muton/Lamb bone Kulambu

This is a dish my sons and their friends who visit me enjoy very much. The sauce blended in the meat left on the bones give them an enjoyment when eventually the bones are polished and left clean on their plates.

When you buy mutton or lamb and use the meat to cook a dry Kari, save the bones with little meat on the bones to prepare a Kulambu (thick sauce).

Preparation & Cooking 50 minutes - Serves 4-5

Ingredients

- 500g mutton bones, (preferable if marrow bones)
- 3 cups water
- 2 onions chopped
- ½ cup cows milk, ½" strip of cream coconut
- 2 cm ginger, 4 cloves garlic, crushed
- 3 large tomatoes, cut
- 2tbsp roasted chilli powder, ½ tsp garam masala powder
- 2 medium potatoes, cut into medium size cubes
- 1 sprig curry leaves, few pieces of rampe

For sauting/tempering:

- 2 tbsp oil, pinch of mustard seeds, cumin and fennel seeds
- 1-2 tsp roasted fennel powder, 1/2tsp cinnamon powder

Method

1. In a pan add oil and sauté the onions. Add the tempering ingredients.

2. Clean and wash the bones, add to the pan. Add salt, chilli powder, ground ginger, garlic and cook for 2-3 minutes.

3. Add water cover and cook for 20 minutes. Add the tomatoes and cook for 5 minutes. Add the potatoes, garam masala and milk. Cook over a medium heat for 10 minutes until the potatoes are just cooked.

4. Add the cream coconut; curry leaves rampe, fennel powder cinnamon powder. Allow the sauce to thicken slightly and remove from cooker.

★ This can be served with rice, string hoppers pittu, naan or bread. The meat will start to come off the bone and some like to sit around the table and enjoy getting every piece of the meat.

★ If you are to use a pressure cooker, it is useful to soften the meat on the bones. First sauté the onions and cook the bones for few whistles. Then add the tomatoes potato etc and cook without the pressure knob.

Pork Stir Fry

Preparation & cooking time: 30 minutes
Serves 5

Ingredients

- 500g boneless pork, sliced into thin strips
- 2 medium onions, finely sliced
- 3 garlic cloves, finely sliced
- 4cm size ginger, cut into thin strips
- 3 long capsicum chillies, sliced diagnally
- 3 tsp crushed chillies
- 1 tbsp tomato sauce, ½ tsp soya sauce
- salt to taste, ½ tsp black pepper powder
- 2 tsp coconut powder mixed in ¼ cup warm water
- 3 tbsp oil
- 2 green chillies, chopped fine
- 1 tsp cinnamon powder

Method

1. In a heavy-based pan place 2 tbsp oil and fry the pork slices on both sides. Add the coconut milk, salt, garlic and ginger and cook for 4-5 minutes. Remove and place the pork slices on a plate.
2. Add 1 tbsp oil to the pan and fry the onions, capsicum, chillies. Add the tomato sauce, crushed chillies, soya sauce and cook for a minute. Add the fried pork and cook (allow to fry) with the onions and capsicum. Add chopped green chillies, cinnamon powder and remove from cooker.

★ **Serve with rice, noodles, string hoppers etc.**

★ Instead of the tomato sauce can add chopped tomatoes to the capsicum to get a thick sauce.

Pork Chops

Preparation & cooking time: 35 minutes
Serves 2

Ingredients

- 4 chops about 2½ cm thickness
- 2 tsp roasted chilli powder
- ½ tsp roasted fennel powder
- ½ tsp turmeric powder
- 1 sprig curry leaves
- ¼ cup milk or piece of cream coconut
- 1 medium onion, diced
- salt to taste
- 4 garlic cloves
- 1 tsp lime juice
- 1 tsp cinnamon powder

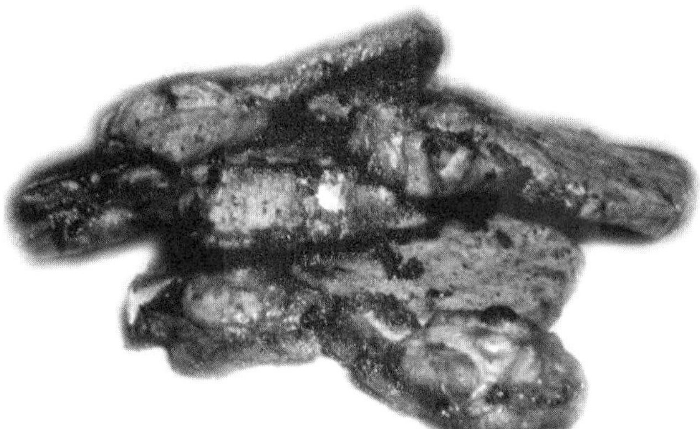

Method

1. Clean the chops and marinate in salt, chilli powder, turmeric, ground onion and garlic paste.
2. Heat a frying pan, add a little oil, scrape the onion paste slightly from the chops to avoid burning quickly and shallow fry on both sides. Next add the onion paste and a cup of water, bring to boil and simmer for 10 minutes.
3. Add milk, curry leaves, cinnamon powder and fennel powder. Stir and cook for 3-4 minutes and remove from cooker.

Variations

After frying as at 2 above, place the chops in an oven proof dish, add onions, water, little milk, cinnamon powder and cook in a pre-heated oven at 180°C for 15-20 minutes. Remove and sprinkle fennel powder and add a teaspoon of lime juice and serve.

Pork Kari dry preparation

Preparation & cooking time: 45 minutes

Serves 4-5

Ingredients

- 1kg pork (shoulder or leg)
- 5 garlic cloves, crushed
- 4cm size root ginger, crushed
- piece of rampe (5cm), chopped
- 2 tsp garam masala powder
- ¼ cup cider (optional) to marinate
- 1 cup coconut milk or normal milk
- tempering ingredients: 1 tsp mustard seeds, 1 tsp cumin seeds 1 red chilli, little oil, pinch of fenugreek
- 2 onions, chopped
- 2 tbsp roasted chilli powder
- salt to taste
- 2 tsp roasted fennel powder
- 1 sprig curry leaves

Method

1. Cut the pork into 2-3cm pieces. Add salt, 1 tsp chilli powder, garlic, ginger, a little water and cider and marinate for 10 minutes.
2. In a thava add oil and fry onions, mustard seeds, cumin, and fenugreek seeds. Stir fry and then add the chopped red chilli and few curry leaves.
3. Add the pork and stir fry for 3 minutes. Add ½ cup water, the rest of the chilli powder, masala powder and bring to boil. Reduce the heat and cook for 20 minutes.
4. Add milk, the rest of the curry leaves, rampe and cook for another 5 minutes on a medium heat. When the sauce begins to dry and the meat pieces leave the sides of the pan, add the fennel powder, stir well and remove from heat.

Variations

★ If you like a bit of sauce or gravy, after 10 minutes of the cook ing add 3 chopped tomatoes, 2 tbsp yoghurt and cook. Add ½ cup milk and cook for the last five minutes. Add chopped coriander leaves or methi leaves.

★ Pork kari should be fairly hot and spicy.

Goat Kari

Dry preparation

Ingredients

- 2 lb goat meat boneless
- Use ingredients as for dry mutton kari

Method

1. Marinate the goat meat in ground paste prepared with ginger, garlic, salt, chilli powder, yoghurt and ½ onion chopped
2. Saute the rest of the chopped onions in little oil and follow the recipe as for dry mutton kari.

★ Goat meat takes about an hour to cook, so if you want you can cook in a pressure cooker for 2 whistles and switch off. Allow for 3-4 minutes and open. Transfer to a pan, add milk and continue with the cooking for 15-20 minutes.

★ Coconut milk or single cream will give a different taste.

★ If you are to going cook it with the bones, add chopped tomatoes and prepare the dish with sauce as for mutton kulambu.

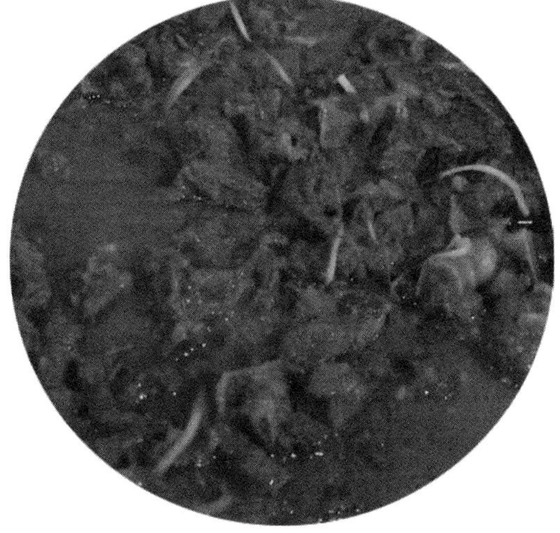

Hot Chilli Oil - with Shrimp

Ingredients

- 150g of dry prawns
- 2 onions chopped
- 1 tsp of ginger paste
- 1 tsp garlic paste
- 1 tsp of mustard ground
- 2 tsp of crushed chillies
- salt to taste
- 1 tsp sugar
- 4 tbsp vinegar
- oil for deep frying

Method

1. Deep fry the shrimps and drain it on a kitchen paper.
2. Mix garlic, ginger, mustard, chilli powder, salt and 2 tablespoon of vinegar.
3. Heat a pan and add 1 tbsp of oil and fry onions. Add the above paste and stir fry.
4. In a blender grind all, including the shrimp, to make a paste. If needed add a bit more of the vinegar and crushed chillies.
5. Add 1 tsp oil and mix well and store in a jar.
6. Have it with noodles, rice etc.

Variations

For vegetarians

1. Omit the shrimp.
   Deep fry 7-8 dry red chillies or slightly butter these and cook over a pan for few minutes. Careful, as you will start to cough.
2. For convenience, you can buy the crushed chillies from the shops and follow as for above recipe.

Baked Fish Buns

Preparation & baking Time: 2 hours

Ingredients For the dough

- 500g white or brown bread rolls mix
- 200g self raising flour
- 1 egg (optional)
- 2 tbsp margarine

.

Ingredients For the filling

- 350g tuna/salmon tin
- 1 small onion, chopped
- 2 green chillies, chopped
- 1 sprig curry leaves (optional)
- 2cm piece rampe (optional)
- 1½ tsp mixed cinnamon and cardomom powder
- 2cm ginger, crushed or 1 tsp paste
- 4 cloves garlic, crushed or 1 tsp paste
- 2 tbsp vegetable oil or margarine
- salt, pepper
- 4 medium potatoes boiled, skinned and cut
- into very small cubes.
- 1 tsp roasted chilli powder (to your taste)

Method

1. Retain 2 tbsp self raising flour and mix the rest with the bread mix . Follow the instructions on the packet and mix into dough adding a bit of margarine or oil and an egg.

2 Cover and leave the dough in warm place to rise.

3. Drain the fish can and leave in a bowl.

4. Heat the oil in a frying pan and fry the chopped onions, add crushed ginger and garlic and stir. After few minutes when the onion turns to a golden colour, add the drained fish and cook until the liquid dries up. Then add the green chillies, curry leaves, chopped rampe, salt, pepper, chilli powder, cinnamon and cardomom powder. Mix and cook for few seconds and remove from heat.

5. In a bowl add the cut-up potatoes and the fried ingredients including the fish. Mix and mash it slightly so that the pieces are not squashed to a paste.

6. Take small amounts of the dough, roll into small balls and flatten to a disc by placing on a floured board.

7. Place 2 tsp of the cooked fish mixture filling. Bring all sides in to get a shape of a roll and place the sealed end on a baking tray. Gently flatten the top with using your fingers.

8. Cover with a wet tea towel and allow to rise for about 15 minutes.

9. Brush the top with a little milk and bake at 190°C for about 20-25 minutes or until done.

★ **Serve with chilli or tomato sauce.**

- Can be prepared in advance and frozen.
- Can be taken for outings/picnics
- Filling can be of your choice and also the spices can be increased or decreased to your taste.
- In Sri Lanka, seeni sambol (onion dish in chutney section) filling is used for bread rolls.

Cutlets

Could be a starter to have with drinks before a main meal. Also a short eat with lots of other eats.

Preparation & cooking time: 1 hour

Ingredients

- 250g fish cod, coley or salmon
- 2 medium onions, chopped
- 2 green chillies, chopped
- 1 packet, golden bread crumbs
- 10 curry leaves, cut finely
- 1 tsp each freshly ground cumin and pepper
- 1 tsp chilli powder (optional depending on hotness)
- ½ tsp ground ginger powder
- 500g potato
- ½ tsp garlic powder
- 2 egg whites
- oil for frying
- 1 tsp salt

Method

1. Cook the fish in a little water and drain the water. Take out the bones and flake the fish.
2. Boil potatoes and remove skin. Mash this slightly.
3. In a bowl place the fish, add the salt, cumin, pepper, onion, ginger, garlic and mix it well. Add the potato and mix it. Use a potato masher to mash lightly. Add the curry leaves.

4. Take a tablespoon of the mixture and shape into a ball. Do this with all of the mixture and leave it aside.

5. Place the egg whites in a bowl and beat until firm and frothy.

6. Take a fish ball, if preferred flatten it slightly, dip in egg white to cover all sides and roll it in the breadcrumbs.

7. Heat a deep pan, pour fresh oil to cover the height of the cutlets. When the oil is fairly hot drop carefully the rolled cutlets and deep fry for a few minutes.

8. Remove with a slotted spoon and leave on a kitchen paper. The surface should be crispy.

Variations & helpful hints

★ Canned fish of tuna, mackerel, pilchards or salmon can be used. This will reduce the cooking time by 10-15 minutes.

★ When deep-frying, ensure the cutlets are immersed in the oil and the temperature is fairly high. This will prevent the cutlets from breaking.

★ Instead of fish, you can prepare using minced lamb, chicken, beef or pork. Cook and saute the meat adding onions, ginger and garlic. Then follow the steps as in above recipe.

Chinese Fish Rolls

Ingredients

For the pancakes

- 2 cups plain flour
- pinch of turmeric (optional)
- 1 cup milk, or more as needed
- 1 egg
- pinch salt

Method

Combine flour, eggs and salt in a large bowl. Using a hand whisk or an electric whisk mix the flour and milk to form a batter.

Ingredients (For the filling)

- 250g potatoes, boiled
- 1 leek, cut finely
- 1 tbsp vegetable oil
- 1 tsp ginger paste
- 1 sprig curry leaves, chopped
- 2 tsp ground cumin and pepper
- 2 green chillies, chopped (optional)
- 1 can (420g) of salmon
- 1 medium onion, chopped
- 1 tsp roasted chilli powder
- 1 tsp garlic paste
- salt to taste

Method

1. Prepare the potatoes by removing the skin and cutting it to small pieces mash it lightly.
2. Open a can of salmon and drain the water or oil. Flake the salmon, add salt, cumin and pepper, mix and leave it aside.
3. Heat a large frying pan, add oil and stir fry the onions for about 4-5 minutes. Add the leeks and stir fry. Add the salmon, chilli powder, chopped chillies and fry for few minutes.
4. Add the potatoes, curry leaves and mix it well. Cook for a minute and remove from heat.

Method

To make the pancakes

1. Heat a frying pan or skillet over medium heat for about 1 minute.
2. Coat the surface of the pan with a little oil or wipe with a piece of cloth dampened with vegetable oil.
3. When the pan is hot, take a ladle full of batter, pour and swirl with the back of the spoon to make a pancake.
4. Cook both sides for a minute and take it out and leave on a plate.
5. Wipe/brush the pan with the oil brush or oil cloth and pour the next pancake.
6. Whilst this is cooking take one tablespoon of filling and place it on the edge of the pancake. Fold the sides inwards and then roll from one end to the other. May need to put a bit of water or batter to the edge to make it stick so that it does not unravel. Turn over and arrange on to a plate.

Make the batter for covering

1. Mix an egg with ½ cup of flour, pinch of salt and a little water (use a hand whisk to do this).
2. Dip the rolls in the batter and then in breadcrumbs.
3. Heat a thava or an electric fryer with oil. Into the hot oil drop a few rolls, deep fry till golden brown and serve hot.

★ Readymade frozen pastry sheets are available, these can be used for covering instead of making pancakes.

★ I have used the medium size to make party size rolls, you need to use two sheets for each roll as they are too flimsy.

Egg and Bacon Roll

Ingredients

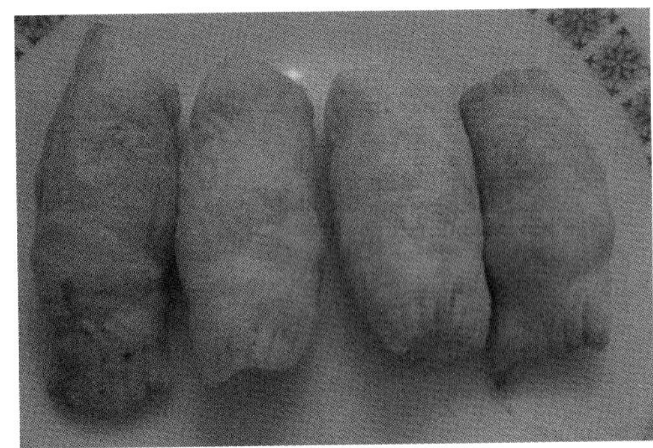

- 500g puff pastry in block
- 6 eggs boiled and shelled
- 200g bacon rashers
- 2 tbsp chilli paste
- 2 tsp chutney
- 1 tsp ground pepper
- 2 tbsp tomato sauce
- 200g cream cheese

Method

1. Mix the cheese, chutney, sauce and leave in a bowl.
2. Cut each bacon slice in the middle to halve the width. Then cut each piece into 6-7cm strips.
3. Cut the pastry into 3½ cm strips. Cut into two halves. Place on a floured board and roll each piece seperately. Cut this into two.
4. Spread ¼ tsp of cream cheese and pinch of pepper to the rolled pastry.
5. Apply little bit of sauce mixture on to a slice of bacon, quarter the egg, wrap the egg with the bacon piece.
6. Place this on the rolled pastry, bring one end of the pastry over and roll so that the egg and bacon are fully covered. Place the open ends at the base. Seal the sides and press with a fork to make indents. Make a few pricks on the top of the pastry.
7. Brush an oven tray with a little oil, place the pastry on this and arrange the rest of the rolled pastry. Brush with little milk and bake in hot oven 190°C for 20-25 minutes.

Variations

If they are large, each half of the eggs can be cut into 4 pieces.
Minced lamb and potato kari filling can be used.
Good item for parties.

★ It is a very popular finger food.

Prawn Puffs

Ingredients

- 1 packet 375g cooked prawns·
- 1 green chilli chopped
- 6 shallots chopped
- 3 tsp olive oil
- 1 tsp ginger paste, 1 tsp garlic paste
- 50g grated cheese
- 1 tsp corn flour mixed with little milk and water
- 2 tsp coriander powder
- 1 tsp butter, 2tbsp chilli sauce, salt to taste
- 500g Puff pastry
- ½ tsp pepper corn roasted and coarsely ground

Method

1. Place the cooked prawns in hot water for 2-3 seconds and squeeze the water out.

2. Chop the prawns into fine pieces. Add green chillies and then the prawns salt, pepper and cook for further minute.

3. Add the cheese corn flour mixed in milk and water. Stir and cook for few seconds and add the chilli sauce .

4. Roll out the puff pastry into thin strips as for the egg and bacon roll recipe. Cut rectangular strips appx 4" by 2". Place a teaspoon of the mixture on one end and then roll it over so that it is covered. Seal the edges and indent (press) with a fork.

5. Arrange on a oiled tray, brush with milk and bake on high temperature for 20-25 minutes.

Fried Mutton Delights

(Finger Food) Good to serve for parties.

Children will love this but make it milder.

Ingredients

- 1 kg lamb/mutton cut to 2" strips·

Add the following in powder or paste form, according to your taste

- salt, garam masala,,chilli powder, coriander powder, garlic, ginger, lemon juice
- oil for deep frying
- 1 cup plain flour, ½ cup rice flour mixed with 1tsp chilli powder, water and a bit of salt

Method

1. Marinate the lamb pieces in masala,salt and other ingredients.
2. Heat 3tbsp oil and cook the lamb pieces on a high heat for 8-10 minutes.
3. Prepare a thick batter with the flour and water. Dip each cooked piece of lamb and deep fry in oil. Remove and place on paper to drain the oil

★ To serve warm and crispy

★ Place the pieces on a tray and heat in the oven on the highest temp for 10 minutes.

★ Chicken, pork can be fried using the same method.

Helpful Hints

- Leave pickle, ghee in glass bottles or jars.
- When cooking vegetables to make a mild dish add just enough water, add salt and cook. Any excess water can be drained and used as stock.
- If you cook the dark brown rice 'Kutharisi' which is available in Sri Lankan shops, add double the quantity of water that you would use for normal basmati rice. When the rice is cooked, drain and save the drained water, add salt, a little warm milk, and drink as a beverage. (Usually coconut milk is added)
- When peeling onions try and put the onions in water then your eyes won't water/tear.
- If rice is overcooked sometimes it helps if you squeeze the juice of one lemon and mix it.
- When frying potato, to make it crispy you can sprinkle a little rice flour and green gram flour on the potato pieces and then deep fry.
- To retain the colour of the fried potato, cut the potato, wash and soak in salt water for 15 minutes, then drain wipe in a towel and deep fry.
- If thosai, hoppers and pan cake do not come off easily, use a small piece of cotton cloth dipped in oil and give it a rub. Using the same oil cloth with a copper coin (two-penny piece) give a rub to the inside of the base. This will make it smooth.
- Sometimes, for pancake, you may have to use a bit of salt and yoghurt mixture and give it a rub. This will make it easy to lift the pancake.
- But it is always better to use a non stick pan.
- To make fried pakodas crispy you may put the pakodas on a tray and cook in the oven for 15 minutes on high, and then take them out. This will keep them very crispy.
- If you add too much salt while cooking, cut up two potatoes into small pieces and add it to the dish.
- To get rid of the water content from an aubergine, cut it and slightly salt and leave in a colander allowing for the water to drain. Then deep fry the aubergine slices, they will be crispy.

A good meal ready in 45 minutes

Main: rice, pasta,noodles, flour.

Side dish: tomato - a can, puree, fresh or frozen.
potato, fresh onions or even dried flakes

Lentil: red lentil, dhal grains or a from a can

Spice: salt, pepper, chilli powder, few spices ginger, garlic paste, powder or fresh.

Veg: fesh carrots, greens, courgette or frozen spinach
From the above you could make a main dish and three side dishes.

Rice: cook rice as normal and can add bit o butter towards the end.

Vegetable: Prepare dhal, carrots and a potato dish either a dry one or with tomato and sauce (gravy)

Dhal: See lentils section but to be quick put ¼ cup of red lentils in a pan wash and boil in 1 ½ cups of water. This will be about 10 minutes. Whilst it is boiling cut up onions, chillie and stir-fry this in a little bit of oil or butter. Add the spices of mustard seeds, cumin green curry leaves. When the dhal is cooked pour this in to the pan with fried ingredients add turmeric asafoetida bit of milk, ground pepper and cumin. Remove from cooker.

Carrot: Clean and dice into small cubes. Either cooks as a mild dish (milky) following the recipe and add lime juice. Alternatively, fry chopped onions in 1 tsp of oil add carrots, salt and let it cook in its juice. In two minutes, add milk chilli/curry powder. Cook half covered. Finally add fennel powder. Here this is done.

Potato: Boil with skin and peel. Chop to small pieces stir-fry onions. Add all the spices(mustard cumin 1 red chilli cut to small pieces bit of turmeric). Here you may use the chilli flakes. Add salt and chilli flakes to the cut up potato. Toss it and add to the fried stuff. Stir-fry, add curry leaves and remove from cooker.

Another dish:

Chop tomatoes, potato, onions and brings to boil in 1 ½ cups of water. Add salt, chilli powder, cumin, masala , ginger, garlic and cinnamon powder.

Finally bit of milk or coconut and cook for a minute or two. Remove from cooker to the consistency you like.

Here you are you can have a good meal with yoghurt and a packet of crisps or so instead of a take away.

INDEX